THE CHRIST

THE CHRIST

by CHARLES GUIGNEBERT

Translated by Peter Ouzts
AND *Phyllis Cooperman*

Edited and Revised by
Sonia Volochova

UNIVERSITY BOOKS   *New Hyde Park, New York*

FOREWORD

CHARLES Guignebert died aged 72 on August 27, 1939, almost unnoticed amid the frenzy of France's mobilization for the first disastrous phase of the Second World War. He left behind him the unfinished manuscript of a great work entitled *Le Christ*, subsequently published in 1943, and notes for its sequel, *L'Eglise*. These were the fruits of thirty years of teaching and research at the Sorbonne, first as lecturer, and since 1919 as Professor of the History of Christianity at the University of Paris. This intense effort had already resulted in the publication of two fundamental works on Christian origins, *Le Monde au temps de Jésus* (Eng. trans. by S. H. Hooke as *The Jewish World in the Time of Jesus*) [1] and *Jésus* (translated also by Dr. Hooke).[2] Both were in every sense great works, which placed its author among the foremost scholars in Europe. Indeed, Guignebert, Loisy (died 1940) and Goguel (died 1956) form a trio of historians whose writings and ideas dominated New Testament scholarship in the period between the two World Wars. Theirs was scientific research *par excellence* applied to the field of religious studies. On this foundation, the postwar generation of historians of Christian origins have built.

1. Published by University Books, New Hyde Park, N.Y., 1958.
2. Published by University Books, New Hyde Park, N.Y., 1956.

The author of *The Christ* was born of artisan parents at Villeneuve Saint Georges near Paris on June 18, 1867. His father died when he was in infancy, and his mother married as her second husband a schoolmaster, by whose efforts Charles was able to enter the Lycée of Versailles. He was an average, if rather nervous, pupil developing his gift for research late, and he very nearly became a professional singer, for he had a fine tenor voice and a love of music which he retained throughout his life. He was, however, persuaded to take his *licenciat* first, and as a student at the Sorbonne decided to make teaching his career. His early enthusiasm was for the Conciliar period of Church history (1400-1440) and he wrote his Latin thesis in preparation for his doctorate on Pierre d'Ailly, the Conciliarist leader from the University of Paris. Gradually, however, he became attracted to the problem of the Church in the Roman Empire, and while a senior history master (*professeur agrégé*) at the Lycée of Toulouse he produced a monumental work on Tertullian. This was published in 1901 and Guignebert became Docteur ès Lettres.

Tertullien. Etude sur ses sentiments à l'égard de l'empire et de la société civile was a pioneer work, a new step forward in the interpretation of the development of the Church's relations with the Roman Empire. He set out, as he stated in his Introduction, to place Tertullian "not only in his pagan and Christian background but as part of the great movement that was pushing Christianity towards its triumph." [3] Indeed, in the 600 pages of this monograph there was no aspect of the Church's relations with pagan society between A.D. 150 and 250 that the author did not touch upon. He was as much at home with the anti-Christian polemic of Celsus and Cornelius Fronto, and with the Alexandrians Clement and Origen as he was with Tertullian himself. Above all, he grasped the essence of the Christian movement at the turn of the 3rd century as a social force, a movement protesting against the entire way of life of the Roman Empire based on the worship of the traditional Roman and provincial gods. "It would be impossible," he said, "to make a social revolution more radical than that which Tertullian was preparing for the pagan world." [4]

His view of Christianity as a social as well as a religious movement was in advance of the ideas of his time, including those even of Harnack. He was preparing the ground for the studies of A. D. Nock, Marcel Simon and above all, of J. B. Brisson, whose *Autononisme et Christianisme dans l'Afrique romaine* (Paris, 1958) may be read as a companion volume to Guignebert's *Tertullien*.

3. Introduction, p. iii.
4. *Tertullien*, p. 277.

Guignebert's gifts lay in the direction of synthesis. He could command and assimilate a vast amount of the most varied sources, and it is probably no accident that in many ways the most satisfactory of his later works was *The Jewish World in the Time of Jesus* in which these gifts found fullest scope. Long before he wrote this he had committed himself to what he believed to be a fundamental task for his age, the understanding of Christian origins.

Guignebert was a man of his time, energetic and passionately convinced by the liberal causes he adopted. France in the decade before the First World War was a prey to two great religious crises. First, the government of the Republic sought the complete separation between the French state and the dominant Roman Catholic Church and the diminution of the latter's influence on education. The administration of Waldeck-Rousseau (1901-1905) was strongly anti-clerical and it was determined, in the words of Emile Combes, his successor, "to secure the victory of the spirit of the Revolution in religious policy," and to substitute lay for clerical influence in education. Added to this, there was arising within the Roman Catholic Church a deep movement of unease, of discontent with traditional ideas and traditional doctrines, coupled with fresh interpretations of the history of the Church which paid full regard to the discoveries of critical scholarship. Alfred Loisy's *L'Evangile et l'Eglise*, published in 1902, marked the onset of the Modernist crisis in France.

Both movements appealed to Guignebert. His upbringing had been lay and non-religious and in *Tertullien* he had already set the example of a study devoted to the examination of religious issues "according to the rules of historical criticism." He now sought to apply these principles to what had become the burning issue of Christian origins. Behind this conflict of scholars and clerics lay the wider issue of the relevance and meaning of the Church's claims in France.

In 1905 the French Government, anxious to establish a non-confessional school of religious history, appointed Guignebert as lecturer at the Sorbonne. In his inaugural lecture he pointed a road along which he was to move the rest of his life. He would demonstrate "that Christian history was history like any other, that the facts that composed it were facts like other facts, known from texts accessible as are other texts to critical research, that transcend all confessions of faith in the serene atmosphere of scientific impartiality." [5] This statement, obvious though it seems to us today, was a bold one to make in Paris in 1905, the era of Claudel, Huysmans and Bloy.

5. Cited from M. Brunot's appreciation of Guignebert's life and work, published in *Annales de l'Université de Paris*, July-Oct. 1939, pp. 365-80.

With this end in view he wrote two works in 1906-1907, a *Manuel
d'histoire ancienne du Christianisme*, and a critical study of the historical
basis for the Primacy of Peter which included a review of the evidence for
Peter's stay in Rome. The *Manuel* was a massive work, a foretaste of his
later productions including *Le Christ*, in which he examined the evidence
for the development of primitive Christianity in the light of what was
known of the Jewish and the Greco-Roman worlds into which the new
religion had been born. He sifted the evidence provided by the Gospels
for Jesus's life and teaching, insisting, as he was to later on, on his membership of a normal family with brothers and sisters. He included a study
of Paul and the churches which he founded, and ended with an account
of the Church at the end of the first century. The foundation for his
future work had been surely laid.

He was now well established at the Sorbonne, and at the end of 1907
he wrote a series of articles in the *Grande Revue* on the subject of Mod-
ernism and the Catholic Tradition in France. It was the time of *Pascendi
Gregis*, which Guignebert described as "a peremptory demonstration [on
the part of Pius X] of the impossibility of any understanding between
the critical approach and Roman dogmatism." [6] The author described the
plight of the French clergy caught between loyalty to the Pope and the
demands of intelligence. How could it be supposed, Guignebert asks, that
an Israelite patriarch living some 1500 years before Christ set himself
down to write the five books of the Pentateuch? Yet that is what the
Pontifical commission on the Bible had solemnly affirmed on June 27,
1906.[7]

He felt deeply the massive ignorance of his countrymen about the
history of religion and the utter lack of tolerance that characterized religious attitudes of the day, and these "scandals" he was prepared to set
about ending. In this, indeed, he was not alone, for one feels the same
educative mission at work in Mgr. L. Duchesne's three volumes on the
Early History of the Church, modernist in their approach but always just
within the bounds of Catholic orthodoxy. Guignebert's own *Evolution
des Dogmes* appeared in 1910 at the height of Duchesne's influence. This
was an excursion into the field of comparative religion, an attempt to
show how all religions underwent a process of evolution and elaboration
despite their claims to represent unchangeable revealed truths.

The outbreak of the First World War ended Guignebert's first period

6. *Modernisme et Tradition catholique en France*. Collection de la Grande Revue,
Paris, 1908, p. 163.
7. *Ibid.*, pp. 20-21.

of creative activity. In a dozen years he had written three major works as well as many other contributions. A thinker and a man of action, he seemed destined to go far in the energetic, prosperous and anti-clerical France of the first decade of this century. The war delayed the full harvest of his thought. At 47 he was too old for the front, but served in the Ministry of Information as well as continuing his lectures at the Sorbonne. In 1916 he became director of studies in history and geography, which he undertook at the same time as his other duties.

The proliferation of lecture courses and administrative duties gave him less time for writing but in 1919 he was promoted professor. He became an active member of the Société Ernest Renan and firm friend of Loisy. He was gaining a tremendous reputation as a teacher and lecturer. While not abandoning his aim of writing specialist studies, it was to be in the *Evolution de l'Humanité* series, published by Henri Berr, that Guignebert, like the mediaevalists Ferdinand Lot and Louis Halphen, was to make his deepest impression.

His approach was slowly to become warmer and more mellow. In the work which he published in 1921 entitled *Le Christianisme antique*, he was to cite the declaration of Anatole France, "Science is not concerned with pleasing or displeasing. She is non-human" (*Elle est inhumaine*). Twelve years later, however, while applying the same strict categories of scientific study to his subject, he was prepared to affirm, "Christianity that originates from that past which is so foreign to the spirit of to-day, is ever-living. . . . Therefore let us not remain closed in spirit to the hopes which inspired the contemporaries of Paul of Tarsus." Pauline mysticism had its relevance for his own day. While he did not believe in the divinity of Christ he believed in what he called the "rêve humain," the deep aspirations of mankind that turn each generation back to the challenge of the life and death of Jesus Christ.

The Christ is the fifth volume in a series planned by the publishers in the 1930's to cover the general theme of the origins of Christianity and the moral crisis of the ancient world. The first two volumes by Adolfe Lods, *Israel* and *The Prophets of Israel*, had become standard works. Guignebert's assignment was to take up the story from the end of the era of the prophets and continue through the ministry of Jesus and the apostolic period into the early history of the Church. His picture of the Jewish world at the time of Jesus, written with lucidity and learning, almost suggests the inevitability of Jesus's life and work.

Written more than a decade before the discovery of the Dead Sea Scrolls, *The Jewish World in the Time of Jesus* remains one of the essential handbooks for understanding the two centuries of Jewish history before the birth of Christ. As in all Guignebert's works there is a detailed discussion of sources at the outset, a judicious and complete piece of scholarship in itself. Then the structure, ideas and organisation of the Jewish people in the Hasmonean age is unfolded. Rightly the author stressed the great importance of the sects, the Zealots, Essenes and the Nazirs in Jewish life at this time. He showed how from the Maccabean period onward these sects formed the powerhouse of intense apocalyptic hopes. Israel might find herself occupied by the idolatrous empire of Rome: but Yahweh would send his Messiah and he would deliver her. In this hope Zealot and Pharisee were at one. They were divided only by calculation and prudence in face of Roman power. Outside Palestine was the Judaism of the Dispersion and here Jewish thought was evolving towards an essentially Jewish syncretism [8] which the author believed was one of the main legacies of Hellenistic Judaism to Christianity. Finally, the phenomenon of Gnosis could be traced directly to the religious currents prevalent among the Dispersion Jews, those who occupied themselves with speculations on "the birth, organization, government and life of the Cosmos." [9] In all this Guignebert's ideas have been justified by later discoveries.

The *Jewish World* was designed as an introduction to the author's study of Jesus. This, many of Guignebert's critics have come to regard as the crowning achievement of his career. For the author develops to the full his superb analytical gifts concentrated on a single field, the study of the New Testament documents. With immense learning and patience every scrap of information bearing on the life of Jesus is subjected to scrutiny. The author declares, "The historian must permit himself to be swayed by no other presupposition save that he may believe nothing, and that he knows nothing: he is nothing more than a seeker." After 132 pages of discussion of every detail known about Jesus's birth and family, the reader is at last told "Jesus was born somewhere in Galilee in the time of the Emperor Augustus, of a humble family, which included half a dozen or more children besides himself." That said, and Jesus himself put firmly into the framework of the prophet of Nazareth who spoke nearly always to "audiences of peasants and common people," not a great deal else remains. "We do not believe in the mission of the Twelve, and have little more faith in the choice of the Twelve by Jesus" (p. 223). The mission of the *nabi* was short. "Five or six weeks in Galilee, and the

8. *The Jewish World in the Time of Jesus* (Eng. tr., p. 242).
9. *Ibid.*, p. 245.

same, at most, on the outskirts" were all that preceded Jesus's move to Jerusalem. He went thither not of his own accord but because Galilee became too hot for him. There he met his fate as an agitator at the hands of the religious leaders of his people and the Roman authorities. His message had been a reiterated prophecy of the imminent arrival of a celestial transformation which was significant only to the Jewish people. Other factors, such as popular Jewish eschatological hopes and Hellenistic-Jewish yearning to understand the mystery of salvation, brought the Church into existence. Christianity had "a favorable soil for syncretistic influences, by virtue of which the Jewish Messiah, unintelligible and uninteresting to the Greeks, became the Lord, the Saviour, the Son of God, the supreme Master of the Universe, before whom the whole creation bends the knee. The ground was prepared for it throughout the oriental world by the ancient myth of the dying and rising God." (p. 536). And the author ends his study with Wellhausen's dictum "Enthusiasm engendered Christianity, but it was the enthusiasm of the disciples, not that of Jesus" (p. 538).

The Christ is the sequel to *Jesus*. Once again, there is the long and careful assessment of sources in which Guignebert draws attention to the comparatively late date (mainly 9th and 10th century A.D.) of many of the existing manuscripts of the New Testament and the fact that "no text in our possession goes back from copy to copy to an original text." The task of the historian forced to rely on such incomplete material was indeed a hard one. Nonetheless, in the generation before the appearance of written texts, the religion of Christ was beginning to develop in three different ways. There was first the strictly Jewish sect, held together by the disciples in Jerusalem awaiting the promised Coming of their Master. They were the Believers in Christ as opposed to the mass of their unbelieving fellow-countrymen. Then, beyond Jerusalem were the Jews of the Dispersion, combined with whom were the ever-widening circles of proselytes and God-fearers. For them, deeply influenced by their pagan surroundings, the Jesus-Messiah had already become Savior and Lord of the Cosmos. Finally, Christian doctrine was becoming established under the influence of an all-pervading philosophic syncretism. The figure of Jesus developed and increased from Prophet to Messiah, and from Messiah to personalized Yahweh and finally to God.

The author traces this development through what can be established from accounts of the Church in Jerusalem, attributing a major role to the Hellenists and Stephen. The description of the Greek world and its relation to the Dispersion Jews in its midst is a masterly piece of work, in particular the author's analysis of the development of the Mystery cults out of age-old oriental cults of vegetation. The inhabitants of the Near East "were in the habit of practicing rites reputedly effective in aiding the work of the sun and vegetation, a work requisite for the preservation of life. These rites were gradually transposed and were adapted to preparing men for the *true life*, the life expressed by the concept of salvation." Anatolia, Syria and Egypt were dominated at the time of Christ by these great religions of salvation in part derived from traditional gods of nature and vegetation.

Such was the background against which Paul grew up in Tarsus, and Tarsus, Guignebert points out, was far more an oriental than a Hellenistic centre. The author is highly skeptical of the statement (Acts xxii.3) that Paul was educated in Jerusalem and that he sat "at the feet of Gamaliel," since Paul himself admitted in Galatians i.22 that before his conversion he "was unkknown by face unto the churches of Judaea." To him Paul was purely a product of the Dispersion whose literary knowledge went not much further than the Septuagint, Enoch, the Wisdom literature and some Jewish apocryphal works which contained the tags of Aratus or Menander which Paul quotes. But this environment did inspire those profound hopes of mystical salvation which were to become characteristic of Pauline Christianity.

The dominant authority on this aspect of the thought of the early Church was Loisy's *Les Mystères païens et le mystère chrétien* (2nd ed., Nourry, Paris, 1930) and for much of his assessment of the origins of Christian sacraments, the Eucharist and baptism, Guignebert is deeply in Loisy's debt. He did not believe that the eucharistic meal was derived from Judaism at all, but came from current practices among initiates in the Mystery religions, in particular those of the Bacchi, of Attis and Osiris. The religion which Paul preached was above all "a Mystery," and like all Mystery cults of the day, the aim of Christian rites was to establish the closest unity between the initiate and his god. To Paul this god was the Christ Crucified. Almost among the last words that Guignebert wrote was the affirmation that "Paulinism represents and comprises a simplified, enlarged, and perfected Mystery." [10] Paul's service to the religion he had adopted was that he had transported a belief which orthodox Jews had repudiated into the Hellenistic world. It was this transposition

10. Compare Loisy's statement "L'Evangile de Jésus est véritablement devenue un mystère dans le christianisme" (*Les Mystères païens et le mystère chrétien*, p. 333). Loisy considered the process complete by the time Mark wrote his gospel.

that made Christianity a new and independent religious force in the ancient world.

Such is the gist of Guignebert's two marathon works. Both in their way marked an important phase in the study of New Testament times. Both were written in a period of revolutionary reappraisal of the teaching of the primitive Church and its Master. Guignebert's peers were Schweitzer, Loisy, Kirsopp Lake, Goguel and Lagrange. In retrospect it may seem curious that he felt himself out of sympathy with the emerging school of Roman Catholic Biblical scholars represented by Lagrange, whose contribution to an understanding of the Jewish world in the time of Christ was equal to his own. But Guignebert was also critical of the rationalists, the school of Eysinga and van Manen who sought to pin their own nostrums onto Jesus, and to portray him as a "dromomaniac" or an "Oedipist," or a "sitophobiac," whose fasting for forty days was due to a compulsive urge. Guignebert's account of Jesus and the rise of Christianity represents however about the furthest one can go along the road to skepticism without abandoning completely belief in the Christian ménage and the Christian life. Were it the last word on the subject, Jesus himself would be left as an improbable figure, flitting for a few weeks across the stage of history before his arrest and execution. His disciples would fade into myth. The Christian tradition would be that of Paul, the questing, unquiet Jewish mind that seized on the enthusiasm generated by the obscure Galilean prophet to proclaim a new Mystery religion to the world. Is that adequate?

The great merit of Guignebert's approach has been to clear away an immense amount of dead wood which still cluttered the way towards understanding the New Testament period. Today one can read with amazement Seeley's confident assertion "No other career [than Jesus's] ever had so much unity, no other biography is so simple or can so well afford to dispense with details." [11] Even T. R. Glover, who had an almost unrivalled command of the life and thought of the Greco-Roman provincial world, was still too apt to treat the Gospels as biographies in *The Jesus of History*. Headlam's *Life and Teaching of Jesus Christ*, published in 1923, perhaps still the most satisfactory of all the attempts in English to portray the "Jesus of history," lacks the depth of Guignebert's penetration into the sources and takes no account of the findings of Form Criticism. In none of these works is there awareness of the possibility that

11. Sir J. R. Seeley, *Ecce Homo: a Survey of the Life and Work of Jesus Christ*, Macmillan, 1916, p. 20. Seeley was Regius Professor of Modern History at Cambridge.

the words attributed to Jesus in the Gospels might reflect more accurately the views of the community in which the Gospel was produced than of Jesus himself. Guignebert showed at the conclusion of three decades of painstaking work just how little we could know from existing sources of the historical figure of Jesus. His successors have tended to agree.

The Christ is valuable for similar reasons. The rise of Christianity is portrayed in terms explicable by cause and effect and is stripped of mythical accretions demanded by dogma. One can see how, given the religious climate of the day, which the author describes brilliantly, the message of the Galilean prophet designed for the Palestinian countryside could be transformed into a promise of salvation for the Mediterranean world as a whole. Jesus of Nazareth is elevated stage by stage into the cosmic Christ of the early Church. After nearly thirty years, few would wish to challenge the basic thesis that Paul attempted to present Christianity "in the form of a Mystery" to an audience largely composed of those on the outer fringes of the Jewish synagogue. The emphasis of Christianity as a life-giving Mystery one finds in Justin and Clement; and one has only to read Basil of Caesarea's *De Spiritu Sancto* (written *circa* 372) to see that to some of the Christian leaders of the fourth century the Christian religion was indeed a "mysterion" whose "secret teaching was preserved in silence out of the reach of curious meddling and inquisitive investigation." [12] Here Basil, like Paul, was speaking to those who understood salvation as the destruction of demonic powers. *The Christ* will remain the classic presentation of the historical origins of that view.

Throughout Guignebert's life the material finds discovered by the archaeologist were continuously increasing the evidence available to the historian of the social and religious life of the ancient world. The names of Ramsay, Deissmann, Keil and Premerstein, Cumont and Rostovtzeff will always be associated with the "archaeological explosion" of the first decades of the present century which resulted in the amassing of an enormous amount of detailed evidence bearing on the religious situation in the Roman Empire. Even in the strictly New Testament field, to the Oxyrhynchus *Logia* discovered by Grenfell and Hunt in 1897 and 1903 were added the Unknown Gospel [13] and numerous fragments of non-canonical and apocryphal works. Guignebert was no stranger to these developments. Indeed, at the end of a striking section in *The Christ* describing the religiosity of the age of Paul in Asia Minor, he demon-

12. *De Spiritu Sancto*, xxvii. 67. Also, *ibid.*, 68.
13. Published by H. I. Bell and T. C. Skeat, *Fragments of an Unknown Gospel*, London, the British Museum, 1935.

strates how inscriptions, ostraka, papyri, and other finds have corrected the view presented by moralists of the age that the first century A.D. was a period of religious skepticism. Yet despite this appreciation of the insights which archaeology could provide, there are those who feel he was never really at home with the subject. His handling of the Oxyrhynchus *Logia* provides a useful example. These "Sayings of Jesus" were exhaustively discussed among scholars in the decade leading up to the First World War, yet Guignebert's assessment of them in *Jesus* is among the more peremptory sections of the book.[14] He is content to rehearse briefly the various theories regarding the relation of the *Logia* to the *Gospel according to the Hebrews*, and to the Synoptics, and concludes that "this interesting find is disappointing. It tells us nothing that we did not already know, and in the opinion of the writer, there is not much hope of anything better from future discoveries." [15]

The Oxyrhynchus *Logia* proved in the end to be incomplete but slightly variant versions of the *Gospel of Thomas*, a complete copy of which was found among the Nag Hammadi documents.[16] These were not published until after the Second World War. All the time, however, the discoveries made by Biblical archaeologists were rendering the position of the radical critic of the New Testament more precarious.

The discovery of the Dead Sea Scrolls had been preceded by a century and a half of piecemeal and often arduous archeological discovery. In Guignebert's day, the *Manual of Discipline*, similar to that found among the Scrolls, belonging to a sect of Jews living in Damascus had been discovered in the *geniza* (or repository) of the synagogue at Cairo and published by Canon R. H. Charles.[17]

The Scrolls have opened up new perspectives in the study of Christian origins. Put at the lowest estimate, these discoveries have thrown an unexpected flood of light on the Palestinian religious environment in which Jesus's mission took place. Guignebert's emphasis on the role of the sects and the excited atmosphere of apocalyptic which sustained their hopes and vitality has received startling confirmation. A large proportion of the manuscript fragments that littered the floor of Cave iv were connected

14. *Jesus*, pp. 57-59.

15. *Jesus*, p. 58. Contrast perhaps F. C. Burkitt's comments on the possible importance of future discoveries of *Logia* in unravelling the literary relationship between Matthew and Luke, in "The Early Church and the Synoptic Gospels," *Journ. Theol. Studies*, V (1904), 341.

16. See J. A. Fitzmyer, "The Oxyrhynchus *Logoi* of Jesus and the Coptic Gospel according to Thomas," *Theological Studies*, XX (1959), 505ff.

17. R. H. Charles, *Apocrypha and Pseudepigrapha of the Old Testament*, Oxford, 1913, Vol. II, pp.785ff.

with apocalyptic literature, now dated with some reasonable degree of security to the half century either side of the beginning of the Christian epoch. As Frank Moore Cross has claimed,[18] the Essenes, as he considers the Covenanters to have been, "were the bearers and in no small part the producers of the apocalyptic tradition of Judaism." Indeed, we see Palestine in the time of Christ saturated in this tradition. But its reality lends reality also to some of the chief incidents recorded in the Gospels. The temptation that Jesus faced at the outset of his ministry, whether to set himself up as a second Judas Maccabeus and challenge the might of Rome was no more than the truth. The symbolism contained in the Synoptic account of the Temptations masked grim reality. Nationalism and Jesus's reactions to it become one of the most compelling themes of the Gospel story. There is no need to play down the background role of Zealotry among Jesus's intimate followers. It was perhaps only in Gethsemane itself that Jesus saw the will of his Father clearly. The disciples were ordered "to put up the swords" (Matt. xxvi.52) they had previously been enjoined to buy (Luke xxii.36) and their Master trod his lonely way to the Cross.[19] The events narrated by the Synoptists in the New Testament will henceforth need no apologists. The Bible is in a literal sense true.

Equally drastic has been the effect of the discovery of the Scrolls on accepted views of the Fourth Gospel. Guignebert and his contemporaries could confidently dismiss its testimony as being of any value as a source for the life of Jesus. Here and there one of the redactors of the Johannine account may have brought in some historical fact that is worth keeping, but in general the Gospel of John "seems further removed from historical probability than the other three." [20] Today one must be much more careful. As F. M. Cross points out, "linguistic and conceptual contacts between the scrolls and the New Testament are nowhere more in evidence than in the Gospel of John." [21] The symbolism of light and darkness, of "doing the truth," and "life eternal" so prominent in John is also the language of the writing of the Dead Sea community. Far from the writer of the Fourth Gospel being steeped in the thought of the world of the Hellenistic Mystery religions, he seems to come from an environment "where Jewish Christianity was dominant, and Essene

18. *The Ancient Library of Qumran and Modern Biblical Studies*, London, Duckworth, 1958, p. 147.

19. See the survey of the evidence in my work on *Martyrdom and Persecution in the Early Church*, Oxford, Blackwells, 1965, pp. 93–95, and S. G. F. Brandon, *Jesus and the Zealots*, Manchester University Press, 1967.

20. Guignebert, *Jesus*, p. 28.

21. Cross, *op. cit.*, p. 153.

influences persisted." [22] A complete reassessment of John based on these conclusions appears to be due.

Similarly, the study of the development of the primitive Church in Jerusalem has benefited from the Scrolls. Much light has been thrown on the dark places which Guignebert and Loisy were inclined to attribute to myth and forgery. The dreadful punishment that befell Ananias and Sapphira, for instance, can be seen as a more drastic penalty in keeping with the eschatological times in which the Church believed itself to be living, for a misdemeanor which at Qumran would have been punished by a severe loss of rations. There is no need now to search for the rituals of Baptism and the Eucharist from the ways of Hellenistic cults, or for its constitution from the same source. "The Jerusalem church," as S. E. Johnson points out, "as we see it in Acts, is in several ways reminiscent of the Qumran sect." [23] Reception of the Spirit, communal sharing of possessions, hallowed poverty, the sense of "election," of belonging to the Sons of Light, are all factors common to the two groups. Contrasts between "flesh" and "spirit" recurring in the Pauline epistles begin to take on a different significance from that attributed to them by Guignebert. From now on, Paul the Pharisee, the man of zeal, who prepared for his missionary journeys by years of retirement in the Syrian desert, becomes as significant as Paul the Roman citizen from Tarsus, the apostle of a syncretistic cult of salvation.

Archaeological evidence, combined with a clearer understanding of the nature of the literary sources for the study of the ancient world, have tended also to rehabilitate the Gospels and Acts as historical narrative. In a notable analysis of the trial of Jesus the Oxford Roman historian, A. N. Sherwin-White, points out that even "despite many improbabilities and obscurities John yet gives a convincingly contemporary version of the political pressure on Pilate in the age of Tiberius." [24] He points out how Mark and Matthew "supplementing each other even in particular phrases, yet each with his particular contribution, then Luke with his more coherent and explicit account of the charges and less clear version of the activity of the Sanhedrin," give a strong impression of a valid historical tradition. Indeed, the same historian finds it astonishing that while Greco-Roman historians have been growing in confidence concerning the value of their sources, "the twentieth-century study of the Gospel narra-

22. *Ibid.*, p. 161.
23. S. E. Johnson, "The Jerusalem Church in Acts," in (ed. Kristen Stendahl) *The Scrolls and the New Testament*, SCM Press, London, 1958, p. 130.
24. A. N. Sherwin-White, *Roman Society and Roman Law in the New Testament* (The Sarum Lectures, 1960-1961). Oxford University Press, 1963, p. 192.

in the development of form criticism," and "concluded that the historical Christ is unknowable and the history of his mission cannot be written." [25] The evidence is as good as for his best-known contemporary, Tiberius Caesar. Indeed, it is becoming more and more obvious that however we may interpret the words attributed to Jesus himself, the Gospel writers tives, starting from no less promising material, has taken so gloomy a turn provide a unique picture of life in first-century Palestine, and that Acts is a document of great value for the study of the provincial administration of Asia under Claudius and Nero.

In a number of ways, then, the discoveries of the postwar era have carried New Testament scholarship beyond the point where Guignebert left it. The prospects of arriving at a more complete understanding of the religious life of Palestine in the time of Christ have become brighter, and with that the eventual achievement of a more adequate presentation of the life of Jesus. But without the demolition of outworn myth and the thorough clearance of the ground carried out by Guignebert, and his contemporaries, this could hardly have come about. If ever there was a case of old bottles being unable to hold new wine it was in New Testament studies at the beginning of this century. In this context *The Christ* is a notable work. For its assessment of the religious psychology of Paul, of the thought-world of Jewish Diaspora and its influence on the communities of the primitive Church Guignebert's study will stand the test of time. But it is also a historic work, bearing the same sort of timeless stamp as Harnack's *What Is Christianity?* It sums up the results and also the aspirations of a whole generation of Biblical critics. It remains a monument to its author, a thinker and writer to whom the world of liberal scholarship stands in permanent debt.

W. H. C. FREND

Cambridge, England
January 1967

---

25. *Ibid.*, p. 187. See also R. P. C. Hanson's comments in *Vindications, Essays on the Historical Basis of Christianity* (ed. A. Hanson), SCM Press, London, 1966, pp. 34ff.

CONTENTS

PART II: THE BIRTH OF CHRISTIANITY

PREFACE

THE manuscript contains, unfortunately, only one half of the work entitled *The Christ*. In fact, according to the author's plan, it was to comprise four parts. Only the first had been carefully reread and completed by Charles Guignebert; the second had been drafted some time ago and was to be revised; he was working on the third when, implacably, death came to interrupt his task.

The complete work, to judge by the present book, would have been at least as long as the one it followed: *Jesus*. One should remember this in reading the preliminary chapter: "Sources of Early Christian History." Now the length of this chapter seems somewhat disproportionate, but this base was intended to support an exposition double its present length.

Elsewhere the incompleteness of the work is evident in a less precise transition than the author would have made between the first and second parts of the book. This second part was still in the process of organization; two chapters on the Jewish Diaspora had been removed from it to be inserted in *The Jewish World in the Time of Jesus*, which appeared in the interim, and the overall organization is broken by this. A note on the manuscript testifies to the author's preoccupation with this matter: he planned to introduce the second part in a more satisfactory fashion by combining, where necessary, its initial chapter, "Our Information" on the subject of Paul, with the chapter on the "Sources of Early Christian History" of which we spoke—an important revision that we hesitated to attempt.

The third part is in a fragmentary state; it contains the first chapter, which gives the plan for what would have been an exposition of Pauline doctrines. Some notion of how this plan would have developed can be gained from the chapter entitled "The Pauline Mystery," which had been the topic of a lecture and which we reprint, with no changes, in its place. It reveals an essential aspect of the "Paulism" that we have interpreted according to a definition found among the last papers of Professor Guignebert.

There is no draft of the fourth part, which was to include the various aspects of Christianity's development after Paul, whether within the framework of his teachings or according to currents divergent from, or even hostile to, his thinking.

Such is the rough state of the text that was entrusted to us and which we have respected. Hence there are some imperfections of style, such as repetitiveness: habituated by teaching, Guignebert the professor chose to emphasize ideas he judged to be essential; Guignebert the writer would no doubt have deleted some of the repetitions; we, however, have refrained from doing so. On the contrary, we have inserted two chapters already published: "Paul's Conversion" and "The Pauline Mystery." Designed to stand alone, as an article and a lecture should, they contain a certain number of facts or ideas more fully developed elsewhere in the work.

But it is not only the organization of the second part that the author considered to be unfinished; the very basis of his exposition remained subject to revisions. In his retirement, his mind, which remained young and vigorous and wholly uncongealed by acquired convictions, continued, with increasingly acute judgment, to scrutinize the text of the Acts and the Epistles, and to reflect on new hypotheses proffered by exegetes. Certain of the "complementary notes" on Paul in which he noted the conclusions of his reflections and his reading and which were intended for revision of his own text reveal that he had changed his opinion on more than one point.

He had not the time to make this last revision, and we would not attempt to perform so delicate an operation in his stead. Moreover, it is merely a question of details; while in the eyes of specialists all of them are of greater or lesser importance, they do not alter the general portrait of the Apostle and his activity that the reader will find in these chapters.

C. M. B.

January 1942

PUBLISHER'S NOTE

CHARLES Guignebert's posthumous manuscript was edited for publication by Marguerite Brunot, his former student and for many years his faithful secretary and devoted collaborator. She corrected the proofs and compiled the Index, and several notes throughout the volume are signed with her initials.

The Introduction, all of Part I, and the first four chapters of Part II were translated by Peter Ouzts; the Preface, chapters 5–8 of Part II, and all of Part III, by Phyllis Cooperman; the section on Sources of Early Christian History, by Bertha Humez; the Bibliography and Index, by Sonia Volochova.

In the translation of Biblical quotations, the translators followed the King James Bible. In a few cases, however, where Guignebert's rendering is closer to the Revised Standard Bible, that version was used. Renderings based on the Revised Standard Version are indicated by the initials RSV. In any event, Guignebert takes care to give the Greek term where a difference of opinion may arise.

Italicized roman numerals in the footnotes refer to publications listed in the Bibliography.

Except for a few modifications to conform to American usage, footnotes and bibliography follow Guignebert's special usage.

October, 1967

THE CHRIST

INTRODUCTION

> The history of primitive Christianity· is a kind of pre-history which has to be reconstructed—one might almost say to be guessed—from texts which reflect it, but were neither originally conceived nor later edited, for the purpose of putting it on record.—(Loisy, *The Birth of the Christian Religion,* p. 18).

I. Jesus, the Primary Cause of Christianity

THE primary cause of the birth of Christianity was Jesus of Nazareth, who lived in Palestine in the age of Augustus and Tiberius. The Biblical texts do not give us much information about him, but at least we learn from them that he was a real man and not the mere embodiment of myths and symbols. We know that he saw himself as the successor of the prophets of old in Israel. Like them, he had arisen to announce the approaching realization of the hope of his people. He thought he had seen the dawning of the Day of Yahweh and had sensed the first stirrings of the new creation. This Day, the object of both dread and ardent desire, was called by the Jews the *Kingdom* or the *Reign of God.*

And because we know this, we also know that Jesus had no intention of working for a distant future; that he neither foresaw nor willed the Christian Church; that he did not see himself as the founder of a religion, nor even as a religious reformer. Herald of the Good News (which was precisely the affirmation that Yahweh would perform a mighty deed to establish in the world his justice and glory), he had indeed no reason to think of setting up a new religion. That idea could not have occurred to his mind, which was that of a pious Jew, except as an absurdity and a sacrilege.[1]

His religion was that of the Torah, as it was understood by the *anavim* the *poor* of Israel. A few pronouncements, authentic or not, which at times make the legal obligations more flexible than they were commonly taken to be, and at times more rigorous, must not be confused with the desire nor the will to effect reforms. At the most, these sayings are an example of the personal interpretation that each prophet, and even each rabbi, could and did permit himself, as the Mishnah bears witness. There was nothing in them that went beyond the bounds of practical advice offered to meet the needs of specific situations.

In his case, it was only a matter of pointing out to men of good will the most certain way of attaining to the gates of the Kingdom and of entering it. It does not seem that Jesus's message was anything more than that of the Baptist, who had repeated before him: "The time is fulfilled, and the Kingdom of God is at hand; repent, and believe in the Good News" (Mark i.15).

If we had to admit that Jesus belonged to a Jewish sect—a possibility to be taken into account—the certainty and the evidence that he thought, felt, and acted as a pure son of Israel would not be weakened, even if we imagined that the sect had a few peculiarities in the modalities of its Messianism and in the forms of its piety.

Since Jesus did not want to found a new religion, he did not found Christianity. However, without knowing it, he did father the faith of which he is the center and the Church which was soon to be accounted his. This paternity, in fundamental contradiction with all that he believed, desired, and expected, would have driven him to despair if he had but foreseen it. Christianity is grounded in the love and in the trust that the Master inspired in his disciples, but its roots owe just as much to his fundamental error, to his lamentable failure. His message had been conceived "almost outside human history, and as the ultimate terminus of this history." The unending Reign of God was to replace all the frenzy and the schemes of men. But what had occurred was the unexpected and horrible agony of the cross.[2]

1. This chapter, and all of the first part of this volume, had already been written when Loisy's *The Origins of the New Testament* appeared. I have naturally taken it into account, but I have made no essential change in my own presentation. A comparison of my conclusions with those of my illustrious colleague will perhaps be of interest. In particular, for this Introduction, cf. the admirable section in *Origins*, pp. 33–40. I assume that the reader has at hand my two preceding books: *The Jewish World in the Time of Jesus* and *Jesus*.
   2. *CX*, p. 43.

The sensibility of the disciples corrected and rectified the blunt fact, and then interpreted and justified it through the power of a touching illusion which turned the work begun by the Nazarene, apparently definitively halted by the disaster, towards a brilliant future.

Jesus, therefore, in announcing the approaching advent of the Kingdom, had been mistaken, and like many another Messianist, he had perished for his dream. But the faith of the disciples did not accept this defeat, and through them he conquered death. They were convinced that he was alive, with God and in glory, and that he was being held in reserve for the great work of establishing the Kingdom on earth. They found a satisfactory explanation for his Passion and Crucifixion. They believed that he was no longer dead, that his wretched (and, according to the common opinion, scandalous) crucifixion had been nothing more than the means by which God had elevated him, in resurrecting him from the dead, from humanity to his magnificent and sovereign role: the Kingdom would be made manifest at any moment, and Jesus would inaugurate it with the grandiose pomp foreseen and predicted by the prophet Daniel.

But we must insist on the fact that this belief and proclamation of the disciples, which surpassed the teaching of the Master and exalted beyond measure his claims, was not a denial of his spirit. The disciples remained in his line. They had no idea of giving offense to their Mother, the Jewish religion, and had no intention of stepping outside its limits. They were simply attached to a special interpretation of the Messianic hope, a hope as yet so vaguely defined that their way of expressing it would, they thought, necessarily arouse opposition. But they did not in the least suspect that this hope must lead them outside Judaism and make Christianity inevitable.

If the *parousia*, the return, the manifestation of the glorified Jesus who had become the Messiah had been accomplished as they expected; if the Kingdom had been brought to men in the way they proclaimed it, their faith would at once have been justified and fulfilled, and need not have transcended its first limits. And the great miracle would in fact have enlightened no one but the Jews. But it did not occur. The faith of the disciples survived this second disappointment, but *it could continue to live only by an expansion and a transplanting*.[3] It was *expanded* by its insistence on the point it accounted essential, which already distinguished it from authentic Jewish religion. That point was its presentation of the person and mission of the Nazarene (who for the pure Jews was only an impostor or misguided individual) as being that of the designated Mes-

3. For the necessity of this process in every living faith, cf. XX.

siah. Thus began the real formation of Christology, the doctrine of the Christ, the center and pivot of all Christianity. The faith was *transplanted* because the Jews in general did not accept it and became so hostile to its promoters that the latter were forced to part company and to organize as well as they could while they awaited the late-arriving *parousia*. They were forced to see themselves as their own *raison d'être*, and to drift gradually towards characteristic rites, towards a cultus which, although not yet rejecting legalistic practices, was no longer purely Jewish. Finally, they were forced to attach an ever-increasing importance to faith-as-belief-about as well as to faith-as-trust-in Christ Jesus.

These then are the phenomena, some belonging to the realm of religious psychology, others to that of practical and vital necessity, which surround the historical causes of the birth of Christianity as a new religion.

II. The Establishment of Christian Autonomy

If we look at the overall facts of the period covered by the present study, which comes to a close more or less with the first half of the second century, we see that the establishment of Christian autonomy was effected in three phases:

1. After the faith-as-trust of the disciples had lifted them from the despair into which they had been cast by the arrest and crucifixion of Jesus, they came back from Galilee to Jerusalem, there to await the *parousia*. Why? Probably because they derived from their Master the expectation that the establishment of the Kingdom was to begin in the Holy City.[4] Lost in the crowd which at first did not detest them, but which did find them odd (and which they found strange because it would not believe what they believed), they were subject to the *law of the sect*: they formed a group, huddled together to comfort one another, to help each other, and to await patiently the external confirmation of their inner certainty. Thus they formed the first community, not of *Christians*, for the word would lend itself to misunderstanding, but of *believers* in Christ Jesus.

It was an inorganic community, in which the emanations of the Spirit multiplied, dominating hearts and minds. But it was also a community in which some of the most beloved friends of the Master exercised their personal influence for the spiritual and moral well-being of all. Perhaps we may be permitted to name among them Simon Peter; the two sons

4. Cf. *LXXXVI*, pp. 507f.

of Zebedee; and James, a brother of Jesus, who was probably won over by the Easter faith. All these men were Jews, good Jews, and better Jews than the others since they were shown, we are told, to be capable of edifying them by the exactitude and ardor of their piety.[5] They frequented the temple assiduously.[6] Their only apparent originality was that they met in the house of some Hierosolymitan who had been won over to their convictions. There they rekindled their hopes and *ate together*. The secret power of table communion, so active among the Ancients, bound together firmly these simple and eager men, while the meal brought their thoughts back quite naturally to the person of the Master, because they re-enacted his gestures and repeated the words of blessing he had been wont to use when he was among them.

Abroad, they sought to win acceptance of their faith from others. Did they elaborate an organized propaganda, preoccupied with a future filled with conversations? Hardly. What future would they have counted on? Merely on a short delay. Their methods were those of simple conversions; ardent preaching to two or three persons who happened not to be busy; gentle obstinacy in coming back to the same subject, using as a starting point postulates that the auditor already accepted—all seeming so many madmen's ways to those resistant to their conviction, but also the well-known and efficacious procedure of the spot of oil slowly spreading, the only procedure that could be suitable for them. More boldness, or a more methodical plan of winning converts, would have brought down on their heads the dreaded attention of the Jewish, and perhaps of the Roman, authorities. And notice by the first was especially to be feared, since the imperial procurator would not on his own become very uneasy over the sterile agitation of a handful of poor folk, who expected nothing but the return of a dead man.

At the end of a certain period of time—its extent we cannot gauge with certainty, but it can hardly have been very long, no longer perhaps than a few months—the disappointing delay of the *parousia* imposed on the little community (somewhat enlarged by sporadic gains) the need of some kind of organization, in order to reinforce the zeal and assure the survival of the brotherhood. A source of authority was fixed, which was, or would be, that of the *Twelve*, and appreciably later, I think, that of the *Apostles* [7] and the *Elders*.[8] Procedures were established to meet the needs of the faithful. Divergent tendencies can perhaps, even at this early date, be

5. Acts ii.47; v.13.
6. Acts ii.46; v.42.
7. Gal. i.19; ii.8f.
8. Acts xv.22f.: οἱ πρεσβύτεροι ἀδελφοί.

glimpsed in the little group. *Only at this point could propaganda, properly speaking, be born*; or at least not until then could it assume definite proportions, become strong, and spread abroad, giving rise to the first serious difficulties with the recalcitrant: insistence provokes resistance.

At the same time, *the faith was fortified* by expansion: the bases of Christology were founded and the legend of Jesus began to take shape, the affirmations of the eschatology of the first hour having proven themselves to be insufficient, not only because they had not been realized, but also because the brethren, who found themselves drawn into debate with non-believers, gradually added to the store of doctrines in order to have an answer for all the objections they encountered.

Finally, *rites* which can already be called sacramental became prominent: *initiatory baptism, the laying on of hands, the communion meal.* Now the primitive *community of Jerusalem*, which was certainly always Jewish in intention, tended, without quite realizing it, to be transformed into the *Church* of Jerusalem. Faith in Christ Jesus gradually took precedence over every other religious concept in the spiritual life of the *apostolic world.* The Christian religion was on the move, and the hatred the pure Jews had for it began to give it some notion of its own existence.

It was on the move, and we realize that it had taken its first steps. But the contemporaries on the outside were no doubt less perspicacious. In their eyes, the hope and faith of the brethren simply represented a *Jewish heresy*, the error of a handful of foolish visionaries. What chances of lasting could it have since the immense majority of the Jews rejected it? The young Church seemed condemned to vegetate, as a humble sect can, and to be soon extinguished, since nothing it expected would come to pass.

2. *The second phase saved the Church.* Thanks to it, the limited first faith widened its bounds to the proportions of a universal religion. The second phase gave it a new spirit and even a new substance, new intentions and new ambitions, all equally fruitful. The first faith really underwent a new birth in the cradle of the Hellenistic environment.

The beginnings of this most important movement are marked by the success the brethren achieved in converting certain pilgrims who had come to Jerusalem from the ghettos of the Greek world. These men could be much more open to the Christian hope than the Judeans, but they did not receive it in a spirit as strictly and correctly Jewish. They did not fail to interpret it in line with their own habitual modes of thought. In their synagogues—the synagogues of the Diaspora—they had set aside to a greater or lesser extent the narrow legalistic interpretation of the Torah, both because it would scarcely have been possible to conform to it, living as they did in the midst of the Gentiles, and because they were subject in various degrees, in one place or another, to the influence of that Hellenistic habit of combining and blending together myths and beliefs which is called *syncretism*. In the Hellenistic world of that time, religions that pretended to reveal to men the way by means of which, after earthly misfortunes, they could attain an eternally blessed life, were widespread and flourishing. To take its place beside them, the as yet stuttering Christianity, adaptable because it was formless (but even more because it was obliged to turn in some practical way from the ever more distant *parousia* and to substitute for it something else which would in itself be a reason for being), was going to find itself pushed to resemble them, to present itself as also *a religion of salvation* to men for whom Jewish nationalism and its narrow Messianism held no true interest.

This evolution was all the more easy for it, since, having at first run into the obstinate resistance of the true Jews, it had to direct its propaganda toward the proselytes, the semi-Jews who haunted the synagogues of the Diaspora. These men were much more susceptible than the Israelites, but they were more dangerous if the faith was to be maintained in its first forms and content.

Powerful forces were at work on all sides, forcing the faith to define more precisely its content and to extend its claims, to undergo the expansion to which I have already alluded. These forces stirred most energetically in the places and directions where the thinking of *apostolic* times had already been at work. But greater vigor and saturation was now possible, for the powerful forces were now relieved of the counterweight that the apostles' effort to defend their orthodoxy had proved to be in Jerusalem.

The forces first actively developed the virtualities of Christology: the Jesus-Messiah, the Christ of the Judeo-Christians, became the *Savior* and the *Lord* of the Cosmos. Broad cosmological myths surrounded its speculations, under which the historical person of the Nazarene disappeared. Almost imperceptibly *the Christ was elevated to a plane approaching that of God himself*. The Jews could only be scandalized and indignant.

Secondly, the cultus assumed a more important and commanding role. The two old rites, baptism and the Eucharist, tended to become freighted with the essential content of the pagan salvation Mysteries. And this was a development equally unacceptable to the Jews.

Finally, the communities, compelled by Jewish hostility to separate from the synagogues, set up an organization, and soon an administration, which strengthened them by binding them close to one another and distinguished them from Jewish groups.

The foregoing considerations may be called both the *raisons d'être* and the ingredients of Christianity as an autonomous religion. Henceforth, the old Church of Jerusalem was left behind and whatever the respect its transformed sons retained for it at first, it was virtually doomed to impotence, scorn, and fast-approaching extinction. There would remain only the necessary but illusory hypothesis of *apostolic tradition*, the notion that because of the *Apostles* it was the repository of all truth, and that through the labors of its *missionaries* the faith shone on the entire world. Similarly, scarcely more remained of the real Jesus the Nazarene than his reputedly prophetic name (Matt. ii.23), a strand of tendentious anecdotes and miraculous events, the pseudo-narrative of his Passion (interpreted as a salvation Mystery), and the postulate of his inviolable teaching.

This twofold elimination of the historic Jesus and of the authentic apostolic faith was obviously necessary before Christianity could become an independent religion. Two legends, one *evangelical*, the other *apostolic*, replaced the reality that had been bypassed, for *facts* proved the inanity of the first very simple eschatological presentation.

The tiny Jewish seed, sown on Greek soil, found there a rich and prolific substance for its enrootment and nourishment. It became so acclimated that it changed its own nature and denied it. At last it blossomed out as an immense tree, some of whose branches have been cut down through the ages, but which still covers with its shadow an area much greater than the known world of the Ancients.

3. Although it already contained a more or less firm doctrinal basis concerning the person, mission, and role of the Christ, the new religion was not presented as an organized and coherent doctrine, but as a hope to which were related a salvation myth and rites supposedly efficacious in granting the faithful access to the way of salvation and in safeguarding them thereon. From another point of view, the new religion appeared as a *way of life* that corresponded to a certain ethical ideal. The realization of this ideal, regarded as being in conformity with God's will and pleasure, was almost as important for salvation as faith. There was nothing in this presentation to satisfy the cultivated minds of the Greco-Roman world. Their religious concerns generally demanded a metaphysical explanation, and when they began to be interested in Christianity, they asked it questions it was not in a position to answer. They answered for it, projecting unto its elementary postulates the concepts and the spirit of their own

philosophical speculations, that is, the speculations to which their training in the schools had accustomed them. They reasoned about each of its postulates and discovered antecedents and consequences which the first generation of the faithful had not suspected. Moreover, polemic—which was soon to rage between Christians and Jews, Christians and pagans, and between Christians of diverse tendencies—released problems which had to be considered and solved. Finally, the notions which had surged from the minds and the often too ingenious imagination of individuals, without benefit of discipline and control, required the establishment of some co-ordinating authority.

Thus, Greek intellectualism, with its philosophical and religious syncretism, reacted on early Christianity to produce Christian doctrine. The indefinite delay of the *parousia* favored its genesis and soon permitted its ascendancy over the rather naive hope, the living but summary mystique, which had from the start separated Christianity from the religion of Israel.

If Christianity had been, as Catholic orthodoxy still maintains, a religion which really had its roots in the revelation of God through Jesus, a religion constituted by an act of his conscious will, and made so clear to his first and future disciples that no fundamental divergence between them would be admitted, then Christianity, especially during its first years, would have offered a visible unity of direction and intention. The inevitable reflection on its essential principles, with the consequence of doctrinal speculation, the necessary food of faith—and of heresy—would by itself have been enough to create streams of thought and life more or less divergent in relation to those of the authentic first tradition. But it is precisely this tradition that cannot be seen in the beginning. This tradition, which living faith invented in the midst of its hesitations, stumblings, trials, successes, false starts, and acts of penitence, does not exist.

Primitive Christianity, then, is the painfully ripened fruit of a *life experience* which enabled it to multiply its acquisitions *in the field of doctrine* until it had settled on a *rule of faith* generally accepted. Then, from more or less disputed doctrinal affirmations, it developed a so-called orthodox *creed*, which already belonged to the realm of theology. In parallel fashion, the life experience *in the area of pragmatic piety* enabled primitive Christianity to elaborate a practical moral and mental discipline whose importance in fact surpassed for a long time the rule of faith. The lack of that fundamental revelation which evolved Christianity that is nevertheless supposed to be at the base of its doctrinal edifice has made the study and explanation of the ancient Christian phenomenon—especially in the period we are here considering—a very complicated and often very obscure matter. The *internal* fact which no doubt marks the end of this stage of evolution towards *orthodoxy*, by which I mean the acceptance of an approximately fixed and coherent core of beliefs, is represented by the failure of the *Montanist pneumatism*, in which the liberty of individual inspiration still survived in the first quarter of the third century.[9]

III. *The Principle of the Evolution of Primitive Christianity*

If one were to look for the principle of unity which dominates and coordinates the three phases in the evolution of primitive Christianity, he would find it in the constant concern to magnify and embellish the person of Jesus, who became successively *Messiah, Vice-God, Lord of the Cosmos,* and (we say this provisionally, in order not to prejudge the solutions theology would bring) at least one of the aspects of the one *God.* Autonomous Christianity became the *religion of Christ Jesus.* Under the name of *Christ* there was no longer subsumed the narrow notion of the Jewish Messiah, but the whole grandiose idea which was to find its adequate expression only in the creeds of the fourth century.

And that is why the title of this book is *The Christ.*

9. *CVII*, p. 441.

SOURCES OF
EARLY CHRISTIAN
HISTORY [1]

**I. Scarcity of
Documents; Causes**

ONE of the most discouraging and
surprising disappointments encountered as one begins the study of Christian antiquity is the paucity and slenderness of documents: the preachings
of the Apostles, the founding of the Pauline communities, and the establishment of the new religion in the Greco-Roman world appear to have
attracted no more contemporary attention than the rise of Jesus itself had
done. How can we explain the silence of Jewish and pagan historians on
such events? We begin by seeking reasons for the strange neglect; then,
since no satisfactory ones appear, we finally begin to wonder whether we
are not, quite simply, the victims of an illusion: was something that we
now judge so enormously important really enough to kindle the emotions
of the Ancients, or have its growing effects over the years falsified our
judgment of the initial causes? I believe that the latter is, in fact, the case.

Suppose that the cult founded by Anthony the Healer, who lived at
Jemeppe-lez-Liège some forty years ago, were to achieve brilliant heights
after two or three centuries: what traces of its founding and its present

1. The bibliography is immense: I shall indicate here only some books in current
use: (1) Two invaluable manuals: *LXVI* and *LXI*. (2) On Christian literature: in
French, *XIII, XLII, LII*; in German, *XXII, II, XXXVI*; for a systematic exposé by
genres, *LXIV*. (3) On the New Testament: in French, *XXXII, XVIII, CX*; in
German, *XXX, XXXVII*; in English, *XLVIII*. (4) On the N.T. Apocrypha: *XXVIII*.

existence would the faithful of those future times be able to find in today's lay literature? Only our newspapers will by chance have said something on the subject; and we do not have newspapers from the first century. So far as public attention is concerned, the Anthonist propaganda is lost in the confusion of daily life, and people judge it, on the basis of a few apparent data into which they normally do not bother to inquire, to be eccentric and negligible. Nine tenths or more of the Parisians have never heard of it, even though it has built a church in Paris which has regular attendants. Similarly, the Christians very early, as soon as they began to be distinguished from the Jews, seemed in the eyes of reasonable pagans to be gesticulating madmen. They would have made a mark on history only if they had caused a disturbance in public life, either directly, by their revolts, or indirectly, by the prosecutions instituted against them. Nothing of the sort took place; the brethren submitted on principle to the powers of the age, even when they were tyrannical or cruel. As for the persecutions which the Church has—understandably—dramatized and raised above all contemporary events, they were certainly looked upon by the pagans, at least until the middle and perhaps until the very end of the third century, as merely police measures: sometimes rigorous and capable of deeply disturbing the faithful who were forced to endure them, but nonetheless in themselves episodic and without general importance.

Furthermore, in some special cases, for example certain testimonials by Jews that might have been made and were not, silence may have been imposed by a concern for immediate interests as well as by the effects of ignorance and scorn. Thus, when Josephus published his *Antiquities of the Jews* in the last years of the first century, the Church was already sufficiently distinct from the Synagogue to be repudiated by it. The state itself was ceasing to confuse them, and the Christian "fraternity," firmly established in pagan territory as a nonauthorized religious society, was sufficient in itself to attract the attention of the imperial police. A Jewish writer could well consider it fitting and prudent not to remind his readers that this punishable enterprise issued from Israel. In any case, in the majority of situations all that comes to our ears is the sound of the Christian churchbell.

It is true that certain passages in Jewish works [2] give us a text in which Christianity can be glimpsed; but this impression is the work of a Christian hand, which either recast the original text or introduced some para-

2. List in *XXII*, I, p. 864. It includes 16 numbers, but hardly any, aside from no. 14 on the pseudo-testimony of Josephus (cf. *LXXXVI*, p. 19), has to do with events properly speaking; the others deal with doctrinal interpretations.

sitical sentences into it. In fact, *we possess no Jewish attestation whatever from the first century concerning the earliest Christian communities.*

Pagan literature is not much more helpful.[3] There is the remark by Suetonius (*Claudius,* 25): "The Jews, who were flung into constant agitation by the excitations of Chrestus, he expelled from Rome." However, the opinion is generally held today that the Roman writer, deceived by the resemblance between Christos and Chrestos, a proper name that was fairly common in his time, took Christ himself, whose name doubtless often arose in the arguments between Christians and Jews in Rome, for an agitator contemporaneous with Claudius. From this we can doubtless conclude that he had no very good idea what he was talking about. There are also a few words in the *Annals* of Tacitus (15, 44) on "those whom the common people called Christians." This text can be compared to another fragment of Suetonius (*Nero,* 16): "Many torments were heaped upon the Christians, men who adhered to a new and harmful superstition." It should not be forgotten that Tacitus and Suetonius were already men of the second century. Tacitus died after 117 and Suetonius about 160.[4]

A papyrus acquired in 1921 by the British Museum and published in 1924 [5] gave us a letter from Claudius to the Jews of Alexandria, dated 42, which refers to the grave disturbances in the country provoked as much by the anti-Semitism of the Greeks as by the agitation of the Jews. Salomon Reinach believed that he could glimpse between the lines of this curious document an allusion to Christian propaganda, thus theoretically sufficiently developed at that time to give anxiety to the Emperor. Certain people have found this hypothesis tempting, even seductive; but after the copious exchange of arguments and impressions that it provoked I am still convinced that it is absolutely not justified by the text, which has no claim whatsoever to take its place in the very spare list of pagan testimonies that really have to do with Christianity.[6]

I have just enumerated all the data that really ancient sources, Jewish or pagan, place at our disposal on the beginnings of the Christian movement, in the first century: it is as much as to say that there is nothing at all. Inevitably, forgers of varying skill later took advantage of this silence on the part of known writers to try to gain the credence of the naive, sometimes in favor of Christ and his followers and sometimes to their

3. List in *XXII,* I, pp. 865f.

4. *LXXXVI,* p. 16.

5. *VI,* pp. 1–37. The papyrus came from Philadelphia, now Darb-el-Gerza, in Egypt.

6. On Reinach's arguments and mine, cf. *RHR,* LXXXIX (1924), 123f.; W. Seston, "L'Empereur Claude et les chrétiens," *RHPR,* May–June 1931.

detriment. Some of their inventions are known to us by name; others have come down to us. I have lately pointed out those that have especially to do with Jesus.[7] Nevertheless, it is certain that in the course of the second century there existed polemical writings directed by the Jews against Christ and, shall we say for the sake of simplification, the Apostles. The *Dialogue* of Justin with the Jew Trypho perhaps allows us to grasp something of their spirit and their arguments. It is very probable that they aimed far more at ruining the Christian interpretation of the Prophecies, and at contesting those in the traditions of the Church that claimed to justify the divinity of Christ, than at rectifying or completing the history of the Christian beginnings as such.[8] Celsus, Porphyry, Julian, Hierocles, the great pagan adversaries of the new religion, would go about it in that way and no other: a proof that they no longer had any historical memory of the facts themselves. Further, we have lost all these books of battle, pagan as well as Jewish: the Church disencumbered itself of them early, and it is only through the Christian refutations that they provoked, and that partially survived them, that we barely glimpse their content.[9]

Some lines encountered in the two enormous compilations that compose the Talmud are of no more value for criticism than the late inventions of the Christians.[10] In several passages there is mention, in insulting terms, of the *minim* or *heretics*, which are the object especially of a curse introduced, apparently towards the end of the first century, into the Shemoneh Esreh, the Eighteen Blessings which the pious Jew must recite three times a day. But are the *minim* the Christians or, more generally, bad Jews, apostates, or heretics? The question, which has been much argued, has not yet been finally solved. Even if we were to concede that the reference is only to the Nazarenes—a term which in the East still designates Christians—we would merely learn that the rabbis did not like them, which would be neither surprising nor very helpful.[11] The poverty of that whole Talmudic tradition, on Jesus as well as on his first Church, is such as to make one wonder whether it did not result from prudent

---

7. Cf. *LXXXVI*, pp. 17 and 23. One can arrive at an idea of these audacious inventions by studying the claimed *Edict of Nerva against the Apostle John* (cf. Gebhardt, in *TL* (1876), p. 642 and the *Letter of Governor Tiberianus to Trajan* (*XXII*, I, p. 866).

8. *LXX*, p. 454.

9. *LXX*, p. 457, which gives useful references. Cf. *CLXVI*.

10. *CCLXII; CXXV*. In these two works there is an annotated translation of all passages in which an allusion to the Christians has been believed to exist.

11. A text of the Shemoneh Esreh discovered in the synagogue of Cairo and published in 1897 says explicitly: "that the *nosrim* [Nazarenes] and the *minim* [heretics] may be swiftly annihilated"; but the date of this precise statement is uncertain. Cf. Strack, *Einl. in Thalmud*,[4] Leipzig, 1908.

purifications in the Middle Ages. I doubt this, myself, on the ground that the text that came to be printed in the Renaissance contained more than enough to be exasperating to the Christians! [12]

II. The New Testament; Its Origins

More serious for us, it seems to me, than the ignorance of the pagans and the Jews with regard to early Christian history is that of the Christian writers themselves, starting with the earliest, with the provisional exception of the writers of the New Testament. As soon as we study, for example, the apologists of the second century,[13] we perceive that they do not seem to know any more than we do, at least for certain, on the subject that concerns us, and that they have available hardly any more sources than those that have come down to us. The same is true of all the Church Fathers who were nearest to the beginnings, hence *a fortiori* of the others. The bishop of Caesarea, Eusebius, who, at the beginning of the fourth century, applied himself with zeal and competence to the task of gathering together the elements of a sort of historical apologia of the Christian faith, and who doubtless had at his disposal all the books, in the libraries of Jerusalem and Caesarea, still known to the Greek East,[14] teaches us practically nothing on the beginnings that we do not know from other sources. And yet, he was still reading the works of Papias of Hierapolis, who had lived in direct contact with the apostolic generation, and those of Hegesippus, born probably ca. 120, who seems to have had excellent knowledge of the Palestinian world of his time and of the Judeo-Christian communities, whose memories of the first period of the faith had, it is possible to believe, undergone less alteration than those of the Churches of Greece. The general interest of what he found there with regard to the history of the first century of Christianity appears insignificant.

12. In fact, in the sixteenth century the Talmud was obliged to undergo Christian censure: the Basel edition of the Babylonian Talmud (1578–81) suffered serious mutilations on this score, but they were corrected by the Amsterdam edition (1644–48). There is reason to believe that we know the form of the text as it circulated in the Middle Ages. I do not, of course, deny the mutilations and deletions inflicted on Jewish writings in various times and places (see the curious plates cited by Eisler, ΙΗΣΟΥΣ ΒΑΣΙΛΕΥΣ, Heidelberg, 1930, 2 vols., in the appendix to Vol. 1); I only note that they did not succeed in causing the worst rabbinical abuses to disappear completely.

13. *LII*, II, pp. 110f.

14. The former had been created by Bishop Alexander in the third century (cf. *H. E.*, VI, 20), the latter by Origen and Pamphilus.

In the last analysis, everything that is essential in our information comes from the New Testament and, in a subsidiary fashion, from some writings that have remained marginal to the Canon—such as the *Teaching of the Twelve Apostles* (the Didache), the Epistle said to be from Clement of Rome, or the Epistle of Barnabas [15]—and in the Apocrypha of the New Testament and the Apostles. At that, experience has shown that the contribution of this last category of writings presents real interest only in regard to the history of Christian legend, into which the actual events promptly disappeared. Obviously nothing prevents us from hoping that the methodical and thoroughgoing exploration of the conventual libraries of the East [16] or a happy chance discovery in the papyrus heaps of Egypt will one day make some profitable additions to our information.[17] Unfortunately, it is to be feared that they always pertain only to details; later parts of this study bear convincing evidence of this. Since neither Christian epigraphy nor archaeology is of help to us in picturing those far-off times, we must always come back to the New Testament, the foundation and point of departure of our knowledge.

The New Testament is the name given to twenty-seven writings called "inspired": they constitute the second part of the Christian Bible, the first and much longer part being represented by the Old Testament. The word Testament (διαθήκη) meant, in the Hellenistic tongue, first alliance, then pact or treaty, and by extension "divine disposition" or "law." [18] It is probably used in the last sense in the parallel expressions "Old Testa-

---

15. The authors of these writings are universally known as the Apostolic Fathers. Edition and translation in the Hemmer-Lejay collection: *Les Pères apostoliques*, by Hemmer, Oger, Laurent, and Lelong, 4 vols., Paris, 1907–12. A good German commentary, with translation, follows Lietzmann, *Die Apostolischen Väter*, I, Tübingen, 1920–23.

16. Thus the important treatise against heresies known as the *Philosophumena* was brought back from Mt. Athos in 1840, and the Didache, mentioned above, was discovered in 1883 in the library of the Hospice of the Holy Sepulchre in Constantinople. More recently (1904), a treatise by Irenaeus, a bishop of Lyon at the end of the second century, entitled the *Demonstration of the Preaching of the Apostles* (Εἰς ἐπίδειξιν τοῦ ἀποστολικοῦ κηρύγματος) was rediscovered in an Armenian translation among the books of the Church of Erivan. Western sources, too, probably still hold some surprises: the *Apostolic Constitutions* were recognized in a Syriac manuscript in the Bibliothèque nationale in 1854, and in 1903 the Library of Propaganda in Rome delivered up an Arabic version of the same book. Cf. Funk, *Didascalia et Constitutiones apostolorum*, Paderborn, 1905, 2 vols.

17. Up to the present time, the contribution of papyri to the history of Christian beginnings has been very modest: it is limited to a few fragments of lost gospels or collections of sentences attributed to Christ, and to a few scraps of apocryphal writings. Cf. *CXXXIII* and *XLV*, nos. 3, 8, 11, and 31.

18. *CLIII*, pp. 240, n. 2, and 253, and *LXIX*, *ad verbum*.

ment" and "New Testament" (ἡ παλαία διαθήκη and καινὴ διαθήκη).[19] The twenty-seven New Testament writings are the following: the four Gospels, according to Matthew, Mark, Luke, and John; the Acts of the Apostles; fourteen Epistles attributed to Saint Paul: one addressed to the Romans, two to the Corinthians, one to the Galatians, one to the Ephesians, one to the Philippians, one to the Colossians, two to the Thessalonians, two to Timothy, one to Titus, one to Philemon, and the Epistle to the Hebrews; the seven Catholic Epistles: one of James, two of Peter, three of John, and one of Jude; and the Apocalypse. These various works are called *canonical*, because they are all inscribed in the *Canon*: that is, they belong to the collection of books that the Church has consecrated as authentic.[20]

The "Holy Scripture" for the first Christians was only the *Old Testament*, the Jewish Bible: they accepted its most widespread Canon, which seems to have corresponded to the Greek translation in use particularly among the Jewry of Alexandria. A first problem therefore arises: how did the Christian communities come to ascribe an authority equal to that of this Jewish Old Testament to a certain number of new writings? It would have been natural, certainly, for them to do so if Christ had written or dictated anything, but he had not done so. Aside from the fact that it is hard to believe that he knew how to write, he had not come to add a book to other books, but to announce the imminent realization of the Great Promise. Why write down instructions, even divine ones, for a humanity which was on the point either of disappearing or of entering into the Messianic Kingdom? However, since what the Lord had expected and announced had not happened, his disciples had had to put off his hope by transposing it. He himself had preached the Kingdom of God; they preached, first, his person and his forthcoming manifestation, his *pa-*

19. The first mention, to my knowledge, of the use διαθήκη in the Christian sense is found in a letter of Melito of Sardis (mid-second century) quoted by Eusebius, *H. E.*, IV, 26, 14: τὰ τῆς παλαιᾶς διαθήκης βιβλία, which implies that there is also τὰ τῆς καινῆς διαθήκης βιβλία.

20. The word κανῶν is related to κάννα, κάνη, a reed; it means first a measure of length and finally a *rule*, a *norm*, a *law*. In its application to the Holy Scripture it appears in canon 59 of the Council of Laodicea (360?): βιβλία κανονικά. There is still disagreement on the meaning intended by those who drew up these conciliar canons. My own translation would be: "books conforming to the rule [of the true faith]." The sense of *collection*, which has since prevailed, is a later one. Cf. *EB*, art. "Canon." There are numerous books on the history of the N.T. Canon. Bibliography in *XLVII*, pp. 301f; a copious résumé in *LXIX*, a short one in *XXIX*; in French, *XXXIII*. Cf. in English, *XIX*, *LXIII*. Cf. J. M. Lagrange, *Histoire ancienne du Canon du Nouveau Testament*, Paris, 1933.

rousia.[21] Further, they remained convinced, and the Christian generations following them believed it even more firmly than they, that he had spoken by virtue of an authority (κατ' ἐξουσίαν), an authority lent by God, for he had been full of the Holy Spirit(πλήρης πνεύματος ἁγίου)(Luke iv.1). This privilege placed him on the same level as the prophets of Israel. It would soon be said (2 Cor. iii.17 and John i.1–18) that he had been the *Pneuma* or the *Logos*, the Spirit or the Word, hence that there had been incarnate in him a quality emanated from God himself, a divine *hypostasis*. This affirmation raised him well above the prophets, identifying him with the very principle of their inspiration. This is why, as soon as events forced the conviction that the last day was yet to be delayed, it seemed natural and in a way inevitable that divine value and authority should be attached to the instructions and precepts attributed to the Nazarene Master.

It would be a serious error to think that the first disciples had copious memories of the life and teaching of Jesus and that they felt nothing to be more urgent than to transmit them to new converts. In reality, the evangelical stories probably did not begin their career until thirty or forty years after the Crucifixion. Until then, there was no more story of the life and teaching of Jesus than we find in the Apostles' Creed (Burkitt).[22] No doubt the disciples did not hesitate to speak of the Master and call his words to mind, but they did not turn all this matter into a catechesis for either themselves or newcomers to the faith. The hope and expectation that united them all placed them on another and higher plane, and this hope and expectation were entirely contained, so to speak, in their common confidence in the *parousia*. To sustain the ardor of their faith they probably depended more upon apocalyptic revelations than on edifying stories.

The likelihood is, therefore, that the first Christian generation felt no need nor desire to write down material of any kind about Jesus. An oral tradition (*paradosis*), entirely spontaneous in nature but with no defense against legendary embellishments and without official supervision, doubtless circulated among the faithful side by side with eschatological statements. Since the development of the oral and eschatological was parallel, the former was not compared with and did not influence the latter, at least consciously. It was only when the eschatological statements began to

---

21. The word παρουσία means *presence, coming, approach,* and even more *manifestation.* It is often taken in the sense of *return* when applied to Jesus, because it is his *return* that will *make manifest* his divine dignity.

22. *CCLVII,* p. 142. Cf. *CVII,* pp. 46f, along the same line and with excellent points.

waver that the oral tradition experienced a growth in importance, and a catechesis with historical pretensions began to be constructed and established. Then the tradition simultaneously created a supposed life and a supposed teaching of Jesus, artificially disposed to justify the new representation of the faith. I could readily believe that the first lineaments of this work, from which the evangelical literature was to emerge, are represented by little disinterested collections, manuals of a sort for the curious.[23] Afterwards there were indeed collections of the *sayings* and *deeds* of the Lord, in order that a catechesis might be derived from them that would be on the one hand *doctrinal* and on the other *liturgical.* The shaping of the Sermon on the Mount, for example, has to do with the former preoccupation, that of the Passion with the latter: although in neither case did the Evangelists bring much sequence, logic, or coherence to bear upon their task. These vulgar qualities were not in their spirit.

What the Lord said and what the Lord did—these were what must logically constitute the core of the "new Scripture" of the Christians. It can thus be foreseen that, in the formation of the New Testament Canon, the writings that would later take their place beside those believed to include the words of Christ would derive their credit from the opinion that they too proceeded more or less directly from his authority. This would be the case, for example, with the various books attributed to the Apostles, and with the Epistles of Paul, who was considered to share the knowledge and inspiration of the Twelve. Further, the first communities lived in familiarity with the Holy Spirit: it was that Spirit that guided, illumined, and completed their faith, by an ever-present influence, and this practical pneumatism would continue so long as there did not yet exist a well-defined clergy that would be hostile to the fantasies of the inspired. How could the multiple revelations that favored the "saints" fail to be revered, when they came from the same source as the genuine communications of Christ to his disciples during his life on earth? Yet it is not difficult to guess that many a writing was not accepted without hesitation and argument: for, in the last analysis, inspiration in those times could be evaluated only by the opinion of the community where it manifested itself, and its ultimate fate depended entirely upon the adhesion of the other communities.

In the first centuries, there was no central authority in the Church that could settle individual disputes: for the Church was not yet a constituted organism, but merely the total of the faithful, *mystically* regarded as a single *body* of which Christ was the *head.* Every local Church was sov-

23. Cf. *LXXXVI*, pp. 41f.

ereign in its own community, because it alone represented both a service and a visible authority; and the opinions produced within one of them penetrated the other communities only through a kind of endosmosis that was frequently slow. Besides, in those ancient times the custom of pious forgery was current; a zealous Christian would write down his ideas or his reveries, would think them useful, and would ingenuously seek out a patron for them whose luminosity would brighten his own obscurity. He would produce them under the name of this well-known personage. Pseudepigrapha are one of the plagues of ancient Christian literature. This is why from the outset we can consider it probable that pseudo-apostolic books were circulated, and that fairly long debates were necessary before a decisive majority for or against them was established in the Churches.

These preliminary remarks warn us that the history of the Canon is confused, obscure, and complicated, and that the Canon itself, as it finally became fixed, after many quarrels and painful hesitations, does not contain solely writings that are of an unquestionable authenticity and worthy of our confidence.

A certain number of small books appeared, then, increasing in quantity as the period of waiting increased; they went from hand to hand, were copied, and some were used to complete others.[24] It would be absurd to suppose that the intent of the editors of these little collections was to prepare the elements of a new Canon; they intended merely a book that might take its place as a continuation of those of the Old Testament. When, in the oldest Christian texts, we find the words "Scripture" (γραφή), "the Scriptures" (γραφαί), or "it is written" (γέγραπται), the reference is always to the Old Testament. The first time that the word "Scripture" is definitely applied to one of the texts of the future New Testament Canon is in a homily, known as the *Second to the Corinthians* of Clement of Rome, which critics generally agree in placing within twenty years or so of the middle of the second century.[25] In fact, as of that date more than one book had already acquired a deeply canonical authority in the Church—before the Canon.

It was thus first the *sayings of the Lord* (λόγια κυριακά) that were

24. The beginning of the third Gospel gives another testimony of their existence. Luke i.1: ". . . many have taken in hand to set forth in order a declaration of those things . . ."

25. Clement of Rome, 2 Cor. ii.4: καὶ ἑτέρα δὲ γραφὴ λέγει ὅτι οὐχ ἦλθον καλέσαι δικαίους = "And another Scripture says this: I am not come to call the righteous . . ." He is speaking of Matt. ix.13. Barnabas iv.14 is also cited: "Let us take care lest we find [among us], as it is written (ὡς γέγραπται), many called, but few chosen," in which some see a quotation of Matt. xx.16. The quotation is not uncontestable, and besides, the date of the *Epistle of Barnabas* is still uncertain.

clothed with a similar authority. From the apostolic age on, we encounter references to these sayings, to fortify an instruction,[26] resolve a difficult question,[27] or authenticate a rite.[28] Their value inhered in them, and the manuscript that contained them was not yet considered as a book to be venerated. The proof is that Papias, bishop of Hierapolis in Phrygia, in the first third of the second century, had more confidence in the oral tradition than in the partial editions already existing in his time. "I did not believe," he writes, "that what was in books was as profitable to me as to hear things expressed in still living words." [29] And yet, according to Eusebius, the old bishop had composed a five-volume work entitled *Explanations of the Sayings of the Lord* (λογίων κυριακῶν ἐξηγήσεις). The first position taken by the Christians toward writings attributed to the Apostles was analogous: what was important was the apostolic tradition itself, hence its authoritative evidence about the Lord, not the books containing it.

The ritual utilization of the oldest Christian writings was one of the elements that determined their canonical future. The ritual of the Jewish synagogue consisted essentially of prayers and readings, with more or less commentary, of the Scriptures. Naturally the Church, which descended from the Synagogue, would make liturgical use, in that Eucharistic gathering (*synaxis*) out of which the Mass was to develop, of edifying readings drawn from the same collection of writings. We find Paul placing at the end of his first letter to the Thessalonians the express adjuration "by the Lord" to read it "unto all the brethren," that is, to the assembled community.[30] Similarly, the Epistle to the Colossians (iv. 16) carries the final admonition: "And when this epistle hath been read among you, cause that it be read also in the church of the Laodiceans; and that ye also read the epistle from Laodicea." [31] The Apostle rightly thought that an exhortation of a general character could be beneficial also to "brethren" other than those to whom it was immediately addressed. The communities

26. For example, in Acts xx.35, Paul is supposed to say: "Ye ought to support the weak, and to remember the words of the Lord Jesus, how he said, It is more blessed to give than to receive." Our Gospels have not retained this *logion*.

27. 1 Thess. iv.15 leans upon the word of the Lord (ἐν λόγῳ κυρίου) to guarantee the resurrection; and 1 Cor. vii.10, says on divorce: "And unto the married I command, yet not I, but the Lord, Let not the wife depart from her husband." We are reminded of Matt. xix.6, and v.32.

28. In 1 Cor. xi.23, Paul says of the Eucharist: "For I have received of the Lord . . ."

29. Eusebius, *H. E.*, III, 39, 4: τὰ παρὰ ζώσης φωνῆς καὶ κενούσης.

30. 1 Thess. vi.27: Ἐνορκίζω ὑμᾶς τὸν κύριον ἀναγνωσθῆναι τὴν ἐπιστολὴν πᾶσιν τοῖς ἀδελφοῖς.

31. Laodicea and Colossae, both situated in the valley of the Lycus in Phrygia near to Hierapolis, communicated easily between them.

soon came to share this point of view, and (to remain with the Pauline literature) we now possess manuscripts of the Epistle to the Romans which, in the initial salutation (i.7), have suppressed the mention of Rome to address the letter "to all the beloved of God, to the elect, to the faithful."

Obviously, epistles so heavy with doctrine as those that I have just mentioned were not read only once: they were reread, and referred to on every appropriate occasion. And thus they tended to find a place in divine services, even before they had been clothed in canonical authority and before the faithful had any other "Scripture" than the Old Testament. They came to stand side by side with the extracts of Holy Scripture that had been early chosen as being especially edifying and improving, and which were probably the only parts of the Bible ordinarily read in public.[32]

The books in which, a little later, the matter of our Gospels—and others than ours—was gathered, in their turn found use in the meetings of worship, because they appeared to be historical documents that would help to bring the Prophecies nearer, to spread the catechesis, and to fortify the growing apologia.[33] This is indicated very clearly by a celebrated passage of Justin, written towards the middle of the second century: "On the day that is called the Day of the Sun, all in the cities and country come together in one place: they read the Memoirs of the Apostles and the writings of the Prophets." [34] Indeed, the two writings brought together here are logically complementary, for the Memoirs of the Apostles are surely the collections of the *deeds* and *sayings* of the Lord that were already called "Gospels." Justin himself reports this explicitly.[35] It has been thought possible that these Gospels known to Justin were exactly the four that appear in the Canon. In any case, their subject matter was the same; and what we read in another work by the same author, the *Dialogue with the Jew Trypho* (103, 8), "For, in the Memoirs that I have said that his Apostles and their disciples composed. . . ," corresponds rather well with what tradition reports of the two pairs, Matthew and John, Mark and

32. *CXX.*
33. *CXX,* I, p. 63, observes accurately that Irenaeus's treatise *On the Preaching of the Apostles,* which was recently found and can give us an idea of ancient apologia, still rests fundamentally on texts drawn from the Prophets.
34. I *Apol.* 67, 3: καὶ τὰ ἀπομνημονεύματα τῶν ἀποστόλων καὶ τὰ συγγράμματα τῶν προφητῶν ἀναγινώσκεται.
35. I. Apol., 66, 3: Οἱ γὰρ ἀπόστολοι ἐν τοῖς γενομένοις ὑπ᾽ αὐτῶν ἀπομνημονεύμασιν ἃ καλεῖται εὐαγγέλια . . . = . . . for the Apostles, in the Memoirs that they have left, which are called Gospels . . ." The subject under discussion is the evangelical tradition concerning the institution of the Eucharist.

Luke: according to tradition, two Apostles and two disciples of the Apostles.[36]

The attribution of a book to an Apostle, a man who was believed to have known the Lord on familiar terms, naturally lent it the best possible authority. It is by a sort of extension of this confidence in the apostolic tradition that several writings, attributed to disciples of the Twelve or to men who were supposedly close to them, had considerable authority, at least in certain Churches, and were formally accepted there for the needs of worship. This was the case with the first *Epistle of Clement of Rome* in the Church of Corinth; [37] furthermore, several manuscripts containing our Canon contributed very directly to prove that some books finally rejected by the Church were "received" by various communities and, it seems likely, placed by them for a fairly long time on the same level as the most venerated of the texts. Thus Codex A, called the Codex Alexandrinus (fifth century, London), gives us the first and second epistles of Clement of Rome. The Greek Codex Sinaiticus (fourth century, Leningrad) contains the *Epistle of Barnabas* and the *Shepherd* of Hermas.

III. *The Formation of the Canon*

As we know, it was not only in worship and in teaching (catechesis) that the most ancient Christian books were used and became established; it was also in controversy, first with the Jews, and then with the various kinds of Christians, with philosophers from outside, and with eccentrics of all kinds. All of these could shake the confidence of their brothers, in a time when, I repeat, there was still no central authority to guide and govern the Church of Christ. Obviously the reputation and authority of a book grew in proportion to the services it rendered. Jerome (*De viris,* 4) was entirely right when he noted that the various writings of the New Testament had earned their authority by *age* and *use*: it was not for the real apostolicity of their content. "The formation of what is known as New Testament literature was conditioned by the evolution of Christian propaganda; it became, so to speak, stabilized precisely when the "Catholic" Church took final form and declared itself the guardian of what it wished to consider the authentic tradition of Christianity" (Loisy).

It is, after all, noteworthy that it was certain heretics, men from whom

36. On the evangelical literature, cf. *LXXXVI*, pp. 27f.
37. Eusebius, *II. E.,* IV, 23, 11, after a letter of Dionysius, bishop of Corinth in the last third of the second century.

most of the faithful held themselves aloof, Gnostics of certain schools who were eccentric in their faith and sometimes in their customs, who first showed themselves disposed to construct a Christian canon, and thus obliged the Church to make one of its own to oppose theirs. Basically, most of them wished to reject the use of the Old Testament in Churches; they refused to recognize divine inspiration in the Jewish books, and they sought to put forth a New Scripture in their stead. In the time of Hadrian, roughly between 117 and 138, the great heretic leader Basilides was already using, in citing texts that would later enter the Canon, the words "the Scripture says" or "as it is written." And it was another Gnostic, the famous Marcion, who was the first, around 140, to attempt to sort out the books circulating in his time and to *canonize* a certain number of them. Finally, it was a heretic, Heracleon, a disciple of Valentinus, who wrote, around 170, the first commentary on a canonical writing.[38]

The influence of polemics on the construction of the Canon was certainly of the first importance. In the second century, the Christians still had only a single criterion to settle their quarrels or relieve their doctrinal hesitations: *the apostolic tradition.* Unfortunately, everyone claimed to have its secret, and it was perceived fairly quickly that the tradition could be recognized with certainty only through comparison of the various writings that claimed to contain it. This comparison led to a choice which was not inspired by any rule of textual criticism, but only by impressions which it is difficult for us to know of, and which it would be even more difficult for us to evaluate. It had to do chiefly with considerations of immediate utility, which are too often impossible for us to grasp. It was *the true faith*, that is, the faith of the majority of the Churches, that they were trying to authenticate and consolidate; the men of the second century were not hampered by our scrupulous notions of exegesis.

It took a very long time for the general consent of the Churches to fix finally upon a list of works *recognized* as inspired and as holders of the true apostolic tradition. It would be impossible to trace the history of these beginnings without going into more detail than is proper here. It is possible, however, to give a summary sketch.

If we take the end of the fourth century as the terminal point of our study, that being an age by which the Canon was virtually fixed, we see that a natural division in the sequence of events occurs around the year 200, splitting the four centuries into two periods. The first opens with the

38. It was John. We have some idea of this work through Origen, who used it in making his own commentary on the fourth Gospel. On the importance of Gnosis in general, and of Marcion in particular, concerning the origin and formation of the N. T., cf. *CVII*, pp. 395f; *CX*, p. 347.

creation of a *Pauline collection* (*Corpus paulinum*), followed a little later by an *evangelical collection* (*Corpus evangelicum*). If we could be certain of dating the *Letters* of Ignatius of Antioch [39] and of Polycarp of Smyrna in the first years of the second century, around 110, we would be able to prove that as of that time several Pauline Epistles, and perhaps collections of them, were circulating in Asia and Syria. This certainty eludes us, however, for it is difficult, after the interminable arguments waged over these texts, to fix them at the time in which orthodox tradition places them; and it is probably appropriate to place them fairly far into the second century.[40] But at least we do know that, in about 140, Marcion produced a true Pauline *Corpus* which includes ten of our Epistles. He rejected the three Pastoral Epistles and the Epistle to the Hebrews, in doing which, it may be added, he showed some discernment. His initiative, inspired by the suggestions of the controversy, obliged the orthodox Churches in their turn to arrive at a firm opinion on the content of the *Corpus apostolicum*; and this apparently they accomplished fairly easily.

The evangelical collection was certainly more difficult to establish, because each Church, or group of Churches, could cling to its particular collection of the deeds and sayings of the Lord, and because the diversity of editors caused a kind of competition among them that was difficult to overcome. What makes the path that was followed very obscure for us is that nothing gives us the right to conclude, when a Christian writer quotes some *logion* (or *word*, attributed to Jesus), in current use and *authorized* in his Church, that he is quoting from the evangelical collection in which it is to be found today.[41] The acquaintance with evangelical writings of the Apostolic Fathers, and even of Justin, is a perplexing question. If they did not have our Gospels precisely in their present form, at least they seem to have had all their essential elements; but they also used other books, of which our knowledge is imperfect or nonexistent. It is impossible to say that they were already using a completed *Corpus evangelicum*, or even that they had a precise idea of one. The contrary has also been argued, without powerful reasons. It is true that there is a progress in this

39. Ignatius knew Rom., 1 and 2 Cor., 1 and 2 Tim., and Eph.; Polycarp used Rom., 1 and 2 Cor., Gal., Eph., Phil., and 1 and 2 Tim.

40. H. Delafosse (Turmel), *Lettres d'Ignace d'Antioche*, Paris, 1927, 12f.

41. For example: In Chapter VIII of the Didache—written from the end of the first century to the first quarter of the second—we read: "Do not pray like the hypocrites, but instead as the Lord commanded in his Gospel (ἐν τῷ εὐαγγελίῳ αὐτοῦ); pray thus: . . ." The *Pater* follows, in a text analogous but not identical to that in Matt. vi.9–13. If we consider that for a long time the word "gospel" meant exclusively "good news," nothing whatever assures us that the Didache is referring to a book, a Gospel in today's sense, having authority in the Syrian Churches from which it probably came.

direction from Clement of Rome to Justin; for, in going from one to the other, we pass from an allusion that can be identified only with considerable good will to one that is an unquestionable quotation.

We do not, in fact, begin to see our way clear until Tatian, Justin's disciple, who, around 150–160, undertook his *Diatessaron* or *One Gospel from Four.*[42] This is the first harmony of the canonical writings that we know. Tatian's undertaking proves, first, that the four Gospels that stayed in the Canon were already preferred over the others, and had possibly even generally supplanted them. Why? It is hard to see; but a plausible reason would be the fact, very important at the time, that all four carried the warranty of an authoritative name, whereas their competitors were anonymous. Perhaps each of them had the support of a large Church as well. In any case, these four—edited, then touched up in different places, disagreeing and indeed contradictory in many of their parts (almost in their entireties, if John is compared to the three Synoptic Gospels)—had finally asserted themselves, at least in the Syrian Churches for which Tatian was writing. The *Diatessaron* proves further that, in the milieux that it was addressing, the contradictions of the four Gospels were no longer felt as such; they were looked upon as *complementing* each other and as representing four different presentations of the *same and unique Gospel.* This is the thesis that won out in the Church. Its triumph obviously arose out of the preliminary conviction that these four books, unlike others that claimed to resemble them, were marked by the sacred character of inspiration, just as were the canonical books of the ancient Scripture.

During the second half of the second century, the opinion strengthened and spread in the Christian communities that there were four authorized Gospels, that there should be four and not more, that they were illumined by the Holy Spirit, and that the authority of the Apostles was their warrant.[43] And it is certainly due to the fact that confidence in that apostolic authority grew more and more important in the Church, in proportion as the diversity of opinions and trends demanded a more energetic and less

42. Eusebius, *H. E.*, IV, 29, 6: τὸ διὰ τεσσάρων (εὐαγγέλιον). Some fragments of the work have come down to us, in Greek and in an Arabic translation. Cf. *LII*, pp. 182f.

43. Irenaeus, ca. 180–190, invoked nature's typology in their support: four cardinal points, four principal winds, etc., and concluded (*Adv. omnes haereses*, III, 11, 9): "The Word that is enthroned over the Cherubim and contains all things, having manifested itself to men, gave us the fourfold Gospel that is yet animated by a single Spirit" (ἔδωκεν ἡμῖν τετράμορφον τὸ εὐαγγέλιον ἑνὶ δὲ πνεύματι συνεχόμενον). Cf. *CXXVI*, pp. 8f.

questionable principle of reduction,[44] that the Catholic Epistles, which claimed to be apostolic, and the Apocalypse itself, strange and obscure as it was, tended to rise to the same rank as the Pauline Corpus and the fourfold Gospel. Besides, the evangelical books, reduced to apocryphal rank by the ascendancy of Matthew, Mark, Luke, and John, did not lose their credit all at once; it is notable that, in the last years of the third century, Clement of Alexandria, an erudite man, was still quoting the *Traditions* of Matthias and the *Gospel according to the Hebrews* without expressing any reservations about their authority.[45]

An invaluable text, the *Muratorian Fragment*, discovered by the famous Muratori in an eighth-century manuscript in the Ambrosian Library in Milan, gives us a list of the books that the Roman Church "received" at the end of the second century.[46] It contains the Catholic Canon of today, less the Epistle to the Hebrews, the Epistle of James, the Third Epistle of John, and the First and Second Epistles of Peter. The omissions by no means indicate that these writings were not accepted elsewhere at the same time; in fact, the canonical list properly speaking ends with the following sentence: "We also receive the Apocalypses of John and of Peter, which certain among us do not wish to be read in the Church"; which proves that some communities carried their resistance further than the Roman community did. Similarly, while affirming that the so-called letters of Paul *to the Laodiceans* and *to the Alexandrians* were false fabrications supporting the heresy of Marcion and his associates, and that they must not be received in the Catholic Church, the *Fragment* permits it to be understood that not everyone was so severe.[47] Finally, although the *Shepherd* of Hermas is mentioned with approval, it is not granted reading *in ecclesia*.

Here, then, is a highly important text. First, it bears witness that at the end of the second century the Churches had a New Testament Canon; next, it establishes that if the core of this canon—the *Corpus evangelicum*

44. Tertullian, *Adv. Marcionem*, 4, 5, strongly indicates the idea (in 207 or 208) that the authority of the Church is based upon that of the Apostles, and that it is the Church that has the right of *prescription* against every heretical or exaggerated innovation.

45. *Strom.*, 2, 9, 45: Ματθίας ἐν ταῖς παραδόσεσι... τῷ καθ' Ἑβραίους εὐαγγελίῳ...

46. It was published in the *Antiquitates italicae medii aevi*, Milan, 1740, III, pp. 855ff. A good text will be found in *LXIX; XLV* (No. 1, 1902), reproduced in *XL*, pp. 86ff, and in *LI*, pp. 129ff; bibliography, p. 137; *XLVII*, pp. 286ff, also gives it, accompanied by an English translation and a bibliographical note.

47. Lines 63ff: Fertur et ad Laodicenses, alia ad Alexandrinos Pauli nomine finctae ad haeresem Marcionis et alia plura, quae in catholicam ecclesiam recipi non potest: fel enim cum melle misceri non congruit.

and the *Corpus paulinum*—was doubtless the same everywhere, there was still a good deal of difference of opinion from Church to Church on the rest. The canon principle was accepted, but unity was still lacking in its realization.

This would be the work of two more centuries. From time to time, as this obscure story developed, a ray of light comes to us from a single Church or a group of Churches which allows us a glimpse of the path taken. Thus the report of Origen,[48] which has to do with the whole first part of the third century and particularly with Egypt and Palestine, convinces us that a debate was still going on in the Churches between the *uncontested* books—such as the four Gospels and the ensemble of the Pauline Corpus—the *generally received* books—such as the First Epistle of Peter, the First of John, the Apocalypse—and the *doubtful* books: the Epistles of James and of Jude, the Second of Peter, and the Second and Third of John. As for the Epistle to the Hebrews, Origen judged it to be worthy of the Apostle but nevertheless inauthentic.[49]

Eusebius in turn, in the first half of the fourth century, makes an inventory [50] of the "received" books (the four Gospels, the Acts of the Apostles, the Epistles of Paul, including the one to the Hebrews, 1 John, 1 Peter, and, if one judged well to do so [ἔτι γε φανείη], the Apocalypse); the *contested* books (James, Jude, 2 Peter, 2 and 3 John); the *apocryphal* books (Acts of Paul, *Shepherd*, the Apocalypse of Peter, Barnabas, the Didache, the *Gospel according to the Hebrews*); and the *rejected* books (all products of the heretical literature, falsely attributed to the Apostles). The reservations with which our author accompanies his classifications give abundant proof that the Churches were still far from being in agreement on all points.

A list discovered in 1885 by Mommsen in a Cheltenham manuscript [51] appears to give us the Canon accepted in Africa toward the middle of the fourth century. The Epistle to the Hebrews and those of James and of Jude do not appear, and the writer of the list makes a personal protest against 2 Peter and 2 and 3 John. [52]

Even at the end of the fourth century, in the time of St. Augustine, debate on canonical questions still continued in Africa, even though two

48. Born in 185 or 186, died in 254 or 255.
49. Eusebius, *H. E.*, VI, 24, 4–14.
50. *H. E.*, III, 25.
51. English city in Gloucester County. Text in *Ll*, pp. 138f, and bibliography, p. 141. Cf. *CCLXVII*, pp. 229f.
52. He noted his protest in parentheses, in a rather curious fashion: Epistulae Johannis III (una sola)—Epistulae Petri II (una sola).

Councils, of Hippo in 393 and of Carthage in 397, had labored to bring them to a close. The faithful were made anxious by these divergencies, and Augustine, in his *De Doctrina christiana*, tried to reassure them.[53] He felt that they should hold in such cases to the opinion of the large Churches, especially the apostolic Churches, those founded by an Apostle. In case of disagreement between equally weighty authorities, they should accept each of the respective canons in its entirety.

Yet, as early as 367, Athanasius, patriarch of Alexandria, had enumerated the books received in his Church in a paschal encyclical.[54] This is the Canon that prevailed. Some years before, the Council of Laodicea (canon 59) had excluded only the Apocalypse; and, in 397, the Council of Carthage, mentioned above, reached agreement on the acceptance of the twenty-seven books of our Canon (canon 30). Thus, at the end of the fourth century, this Canon existed, and it tended to outweigh the others; opposition to it ceased bit by bit to exist. Yet it was not until 691 that the Council known as the Quinisextum would definitively give it official status as the Catholic Canon of the New Testament.[55]

Two books in especial encountered tenacious resistance, the Apocalypse and the Epistle to the Hebrews. The story of their canonization is sufficiently instructive for me to say a few words about it.

The Apocalypse was related very closely in content, composition, and style to Jewish literature of the type of Daniel; it seemed to be carrying the prophetism of Israel forward into the Church. And in the time when preoccupation with the Day of the Lord still haunted the Christian communities, these qualities made the Apocalypse seem destined for a brilliant future. More than any other books destined for canonical glory, it had within it what was necessary to become *Scripture*. And, in fact, in the beginning it had a rapid success, as did the Apocalypse of Peter and the *Shepherd* of Hermas, and for the same reasons.[56] But the delay of the

---

53. *De Doctr.*, 2, 8, 12.

54. In Egypt the patriarch fixed the date of Easter every year by means of a "festal letter" to his Churches: this is the 39th of Athanasius. Text in *LXIX*, pp. 87f; *LI*, p. 144, and *XLVII*, pp. 297f, where it is followed by an English translation.

55. It should be noted, however, that this decision did not remove all hesitations. At the present time, the Syrian Church still rejects James, Jude, 2 and 3 John, and Apocalypse; the Armenian and Ethiopian Churches make additions to the orthodox Canon, the former the apocryphal correspondence of Paul and the Corinthians, the latter the *Apostolic Constitutions*, a compilation arising out of a writing attributed to Clement of Rome.

56. The sixth-century Greco-Latin New Testament MS. D_2 (*Claromontanus*) still contains these two works at the end of the Pauline Epistles, together with the Apocalypse of John.

parousia shook its credit, and provoked a lively reaction against it in the course of the third century. It was perceived then that its attribution to the Apostle John was not without its difficulties; it was realized that the work, taken by itself, seemed difficult to understand; some even came to the point of calling it "unintelligible" and "incoherent." [57] Dionysius, bishop of Alexandria († 265), confessed that he could understand little of it; yet, as many of the brethren held it in favor, he did not wish to reject it and preferred to suspect, when he lost his way in it, that the words concealed a very deep meaning. I have already noted in passing the hesitations of Eusebius († 340?).

A half-century later, Cyril of Jerusalem († 386) rejected the book, while Athanasius († 373) accepted it; John Chrysostom († 407) made frequent use of it without, however, ever appearing to see it as Scripture; and the Syriac translation of the Bible known as the *Peshitta* (the Simple) excludes it. In all, and in spite of the notable exception of Athanasius, who was perhaps influenced by Rome, the East was rather hostile toward the Apocalypse. The Churches of the West, on the contrary, remained generally favorable towards it. It is not that they understood it better than their Oriental sisters, but rather that they read it, so to speak, mechanically, as they did the Hellenic writings that were beyond them, pausing only over grandiose scenes. Even so, they left the book at the end of their lists. Finally their tenacity won out and imposed the book on the East, or at least on most of its Churches.

The case of the Epistle to the Hebrews is of another kind: it posed a direct problem of authenticity, which the Church of Rome and the African Churches resolved in the *negative*, and their opinion drew with it that of the West: the work was not apostolic, hence it should not be "received." The Eastern Churches, on the contrary, and in spite of some individual divergences, arrived at the *affirmative*, although without ever stating very precisely what connection they thought themselves to be establishing between Paul and the Epistle. Their feeling—it was nothing more—then acted upon that of the West and little by little modified it. Augustine and Jerome accepted the Epistle and brought it to triumph in the Latin-language Churches. Thus the West passed the Apocalypse to the East, while the latter passed the Epistle to the Hebrews to the West.

Here, in this double contestation, we catch the quick of the exchange of concessions and civilities that permitted the Canon to take form. The

---

57. Ἀγνωστόν τε καὶ ἀσυλλόγιστον, according to Dionysius of Alexandria, in Eusebius, *H. E.*, 7, 25, 1.

various Churches, little by little and turn by turn, consented to incorporate into the canon that each had fairly quickly worked out for its own use all the canon elements of the others.

The canonical collection that thus slowly and painfully established itself owed little or nothing to the authority of the Church; or at least the Church entered the matter, under the form of conciliar decisions, only late in the day (fourth century). It was by a sort of instinctive judgment of faith that each Church decided and prepared the eventual fate of each writing or each little group of writings, *in isolation*. It is also possible to believe that, after their hesitations were over, the instinct and experience of the communities finally chose what was by and large the best of the first Christian literature: I mean what was most reasonable and, from another point of view, most living and most active, most useful for both edification and propaganda. This is at least the impression received from a comparison between the books of the New Testament and the Apocrypha of the second century. In any case, I say "by and large" because writings like the Didache, the Epistle of Barnabas, the Epistle to Diognetus, the First Epistle of Clement of Rome, and even the *Shepherd*, would not seem out of place in the Canon. It was special circumstances, or certain details of their content, that hurt them. Thus the Didache, in its liturgical and so to speak ecclesiastic precision, corresponded too closely to stages in the form of worship and in the community organization that were too swiftly left behind; Barnabas was too closely connected with polemics that soon fell into disuse, etc. As for the circumstances that certainly were determining factors in a number of other cases, it is not astonishing that they usually elude us.

IV. The Textual Value of the Canonical Writings

When one reflects that the books that successively entered the Canon had first circulated for a long time among the Churches, some of them for two or three centuries, at a time when we know that respect of texts was not one of the cardinal virtues, we cannot escape a troublesome uneasiness. We wonder what the text of these writings is worth today, and how much of the authentic thought of their true authors they still contain, after all the risks they underwent, amid controversies and quarrels, during that time when dogma and orthodoxy were coming laboriously to life. To tell the truth, the first observations of the critic are not very reassuring.

There is no longer any trace of autographs of our New Testament books.[58] Entrusted to a fragile medium, papyrus, they must have perished fairly early, simply because in the beginning they were not accorded that status of sacred books that would have protected them. Naturally, in antiquity and even in modern times it has been believed several times that these venerable originals had been recognized or rediscovered: in each case the discovery proved to be either a pious illusion or a reprehensible hoax, nothing more. It is, for example, possible and even probable that certain apostolic Churches, 150 or 200 years after they had supposedly produced an apostolic book or received it in their care, still claimed to possess its authentic manuscript. This is no reason for us to believe it.[59] Since then, there has been talk of the discovery of the original of Matthew in Barnabas's tomb at Cyprus, and of the discovery of the original of Mark in Venice; there has been an attempt to make us accept various fragments of papyrus as remnants of the initial edition of Matthew, of James, of Jude —all without the least verisimilitude.

We have at our disposal, then, only copies of copies, separated from the archetypes by very numerous degrees.[60] And unfortunately the exactitude of the first copies, those which in the end gave birth to all the others in families of varying sizes, is still very ill assured. It is a difficult labor to copy a manuscript of some length exactly, and it was particularly so in an age when the custom of writing without separating the words in a line laid numberless traps for the inexperienced or inattentive scribe. Furthermore, we have every reason to believe that the first Christian copyists were not professionals, and they were doomed in advance to commit many minor or gross errors in transcription. Today, a bad *printed* text at least has the advantage of being fixed; it does not vary from one copy to another. In antiquity, a bad *copied* text ran a great risk of becoming worse and worse with each reproduction. In addition, the scribes had no scruples about

58. On everything concerning the text of the New Testament and its history, see *XLVII; XXXIX; XXXIII*, II; *CXXVI*, Part I; *L*, first part, pp. 1–59; and the briefer account of *LII*, I, pp. 475–86; H. J. Vogels, *Handbuch der neutestamentlichen Textkritik*, Münster-in-West, 1923. All give useful bibliographic information.

59. As Tertullian seems to do in *De praescript. haeretic.*, 36, 1: "Percurre ecclesias apostolicas, apud quas ipsae adhuc cathedrae apostolorum suis locis praesident; apud quae ipsae authenticae litterae eorum recitantur sonantes vocem et repraesentantes faciem uniuscuiusque." I think that he is speaking of the seats or chairs in which it was believed that the Apostles had actually seated themselves in *their* Churches, and of the originals of their writings.

60. An excellent résumé of the principles of textual criticism will be found in *CXXVI*, pp. 308f. Appendix I of the same book gives instructive examples of the various faults of handwriting that are found in the MSS.

correcting, according to a fancy that might or might not be enlightened, the passages that they had difficulty in understanding. Dionysius of Corinth, obliged to observe that his letters were circulating in a falsified form, consoled himself with the reflection that they were not worse treated than the Scriptures.[61] And he was right.

In addition to this, we must take account of the intentional alterations, the tendentious ameliorations intended to put the ancient text into accord with the doctrinal convictions or knowledge of the copyist. Soon complaints arose in the Church against these alterations, accidental or voluntary, of the most venerated books. Irenaeus, toward the end of the second century, was already adjuring the copyists, "in the name of our Lord Jesus Christ and of his glorious parousia," to pay attention to what they were writing.[62] And he complained of those who believed themselves "more able than the Apostles" (*peritiores Apostolis*) in matters of textual tradition, as they had no fear of correcting them.[63] Clement of Alexandria [64] in the third century and the fourth-century commentator known as the Ambrosiaster [65] echo the old bishop of Lyons. The evil appeared incurable, and in truth, at least up to the time of the fixing of the Canon, our unhappy texts were exposed to a quadruple peril: the malice of the heretics,[66] the orthodox zeal of successive scribes, their indiscreet exegesis, and their inattention. It is a great deal, and we begin to understand why our manuscripts of the New Testament contain so many variants.[67]

Well informed Christians did not fail to notice the offenses that these renowned apostolic writings had undergone, and this knowledge led to several serious efforts to restore the true text. In the third and fourth centuries, textual corrections of the Gospels and of "the Apostle" went out from Alexandria, Antioch, Caesarea, and Palestine. We examine them with interest, but we are still perplexed as to their critical value. It is unfortunately probable that their authors had hardly risen above a very chancy empiricism, a criticism of appearance and of pseudo common sense, extremely dangerous to the original text. Today we can hardly count on anything except a minute and patient comparison of the manu-

---

61. Eusebuis, *H. E.*, IV, 23, 12.
62. Eusebius, *H. E.*, V, 20, 2.
63. *Adv. omnes haer.*, IV, II, 1.
64. *Strom.*, IV, 6.
65. *Comment. in Gal.*, II, 1.
66. Had Marcion not given out an *ameliorated* edition of Luke?
67. There is a formidable number of them. The great majority do not change or seriously alter the sense, but there is still an imposing minority that are more difficult to set aside. *XXXIX*, Index II, p. 380, will give an idea of these variants.

scripts, first to determine the value of each and secondly to determine, with the least risk possible, their most indicative lessons.

At the present time, we possess more than four thousand Greek manuscripts having to do with the text of the New Testament.[68] Their number will certainly grow, and we must place beside them the formidable mass of *versions* left us by all the ancient languages, because they sometimes bear witness to a textual state previous to that of our oldest copies in Greek, or because they echo variants that we do not know in Greek. The scholars have not yet come to entire agreement on the age of our oldest Greek manuscripts. Until recent years, they usually agreed that none was older than the fourth century, except for a few papyrus fragments which may perhaps be older. Recent discoveries have somewhat modified these conclusions. The Chester Beatty Papyri, named after their discoverer (1931)[69] and published from 1933, then the *Fragments of an Unknown Gospel* found in 1934 and published in 1935,[70] have every appearance of going back respectively to the third and the course of the second centuries. They brought us nothing revolutionary, either from the point of view of the establishment of the canonical text or from that of our knowledge of events. The manuscripts that may be called *classic*, those upon which exegesis founded its essential theses, still retain their rank and their dignity.

For the sake of orientation, here is the chronological classification proposed by Von Soden, to whom we owe the most complete work on

68. In 1912, Gregory put the count at exactly 4,105: majuscules, minuscules, papyri, lectionaries (collections of extracts read in Church services), various fragments. Since then the list has grown to some extent. On all these MSS., see especially *L*, p. 77, and *XLVII*, 3–33.

69. F. G. Kenyon, *The Chester Beatty Biblical Papyri* (description and text of twelve manuscripts), London, 1933ff. Cf. *DACL*, art. "Papyrus," XLVIII, col. 1175ff. The matter of these scraps of a Greek Bible (Old and New Testaments) covers, for the most part, the third century, although some pieces of the O. T. are earlier (second century) and others later (fourth century). [H. A. Sanders edited a codex based upon these papyri: *A Third-Century Papyrus Codex of the Epistles of Paul*, Ann Arbor, University of Michigan Press, 1935. M. B.]

70. H. Idris Bell and T. C. Skeat, *Fragments of an Unknown Gospel and Other Early Christian Papyri*, London, 1935. These evangelical fragments, unfortunately very much mutilated, gave rise to some interesting observations, chief of which is that, while the fragments are obviously related to our canonical writings (the Synoptic Gospels and John), they nowhere conform to any of them. We do not know exactly where they came from, but it is not impossible that they date back as far as the middle of the second century. They appear to represent separate compositions utilized as sources for our canonical writings but not mingled with them. On the other hand, they have no odor of heresy. They teach us little that is new (nothing at all regarding Jesus); their value in general is that they attest to the already known existence and circulation of collections of pericopes and evangelical books of varying lengths, before the formation of our Canon.

all these texts: [71] Of the 167 *codices* that contain the entire or nearly entire New Testament, two are from the fourth century, two from the fifth, one from the sixth, three from the ninth, two from the tenth; all the others arc later. Among the 1,277 manuscripts of the Gospels alone, three, perhaps four, go back to the fourth century, nine to the fifth, three to the fifth or sixth, twenty-three to the sixth, from sixteen to nineteen to the eighth, twenty-six to the ninth, 282 to the tenth; the rest are more recent. Thus most of the manuscripts were copies in the Middle Ages. Also, much more important than the age of the copies is the age of the text that they reproduce with differing degrees of accuracy: it is, as Streeter says, their "pedigree." A codex of the tenth century can perfectly well give us an older text than a codex of the fourth, and above all it can have many fewer intermediate copies—thus fewer dangers of alteration—between its archetype and itself.

The long, minute, painful, admirable effort of textual criticism of the New Testament has established that *no manuscript in our possession goes back, copy by copy, to the original text.* All have only an ancient *revision* as their archetype. It seems to be proved that they represent the descendants of four such revisions, called the Neutral, the Alexandrian, the Syrian, and the Western.[72] Each of these represents an ancient edition (third-fourth century) of the text, reviewed and corrected, as I said above. And these editions can differ sufficiently to enable Blass, on comparing the two texts of Luke and of the Acts of the Apostles in the Neutral and Western revisions, to support the thesis that the author of the two books had given two editions of them himself. The comparison of the Western text, with regard to the Gospels and the Acts, with what is called the "received text" [73] has led exegetes to even more interesting observations. In general terms, Codex D (codex Bezae, principal witness to the Western text) presents, in relation to the other manuscripts, now additions, now omissions, now transpositions, now a different choice of words to say the same thing, etc. All these dissimilarities are not sufficient to lead us to conclude that Codex D represents a text that is uniformly older or better

71. Von Soden, *Die Schriften des Neuen Testaments*, 2 vols., Berlin, 1902 and 1913; one gives the Prolegomena, the other the text with the richest possible critical apparatus. There are interesting reflections on the ancient N. T. texts, especially the Gospels, in *CXXVI*, pp. 27f.

72. *XXXIII*, pp. 344f; *XXXIX*, pp. 314f. Cf. *CXXVI*, entire Part I, which has its own hypotheses: they are not, in fact, irreconcilable with the consensus of the canonists.

73. The expression used by Elzevir in his 1633 edition to designate the text used by the Greek Church in the Middle Ages, which spread throughout the West when the interest in Greek revived there. The text seems to be based on a recension made by Lucian of Antioch ca. 300: *CXXVI*, pp. 145f.

than the others; but they attest to the fact that the codex represents an edition which is not theirs and diverges noticeably from it. Every variant requires separate examination [74] and recourse to the ancient *versions* which, as I have said above, may have been established upon *earlier* texts than those that have come down to us, thus earlier than the revisions that separate us from the originals.[75]

These originals were written in Greek; none was directly translated from the Aramaic. After rather keen debate, there now seems to be agreement on this point. New Testament Greek is not the classic Greek of Attic prose, but neither is it, as was believed for a long time, a special and exceptional language: it is, quite simply, the language that was spoken by the people of the Hellenistic world. Methodical study of the inscriptions and papyri of the time demonstrated this, and it is somewhat surprising that the exegetes were so long in realizing that such comparisons were necessary.[76] There is no doubt that the linguistic and philological studies carried out on New Testament texts during the last thirty-five or forty years have clarified this fact and given us a more solid assurance that our understanding of the situation is correct.[77]

74. It must be noted here that the moderns, accepting no MS. as correct and no ancient edition as perfectly faithful, and seeking the probably authentic text among the variants, have ended by creating new families of texts which are not to be found entire in any MS., but are made up of borrowings from all. Thus there are the Tischendorf-Gregory family (1869–1894), the Westcott-Hort family (1882), and the Von Soden family (1902–1913), each corresponding to a new edition. On internal criticism and its rules, results, and establishments of fact, cf. *XXXIII*, II, pp. 313; *XXXIX*, 1f; *L*, pp. 118f.

75. On these versions, see *XXXIII*, II, pp. 188f; *XXXIX*, pp. 145f; *EB*, art. "Text and Versions," §§13f; *L*, 77–114.

76. The publication of Deissmann's *Bibel Studien* (1895) marks a date of major importance in the progress of these studies. *CLIII* is still the fundamental study of its kind. The language of the inscriptions is ordinarily more careful than that of the papyri, and even more so than that of the ostraca, the potsherds used as writing materials by poor folk for lack of anything better; but all were basically the same. As Moulton picturesquely puts it, "In the inscriptions the Greek is in its best clothes, in the papyri it is in corduroys" (A *Grammar of New Testament Greek*, I,[3] Edinburgh, 1908, p. 28).

77. Cf. *XLVII*, pp. 35f, and *XXXV*, pp. 8f. The most usable text is that of E. Nestle, *Novum Testamentum graece*,[6] Struttgart, 1907; the same author provides a *Novum Testamentum graece et latine*, which places a good Latin Vulgate text opposite the Greek. Nestle gives all the really important variants; for the others, the reader is referred to Von Soden, *Die Schriften des Neuen Testaments*, II, Berlin, 1913. O. Schmoller, *Handkonkordanz zum griechischen N.T.*,[5] Gütersloh, 1923, must not be neglected. There are good translations into modern languages: today nearly all commentators translate the texts that they undertake to explicate. Among these are Loisy for the Gospels, the Acts, the Epistle to the Galatians, and the Apocalypse, and Lagrange for the four Gospels, Rom., and Gal. In French, three general translations are recommendable: Abbé Crampon, *La Sainte Bible*, Paris, 1905, second part: *Le Nouveau Testament*; la Bible du Centenaire, *Le Nouveau Testament, traduction*

Besides, as New Testament Greek was in process of losing its supposed identity as an original language, the literary characteristics of the canonical books were also losing their appearance of being exceptional. They took their place in a genre which they did not constitute by themselves. There was hardly any way to realize this so long as comparison was made only with purely literary works. The papyri, which extend over some thousand years, from the end of the fourth century before Christ to the seventh after him, and which have given us quantities of little writings entirely foreign to literature (familiar letters, accounts, petitions, inventories, etc.), have made it possible for us to modify our points of view.[78]

With regard to the form given by their writers to the books of the New Testament, especially the Gospels, a question arose some years ago that has caused rather lively discussions.[79] It was asked whether it would not be proper to extend to the entirety of the New Testament the comments provoked, for example, by the whole Apocalypse [80] and by certain verses in the Pauline Epistles [81]—comments having to do with a regular rhythm in the style and the establishment of veritable stanzas. It would not be at all surprising if certain pericopes that may have been used in the liturgy, such as the one in 1 Corinthians xi.23 relating to the Eucharist, had been introduced into the text in the psalmic form required by their liturgical use. Similarly, it is not astonishing if a vision conceived in a sacred delirium takes the form of a poem. But if the whole New Testament, or even only the Gospels, is of the same making, this fact leads us to grave consequences: these writings, which we have become used to seeing as very simple and devoid of literary artifice, become works that

---

nouvelle d'après les meilleurs textes avec introductions et notes sous la direction de M. Goguel et H. Monnier, Paris, 1929; and Loisy, *Les Livres du N.T.*, Paris, 1922. The best dictionaries are: Grimm, *Lexicon graeco-latinum in libros Novi Testamenti*,[4] Leipzig, 1903, which is best used in the enlarged and improved adaptation by Thayer, *A Greek-English Lexicon of the N.T.*,[4] Edinburgh, 1914; Preuschen, *Vollständiges griechisch-deutsches Handwörterbuch zu den Schriften des Neuen Testaments*, Leipzig, 1913; W. Bauer, *Griechisch-deutsches Wörterbuch zu den Schriften des N.T. und der übrigen christlichen Literatur*, Giessen, 1928. Indispensable supplements are Cremer, *Biblisch-theologisches Wörterbuch zum N.T.*,[9] Gotha, 1915; Moulton and Milligan, *The Vocabulary of the Greek Testament illustrated from the Papyri*, etc., London, 1914f.; and G. Kittel, *Theologisches Wörterbuch zum N.T.*, Stuttgart, 1932f. The best grammar is Blass-Debrunner, *Grammatik des neutestamentlichen Griechisch*,[5] Göttingen, 1921. To supplement this, Radermacher, *Neutestamentliche Grammatik*, in vol. I of *XLIV*.

78. *XLVII*, pp. 83f; *XXXV*, pp. 181f; *CLIII*, pp. 100f.

79. Cf. *LXXXVI*, p. 33.

80. On the Apocalypse considered from this point of view, cf. R. H. Charles, *The Revelation of St. John*, Edinburgh, 1920, 2 vols.

81. For example, 1 Cor. xi.23f; xiii.1f; etc.

were laboriously organized and follow the rules of an art very distant indeed from spontaneity. In addition, all the problems having to do with their content and their basis are relegated to second place: the intention of shaping the text for recitation and for use in worship takes precedence over all the rest: we are in the presence of, *first of all*, the products of a feeling, of a religious and ritual necessity, not the expression of a tradition.[82] Up to the present time, I do not believe that anything absolutely decisive has been said to resolve the question in the affirmative. Certain passages of our texts fall fairly well into stanzas; others—and the greater number, it seems to me—refuse to do so. Nor has anyone found the rule or rules, the principle or principles, that would provide a sure formula for establishing a rhythm that until now has almost completely escaped all the editors. It will be wisest to wait for more extensive studies and not to be in haste to push the results in one direction or the other.[83]

The most striking characteristic of the writings arranged in the new Testament is their nature as occasional works. If we were to consider only the role that they have played in the religious life of humanity, we would be inclined to imagine, for example, that the Gospels were drawn up for history and the instruction of posterity: that the Epistle to the Romans is intentionally a theological treatise on *justification*; that the Apocalypse is an eschatological picture constructed outside of time. Nothing could be less true. The Gospels represent little books written for purposes of propaganda, polemics, or reading in worship, depending on the necessities of the milieu in which they were born; the Pauline Epistles, however interesting their doctrinal content is for us, were basically nothing more than works of a personal apologia, often even simply echoes of polemics, all aiming towards immediate accomplishments; or they were directive letters having to do with particular circumstances. Their exposition of doctrine was there merely to furnish arguments in the pleading of the case. The Apocalypse accidentally brings down to us the reaction provoked in an enlightened mystic, or in two of them in succession, by secular violence.

Of course important nuances can be observed: thus the writer of the Third Gospel and the Acts, he of the Epistle to the Hebrews, he of the *Secunda Petri*, were undoubtedly acquainted with literature and the writer's craft, so that these four books have a continuity of style that is lacking in the other canonical writings; but their intentions, entirely

82. Loisy, who has taken a stand in favor of the extension of rhythmic preoccupations to the whole of the N. T., insists strongly on this conclusion. Cf. especially *RC*, Nov. 1, 1923.

83. Bibliography in *XVIII*, I, p. 8, n. 1, and L. de Grandmaison, *Jésus-Christ* (2 vols., Paris, 1928), I, pp. 201f.

utilitarian, were not different. It can be said that, apart from some phrases of the Lukan writings, especially the Prologue to Luke and all of 2 Petri, which visibly attempt to imitate artistic Attic prose, the men who constructed the Gospels created literature only involuntarily; in any case, these works have remained within the forms of popular literature.[84] Thus, if the works did not suffer from a literary taint as such, they did undergo very deeply the distortion that results from their essential character as apologies of propagandistic or polemical intent, born in a sect in the midst of its birth crisis and its transformation into a religion, amid popular surroundings.

It would be very dangerous to accept such writings, even if their text were supposed—gratuitously—to be certain and well established, as documents worthy of the historian's confidence. They require a rigorous and alert criticism, which is resigned in advance to receiving no answer from them to more than one of the questions that will be asked. It is this criticism, intended for the sake of history to give order and definition to these obscure and mingled writings, that is properly called *exegesis* (ἐξήγησις, explication). Its progress is linked to courageous limitation of its ambitions and to independence of any dogma whatsoever. Its role is not to seek to demonstrate how well founded any doctrinal affirmation may be, but only to try to find the real sense of the texts and to measure their exact meaning. In reality, this discipline has not yet had more than a single century of scientific existence.[85]

---

84. On the particularly controversial question of the place of the Gospels in literature, see especially K. L. Schmidt, *Die Stellung der Evangelien in der allgemeinen Literaturgeschichte* in the *Mélanges* in honor of H. Gunkel, Göttingen, 1923; *LXXIII*, pp. 227f.

85. Holtzmann said with truth, "Our discipline is old, if one thinks of the name only, but young if one thinks of the thing itself" (*XXX*, 1). On the history of exegesis, cf. *XXXI*, pp. 1f; *XXXVII*, Prolegomena; Conybeare, *History of N. T. Criticism*, London, 1910; and especially, G. H. Gilbert, *A Short History of the Interpretation of the Bible*, New York, 1908.

Part I

JERUSALEM

1

OUR INFORMATION[1]

I. Its Overall Poverty O N the threshold of our inquiry one reason for anxiety gives us pause: do we have enough information to insure a convincing presentation of the pre-Christian milieu? Have we not grounds to fear that it, like Jesus, will not be visible to us except through the veils of disturbing intermediaries?

One thing is clear from the start: *faith* and, in a sense, *the Christian life and brotherhood* which would become the Church—*and therefore also the tradition,* for collective life necessarily gives birth to tradition— *preceded the Scriptures.* All the writings of the New Testament are in fact of later date than this primitive period that we are seeking to uncover. The oldest do not antedate Paul, who is not himself a worker of the first hour.[2]

Of course there are two letters in the canonical collection that are attributed to the apostle Peter.[3] I do not believe them to be authentic, and when the time comes, I shall say why. But even if they were, it would still be necessary to grant that they are post-Pauline, for the first (*Prima Petri*) obviously owes much to the ideas of Paul. As for the sec-

---

1. Bibliography: *XXXVII*, Pt. I, chs. ii and iii; *XXXII; XLVI; CX* and *CCXXIV*. See also the great commentaries, especially *V* and *XLIV*.
2. The earliest of his Epistles, 1 Thess., may possibly have been written in 50 A.D.
3. Cf. *XXXVII*, pp. 189, 216; *CCXXIV*, ch. v.

ond (*Secunda Petri*), it comes from a time when it was possible to speak of *all* the letters of Paul, "which ignorant and unstable [men] distort, as they do also the other Scriptures" (2 Pet. iii.16). If, as is probable, this is a reference to Marcion, we are brought forward to the middle of the second century. 2 Peter is, I think, the latest of the writings included in the New Testament, and is to be dated after 150 A.D.

In the New Testament there are also three Epistles credited to John, the son of Zebedee, one of the persons who seems to have played a role of major importance in this tiny world of Christian beginnings. Not one liberal critic—that is, a critic liberated from the constraint of orthodoxy—grants the accuracy of this attribution. However, even if we accepted it, we would still have to acknowledge the fact that these three short compositions are related to the Fourth Gospel, which, Johannine or not, comes long after Paul and obviously springs from a milieu quite different from the one we shall attempt to penetrate.

The Canon contains still another pseudo-epistle, which is presented as the work of "James, a servant of God and of the Lord Jesus Christ." [4] The writer certainly had in mind James the Less, whom Paul calls "the brother of the Lord." This sententious little lesson in morals is supposedly addressed to the "twelve tribes," and it is of great interest, because it appears to be very slightly Christian, very Judaizing, and anti-Pauline. This last characteristic permits one to date it. It would not, I think, be wrong to assign it to the third part of the second century, and towards the end of that third part rather than the beginning.

Finally, one comes to the Epistle attributed to "Jude, a servant of Jesus Christ, and brother of James," and addressed to "those that are called." It stems from a period when the Christian faith was apparently already established as a universalist religion and is directed against "doctors," presumably Gnostics. One must therefore date it well into the second century, a little, but not long, before 2 Peter.

In the writings cited above there is no narrative, nothing that gives us straightforward history; they contain only exhortations and instructions of a general nature. If they were authentic, they would be more embarrassing than helpful, for we would have difficulty in reconciling their diverse presentations of Christianity.

One might think that something more useful would be found in the Didache and the Epistle of Barnabas, two short works which, although not admitted into the Canon, and indisputably post-Pauline, seem to

4. J. Marty, *L'Epitre de Jacques*, Paris, 1935. For a conservative point of view, cf. J. Chaine, *L'Epître de S. Jacques*, Paris, 1927.

share the perspective of the communities of the circumcision, the direct heirs and first outposts of the Church of Jerusalem. But if these works have the same perspective as the Church of Jerusalem, they are neither contemporaneous with it, nor do they share its spirit: for the author of the Didache, pure Jews are "hypocrites;" and the Epistle of Barnabas may well be Christianity's first anti-Jewish pamphlet.

This rapid survey thus brings us back to face the tiresome fact that no text that has come down to us dates back to the primitive community. The late writings which pretend to describe it conceal snares which, though formidable, can already be foreseen.

II. *The Acts of the Apostles*

The best known of these writings is Acts of the Apostles.[5] It is the second volume—the first being the Third Gospel—of a comprehensive work dedicated to one Theophilus, who remains unknown. The first part (chs. 1 to 12) is given as a history of the first years of the Christian community. Unfortunately, the poverty of its information and the incoherence of its narrative are evident to the reader who is to any extent attentive. In the last thirty-five years, the *problem of Acts*, scrutinized from every angle, has constantly remained (for the erudite world) on the order of business for the day. It cannot, however, be said that the considerable research directed towards its solution has definitely resolved, or even enlightened it, in a fully satisfactory manner.[6] The most esteemed authorities have fought, vehemently, over the book's sources, composition, author or authors, date, and historical value, without even the hope of an agreement resulting from their conflict. The debate has grown to such proportions and has probed into so many details that I cannot even dream of summarizing it here. I must therefore confine myself to giving an idea only of: (1) the easily made basic assertions concerning the book; (2) the principal critical difficulties it presents.

It is to be noted at the outset that the first reading of the book does not inspire confidence: there is too much gentleness, kindness, and moderation. The first [Christian] community is nothing but sweetness and light;

5. The title is probably not original. Cf. *XCVII*, IV, p. 1, and *XVIII*, III, ch. i. Harnack thinks it can hardly be earlier than 150 A.D.: Acta = πράξεις, which in this case means *res gestae*.

6. *LXXXIX; XC; XCI; CXC*, pp. 314f.; *CCXXXI; CXV*, III; *CVIII; CXIX; XVIII*, III; *LXXIV; XCVII*, II–V. For a conservative point of view, cf. *XCVIII*; for an excellent résumé of criticism, *XVIII*, III, ch. ii.

its overly moving homogeneity accords ill with what we can imagine of its hesitations and the tumult caused by convictions which, in the process of being formed, clashed with one another. The author seems to have been burdened with preconceived ideas and he launches into long speeches, à la Livy, which cannot fail to disturb. At times he does not seem to know what he is talking about, and we are inclined to give credence to Renan who saw in him "the founder of that eternal fiction called ecclesiastical history, with its insipidity, its habit of smoothing over all the angles, and its ridiculously smug phraseology." [7] A more searching study does not lead to an appreciably better opinion.

Orthodox tradition ascribes the composition of the work to Luke the Physician, friend and companion of Paul, referred to as such in Colossians iv.14.[8] This conviction was confirmed by a decision of the Pontifical Biblical Commission (June 12, 1913), according to which the book of Acts "must be attributed to only one author," the contrary opinion being "devoid of any foundation." This author is, in all certainty, "the Evangelist Luke," who completed his work "in the last days of St. Paul's captivity in Rome," and the authority of the book as history must remain beyond dispute and its agreement with the Epistles of Paul merits our admiration. A peremptory judgment indeed, but actually it can win the support only of those who have read neither the Acts nor the Epistles. I have mentioned it only as one example of those resounding Roman proclamations which reassure the simple faithful.

Nonetheless, Acts has been able to mtaintain its reputation with other than Catholic theologians. Renan and Reuss, for example, despite reservations, regarded it favorably. Subsequently, Protestant conservatives have usually extolled it. The partisans of the traditional opinion were greatly delighted thirty years ago when, with great éclat, Adolf Harnack joined their ranks. But, like the pronouncements of the Biblical Commission, the arguments by means of which he sought to justify his surprising conversion convinced only those who, being convinced already, needed convincing no longer.[9] In this respect, his opinions have been influential in the same way as those of the Biblical Commission.

It is possible that there was, in the first years of the second century, a book from the pen of one of Paul's companions, possibly Luke, which

7. *LVII*, p. 438.

8. "Greet Luke the beloved physician." Other references to Luke will be found in Philemon 24 and 2 Tim. iv.11. [I am unaware of any textual variant which makes Guignebert's translation of Col. iv.14 a possible one, but the inaccuracy does not affect his point. Tr.]

9. For a closely reasoned refutation of these arguments, cf. *XCVII*, II, pp. 161f (Cadbury).

was written for the purpose of giving to one Theophilus, a Roman, information on the activity of the Apostles since the Ascension. This book may have contained reliable information that would be of value to us today, but it is certainly not this book that Acts presents to us. The hope remains that the unknown author of our Acts was not unaware of the authentic *book to Theophilus*.[10] But he has not reproduced it. Indeed, if we must admit that Luke's work possessed all the virtues that Loisy, among others, is inclined to see in it,[11] we must say that our unknown author mutilated, disarranged, and in effect, destroyed it. The purpose of this extreme mishandling was to make the work serve his own ends, ends which had nothing to do with history.

A quick reading of the twelve chapters which bear on our subject reveals a surprising lack of information. If one grants that Jesus perished about 30 A.D. and that Peter's imprisonment, by order of Herod Agrippa, has some basis in fact, one must assume that these chapters cover at least a dozen years; for this Herod died in 44 A.D.,[12] and apparently not much time elapsed between his move against the Apostles and the end of his life. Acts (xii.21–23) puts the two events side by side. Now, once the speeches,[13] which are somewhat in the way and are of scarcely disputable spuriousness, have been put aside, the historian is left with only a pinch of usable facts—very little to come from a man who, so they say, had such good access to reliable information.

To account for this odd fact, an argument has been advanced which would be telling if it were well founded: [14] the author of Acts knew and used Josephus's *Antiquities of the Jews*, which did not appear before 94 A.D., at the earliest; therefore, the publication of Acts must have taken place "in the same sphere as the Epistle to the Ephesians, 1 Peter, and the Pastoral Epistles." [15] If this was the case, the question of first-hand information in Acts could be summarily answered in the negative, and the poverty of a narrative which Josephus could hardly supplement would be explained. Unfortunately, the reasons produced to establish this dependence of Acts on the Jewish annalist are anything but decisive. True,

10. Unless he was himself the author of this book, working from an earlier edition of Luke. This is the hypothesis of Goguel, *XVIII*, p. 352.

11. *CVIII*, pp. 89–96.

12. *XCVII*, V, pp. 446f and 469, which puts the imprisonment and deliverance of Peter in March or April, 44 A.D. (?) and the death of Herod Agrippa in the spring of 44 A.D.

13. For a study of their nature, value, style, etc., see *XCVII*, V, pp. 402–27 (Cadbury).

14. M. Krenkel, *CI*. The possibility Krenkel seeks to establish as a certainty had occurred to others before him. Cf. *XVIII*, III, p. 117; *XXXVIII*, I, p. 41n.

15. *CXXIX*, p. 4.

the similarity of language is not to be denied, and certain parallels are at first sight striking.[16] But what argument can be drawn from these facts if Josephus and the author of Acts were contemporaries who may well have used the same sources? Accordingly, the authorities have been divided on this issue, pro and con,[17] and I see no compelling reason to take one side rather than the other. *I don't know*—and this is an admission that I shall have more than one occasion to repeat.

No more reassuring is the fact that the pseudo-historical account in Acts is interrupted by gaps whose limits cannot be determined.[18] If we follow the account as it stands, we fail to get a picture of the external life of the community, nor can we appreciate its trials, because everything the author says remains so vague and "up in the air." He seems to be a man too far removed from the facts to understand them or to have any idea of what needs to be said to make them intelligible. He presents these facts as if they were not in themselves of any interest, uses them only in order to support his apologetic. They appear in his tale as divorced from their real setting. One wonders, moreover, why a chronicler who was allegedly a close companion of Paul would have left the beginnings of the Church of Antioch in such obscurity. If we pursue the analysis to the remaining sections of the first part of Acts, we are impressed by the incoherence of the information, and the disjunctiveness of the traditions or legends used, as well as by the fundamental poverty of information.[19]

Equally disquieting are the contradictions in the narrative. For the moment, I shall confine myself to only one example, but it is a striking one. In Acts i.8 Jesus is supposed to have said to his disciples: "You will be my witnesses in Jerusalem, in all Judaea and Samaria, and to the ends of the earth." There is no doubt that this is a proclamation of the universalism in store for the Christian faith. What, then, is the meaning of chapter 10, which presents the conversion and baptism of the centurion Cornelius, at Caesaria, as so marvelous a sign? Why do the other Apostles, at the beginning of chapter 11, show disgruntled surprise and accept so grudgingly Peter's association with, and baptism of, Gen-

16. As an example, cf. Acts v.36 and *Antt. XX*, 5:1–2, in which Theudas and Judas the Galilean, two insurrectionists separated in fact by half a century, are to be found as contemporaries.

17. *Pro:* before Krenkel: Renan, Holtzmann, Hausrath, Keim; after Krenkel: Clemen, Schmiedel, J. Weiss, Wendt. *Con:* before Krenkel: Schürer and Schanz; after Krenkel: Bousset, Julicher, Wellhausen, Feine, Ramsay, Stanton, Goguel, etc. Cf. *CVIII.*

18. Wendland, *CXC*, p. 315, contains a study of them.

19. *XVIII*, III, p. 152.

tiles? The probable answer is that our author employed two different sources, which he did not reconcile.

The presence of easily recognizable doublets in the text leads to the same hypothesis. If one reads, successively, the two accounts of the two alleged interrogations of Peter before the Jewish authorities (Acts iv.7f and v.26f), he will find such great similarity in their unfolding and events that it will be difficult for him not to be convinced that the two passages deal with one and the same incident. The speeches of Peter in Acts xi and xv show the same process at work. The same journey, apparently, is related in xi.27–30 and xii.25 on the one hand, and in xv.1f. on the other. In these three cases, the sources probably contained two versions of each incident; unable to identify them, our editor innocently wove both versions into his narrative.

Such confusion would not have occurred had the author been a disciple of Paul. It can therefore be considered certain that Acts was compiled from sources a number of years after the events it pretends to relate. The editor whose work we possess was assuredly "not an eyewitness" of anything that he has related (Norden). To be convinced that the writer was either unable or unwilling to put his sources to work or to blend them into a true whole, one need only note the contradictions and doublets and to add up the number of times threads of narrative were abandoned for no apparent reason, or picked up from nowhere.

It would be wrong to conclude from the fact that Acts does not relate the death of Paul that the work was completed before that event. We agree with Loisy's excellent statement: [20] "If the editor has said nothing about this death, it was because he did not choose to; and if he chose not to say anything about it, it was because what he knew for certain about Paul's death would not easily have served the aims of his apologetic." Finally, it is possible that editorial retouching at various times has added to the initial confusion of the book.

III. The Problem of the Sources of Acts

Some authors have thought it possible to identify a certain number of the sources of Acts. Of Josephus I have already spoken. Other possible sources are: 2 Maccabees, the Epistle to the Hebrews, the Assumption of

---

20. *CX*, p. 206.

Moses, the Testament of the Twelve Patriarchs, Tobit, etc.[21] But these texts are not the ones that concern us most at the moment, and it seems rather useless to make a thorough investigation of them in the fond hope of establishing whatever historical value they may possess.[22]

The basic problem confronting us is establishing whether the principal source was or was not a writing of Luke's. It has long been thought possible to recognize authentic fragments of this writing in the second part of Acts (xvi.10–17; xx.5–15; xxi.1–18; xxvii.1–xxviii.16). These fragments are known as the *Wirstück* (the *We passages*), because the author speaks here in the first person plural: "Having embarked at Troas, we went directly to Samothrace" [xvi.11]. One must immediately set aside the tempting hypothesis that collectively these fragments constitute a fundamentally coherent narrative of the early work. For if we were to assume that these various passages came in the form we know from the pen of Luke, we would have to admit that on rereading his journal or his log notes he no longer understood what he had written.[23] It is preferable to believe that our editor sometimes misunderstood what he read.

If, as it seems, the writer borrowed from the *Wirstück* the framework in which he sets the narrative of the missionary activity of Paul, it is certain that he has not reproduced his source in its entirety. In conformity with his special designs, he has deleted here, added there, and elsewhere interpolated extensive borrowings from other documents, all with the unscrupulous liberty familiar to us from the study of the composition of the Synoptics.[24]

Two questions come immediately to our minds: (1) This source, which seems to be trustworthy, apparently feeds only the second part of Acts; did it affect the first part as well, and did our writer use it? (2) Was Luke really the author of this *direct* source? These questions have been answered in all possible ways—which means that no answer is compelling. My personal opinion is that it is unlikely that one of Paul's companions would have written an account of his journeys which begins with the history of the primitive community. In any event, such a preamble would have had neither the features nor the value of an eyewitness report. But from where do we get the certainty that Luke was the author of the *Wirstück*? I must, in all frankness, say that this certainty is unfounded and based merely on an asumption: that, since the first sentence of Acts

21. *XCVII*, II, pp. 73–75, 81f.
22. *CVIII*, p. 131.
23. *CXC*, pp. 324, 334.
24. *XVIII*, III, pp. 324f.

can be interpreted in the light of the preamble of the Third Gospel, both Luke and Acts were written by the same pen. That pen, says tradition, was Luke's.[25] All this is not very convincing, and one can understand why some men, e.g., Harnack, Norden, Loisy, Goguel, have opted for Luke, while others considered one or another companion of Paul to have been the author, proposing (without, however, giving good reasons) Silas, or Titus, or Epaphroditus. The argument formerly advanced by Harnack, that the abundance and precision of medical terms betrays the pen of a physician, and therefore the pen of Luke, is in fact worthless. It is quite easy to see that the so-called technical terms are not beyond the ordinary competence of any well-educated man. Philo, no doctor certainly, but better educated than the author of the *Wirstück* and the writer of Acts, seems to know more about the medicine than they do.[26]

Since Norden's study, the majority of liberal critics admit that the version of Acts that we know is not the first, but the work of a man who similarly revised the Third Gospel, endowing the two books with the same coloration and the appearance of two volumes of a single work.[27]

This version was preceded by another, which was closer to the facts, and possibly better, since good will permits one to suppose that it was more substantial and coherent. Luke may have been its author. If so, he probably fashioned this work in the manner used by him in the Third Gospel, in whose first verses he tells us of his methods; that is, he diligently assembled the various accounts and put them in order as best he could (Luke i.1–4). How valuable was his work? Opinions differ, but it was undoubtedly more valuable than the work which has reached us, since the latter is the product of a tendentious and not overly intelligent recasting, unconcerned about the authentic face of the past. The task of exegesis today is essentially that of unraveling the skein of trustworthy information from the maze of absurd inventions and fantastic interpretations which constitute the very substance of Acts, and in which the second writer seems to delight.

Unfortunately, the process of sorting out the strands of reliable information is so difficult that the judgments of the critics still diverge, even on the main points. One critic sees the skillful hand of Luke where another does not hesitate to denounce the tiresome intervention of the adapter. Painful and troubling disagreements remain.

25. Cf. Cadbury, *XCVII*, II, pp. 262f, for the extreme weakness of this tradition. Cf. Loisy, *CIX*, for a vigorous defense of the thesis which identifies Luke with the first author of Acts.
26. *CXC*, p. 335; *CCXV*, pp. 7f; and especially Cadbury, *XCVII*, II, pp. 349–55.
27. *LXXIV*, pp. 9–11; *CXXVI*, ch. xviii, pp. 529f; *XVIII*, III, p. 343.

No less disturbing is the presence in our extant manuscripts of such discordant textual variants that some critics have been led to the hypothesis of two versions,[28] a theory that has not found universal favor with exegetes. Nonetheless, these variants indicate that our edition was subjected to radical revision, perhaps long after its completion. Von Soden, although without any proof, attributed this revision to Tatian (second half of the second century).

Another question still being debated is whether our writer knew the Pauline epistles.[29] Although I am inclined to say that he did, because some details of the account seem to me to bear the stamp of Paul's ideas, I shall take great care not to confuse this impression of mine with a sure conviction. But if it is to be admitted that our author was acquainted with the Pauline epistles, why did he not make greater use of them? One especially wonders why he did not try to harmonize Acts xv with Galatians ii. The divergence at this point—and at others—amounts to an irreducible contradiction.

But it may be that our writer *deliberately* departed from Paul's account [30] because the allegations of Galatians ii went counter to his purpose, which was to show that the Church was founded in the concord of the Apostles and the perfect harmonization of those tendencies whose differences Paul, on the contrary, accentuates. Whatever one decides about this issue does not affect the consideration that this book is a work of edification in which narratives and speeches [31] concur towards the same end, which is set down *ad probandum*. That end consists in consummating the proof, begun in Luke, whose basic theme is that Jesus and his work, taken up and completed by his Apostles, mark the culminating point in the history of Israel and remain well within the limits of that *religio licita* which is Judaism. In no way is Christianity an unforeseen phenomenon, since it was foretold by the Prophets. The Gospel, initiated by Jesus, was perpetuated by the Twelve and carried by Paul to the

28. *XVIII*, III, pp. 73f; J. H. Ropes, *XCVII*, III, gives in parallel columns the Codex Vaticanus and Codex Bezae.

29. *XVIII*, III, pp. 108f, gives the bibliography of this debate; *XCVII*, I, pp. 266f, and *XCVII*, II, p. 198, tries to establish the complete reciprocal independence of Paul and the author of Acts, who would represent two different lines of development rather than two points on the same line.

30. *CVIII*, p. 63.

31. These speeches, composed by the writer, are very valuable, because they give us a second-generation Christian's conception of the basic beliefs which nourished the first generation. Cf. Cadbury, *XCVII*, II, pp. 402f, 427f; Burkitt (*XCVII*, II, p. 115) would concede that not everything in these oratorical compositions is an invention of the author. This is a very charitable supposition.

ends of the earth.[32] In Acts we have the first Christian apology.[33] This kind of pseudo-history did not need to be invented: all antiquity abounds with similar examples. But the example of Acts is especially misleading and harmful. For not only are the facts subordinated to the apologetic and hagiographic designs of the writer, not only are they retained or set aside, respected or twisted, and, when substitution seems necessary, replaced by edifying inventions, but the very actors in this drama also disappear before the preconceived plan of its contrived plot.

Acts dwells on Paul, seen from what may be called an external point of view; but it teaches us almost nothing about him that would make him truly known to us as a person. For that we must go to his Epistles. Acts comes to a close without thinking it opportune to tell us what became of him. The other protagonists, with the exception of James (xii.2 mentions his martyrdom), leave the scene when the author no longer finds them useful, and he evidences no concern over their fate, knowledge of which would be of great interest to us. To get an idea of the kind of respect the writer accorded the authenticity of the characters and the truth of the opinions which tradition could supply, one has only to think of the veritable *Paulinisation* imposed on Peter throughout the first part of the book.[34]

IV. *Place and Date of the Composition of Acts*

It is not at all unlikely that Acts is a work of Roman origin. Evidence for this statement has been found in the similarity between the points of doctrine in Acts, the sort of *regula fidei* emanating from the book, and the articles of the Apostles' Creed, generally accepted as of Roman provenance.[35] (Renan,[36] in a moment of fantasy, thought he could see Flavius Clemens, the cousin of Domitian, as its author!) However, it would be imprudent to confuse a likely assumption with a certainty, and

---

32. *XCVII*, II, p. 180.
33. *CXXVI*, pp. 532–52.
34. *CXCIII*, p. 157. The orthodox admire the "striking similarities in doctrine and thought between the speeches of St. Peter preserved in Acts and his teaching as found in his Epistles," i.e., 1 and 2 Peter. (Cf. Dom Leclercq, "Historiens du Christ," *DACL*, p. 2538.) But there is no cause for surprise here.
35. *XCVII*, II, pp. 199f.
36. *LV*, xxiii.

one could as easily imagine our author writing at Antioch or Ephesus as at Rome.[37]

But when? Every date between 60 and 150 A.D. has been mentioned. If need be, the limits can, I believe, be restricted to between 100 and 115 for the first version, and between 130 and 140 for the second. But which date should we accept, if we are anxious to ascertain that of the original book, the one we think most important? Opinions change every time the data are reconsidered.[38] No argument has succeeded in establishing itself so firmly that it seems unshakable. For example, when Goguel avers that the failure to use the Pauline epistles counter-indicates a very late date, his reason seems valid at first: [39] it vanishes if one agrees with Loisy that the writer deliberately discarded Paul's information. Every argument for any one date has its counter-argument; consequently, all opinions have found adherents. I believe, however, that Loisy must be close to the truth when he argues for the period of Nerva or of Trajan, that is, the first quarter of the second century. F. Jackson and K. Lake opt for the Flavian period. The difference is not great, inasmuch as the latter authors finally confine their hypothesis to the last five years of the first century.

Many details of the text resist an earlier dating. There is the evident incomprehension of primitive phenomena, such as *glossolalia*, which is confused with the gift of tongues (ii.3f). The gifts of the Spirit, *charismata*, appear in Acts as though they were schematized and bound to functions in the Church. The expectation of the *parousia* has lost its ardor. In addition, the legend of Judas appears to be more fully developed in Acts (i.16f) than in Matthew, and the story of the Ascension is akin to the latest stratum of traditions concerning the appearances of the Risen One. Another index of the late date is seen in its use of the miraculous. Miracles, which play a large role throughout the book, are introduced as proof of the truth of the Gospel and as the means to conversion. The ones attributed to Peter and to Paul are stamped with a highly magical character (v.15; xix.11–12).[40] Even the language and tone of the book indicate that it is post-Pauline and belongs to the *sub-apostolic age*. In the speeches, the very evident influence of the conventions and motifs of Greek literature also favors the conclusion that Acts belongs to the same period as John and the Pastoral Epistles.

37. *XVIII*, III, pp. 356f.
38. *XCVII*, II, p. 358.
39. It is, moreover, double-edged: if our writer's failure to use Paul's epistles was not deliberate, it means that he did not know their author, and this can lead to an important inference.
40. *CXC*, p. 330.

The partisans of an earlier date of composition attach importance to the fact that the ruin of the Temple and the trials undergone by the Jews in 70 A.D. are nowhere mentioned, nor alluded to, in Acts, and to the nonappearance anywhere in the book of the designation "Christian" as a word that would arouse the hostility of the magistrates, an occurrence they think unlikely (?) in a book written at the end of the first or beginning of the second century.[41] They point out that in Acts ii.29 the tomb of David is referred to as "with us to this day," [42] though it was destroyed in 70 A.D. The book contains no panegyric of Paul, a fact, so claim the partisans, that would indicate unaccountable reticence in a writer who lived at a time when the Apostle had already been aggrandized.[43] And so on. These and similar arguments (e.g., the one based on the archaism of the Christology of Acts) do not appear to be invincible; but perhaps it is not necessary to vanquish them if it be granted that two successive writers produced our book of Acts. That the work of the second was badly adjusted to the work of the first is no cause for astonishment.

V.   Historical Value of Acts

The most important thing to know would be whether our Acts retains any vestiges of recognizable and useful ancient traditions, Lukan or not. One would certainly think so from reading the first chapters, which are not at all representative of the Christology and general aspect of the Church in the period of the second writer. Loisy, however, alleges that this impression is due to the writer's intentional archaism, utilized to give the Roman authorities a misleading idea of the true relation of Christianity to Judaism, in order to assure for the Christians the benefit of the legal recognition which covered the Jews.[44] I find it hard to give such a blunderer credit for that much guile. I can almost believe that his very awkwardness and clumsiness in his use of sources is an advantage of sorts, in that it guarantees the possibility of internal criticism of the text.

Nor is comparative criticism a completely hopeless task, since several notable Pauline assertions permit us to set up such criticism. The Apostle associated with the first Christians of Jerusalem, and was even in conflict with them. For us this is opportune, because opposition accentuates differences. This opposition was not a matter of two or three

41. *XC*, p. 221; *III*, p. 132.
42. *III*, p. 143, n. 1.
43. *LXXXIX*, p. 99; cf. *XCI*, p. 81, for Harnack's conclusions.
44. For the controversy on Loisy's thesis, cf. *XCVII*, V, pp. 1–7.

incidents; it may be said that the whole foundation of the Pauline Corpus consists of struggles and polemics, to the great advantage of the exegete. Another means for comparison is furnished by the Synoptic Gospels, whose basic traditions are no doubt derived from the first Christian Church and reflect its faith.

All these resources are perhaps not of much value, but it cannot be said that they are worthless, and even if it remains established that, as documentation, Acts is execrable, I do not think it can be said that its value is nil.[45] What about the chronological framework of this early history? The series of essential facts which stand out as landmarks? One must not count on learning much; but it is possible to be a little less skeptical about apprehending the basic ideas which nourished the beliefs of the first faithful, and about the evolution of the belief itself. There is reason to believe that the beginnings were not so complicated that reconstruction from mediocre or worse clues is prohibited.

Nevertheless, I wish to state that the restoration I shall hazard has for me only the value of a likely hypothesis. Other hypotheses could no doubt be propounded which would seem no less acceptable. Objective and certain truth escapes us, and probity requires that we admit it from the start.

---

45. I abstain from a judgment on the overall value of Acts as history. (There have been interminable debates; cf. Goguel, *XVIII*, III, p. 364, n. 1, for a bibliography.) I believe it wiser to evaluate separately each assertion of the text.

2

THE FOUNDING
OF THE FIRST
COMMUNITY[1]

I. The Return from Galilee

THE return is shrouded in obscurity, because the memory of those ancient times has disappeared from the texts which remain. It may be that the first writer of Acts knew and said something about it; the second was not interested in it, doubtless because his picture of the origins of the faith and of the Church was drawn from a perspective so different from the reality that he could retain no traces of it that his predecesor may have transmitted.[2] Thus, in the Third Gospel, he painted with bold strokes the picture of the appearances of the Risen One in Jerusalem, and in Acts he told the story of Jesus's *second life* on earth during the forty days and of his Ascension on the Mount of Olives, contradicting, however, the ancient tradition. He breathes no word of what may be called the Galilean tradition, nor does he recall the activity and conduct of the disciples between the time of their dispersion at Jesus's arrest and their return to Jerusalem. He wants

1. Bibliography: Acts and commentaries on Acts, especially those of Wendt, Loisy, Preuschen, and *XCVII*, III–V; *CXIV*, ch. ii; *CXXIX*, chs. iii–v; *CXV*, I, ch. viii; III, chs. iv, vi, vii; *XCVII*, I, Pt. 3; *CXXVII*, Lect. i–ii; *LXXIV bis*, chs. iv–vi. This chapter had already been written when *The Birth of the Christian Religion* by Alfred Loisy appeared. I have made no changes in it since reading this remarkable book, whose striking formulations, in every way excellent, reveal conclusions similar to my own.
2. *CVIII*, p. 55.

us to believe that they did not leave the Holy City and he deliberately ignores their confusion. According to his view of them, there was nothing unexpected, nothing disconcerting in their conduct, for they are the good agents of the divine plan, which develops logically. We are in the midst of a contrived account, which belongs to the realm of apologetics and hagiography, and not to history.

We know that the Easter faith, the precondition of any repentance for the rout of Gethsemane, arose in Galilee and not at Jerusalem.[3] But we also know that only a hypothesis allows us to perceive this important fact, since our texts do not describe it. John xxi and the last known verses of the *Gospel of Peter* give the impression that the disciples, who had gone back to Galilee, returned to the occupations which provided their livelihood before they followed the Nazarene (thus Peter and his brother Andrew again became fishermen on the sea of Tiberias) and disbanded: "Each one, saddened by what had happened, withdrew into his house."[4] Actually John xxi inclines us rather to the belief that the dispersion was not complete, and that the disciples who earned their living by the net stayed together: Simon, Thomas, Nathanael, the sons of Zebedee, and "two other disciples" [xxi.12]. It would be difficult to comprehend how the hopes and confidence of these poor men could have been reborn if at least some of them had not remained together, strengthened by the fellowship of their daily life, comforting one another and compounding their optimistic reactions.[5] I do not think it daring to draw from the few wretched indices we still possess the conclusion that the center and life of this little group was Simon Peter. The conviction that the Master was no longer dead was born in him, and it was through him that it spread.[6]

It may be assumed that as soon as this conviction became articulate, the scattered disciples, certainly not numerous,[7] gradually reassembled around the small Petrine group to absorb its hope. This reassembling must have been very swift, and the decision to return to Jerusalem soon taken, because the feelings awakened in the disciples were not of the kind that are hesitant in giving birth to resolutions. I would, however, be embarrassed, if I had to give an exact figure for the length of time—probably short—which separated the exodus from Jerusalem, after the arrest of

---

3. Cf. *LXXXVI*, pp. 615f.

4. *Ev. Petri*, p. 59.

5. It is appropriate to note that the execution of the Baptist, who proclaimed the same Good News as Jesus, did not discourage his partisans. *CVII*, p. 81.

6. *LXXXVI*, p. 642.

7. *LXXXVI*, p. 260.

Jesus, from the return decided on by the reinvigorated disciples. Was it a few months? Weeks? Perhaps only a few days? We do not know.[8]

So, the little flock headed for Zion. What was behind the return? Was it only to convince the Jews of the truth of Jesus's resurrection and of the authenticity of his divine mission? That has been suggested,[9] but I do not agree. The return of the disciples to Jerusalem was presumably motivated by the same reason as the one that had attracted the Master before them: the conviction that the imminent manifestation of the Kingdom would take place in Jerusalem and that the Messiah would come forward there. The time did not call for preaching to unbelievers, but rather for hastening to be in a favorable spot to await the great event.[10]

The narrative of Acts contains no trace of this first crisis, because the disciples hoped in vain. It thus represents "the change made necessary in the first faith by the bankruptcy of Messianism" (Loisy). The assertion (i.3) that Jesus spent forty days in the midst of the Apostles, between his Resurrection and Ascension, has no basis at all in the primitive tradition, for it can be glimpsed neither in Paul nor in the Synoptics.

Even the number "forty" is enough to reveal the artifice of the account; "forty" may be said to be the *biblical number for a novitiate:* Moses was forty days on Sinai; Elijah walked towards Horeb for forty days; Jesus spent forty days in the wilderness. Perhaps one ought to regard the localization of the Ascension on the Mount of Olives as a kind of compensation for the discounted Messianic event,[11] even as one sees in the Pentecost story, which relates the descent of the Spirit on the assembled Apostles, nothing more than the justification of what our writer of Acts understood by apostolic authority.

It is useless to wonder how many disciples may have returned from Galilee. In Acts i.15 we do find the figure the writer wants us to accept for the total we should like to know: he says "about one hundred and twenty persons"; but I put no confidence in it, because $120 = 12 \times 10$. There is every reason to think this is merely a conventional combination,[12] more or less analogous to the one that gave the seventy-two disciples in Luke x.1 ($72 = 12 \times 6$). I can't quite picture a band of one hundred and twenty persons arriving in a body, and, as it were, in procession, from Galilee. It has been suggested—but on what grounds?—that some dis-

8. *CXIV*, p. 37.
9. *CXIV*, p. 44.
10. *CVIII*, p. 148; *CVII*, pp. 112f, 124f; *XCVII*, I, p. 303.
11. *CVIII*, p. 162.
12. *XCVII*, IV, p. 12 *ad loc.*

ciples, who rallied to and increased the number of the Galilean band, had remained in Jerusalem. In fact, we do not know. But the number of the first faithful was probably very small—I should say a dozen, or at the most, two dozen. Paul (1 Cor. xv.6) does indeed speak of an appearance of the Risen One to "more than five hundred brethren," but this was not at the very beginning of the brotherhood. Besides, this, like the others, is an unverifiable and hardly credible figure.

II. Installation in Jerusalem. The Apostles and the Early Anarchism

What was the *form* of the primitive community? Once again, the absence of chronology, of any true progression, in the narrative of Acts, robs us of an answer. At the very most, it may be conjectured that the Galileans lodged with the hosts or in the inns that they, or their kin, were accustomed to frequent when they came on a pilgrimage to the City, and that they met in some private dwelling, one of those which sheltered their leaders, for the common meal.[13]

Some have wondered how it was possible for the community to be established, and have sought the explanation in the general historical circumstances of the era; that is, in the fact that from 31 (when Sejanus fell out of favor) to 41 (date of the accession of the frivolous and bigoted Agrippa I) Roman toleration was enforced in Palestine.[14] This suggestion offers too broad a framework for a limited undertaking, and projects into the past a very late actuality—the authentic Christian Church—in the same fashion as the writer of Acts. I don't think there would be anything disturbing to any authority in the presence at Jerusalem of a handful of unknown and peaceable poor people. It is superfluous to attribute to the early community the intention of developing a familial organization analogous to that of the rabbinical schools,[15] and subsequently the desire to appear as one of the *existing religious orders* (Essenes?) in order to stay within the confines of the accustomed *forms*.

It is not even necessary to suppose—at least in the beginning—that the Jews regarded them as a sect (αἵρεσις, or φιλοσοφία, in Josephus's

13. Acts ii. 46: Κλῶντές τε κατ' οἶκον ἄρτον. The meaning of κατ' οἶκον is not certain. It can be understood to mean a single house or several successive houses: *CVIII*, p. 220; *XCVII*, IV, p. 29 *ad loc.*
14. *XI*, p. 11.
15. *XI*, p. 11.

language) [16] or that they formed a separate synagogue (*Keneseth*). According to the Mishnah, only ten Jews were necessary for the organization of a regularly constituted synagogue. The brethren could, therefore, have founded the Synagogue of the Nazarenes within the framework of custom and law. Unfortunately, no text authorizes us to believe that they did this: the tiny community, entirely given over to its eschatological expectation, would not take great care to insure its future in the present age.

Since *community* is, in fact, the *raison d'être* of these disciples, we wonder about the composition of their group: what did it consist of? The basic members were direct disciples of Jesus, the best, the most convinced, those who had usually gone about with him and lived with him. Perhaps James, one of the brothers of the Nazarene who rallied to the Easter faith, was already of their number. But was this group simply an inorganic association of men sharing the same conviction, or was it already organized around a definite institution which preceded it? This question raises the problem of the *Apostolic College*.

But if we refer only to Acts, there is no problem: the Apostles instituted by Jesus, having returned *in a body* to Jerusalem, founded the primitive community. They were the ones who governed it, *as a body* (iv.37; v.12, 40–42; vi.6; etc.). Their first care was to replace Judas in order to retain a membership of twelve in their college, the figure willed by the Master.[17] And they took the necessary precautions to insure that the choice of a successor would be as well attested as Jesus's choice of themselves, and that it truly proceeded from the Glorified One in person. Hence, on the initiative of Peter, the Eleven held a meeting, and, having selected two candidates from the number of men who had been by their side "during all the time that the Lord Jesus came and went among us," they prayed, saying "Thou, Lord, which knowest the hearts of all men, shew whether of these two men thou hast chosen, that he may take part of this ministry and apostleship, from which Judas by transgression fell, that he might go to his own place." The will of the Master, who designated Matthias, was revealed by drawing lots (i.15–26). On several occasions (vi.1; viii.1 and 14; xi.1), the writer depicts the Apostolic College as a council existing apart from the brotherhood, and governing and directing it. This is pure fiction, insofar at any rate as it pertains to the earliest

16. *XCVII*, I, p. 304; *contra*, *CXIV*, p. 68.

17. As a supplement to what I said in *Jesus* about the legend of Judas, cf. Loisy, *CVII*, pp. 103f, 113, n. 1. This legend has no basis in fact, and the narrative in Acts of the supplementary election, whose purpose is to authenticate it, is of necessity no better grounded.

days of the community's existence; Acts itself provides the proof, as a mere perusal will show.[18] Moreover, it seems obvious that Paul did not find himself in the presence of a College when he came to Jerusalem, first "to visit Peter" (Gal. i.18), then, fourteen years later, to set forth before the "notables" of the Church the Gospel he was preaching to the Gentiles (Gal. ii.2). At neither of these two memorable meetings did he feel inferior to the men he had come to see, as he doubtless would have if he had recognized them as the authorized and appointed representatives of the Lord Jesus.

If Jesus really chose twelve Apostles, we must ask ourselves what his intention was. If he did not, and if they did nonetheless exist at the inception of the community, it remains to be seen what their origin and functions were.

The evangelical record of the choice of the Apostles (Mark iii.13f.) has provoked disputes and denials before our time.[19] More than one critic has concluded from his study of the evidence that it corresponds to no historical reality. The orthodox, especially the Catholics, do indeed resolutely repudiate these criticisms. Father Lagrange, for example, becomes indignant [20] about an "audacious denial" contradicted, he assures us, by the witness of all tradition. Alas, that does not mean much, for the *entire tradition* does not weigh heavy on the scales and indignation does not add to its weight.

In fact, the basic account of the institution of the Twelve—Mark iii.13ff.—is so confused and so vague that in reading it one cannot escape the impression that its author knew nothing about the institution aside from the very general affirmation given by a list of names. That is not much for an event of this importance. Hence, it is not daring to suspect that this tradition corresponds to no true memory.[21] Luke (vi.12ff) sought to make the Markan scene more imposing and significant: it shows Jesus spending the night in prayer before making his choice and naming his chosen ones *Apostles*. Unfortunately, there is no chance that the third evangelist is better informed than the second, whose account he follows, arranging it to suit his own ideas. What is more, we have every reason to believe that he is often mistaken for the writer of Acts, and are therefore not astonished that he in turn is "dominated by the idea of the

18. *CXIV*, p. 46.
19. *XXVI*, IV, p. 39; *CXXXI*, pp. 6ff.
20. *CII*, p. 144.
21. *CXII*, p. 110. Cf. *LXXXVI*, pp. 260f, and Kirsopp Lake's important study, "The Twelve and the Apostles," in *XCVII*, V, pp. 37-59.

apostolate and the apostolic witness." His disposition of the election and foundation of the authority of the Twelve stems from this concern.[22]

I shall do no more than mention the marked divergences in the various lists of the Apostles which have reached us.[23] Most striking is the fact that the list-makers obviously know nothing about the men whose names they inscribe, with the exception of Peter, and James and John, the sons of Zebedee.[24] It was precisely because tradition knew nothing of their deeds that legends have burdened them with their inconsistent or extravagant inventions.[25]

It is difficult to imagine Jesus, the herald of the imminent Kingdom, surrounding himself with a kind of Council or Headquarters. If he was looking to the future, this precaution would be unlikely, since, in fact, his own mission was to announce that there would be no future. If, on the other hand, he was thinking of present needs, the selection of the Twelve would be explained by the desire he may have felt to enlarge his field of action, to multiply the voices capable of echoing his, in order to reach and to warn a greater number of souls. There could have been no question of sending these trusted men to *preach*, as is so often said through a misconstruing of the verb κηρύσσειν in Mark, but the Master could have charged them to proclaim the Good News of the Kingdom in the places he could not visit in person, and to confirm their proclamation by the signs that he himself manifested.[26] That he had the idea of such an "institution" within these limits is not, of course, impossible, but it is unlikely. The Synoptic tradition knows absolutely nothing about the activity of these *missi dominici*,[27] nor does it at any time give us the impression that they are not with Jesus, even after we have been told (in a passage whose anachronism—I mean parachronism—is an offense against all probability) that he provided them with instructions appropriate to their office and that they departed (Matt. ix.37f.; x.16; Luke ix.1). Luke himself does not dare try to make us believe that they were absent for long, since, having put them en route in ix.6, he notes their return in ix.10. Nothing much happens in the intervening few verses, filled as they are with Herod the Tetrarch's anxious thoughts, which had nothing to do with the activity of the Apostles. The instructions, developed in Matthew

22. *CVIII*, p. 139; *CVII*, pp. 136f.
23. Cf. *LXXXVI*, p. 262.
24. *CCLXIX*, p. 26.
25. *DACL*, art. "Apôtres." Cf. Lipsius, *CV*, for details.
26. Matt. x. 1f; cf. *XCVII*, I, p. 179.
27. Luke ix.10 does not know what to say, except that ". . . when they had come back, the Apostles told him everything they had done." (!)

and abridged in Luke, come from the age which saw the Apostles as missionary leaders and models for the other missionaries. Since my conviction in this instance comes very close to certitude, *I do not believe that Jesus chose the Apostles.* Even when the Twelve did exist, I doubt that in the beginning they corresponded to the apostolic model tradition has fixed: that they were the *missionaries* of the new faith.

Who, then, are they and where do they come from? It has been maintained that Paul did not know them as an organized group, as a College.[28] He mentions the Twelve only once, but in a passage (1 Cor. xv.5) whose literal authenticity cannot be other than suspect. In speaking of the Apostles in other passages, he does not identify them as the Twelve, nor does anyone else.[29] When he comes to Jerusalem, he does not deal with the Twelve, but with one or another influential person: Peter; James, the brother of the Lord; men of repute (οἱ δοκοῦντες); the pillars (στῦλοι) of the community. The force of these remarks is such that a scholar like McGiffert, who is nonetheless convinced that Jesus did distinguish twelve of his disciples by a special call, is obliged to admit that, at the beginning of the primitive period, these elect Twelve did not govern the Church.[30] As a matter of fact, Acts itself leaves us in uncertainty about the actual existence of this role during the primitive period, though it nevertheless presupposes it. For this reason, the shakiness of the supposition seems to me certain; and I deem the existence of the Apostolic College in the very first brotherhood to be equally improbable.[31] Along with Loisy, I am convinced that eliminating the Twelve from history would be the work of a "rather rash criticism," but I think it fitting to displace them. They represent an institution of the second phase in the life of the brethren in Jerusalem, a board of directors and managers made necessary more by the delay of the *parousia* than by the growth of the brotherhood. Even their name suggests that in the beginning theirs was a delegated authority, an office they held as a result of an election, and it brings to mind nothing of what we ordinarily mean by *apostolate.* For the most part, they are not missionaries, and I would not think it impossible that no one of them was. In any case, I doubt that any one of them was a

28. J. Weiss, *CXXIX*, pp. 33f, thinks that the College of the Twelve is quite simply a materialization of the idea of *twelve apostles for the twelve tribes* (Luke xxii.30; Matt. xix.28). This notion was current before the lists were made, and indeed, these lists were its product. The narrative of the institution of the Twelve by Jesus is only a variant, in story form, of the lists themselves. This is quite possible.

29. *CXI*, p. 193; *CVIII*, p. 167. Cf. Gal. i.17, ii.9, where "apostles" are obviously men who perform a task similar to his own: "Those who were apostles before me."

30. *CXIV*, p. 45.

31. *CVIII*, p. 167.

missionary before the dispersion of the Hellenists, which probably marks the beginning of *propaganda* and *missionary activity*. Together they form a kind of ecclesiastical commission which exercises authority over the true apostles, those who initiate and direct propaganda. Paul, an apostle by personal call, will be conscious of the need of gaining their recognition (Gal. ii. 1f.).[32] Their office was essentially one of service, of ministering (διακονία),[33] and even if it were necessary to assume that an attempt was made to spread the Good News before the founding of the Church of Antioch (which we shall soon study), it would not be rash to think that the attempt did not come from the Apostolic College. That it did is simply one of the inventions in Acts, which sets up the *Twelve* as the primitive community's *administrators of affairs spiritual,* as opposed to the *Seven, administrators of affairs temporal.*[34]

Loisy has suggested [35] that the writer of the first version of Acts, whom he took to be Luke, recounted the election of the Twelve, just as he had reported the institution of the Seven (Acts vi.1–6), but that the reviser skipped this account because it contradicted his idea that the College of the Twelve was Jesus's great contribution to regulating the life of the *brotherhood.* But this is no more than a likely hypothesis. At the moment, I need say only that (1) it seems certain that the presentation of the Twelve as authorized missionaries in Christ's name, armed with his gifts and dispensers of the Spirit, and as the appointed leaders of the community, does not belong to the primitive tradition; (2) it seems probable that the Twelve, even if reduced to the status of an influential group, did not exist at the inception of the Jerusalem community.

But there were influential persons in the primitive community. It was only natural that those disciples whose relation with the Nazarene had been more direct and intimate than that of the majority should have special influence. They were heeded and followed. First among them was Simon Peter (Cephas) who appears, in Acts at least, as spokesman for the brethren (i.15; ii.14; iii.12; iv.8; v.2). His status as a very early, perhaps the earliest, disciple of Jesus, the love and confidence accorded him by the Master, and the leading role he played in founding the Easter faith,[36]

---

32. *CVIII*, p. 168.

33. Acts i.17: Peter says of Judas: "For he was numbered among us, and was allotted his share in this ministry" (τὸν κλῆρον τῆς διακονίας ταύτης).

34. *CVII*, pp. 140–42, 158. Loisy, *CX*, p. 154 [p. 143. E. T.]: "The Galilean disciples were never missionaries, to the world, of faith in Jesus. It was not they who founded the hellenic-Christian Church. Nor were they ever the guarantors of the gospel legend."

35. *CVIII*, p. 170.

36. Cf. *LXXXVI*, pp. 642f.

were enough to establish his moral authority and give him the right to be heeded. At his side were the two sons of Zebedee, James and John, no doubt because they too were early disciples of Jesus,[37] and especially close to him.[38] And perhaps only a little later, James the Less, being brother of the Master, acquired some of their prestige and shared their roles. None of these men held the right to command or to govern, for at this early date only *the presence* of the Glorified One, in the Spirit, possessed this right wholly and completely. But they commanded a respect which elevated them to a personal ascendancy that could, on the rare occasions when it was needed, counteract the disadvantages of the anarchy that was undoubtedly the normal state of this primitive brotherhood.

How could this tiny group of devout folk, brought together by their communion in a magnificent hope and the anxious expectation of its approaching realization, even think of organization? They could feel no need for it. Their life was their conviction; they had no doctrine, or if one prefers, it may be said that their doctrine, in its entirety, was contained in the affirmation that Jesus the Crucified had become the Risen and Glorified, and would descend again, at any moment, from his abode with the Father to inaugurate the Kingdom. Disillusionment, imposing on them the necessity of resigning themselves to a long delay, would gradually lead them to submit to its usual exigencies, and force them to give their community the forms of government, even as it obliged them to expand their belief.

37. Mark i.18 seems to indicate that they were chosen by Jesus on the same day as Peter.

38. Mark iii.17 names them after Peter and sets them apart from the others; cf. Mark v.37, ix.2, xiii.3, and Synoptic parallels.

3

THE CHURCH OF
JERUSALEM

**I. The Transformation
of the Primitive
Community**

THE very life of the primitive community was its expectation of the *parousia*, whose delay it could not withstand. The writer of Acts prefers to know nothing of this expectation and the terrible disappointment occasioned by its delay, because in his fictional account everything happened in accord with God's plan revealed by the Christ. He has no reason, therefore, to speak of any transposition of the first hope. He sees *the evangelization of the world* as the aim and primary intent of the apostolic community, and not as the task it undertook as a substitute for the *expectation of the Kingdom*, its first hope. It suits him to overlook the fact that the hope was not realized and that the *apostolate* is nothing more than a strategic redirection, made necessary by the bankruptcy of *Messianism*, of the original faith.

The first brethren reminded one another that "this generation would not pass away before all these things [i.e., the events of the *parousia*] had taken place" (Mark xiii.30). At most, they admitted that the *day* and the *hour* remained the secret of the Father (Mark xiii.32). Our writer takes the precaution (Acts i.7) of extending their ignorance to include even the *age* when the *parousia* will occur: "It is not for you to know the times or seasons (χρόνους ἢ καιροὺς) which the Father has fixed by his own authority." No doubt. But only when the *parousia* did not arrive, neither soon nor late, did it indeed become necessary for the brethren to relinquish their first illusion and come out of their house of dreams. *It was then that the Church of Jerusalem was born.*

In considering this most important transformation, it is perhaps proper to also bear in mind the first manifestations of hostility by the non-believers, who, by making the isolation of the brethren in their own milieu more marked and their separation from the other Jews more definite, forced them to cling more closely to one another and to *materialize* their community by organizing it. Unfortunately, these first difficulties escape us. Acts, it is true, tells us that the healing of a paralytic by Peter and John (iii.4f) provoked great excitement among the people (iii.11), which Peter turned to advantage by delivering an urgent exhortation to faith and *metanoia* (iii.12–26). Before he could finish, men from the Temple arrived, arrested him and John on Solomon's Porch, and dragged both of them before the Sanhedrin (iv.lf). But the entire narrative remains so suspect of editorial adjustment, if not outright invention, that we can no longer discern what, if anything, did happen.[1] Thus, when I speak of the probable effects of the first difficulties, which must have coincided with the *discovery* of the sect by outsiders, I am merely advancing a theory of what seems likely to have happened. On the shifting ground of Acts, one cannot with confidence put his feet down anywhere.

It does, however, seem immediately apparent that, from the Jewish point of view, the position of the men faithful to the Nazarene could not long endure. It is quite probable that they considered themselves to be correct and zealous Jews, as Acts ii.46f confidently assures us they were, but the mere fact that they believed that their Master, who in the opinion of the High Priests and governmental authority deserved the supreme punishment, was in fact "the one who is to come" and the "presumptive Messiah" (Loisy) meant that they would have to be cast out by Israel as soon as "that was known." Cast out against their will, to be sure, but with no possibility of return; it was only a matter of time.[2]

II. The Hellenists

The principal factor leading to the transformation of the primitive community was the entry on the scene of the Hellenists. Who were they? Where did they come from? According to Acts they were Hellenized

1. *CVIII*, pp. 239–51.
2. *CVII*, p. 132.

Jews, Jews whose habitual language was Greek. In ii.5 we read: "Now there were dwelling in Jerusalem Jews, devout men out of every nation under heaven." They were the Jews and proselytes who came to the City for religious festivals, pilgrims who stayed a more or less long time.[3] Acts vi.9 mentions the "Synagogue of the Libertines [Λιβερτίνων], and Cyrenians, and Alexandrians, and of them of Cilicia and of Asia." The text is certainly not wholly enlightening,[4] but I do not think it overly bold to find in it support for the view that each of the large geographical communities formed by the ghettos established in pagan lands had its own place of assembly and prayer at Jerusalem.

Some of these Hellenists joined the community of the brethren. How and when? We do not know, but I should think through chance contacts in the homes of their mutual hosts, or through accidental meetings. The outlook of these men, made flexible by their familiarity with the Greeks, must have been less refractory to the revelation of the Good News than was the more narrow mind of the Judeans. Why, then, did they not return, once they were converted, to their homes to spread their hope? For it is our impression that they remained in the City. They did so, I think, because they were awaiting the *parousia*; hence they would not as yet have had any idea of propagandizing. However, I willingly believe that the first sustained attempts in Jerusalem itself to enlarge the community were the work of the Hellenists, because in their synagogues at home they were in the habit of attempting to gain the good will of outsiders and to seek them out in order to proselytize them. Were not some of the Hellenists themselves "proselytes of righteousness," men who had been pagans? The assumption is certainly a possible one.

Now, despite the soothing assertions of Acts, everything makes us suspect that the accord between the Hellenists and the disciples who constituted the first community was of short duration. We don't know why. At the most, one may conjecture[5] that the Hellenists were more daring than the other brethren in emphasizing the distinctive ideas and special beliefs of the sect; that, unlike the others, they were inclined to accentuate the points which virtually separated them from pure Judaism rather than the ones that would tend to draw the sect back into legalistic correctness. *They were by nature inclined to a "high" Christology,* and I think it likely that the first moves in this direction were theirs.

In Acts vi.1–7 there is an obscure vignette which contains, but hides

---

3. *CXXIX*, p. 119, thinks they were Palestinian Hellenized Jews of the Hasmonean and Herodian periods. I do not agree with this hypothesis.
4. *CVIII*, p. 307; *XCVII*, IV, pp. 66f.
5. *CVIII*, p. 391; *XI*, p. 65.

from us, everything we should like to know. "*In those days* [guess which!] *when the number of the disciples was multiplied, there arose a murmuring of the Grecians* [γογγυσμὸς τῶν Ἑλληνιστῶν] *against the Hebrews.*" They complained that their widows (αἱ χῆραι αὐτῶν) were neglected in the daily distribution of food on the common table. Then the Twelve, having "called the multitude of the disciples unto them," observed that they could not neglect the word of God to serve tables and proposed to charge with this task, by election, seven brethren "full of the Holy Ghost and wisdom." The suggestion was accepted and seven men—all of them Greeks to judge by their names [6]—were chosen. The Apostles laid hands on them after their election, thereby consecrating them for their duties.

There is reason to fear that the difficulties were not so easily settled and that the soothing narrative of Acts hides a fact of great importance which the author is not anxious to stress.[7] Yet what he tells us, or rather, what he permits us to guess, represents, no doubt, the first consistent datum of his exposition. It is probable that we here have a few odds and ends of the oldest version of the book.

Thus, "when the number of the disciples was multiplied," the concord between the Hellenists and the Palestinians ended. I take the text to mean that the multiplication of disciples occurred among the Hellenists, which is understandable if, as is elsewhere apparent, they were more receptive to the Christian hope than were the Judeans. Because they were accustomed to propagandizing at home, it was logical for them to do so also among themselves in Jerusalem. The example of Stephen, who in Acts vi.9 is shown arguing in the synagogues of the Hellenists, is a valuable hint. There can be no doubt that as soon as these converts were sufficiently numerous, the great differences between their thinking and that of the first disciples became so apparent that frictions had soon to arise. The issue that exposed, and exasperated, their latent disharmony may well have been a material one—food for the stomach. From that day onwards, the primitive pseudo-communism was a thing of the past, and was replaced by an institution known to the synagogues, a relief fund administered by a commission, that is, the Twelve. The notion that the latter were wholly occupied with the "service of the word" (τῇ διακονίᾳ τοῦ λόγου)[8] conforms to the author's conception of the apostolate and not to the real-

6. Stephen, Philip, Prochorus, Nicanor, Timon, Parmenas, and Nicolas, προσή-λυτον Ἀντιοχέα. On the current use of these names, cf. *CXIX, ad loc.*
7. *CVIII*, p. 293f.
8. vi.4.

ity of the period he describes; for who would administer the fund, who would take responsibility for it, if not the Twelve, at whose feet, we are told, voluntary donations were laid? [9]

It is difficult to tell just what sort of neglect the Hellenists complained of: to judge from what follows, it apparently concerned the serving of the *agape*, that is, the distribution of the food at the common meal.[10] Moreover, we do not know who the badly served widows were. Is not the writer, who with the election of the *Seven* is about to create the institution of Deacons, implicitly thinking of the *widows* and *deaconesses* prevalent about him in his day? One wonders, too, if he has not substituted a simple incidental complaint for much more serious grounds for disagreement, grounds that, as we shall soon discover, sprang from the relations between the Judaizers and the simple Christians in the Hellenic Churches.

This much at least seems certain: that the division of labor referred to in Acts—service of the word of God for the twelve Apostles; service of material needs for the seven Deacons—has no basis in fact. As the narrative continues, the Seven, and especially Stephen, are depicted as being so devoted to the word and to propaganda, and not to the labors of the Diaconate, that the activities of Stephen and of the Hellenists who follow his example will impair the relations with the Jerusalem authorities. The Hellenists will be driven out, whereas the apostolic group will remain in the City. (Acts viii.1).

What does this mean? Very probably that *the election of the Seven denotes a split in the primitive community.* The Hellenists formed a group governed by the Seven, while the Hebraizers remained under the leadership of the Twelve. It would be wrong to conclude from this that the two groups did not retain their spiritual ties. But henceforth they separated their material existence, as Hellenistic Jews customarily did in Jerusalem, since they had their own synagogues. The type of ordination that the Twelve supposedly conferred on the Seven has of course neither meaning nor value, except from the perspective of the narrator. He means to intimate that the institution of the Seven was the foundation of the *Diaconate*, which depended on the *Episcopate*, which in turn owed its origin and reason for being to the Apostles. His insistence that these Seven were elected primarily for the service of tables is due to the fact that in his day the Deacons' main task was to attend to the orderly arrangement of the Eucharistic table and the orderly conduct of the Supper, as

9. iv.34 and 37; v.2.
10. vi.2: διακονεῖν τραπέζαις.

well as to insure the distribution of relief to the poor, under the apostolical authority of the bishop. And this, let us note in passing, does not confirm the date assigned to Acts by orthodoxy.

Why *seven?* The question is analogous to the one asked earlier: why *twelve?* It is possible that these undoubtedly symbolic numbers were chosen after the fact out of considerations extraneous to their true origins. But it is equally possible that they were chosen for their symbolic import. The number *twelve* was sanctioned by long traditional usage, whose best known application is to be found in the designation *twelve tribes;* the number *seven* was equally meaningful. Commentators have been hard pressed to explain why the Hellenists chose it,[11] but they have, of course, found reasons, as one always does. They have recalled, for example, that Josephus (Antt. IV, 8:16) speaks of a council of seven magistrates in Jewish cities,[12] that the VII *viri epulones,* who were charged with arranging sacred banquets in Rome, are known as the *Seven,* even when there are *ten* of them.[13] They have also noted that "in the evangelical tradition, seven is the number of the Gentiles or of universality" (Loisy) and that the second multiplication of loaves, in the pagan territory of the Decapolis (Mark viii. 1–9), which represents the conversion of the Gentiles, is effected with *seven* loaves and yields *seven* baskets of remains. This variety of possible reasons for the choice of the number seven means that we do not know the precise significance of this number; but it is enough that it seemed so propitious and so good an omen that it was adopted.

For us, the essential fact is the formation of a Hellenistic community alongside the earlier Hebraist community. This fact enables us to recognize the existence of an elementary organization: on the one hand, the Twelve and their group; on the other, the Seven with theirs. As is natural, each of the two brotherhoods resembled a synagogue. One was instinctively conservative, the other progressive; it is the latter that had life and the future on its side. *There, for the first time, the fecundating action of the Greek spirit became manifest.* Beyond this, we know nothing of the organization or workings of the two groups, except the existence of the relief fund, fed by fraternal charity, and the glimpses we catch of the common meal. Material details did not interest the author of Acts, and his account remains so superficial that he makes no reference to them even in passing, except for some express purpose.

11. *CXIX,* p. 36.
12. Cf. Cicero, *Philippics* v, 7, 21.
13. Dion Cass. 43, 51.

The organization itself was still dominated, and therefore restrained, by the expectation of the *parousia*. The delay in its appearance occasioned exhortations for a little more patience, but the hope was not yet set aside.[14] It is unlikely that either the Twelve, or the Seven, *governed*. They *administered* the material affairs and exercised a personal influence on major decisions. The community, the assembly of the brethren, was still self-governing, under the sovereign direction of the Spirit. It was in fact the Spirit who bestowed on certain members of the assembly the *charisma* (the grace) befitting this government, and caused the *ecclesia* to listen to and follow them.[15] It is still along these lines that Paul will conceive the gift of government (1 Cor. xii.28). And within the communities existing at the close of the century wherein *ecclesiasticism* will set up its authority at the expense of that exerted by inspired individuals, defiance, and possibly scorn, of the elected functionaries who were on the way to becoming the masters of these communities will survive for some time. Thus the Didache (xv.lf), after exhorting the faithful to choose bishops and deacons "worthy of the Lord," will feel the need to add: "Do not despise them, for, with the prophets and the *didascaloi* [the inspired ones], it is they who are in honor among you," that is, "they whom you should honor."

To the question when the reign of the Spirit began we can return no certain answer. Acts dates it from Pentecost, that is, the first hour of the reinstallation of the disciples in Jerusalem, but I doubt the likelihood of this. The phenomenon of this reign should, I think, be related to the delay of the *parousia* and the beginnings of propaganda, which are tied together. *It was through the Spirit that the Church replaced the community.* Under his guidance, the first hope enlarged its horizons and turned towards doctrinal speculation. The Spirit was the vital leaven in the growing faith. Because he conventionalized and remolded everything to fit the experiences of his own day, the author of Acts has greatly blurred our vision. We cannot, at any rate, imagine the Spirit as the personal property of the Twelve, who dispensed it to the converts by the laying on of hands. This is a fabrication designed to "assert the apostolic prerogative" (Loisy). In reality, the Spirit is an imperious force (*dynamis*) manifest when, how, and where it pleases him. He determines and sanctions everything that takes place in the community.

---

14. *CCLXIX*, p. 208.
15. On the ancient and parallel use of *synagogè* and *ecclésia*, cf. *XV*,[2] p. 441 and n. The use of the first term survived among the Judeo-Christians and the Ebionites, according to Epiphanius, *Haer*. 30, 18.

The Spirit is manifest, moreover, in more than one form.[16] He affirms his presence in the ecstasy of some of the brethren; in the prophetic announcements of others, that is, in *edifying*, and not in *predictive*, discourse; in the inspiration which enables still others to make precious commentaries and edifying glosses on sacred texts or on the words of the Lord; and especially in dictating, in the midst of the assembly, and even to the most humble of the faithful, those mysterious and powerful words that come from an "unknown tongue." [17] Those who are favored with this *glossolalia* evidence such exaltation that they appear to be drunk; the malicious laugh at them and say: "They are full of new wine" (Acts ii.13).

Thus the real state of the early community was quite different from the long-standing impression, sanctioned by apostolic legends, of a community governed from its foundation by the College of Twelve, under the chairmanship of Peter. In fact, the early community was an assembly of pietists whose life was ruled by inspiration; there was no neo-legalism, and not even a shadow of sacerdotalism: *the brethren did not yet know that Jesus had founded the Church.*

III. *The Cultus*

However, the religious life of the brethren was no longer solely spiritual; it was already clothed with form and materiality in its cultus and liturgy, which, though undoubtedly still embryonic, were nonetheless the first concrete signs of the emergence of Christianity as a distinct religion. The initial simple notions concerning Jesus and his role began to recede, and one glimpses a speculative thinking which is the first stammering of doctrine.

Needless to say, the origins of the cultus and the liturgy remain shrouded in obscurity. This is understandable. It is, in particular, difficult for a man who knows the organized Church life of today to imagine that the past could have adhered to practices other than those he sees all about him. We run the risk of making the gravest errors when we attempt to interpret old rites by what they have become with the passing years.[18]

16. Eusebius, *H.E.*, III, 37, 2 and 3.
17. *LV*, p. 68; *CCXXV*.
18. *CVII*, pp. 48f.

It was inevitable that a cultus, however elementary and simple it may have been, would soon be set up in the community. The customs of the age required that every faith should express its religious sentiments by *demonstration:* cultic practices established a bond, reputedly indispensable, between men who shared the same belief; a bond that was the visible sign of their communion. Consequently, it was natural that the person of Jesus-Messiah should become for the brethren the focal point and the crystallization of their cultic needs; in his person lay the sole reason for and the sole justification of the community. When they assembled, the "saints" spoke of the Christ and of the hopes they placed in his power; they met, indeed, for no other reason. They asked *him* to come; they invoked *his* name, that is, they named him, in their prayers to God, as their guaranty and their certainty. When a recruit joined their flock, he could do so only by a profession of faith in his name, that is, in his person. And whatever else the admission ceremony may have consisted of, it was only by invocation of the name that the recruit was accorded his status as one of the faithful. We know that there must have been an admission ceremony, for we are dealing with a land and an age in which *rites of passage* [19] prevailed and were obligatory. What circumstance could have been more deserving of its own rite than the passage from the status of *damned* to that of *elect?* It is therefore correct to say, as Diessmann does,[20] that, because of the appeal, prayer, and even near-paean it contains, the word *maranatha* ($=$ may the Lord come! Or, Lord come!) offers us documentation of the primitive cultus.

In the milieu in which the first community was established, it was believed that *every name* had an intrinsic power, a power inherent in its essence and proper usage.[21] Moreover, when the Nazarene was alive, he had proved by his miracles that a divine *dynamis* dwelt in his person; it is therefore probable that among his first disciples, and even more so among the second, his name was thought to convey more than a merely thaumaturgic power: it had veritable magic power. It became both component and potent agent of exorcism,[22] as various texts show, for example, Acts iii.6, where Peter says to the paralytic, "In the name of Jesus of Nazareth, walk;" Mark ix.38, where John says to Jesus: "We have seen someone casting out devils in thy name;" Matt. vii.22: "Many will say to me . . . have we not . . . in thy name cast out devils. . . ;" and Mark xvi.17: "In my

19. Van Gennep, *Les Rites de passage*, Paris, 1909.
20. *CC*, p. 80.
21. Cf. *LXXXVI*, p. 76, n. 1.
22. *IX*, pp. 104f.

name they shall cast out devils." [23] Thus a twofold reason leads, if I may say so, to the use of the name of Jesus the Nazarene in the cult: it is the rallying point and instrumental agent of the community.

On the other hand, it was not possible for the cultic life of the brethren to be divorced from that of the synagogues, since, despite the fact that the hostility of outsiders isolated them as a sect, the circumstances of their life were similar. As in the synagogues, they read the Scriptures, sang psalms, offered prayers. For them, the Scriptures consisted basically of those passages of the Bible that were deemed prophetic, the passages that Jesus was supposed to have fulfilled. Their ingenuity quickly picked them out and assembled them as a *corpus testimoniorum*. The psalms they favored were those that sing of hope and exalt the promise. And their prayer, finally, could not but place in the forefront of their supplications the invocation of the *parousia:* the use of *maranatha* as a kind of refrain is enough to prove this. Together, these preoccupations drew the *essential* religious thought of the brethren back to the same object: *the person and the name of Jesus-Messiah.* This unconscious spiritual concentration already implied, as one can easily perceive, a strong tendency towards separation from authentic Judaism.

It is of little importance that the Scriptures read and the psalms sung were Jewish, that the prayers followed Jewish forms [24] and were recited at the hours of the day fixed by Jewish custom: [25] what matters is the intent and the content, for it is the intent and the content—or at any rate the interpretation of the content—that are moving away from Judaism. The framework remains Jewish, and the brethren are under the illusion that they are still well within it, but they have already begun an important work of superimposition.

May we not, in the meantime, take one further step and at least approximate some more decisive considerations in the cultic evolution of the community? At this point hesitation becomes perplexity.

In going through Acts and the Pauline epistles, without even attempting to establish the obviously needed chronological distinctions, one gets the impression that the Church of Jerusalem practiced three rites which in addition to their liturgical meaning, in itself quite interesting and capable of bearing important practical consequences in separating the Christians

23. It goes without saying that in these various texts, *in my name, in thy name* do not mean *in my place, in thy place;* but rather *through the action of thy, of my name.*

24. *CLXXXIX*, p. 225.

25. *CIV*, I, p. 697. Note that the Didache 8, 4 decrees the recitation of the *Pater* three times a day, a practice that conforms to Jewish procedure. Cf. Acts iii.1, x.30.

from the Jews, had also a special import which may be termed *sacra-mental*. They conferred on their beneficiary what I should like to call a *material advantage* on the *mystical plane*; each of them had, in itself, a saving effect. These three rites are *baptism, the laying on of hands*, and *the Eucharist*.

a) It is important to remember that baptism has no place in the Synop-tic tradition. Only in the final section of Matthew, among the instructions of the Risen One and therefore no part of the Galilean tradition, do we find the words: "*Go ye therefore, and teach all nations, baptizing them in the name of the Father, and of the Son, and of the Holy Ghost*." This formula is so obviously of late origin that there is every reason to believe it to be only an interpolation in the final section, which is itself secondary evidence.

One's first notion on passing in review the remaining examples of the practice of the baptismal rite is that it was even more a rite of separation than a rite of passage and admission; it played the same role in the com-munity of the brethren as circumcision did among the Jews. Just as there were the circumcised on the one hand and the uncircumcised on the other, a fundamental differentiation for the sons of Israel, so will there be the baptized and the nonbaptized, a differentiation still more fundamental for Christian salvationists.

There are several reasons for believing that the baptism of the first brethren retained its completely Johannine meaning only up to the time the first *proselytes of the gate* were attracted to the Christian faith and hope. It was therefore not long before baptism became a kind of successor to circumcision for those semi-Jews of good will who had already been won over by the Synagogue, which had not, however, always succeeded in inducing them to be circumcized. It became, as an inevitable and no doubt immediate consequence, the seal (σφραγίς) of faith, and thus of the Church of Jerusalem. Pagan influence had of course a profound effect on the baptismal rite and on its establishment as a sacrament.[26]

Not even once does the Synoptic record speak of baptism as a rite ad-ministered, or ordained, by Jesus—a surprising fact if the custom was nonetheless copied from his practice.[27] Baptism had already been practiced for some time as the *sign* of adherence to the faith at the time the Synoptics were written; of this there can be no doubt. John iii.22 men-tions it in these terms: "After that, Jesus came to the land of Galilee

26. *CLXXXIX*, p. 224.
27. On the serious difficulty we encounter here, cf., for example, *LXV*, pp. 223f; *XV*,[2] p. 211.

. . . and he baptized." But the Evangelist corrects this statement almost at once: "Though Jesus himself did not baptize, but his disciples" (iv.2). Acts ii.41 asserts that the men who adhered to the faith at the start of the community in Jerusalem were baptized, but this assurance proves only that our author believed that they really were baptized. If he did not err by antedating a habitual practice of his own day, the baptism he mentions could only be that of John the Baptist,[28] for the texts make no mention (with the exception of Matt. xxviii.19, a negligible instance) of the institution of a baptism peculiar to Jesus and his disciples. This, I must insist, would be most unlikely if this practice had already been introduced. Should we then believe that as soon as Jesus appeared his disciples received the seal that marked them as the lambs chosen for salvation (ἐν τῷ ὀνόματι Ἰησοῦ Χριστοῦ τοῦ Ναζωραίου, according to Acts iii.6)? Loisy thinks that "it is not at all impossible that Jesus *himself also baptized.*"[29] It is certainly not impossible and, in fact, one can only wonder who if not Jesus could have begun the practice. But nothing attests that he did and the *disavowal* of John iv.2 remains disturbing. I see no means of clarifying this obscure point except by way of hypotheses.

Hypothesis I. I think that the first men who put their trust in the prophet Jesus and rallied to his Good News, received, either from John or at the hands of Jesus, Johannine baptism as a sign of their vocation and of the remission of their sins. The first hypothesis, then, is that the Nazarene soon lost interest in a symbolic gesture which must have seemed of little importance to him, since he doubtless sought *inner* conversion as the essential thing in salvation. Did his disciples nevertheless continue, at his side and with his consent, but without his direct involvement, to baptize the newcomers? Did not Paul, perhaps sanctioning his conduct by the example of his Master, generally leave to his companions the task of performing the rite?[30] And this was a practice he followed at a time when he nonetheless considered baptism as, in principle, indispensable, and it had already acquired, according to the Paulinians, a much more complex meaning than Jesus himself could have given it.

Hypothesis II. If the Synoptic tradition makes no mention of the rite

28. The only baptism known to Apollos (Acts xviii.25: ἐπιστάμενος μόνον τὸ βάπτισμα Ἰωάννου), an Alexandrian who had not been in contact with Pauline speculation. The *baptism of John* had probably been borrowed by the Baptist from "some mystical sect of Judaism which had been subject to Iranian influence." *CCLXVI*, p. 138.

29. *CVIII*, p. 156. He took up the problem again in *CVII*, pp. 78, n. 5, 85, 133; and in *CX*, pp. 36–38.

30. 1 Cor. i.13–17. Holtzmann, *XXXI*, I, p. 450, already noted the parallel, pointing to John iv.2 and Acts x.48.

being practiced by Jesus, it is perhaps because in his day it was so common and so taken for granted that no reason existed for describing it. Besides, one cannot rigorously uphold the view that the texts say nothing of the origin of Christian baptism if it corresponded at the start to the baptism of John, with which the Markan narrative of the Gospel opens (Mark i.4 and 9). The distinction established therein between the baptism of water that John gives (i.8: ἐγὼ ἐβάπτισα ὑμᾶς ὕδατι)and the baptism of the Holy Spirit that He who is to come will administer (αὐτὸς δὲ βαπτίσει ὑμᾶς πνεύματι ἁγίῳ) is that of the Evangelist himself and dates him as living at a time when Christians have already speculated on their rite.

Hypothesis III. The direct disciples of the Nazarene took no more notice than he of the baptism of John, but quite naturally thought of it when, after the disappearance of the Master and the dispersion of their tiny group, they sought a means whereby to reconstitute their brotherhood, to center it in a belief, and to fortify it with a symbol.

I cannot decide which of the hypotheses is correct, for I have no means of doing so. But what did the rite, spoken of by Acts as though it was naturally one of the customs of the brethren, mean for them? What import did they attach to it?

The essential thing to note is that in all probability baptism existed in the Church of Jerusalem before the dispersion of the Hellenists, and that *it is this rite that made one a saint.* It did so because it imparted the Spirit to the convert. This is precisely the feature which distinguishes Christian baptism from the immersion practiced by John the Baptist (Acts i.5; cf. Mark i.8). The author of Acts even conjures up the existence of disciples baptized by *John alone,* that is, by water, and who, as a consequence, are devoid of the Spirit (Acts xix.1–4). I consider this notion of his to be unfounded and nothing more than a contrivance which barely conceals a thrust at Judaizing Christians.[31]

b) But isn't the bestowal of the Spirit linked to a special rite, *the laying on of hands?* Renan saw in this very ordinary Jewish practice, which was already familiar to Jesus,[32] the sacramental act par excellence of the Church of Jerusalem.[33] Perhaps he was too hasty in trusting the author of Acts, whose authority, as Loisy more prudently indicates,[34] does not suffice

---

31. *CVIII*, p. 78.
32. Mark v.23; Matt. ix.18, xix.13–15; Luke iv.40, xiii.13.
33. Renan, *LV*, p. 95, cites Acts vi.6 and viii.17–19; ix.12, 17; xiii.3; xix.6; xxviii.8. These passages all refer to various kinds of situations in which the rite of laying on of hands was used.
34. *CVIII*, p. 303.

to guarantee the actual existence of this rite in the Church in question. I admit, however, that the fact that it was credited to Jesus by the Synoptic tradition, that is, definitively by this Church itself, seems to carry great weight. Was not, I wonder, the laying on of hands in use before baptism, and was it not therefore the first rite of admission to the sect? The entire question concerning the beginnings of the Christian Church is so vague and obscure that nearly every time the exegete risks a statement, he instantly perceives a reason for contradicting it.

The laying on of hands was a *rite of communication and transmission:* when, reputedly, the Apostles prayed *over* the Seven who had been chosen and laid their hands on them (Acts vi.6), they invoked for them and infused in them the *charisma* needed for their new functions. But I am afraid that their action was anachronistic, conforming in advance to the customs of the Church known by the author. One can, however, easily imagine that baptism was accompanied by prayer and a laying on of hands which transmitted to the baptized light (φῶς), grace (χάρις), power (δύναμις), knowledge (γνῶσις)—all analogous gifts—which were the special property of the Church of Christ, and the co-inheritance of the "saint."

I don't know whether or not baptism was ordinarily administered by the Twelve and the Seven, but I surmise there was as yet no rule conferring on them the exclusive right to administer it: the "saint" who had been able to make a proselyte had also to be able to transform that proselyte into a "saint," [35] for saintliness was still the joint property of all the brethren. Sacerdotalism was far away, but the road which led to it was open, since, inherently, liturgy calls for a priesthood.

c) We would very much like to know exactly what happened and what was said at the community meal mentioned in Acts; we have not attained this knowledge.

The two essential texts on this subject are: (1) Acts ii.42: "And they continued steadfastly in the apostles' doctrine and fellowship, and in breaking of bread, and in prayers." In effecting this grouping, of whose artifice and expediency there can be little doubt, it was the writer's intention to present an image of the total religious life of the community: the brethren are assembled around the Apostles, and breaking of bread and common prayer are expressions of their fellowship. (2) Acts ii.46: "And they, continuing daily with one accord in the temple, and breaking bread from house to house, did eat their meat with gladness and singleness of heart." The breaking of bread and the meal are mentioned together, and

35. *XXV*, p. 117.

form a whole: breaking bread is a constituent element of the meal, which, if we collate the two verses (42 and 46), we may call the common meal. An actual meal, and not a mere form, is certainly meant, for the expression "did eat their meat" (μετελάμβανον τροφῆς) is precise. On the other hand, we can be equally certain that "breaking bread" is not simply a synonym for "eating." Accordingly, it has its own distinct meaning, and our question is: what is that meaning?

First let us note that the rite is set in the context of a meal, probably at its beginning. It is, as we have said, an actual meal, and not a liturgical fiction, like the later-day Eucharist. We note, too, that literally the word "eucharist" evokes only the *concept of thanksgiving*. In the Didache (10) there is no question of anything other than a thanksgiving, while in Paul, who is appreciably earlier, the word covers an entirely different concept. There are therefore grounds for believing that here the Didache had preserved the spirit, if not the letter, of the archaic tradition: thanks are offered over the cup to be drunk and the bread to be broken, as is the case with the Jews.[36]

If this is the case, there can be no question of the breaking of bread in the Church of Jerusalem as a memorial of the death of Jesus.[37] Nothing in Acts presupposes such a memorial, and were the breaking of bread a memorial, it would be incomprehensible that Acts should contain no mention of it. It is extremely important to remember that we are still concerned with the *bread* only, and not with the *wine*, which will represent the blood in the Pauline equation: bread and wine = body and blood (1 Cor. xi.26). We have already noted the fact that the cup is not to be found in the text of Luke xxii.19a, according to the reading of Codex D.[38] It is not difficult to account for the omission if we remember that the incipient faith did not stress the death of Jesus: his death was not yet a salvation mystery.

But perhaps one ought to see in the fraction a memorial of the Last Supper, or—and this is a related idea—a realization of Jesus's intention. The texts, however, do not give us this impression. Were this the case, it would be difficult to account for the fact that nothing to this effect appears in the texts, not even an allusion. Would it not be more to the point to consider the fraction as a reminder of one of the Nazarene's customs, who, acting as head of the family, broke the bread for his disciples before the meal? This notion is not to be found in Acts, but a Lukan

36. *CXXIX*, p. 45.
37. *IX*, p. 90; *LXXXIV*, p. 430.
38. Cf. *LXXXVI*, p. 533 [Cf. *RSV*, which follows Codex D. Tr.]

episode perhaps implies it. In Luke xxiv.30 the Pilgrims of Emmaus apparently recognize the Master by a characteristic gesture as he breaks bread and offers thanks.

"Nothing in the texts permits the establishment of any kind of relationship whatever between the breaking of bread and any memory whatsoever of the Christ" (Goguel).[39] If we adhere to a literal reading of the texts, the remark is just. But if we venture beyond the texts, what is the probable explanation when we keep the Emmaus episode in mind?

That it does not seem likely that the Master was absent from the memories of the disciples as they assembled for the meal; that in all times and for all men a meal is a uniting rite, and if it was such a uniting rite among the brethren, one cannot understand how Jesus could have no place in it; [40] that in all probability the rite was not simply the common Jewish practice of breaking bread at the Sabbath meal; [41] and that this gesture must have recalled a custom of Jesus—and it is here that probability is supported by our reading of Luke xxiv.30. Loisy has maintained [42] that "the recognition of Jesus in the breaking of bread bears witness to the relation which existed from the beginning between faith in the resurrection and the eucharistic supper. Faith in the resurrection and the presence of Jesus in the midst of his own were affirmed at the same time in the community meal; the two form, so to speak, one faith in the ever-living Christ." This statement is perhaps more definite than the facts warrant, but I do believe that the truth lies in this direction.[43] The meal in common was the visible sign of the fellowship of the faithful with one another and with Christ Jesus.[44] The breaking of bread, a reminder or repetition of a practice of the Master, evoked his presence, in some fashion, at the beginning of the meal.

May we perhaps call the rite a sacrament? No, not yet. At this stage it is much more akin to our "grace" before meals than to the Pauline Eucharist, and it is the meal itself that is the sign of communion and that will impose its schema on the subsequent rite: the Eucharist will remain

39. *LXXXIV*, p. 130.

40. Note that in the Didache the words of thanksgiving after the meal (ch. 10) close with *maranatha*. This is, perhaps, indicative.

41. *CXXIX*, p. 41.

42. *CXI*, p. 581.

43. Some exegetes (Jülicher, *XCIX*, p. 247; cf. Goguel, *LXXXIV*, p. 131) have thought that there may have been visions during the course of the common meal. These would have oriented it toward the meaning Loisy has indicated.

44. Loisy, *CVIII*, p. 217; J. Weiss, *CXXIX*, p. 41, stresses that the agape was a *communion* of the brethren.

a meal in theory, even when it is in fact only a sacramental rite. The breaking of bread does not yet grant to the participants a special grace; that will be the work of new and far-reaching ideas, whose advent we shall soon understand. It is, however, restricted to the brethren, and participation in it qualifies them as such when they sit down at the common table. *The fraction is the palpable sign of the brotherhood.* And that is already a step towards sacramentalism.

IV. *The Doctrine*

The last sentence of Acts (xxviii.31) merits our attention at this point. It states that Paul dwelt at Rome for two years, "preaching the kingdom of God, and teaching those things which concern the Lord Jesus Christ" (τὰ περὶ τοῦ Κυρίου 'Ιησοῦ Χριστοῦ). This phrase is a summation of the first preaching of the Church of Jerusalem and the substance of its doctrine.[45] It remains to be seen, however, what ideas lie behind this formulation; they are certainly not Paul's. If we had to rely on Acts alone, we should despair of understanding the text, since all its perspectives are jumbled and confused. Fortunately, we can go for assistance to the Synoptic tradition, whose sole purpose, as we know, was to concretize the meaning its authors assigned to the person of Jesus and to the hope founded on him.[46]

The Master had come *to announce the Kingdom of God* (κηρύσσειν τὴν βασιλείαν τοῦ θεοῦ). But one must not forget that in Israel the Messianic and eschatological ideas were not fixed, that they were set down within several somewhat different frameworks.[47] The Church of Jerusalem believed in the imminent coming of the Kingdom, to be preceded by the *parousia*.[48] In Hellenistic Greek, from the time of the Ptolemies to the second century of the Christian era, the word *parousia* was used to designate the arrival or visit of a king, an emperor, or any persons wielding authority, even troops. Its use was not limited to Egypt, but extended also to Asia. It did not imply a *return*. The current use of the word made it closely related in meaning to *epiphany*. In 2 Thess. ii.8 the two terms are conjoined in a discussion of the destruction of the impious (ἄνομος)

45. *XXIII*, I, p. 75, n. 2.
46. *IX*, p. 3.
47. Cf. *LXXXVII*, pp. 176–81.
48. On the nonreligious use of this word in ordinary speech, cf. *CLIII*,[2] pp. 278f, and *XLIX, ad verbum*.

by the Christ's imminent coming, "by the epiphany of his parousia." [49]
Consequently, *the parousia signified not the return of Jesus, but the manifestation of the glorified Master as the Messiah*. This notion ties in very
well with the exclamation *maranatha*—May the Lord come!

The writer of Acts is scarcely interested in the coming of the Kingdom;
all his attention is directed towards the evangelization of the world, and
it is quite possible that in recounting the bestowal of the Spirit in i.5 he
intended to substitute evangelization for the *parousia*. That this evidently
was not the viewpoint of the Jerusalem brethren is proved by the persistence of the concept of the *parousia* in Paul and in much later writings,
as well as by the use of *maranatha*. The outlook of the pristine faith, presumably in conformity with the teaching of Jesus, can be found in various
passages in the Synoptics, all of which imply a belief in the imminent
manifestation of the Kingdom (Mark ix.1; Matt. xvi.28; Mark xiii.32;
Matt. xxiv.34; Mark xiii.33; Matt. xxiv.42). Although they know that the
hour is known only to God,[50] the brethren try to foresee it, and they draw
up a small list of premonitory signs, probably borrowed from Jewish apocalyptic. The list appears also in the Didache (xvi.6), and it must have
never been subject to much variation. Only when the faith comes to terms
with an indefinite delay of the *parousia* [51] do the signs become confined
to the most commonplace phenomena: wars, pestilence, divers disasters.

In the Didache, on the other hand, the "signs of Truth" (τὰ σημεῖα
τῆς ἀληθείας) are still the following: the heavens will open, the trumpet
will blast, and the dead will be raised up—not all of them, but the saints
of the Lord at least.

What sort of Kingdom will be inaugurated by the *parousia?* Acts i.6
seems to offer an answer in the question, asked of Jesus, which it attributes to the disciples: "Lord, wilt thou at this time restore again the kingdom to Israel?" In other words, they ask if he will re-establish the might
of Israel and its sovereignty, as the elect people, over the rest of the
world. The question is related to the popular Jewish idea of the Messiah

49. Τῇ ἐπιφανείᾳ τῆς παρουσίας αὐτοῦ. In the Pastoral Epistles, ἐπιφάνεια
is used for παρουσία. Cf. 1 Tim. vi.14; 2 Tim. iv.1 and 8; Titus ii.13. The same
synonymy was current in secular usage: CLIII,² p. 284.

50. It must be noted that Acts i.7 takes care not to say that the Christ shares the
general ignorance on this point.

51. An excellent reason would finally be given to explain the delay: the Lord has
not abandoned the intention to effect his promise, as some think; he is exercising his
patience that all may have the time to repent and be saved. (2 Peter iii.9. The
verse is a kind of echo to Mark xiii.10: "And the Gospel must first be preached to
all nations.")

as the earthly ruler of Israel. (Cf. Luke i.32: "He shall be great, and shall be called the Son of the Highest: and the Lord God shall give unto him the throne of his father David"; and i.71 and 74, in which the Messianic task is the deliverance of Israel from the hand of her enemies.)

Various texts, however, seem to imply that the Christ's reign began with his Ascension to the Father. (Cf. Matt. xiii.41, which represents him as sending his angels to keep order in his Kingdom, and Rev. iii.21: ". . . I also overcame, and am set down with my Father in his throne.") The belief these words presuppose marks a step towards the spiritualization of the Kingdom, but only a step. For there is no reason to think that the common understanding of the Kingdom did not remain fundamentally Jewish until the day the Hellenists intervened. To the latter the Kingship of Israel was of much less interest. They were already seeking a less material interpretation of the Kingdom, an interpretation that would *realize a life of blessedness for the individual believer*, for that was the *inheritance*, the exclusive privilege and *raison d'être* of their faith. This conception will arrive, in the communities on Greek soil, at its logical consummation: the notion of *salvation*, with its corollary that salvation's primary concern is not the nation, the people of Israel, but the *convert*, the individual who has *known* and *believed*.

Naturally, the conceptions of the Kingdom and of the Messiah complement each other. Bousset went to great trouble [52] to show that at this period the Christian community was convinced that Jesus was the transcendant Son of Man (*Menschensohn*), and Wellhausen [53] perceived in the second part of Mark the predominance of this quite Jewish conception of the Son of Man over the Petrine Christ. I, however, do not think it very likely that the doctrine of the Son of Man was born on Palestinian soil. I believe it owes its origin to a Greek misunderstanding of the Aramaic term *bar-nascha* = a son of man = a man. Bousset himself admits [54] that the primary documentary evidence in favor of belief in the Son of Man is the Fourth Gospel—which is hardly a good recommendation for either the antiquity or the Palestinian origin of the term and the concept it encloses.

Nor does the first part of Acts present us with so exalted a Messiah. (Cf. Acts ii.22: "Jesus of Nazareth, a man approved of God among you by miracles and wonders and signs, which God did by him in the midst

52. *IX*, pp. 6f. Cf. *LXXVI*, pp. 191 and 197.
53. *CXXX*, p. 70.
54. *IX*, p. 24; cf. John iii.13; vi.62; vii.51.

of you." [55] He was a man armed with the might of God, a truly Jewish figure, and everything leads us to believe that Christology sprang from this foundation. Loisy, who contests this assertion, believes that this doctrinal archaism is but a contrivance of the writer, whose bias leads him "to draw as close as possible to Judaism and to show that Jesus was the Messiah proclaimed by the Jewish Scriptures," and that, under this façade, the writer "conceals a mystical Christology, a fit doctrine in a religion whose very object is the Lord Christ." [56] The writer does indeed profess such a Christology, but I find it difficult to believe that his attributing such remote beginnings to this doctrine was only a simple trick of astute archaism. The fact that, although he undoubtedly knew the Christology of Paul, he did not project it onto the Christology he credits to Peter seems to me highly significant. It should also be noted that the Christological reference in Luke xxiv.19, where the Pilgrims of Emmaus describe Jesus as "a prophet mighty in deed and word before God and all the people," is analogous to that of Acts. It is quite possible that this Christology was derived from the original source; moreover, it accords well with its apparent claims to verisimilitude.

But this prophet, this man with whom God *was* as he went about armed with the might of the Spirit, in perfect conformity with the classic picture of the Jewish *nabi*, had already been glorified by the resurrection and exaltation to the right hand of God, as we can see in reading Acts ii.36: "God has made him Lord and Christ" (Κύριον αὐτὸν καὶ χριστὸν ἐποίησεν ὁ Θεός). It was impossible for the faith not to build higher on this fundamental affirmation, for the following practical reasons:

1. The Messiahship attributed to Jesus placed him on a plane other than that of the prophet.

2. It led the brethren to assemble the Messianic prophecies and to apply them to Jesus. At times they went *back* to his earthly life and projected onto the memories they had, or thought they had, of it the data of the prophecies. At other times they went *forward* and built the apocalyptic picture of the *parousia* with details garnered from other prophecies (Mark xiii.26).

3. The Jews would not believe that this Galilean was the Messiah; they thus set the course for the trend that would remove him from their own Messianic notions. As a result, Jesus's Messiahship became highly individualized and conformed *increasingly to Messianic patterns which were not*

55. Cf. Acts x.38: "How God anointed Jesus of Nazareth with the Holy Ghost and with power; who went about doing good, and healing all that were oppressed of the devil; for God was with him."
56. *CVIII*, pp. 113f.

theirs. This trend was of course accentuated by the Hellenists. In the expression *Lord and Christ*, the word *Lord* referred to the Greek *Kyrios* rather than to the Aramaic *Maran*; it was becoming Jesus's own title, perhaps already in cultic use,[57] as would become more clearly apparent in the Hellenic community. The word *Christos* seemed gradually to lose its precise meaning, which was *Messiah*, to become part of the proper name of Jesus; a tendency developed to use the formulas *Jesus-Christ Lord*, or *the Lord Jesus-Christ*, terms devoid of the Jewish conception of the Messiah. As we know, the Ancients did not believe that names were impassive or neutral.

4. The brethren were persuaded that, through the Spirit, the Lord was present in their midst. This conviction favored cultic invocation of his name. Besides, miracles were accomplished *by his name* (Acts iii.16).

5. Above all, necessity imposed the need to reflect upon the meaning of Jesus's death,[58] for this death was the source of scandal and the chief counter-argument of the nonbelievers. For the faithful, it was perhaps only the great mystery of this death that they had to explain, for unless they did, their faith was stopped, unable to free itself from the fearsome text of Deuteronomy xxi.23: "Accursed of God is he who is hanged on the tree!"[59] There was no question of introducing the idea of redemption into this death. That conception was foreign to the milieu, and we shall soon discover where it originated. It was only a matter of explaining how this death was a part of the divine plan in the advent of the Messiah,[60] and it did not exclude faith in Jesus as Messiah.

We begin with the undeniable fact, the *raison d'être* of the community, that after the crucifixion of their Master the disciples were immediately forced to face questions and objections, even if at first their hearts alone had restored their confidence in him and in his wonderful destiny.[61] By the simple fact of facing the difficulties, they had become *witnesses* of Jesus's resurrection, for they must necessarily have said: God's raising him from the dead, must be a mark of his wonderful favor and a token of his exalted design for him; there cannot therefore be any notion of a curse in his death. But an affirmation is not an explanation. It seemed natural to think then of the willing sacrifice, and this idea did indeed take root

---

57. *CVIII*, p. 212.

58. *XXIV*, p. 163; *XCV*; *XV*, p. 190.

59. Feigel, *LXXVIII*, p. 9, recalls the saying of St. Jerome, *Ad Gal.*, 2: *Famosissima quaestio est.* [Guignebert's translation of Deut. xxi.23 results from a conflation with Gal. iii.13. Tr.]

60. *CVI*, p. 195.

61. Cf. *CX*, ch. ii, for a consideration of this idea and for the completely eschatological character of the earliest faith of the Jerusalem brethren.

rather quickly in the Christian tradition. When one reads Mark x.45 (Luke xxii.27), "The Son of man came not to be ministered unto, but to minister, and to give his life a ransom for many;" and the words at the Last Supper, "This is my blood of the new covenant, which is shed for many" (Mark xiv.24), one thinks of the scapegoat and the Jewish ideas on vicarious sacrifice.[62]

I do not, however, believe it probable that the earliest explanation of the Christ's death was based on this conception. It is easy to see that it is not to be found in the first part of Acts. *Therefore it was probably the Hellenistic community that first thought of it.*

The Church of Jerusalem seems to have thought that Jesus's death was the means of passage from an earthly state to celestial dignity. Therefore the Lord who was to come was no longer the man Jesus, but the glorified Risen One, who was seated at the right hand of God, awaiting his assigned day. This semi-divine being was already quite different from the Jewish Messiah, and more different still from the Galilean prophet known by the first disciples. He had become the agent of the works of God, the depositary of his spirit, his intermediary. This notion was as yet badly defined, vague and uncertain in its contours, but it was potentially rich in meaning.

At first this essential transformation of the Nazarene was effected by *adoption*.[63] The *Prophet* had only authority (ἐξουσία); that was his characteristic. The *Glorified One* possessed *the Spirit* (πνεῦμα), which he poured over his saints. That was something else again. He was, at the very least, anointed by God (Acts iv.27) with the Holy Spirit and with *power* (δύναμις) (Acts x.38). Was he also the *son of David*? Yes, but this notion played only an insignificant part in the ancient Synoptic tradition and, I should say, in the primitive community. It would become important only with the apologetic which is to be found in the prehistories of Matthew and Luke. [I.e., the infancy narratives. Tr.] The Church of Jerusalem preferred to stress the Christ's close fellowship with God, his possession of the Spirit, and his collaboration in the divine works. Thus *the ascension of the Christ towards divinity*, towards the acquisition of his status as Jahweh's general legatee, had begun.

62. *IX*, p. 89, and *VII*, pp. 228f.
63. *CXXIX*, p. 85; *CLXXIX*, p. 48, n. 3.

Conclusion

The Church of Jerusalem, though it remained on Jewish soil, already bore within it all that would be needed for leaving it. The elements of opposition to Israel and the grounds for the separation that would have developed and been operative, even without the added leaven of the Hellenists, are clearly evident. The Hellenistic leaven, which had already infiltrated into the brotherhood, even in Jerusalem, began therein that work of transformation which it could finish only where it alone was dominant, that is, on Greek soil. It was through the activity of the Hellenists that the pure Jews became aware of the true status of the disciples in relation to themselves. This discovery marked the beginning of fruitful tribulations which would force the faith out of its Jewish rut and into the potent life of the Hellenic world.

4

THE LIFE OF THE
FIRST BROTHERHOOD

To isolate the features that are truly part of the primitive period of the community from those character-istic of the succeeding years, the years in which the brethren organized for survival, is a difficult undertaking. Neither the simple task of assigning definite dates, nor the more modest one of fixing approximate limits for the era of the beginnings, is easy for us. The author of Acts did not make the necessary distinctions, nor did he set up boundary stakes. Besides, any possible surmises are deplorably limited by the paucity of his narrative. Close examination of his first chapters leaves the impression that he had only a meager account at his disposal. He seems to have fragmented it, and used the pieces several times over, with editorial variations more or less likely to convey the illusion of progression. Critics too often view the community's entire history as a single unit about which they assemble and amalgamate the testimonies of Acts and the Pauline epistles.[1] It is useful, however, to make a few distinctions.

Three points, especially, deserve to hold our attention. (1) *How did the brethren manage to exist?* Even in the Orient, once the first days had passed, insuring their material existence must have been a rather diffi-cult problem for the brethren to solve. (2) *What was their religious life*

1. For example, J. Weiss, *CXXIX*, pp. 32f.

like? Were these Jews distinguished from the others, and if so, exactly how? (3) *How was their existence as a sect conditioned?* Did they conform to a special way of life, to customs peculiar to themselves, which set them apart and cut them off from other people? And did they seek to enlarge their group? If so, what was their purpose and how did they go about it?

I. Material Existence

We do not of course know what resources the disciples who had come back from Galilee may have brought with them. It is not at all certain that they were all destitute; the Synoptic account does not give this impression. And if it is true that Jesus found a generous response among some well-to-do men, such as Simon the Leper (Mark xiv.3), it is possible that his disciples retained the support of these men. It is also likely that, insofar as it was possible, our Galileans disposed of their property before leaving their homes.

On their arrival in Jerusalem, they settled in inns or with friends. I think that as soon as some of their hosts were won over to their belief—which no doubt happened quickly in some cases—the disciples assembled in small groups in their dwellings. No hint permits us to believe that they sought work in order to live, although most of them were doubtless jobbing workmen. The famous Pauline texts, in which the Apostle proclaims his intention to live only by the work of his own hands,[2] have no bearing on the situation in Jerusalem; they pertain only to the Tarsiot and his companions; furthermore, they correspond to another time and another place. It is uncertain whether the brethren had trades that would be useful in Jerusalem. What seems likely, from the impression given by Acts and examination of their general religious psychology, is that *they had no desire to work*, for one worked only to insure *continuation of temporal existence*, and it was their firm expectation that there would be no more continuation. They mustered around the certainty of the imminent end of this world, in which men suffer and travail.

Let us not forget that they were Orientals, abstemious, easy to feed, seeking only to exist come what may until the expected Day. Since a common conviction had united them, it seemed obvious to them that the best means of subsistence was to communalize their resources, as those among

---

2. 1 Cor. iv. 12:καὶ κοπιῶμεν ἐργαζόμενοι ταῖς ἰδίαις χερσίν;1 Cor. ix. 11f; 2 Thess. iii.8.

them who had been the companions of Jesus were already accustomed to doing.

Acts tells us that this is just what they did; but its account is hardly satisfactory. Let us look first at the texts. In ii.43ff we read: "And fear came upon every soul: and many wonders and signs were done by the apostles. And all that believed were together, and had all things common [ἐπὶ τὸ αὐτὸ εἶχον ἅπαντα κοινά]; and sold their possessions and goods, and parted them to all men, as every man had need." A little farther on, in iv.32ff, we find: "And the multitude of them that believed were of one heart and of one soul: neither said any of them that aught of the things which he possessed was his own [ἴδιον εἶναι]; but they had all things common [ἀλλ᾽ ἦν αὐτοῖς ἅπαντα κοινά] . . . and great grace was upon them all. Neither was there any among them that lacked: for as many as were possessors of lands or houses sold them, and brought the prices of the things that were sold, and laid them down at the apostles' feet: and distribution was made unto every man according as he had need."

Examples follow: one edifying, the story of Joseph the Cypriot, called Barnabas (= son of prophecy?) by the Apostles, who sold a field (iv.36f); the other terrifying, the story of Ananias and Sapphira. This couple sold their property but conspired to hold back a portion of what they received from the buyer. Ananias then came to lay at the Apostles' feet what he had decided to give them. But Peter had seen into the soul of the unfortunate man, and reproached him with having foolishly and unnecessarily lied to the Spirit, since what he had sold was his and he could have kept it. Ananias fell down dead on the spot, as did Sapphira, who arrived soon after. Unaware of what had happened, she thought to strengthen the deception by a lie. To Peter's insidious question (v.8); "Tell me whether you sold the land for so much?" she replied, "Yea, for so much." And the author repeats, like a refrain, "And great fear came upon all the church . . . by the hands of the apostles were many signs and wonders wrought among the people" (v.11–12).

Not one liberal exegete would, I think, be inclined to believe that all this is to be taken literally. The difficult thing is to discern, underneath the fantasy and fabrication, the few hints which may perhaps correspond to an authentic and exact memory.

The two passages I have cited, Acts ii.43ff and Acts iv.32ff, are apparently doublets: the writer repeated himself, because he had nothing more to add to what he had already said, and because he wanted to make comments, which mean little, on his two examples. If all the faithful relinquished their property, the example of Barnabas is valueless, and if so-called "communism" was the rule, why did Peter remind Ananias that he was permitted to keep for himself his land or the money he had received for it?[3] In view of this, it is not difficult to extract from the texts a few sensible observations that cause some uneasiness about the consistency of this so-called "communistic" experience.

1. These men, who no longer called anything their own, have pooled their resources. What, then, are we to make of the distribution of aid to the needy? To set up a relief fund was to enter into the framework of Jewish charity, and not to establish community of property.[4] Furthermore, there is mention in vi.1f of discontent among the Hellenistic brethren caused by partiality in this distribution of charity. I incline to the belief that the author knit together two successive and different situations. *Initially*, the brethren did in fact hold their meager resources in common, and lived from hand to mouth in urgent expectation of the *parousia*. *Then*, when it became obvious that patience would be necessary and that the supreme hour might be late in striking, the relief fund replaced the rule-of-thumb pseudo-communism.

2. A life of communal sharing is indeed conceivable as a practical means of subsistence for the very first *small* group; but, prior to speaking of this mode of existence, the author notes Peter's conversion of some three thousand souls (ψυχαὶ ὡσεὶ τρισχίλιαι) (ii.41). Thus his description, so fuzzy under its apparent clarity, no longer seems acceptable. One may very well grant that these three thousand and the first community had only "one heart and one soul," but it is difficult to envisage them all sitting down at a common table, maintained by joint resources.

3. In a burst of enthusiasm, which costs nothing, the author invites us to admire these good brethren who sell lands and houses to supply the common fund;[5] but may not this indifference to possessions be considered quite natural in people who believe that they are living their last days in this world? Our narrator does not seem to suspect that these zealots of the Kingdom are going to put the brotherhood in a very embarrassing position: where will it lodge its members if they have divested themselves of their homes?[6] He is obviously not worried about these problems, for which positive solutions would be sought in vain, and utilizes devices most likely to implant the notion of a complete relinquishing of all private interests for the benefit of the community, whose

3. *XVIII*, III, pp. 184f.
4. *CXXIX*, p. 52; *CVIII*, p. 270.
5. For a thorough note on this alleged event, see *XCVII*, V, pp. 140f (K. Lake).
6. *CVIII*, p. 261.

existence he would have us see as a kind of prefiguration of cenobitic life.[7]

It is a likely supposition that the author's source gave no such impression, but presented the sale and renunciation of private property as an exercise in perfection, in line with Jesus's alleged recommendation to the young man who desired to win a share in the Kingdom (Mark x.21 and Synoptic parallels). The man who succeeds in this laudable endeavor is Barnabas; the one who fails is Ananias, both because he meant to deceive the Apostles in whom the Spirit dwelled and because he forgot that a sin against the Spirit is unpardonable. In addition, I am inclined to believe that before recounting the dramatic story of Ananias and Sapphira (v.1ff) the writer had reread Joshua vii,[8] where it is stated that a certain Achan aroused the anger of Jahweh against Israel because he had misappropriated *dedicated things*. The divine wrath was not appeased until the guilty one had been punished. He confessed and, along with his wife, children, and cattle, was stoned. It is therefore possible that the only two concrete details in the Acts account under discussion have no basis in reality.[9]

Similarly, the assertion that "neither was there any among them that lacked" may very well have been only a probable deduction bolstered by the Scriptural text in Deuteronomy xv.4 which, in describing the Promised Land, states: "There shall be no poor among you."

The passages thus bear the marks of an idealization which it would be imprudent to receive as history.[10] It seems impossible to believe in this absolute, organized, and systematic communism. System and organization do not harmonize with the spirit of the first hour; absolute communism is incompatible with that of the second. The concrete instances cited by the narrator contradict his general assertions.[11] However, I agree with Loisy [12] that the account contains "elements of truth assembled in a false perspective." These elements of truth should be seen as follows:

During the first weeks, perhaps the first months (how can one estimate the capacity of the Galilean disciples for illusion?) the brethren, as long as they firmly believed that the *parousia* would come on the morrow, or the day after, or at the worst, on the very next Sunday, lived hand-to-mouth, thanks to a spontaneous pooling of their resources. In doing so

7. *CVIII, ad* Acts iv.32.

8. I would say that positive proof of this contention is provided by his use of the rare word νοσφίσασθαι (καὶ ἐνοσφίσατο ἀπὸ τῆς τιμῆς) which he found in Josh. vii.1: ἐνοσφίσατο ἀπὸ τοῦ ἀναθέματος. Cf. *XCVII*, IV, p. 50, *ad loc.*

9. *CVIII*, p. 271.

10. *CXXIX*, p. 49.

11. *CXC*, p. 315.

12. *CVIII*, pp. 222, 229.

they had no wish to apply a *social* theory—which would not make sense in their day [13]—nor even a *moral* or *religious* one. Communal life was imposed by the fact that *fraternity* made fraternal existence necessary as they shared in the common waiting for the *parousia*. The primitive group constituted a visible *family*, that of the Messiah Jesus; it continued the family that had lived with him in Galilee during his earthly mission.

The first group was recruited, with rare exceptions, only from *among the poor in spirit* (*anavim*) and *the poor in material means* (*ebyonim*). A twofold consequence resulted: (1) These men thought it an advantage and a blessing to be poor, because the Kingdom was promised first of all to them (Luke vi.20, 24f). Poverty was also the essential sign of election.[14] (2) The sale of property and the use of the money thus gained to feed the poor constituted the pre-eminently excellent act (Luke xii.21 and xii.33: "Sell that ye have, and give alms; provide yourselves bags which wax not old, a treasure in the heavens that faileth not"). It affirmed a precious detachment from the world and realized that precept of Jewish ethics which recommends to the rich the succor of the needy (cf. Luke xvi.9: "And I say unto you, Make to yourself friends of the riches of unrighteousness"). These Lukan texts are in perfect correspondence with the practices that, I imagine, must have existed among the first brethren. They also evoke the Jewish custom of setting up in every community a fund to aid the impoverished: it was called *kûppah* = basket, or *tamhui* = tray.[15]

It is therefore, in my opinion, quite probable that the small primitive group held the brethren's property jointly, as much through pious resolution as material necessity, each member bringing from day to day what he had to contribute to the common subsistence. But where did the author of Acts get the data for his description? Opinions differ, which means that nobody knows. Some think he got them from Josephus's description of the Essene cenobitism,[16] noting as well that the author may have known the Essenes directly. Others prefer to attribute them to influences from the Pythagorean community.[17] But the source matters very

---

13. I cannot put the *lector candidus* too much on guard against tempting, but illusory, identifications. The pseudo-communism of the first brethren of Jerusalem is as foreign to what we today call communism as the Lukan darts directed against the rich (Luke vi.20–25)—the wicked rich—are from our socialism. We do well to be wary of words; though they convey ideas, they are not themselves to be taken for ideas.

14. *CXXIX*, p. 53; *CVIII*, p. 261.

15. *XCVII*, V, pp. 148f.

16. Josephus, *War* II, 8; III, 4; *Antt.* XVIII, 1, 5.

17. *CXIX*, p. 38.

little; what is important is to understand the author's intent, which was to present an exalted picture of the primitive community's fraternal perfection. The Fathers interpreted his text in this sense: they used it as an example to encourage philanthropy among the faithful and indifference to earthly possessions.[18]

This state of affairs was of short duration; inevitably, it ended with the beginning of propaganda, which increased the size of the little flock. Pseudo-communism gave way to the relief fund, maintained by voluntary donations laid *at the feet of the Apostles.* Indeed, the institution of the Twelve, as administrators of this fund, may date from this period.[19] The need to administer a fund may have been, as is often the case elsewhere, the beginning of organization: the till created the Church.[20]

When the local resources are exhausted, which must not have taken long, the community would be in danger of starvation. Charity from the communities of the Diaspora, which had already swarmed from it, would then come into play, and *collection* for the *saints of Jerusalem* would become a current practice and a duty.[21]

II. *Religious Life*

There is no doubt that the writer of Acts saw the first faithful of the Christ as strict Jews. He showed them as steadfast in daily attendance at the Temple (ii.46), praising God with one accord (ὁμοθυμαδόν) : this God is Yahweh. Such edifying conduct earns them the good will of the people (ii.47). I grant that there is something artificial and far-fetched in this idyllic picture, but I find it difficult to believe that everything in it is an invention.

If these men were not authentically pure Jews, what brought them to Jerusalem? By *pure Jews,* I mean men bound to the yoke of the Torah. Let us reread the *logia* in Matthew v.17f: "Think not that I am come to destroy the law, or the prophets: I am not come to destroy, but to fulfill. For verily I say unto you, till heaven and earth pass, one jot or one tittle shall in no wise pass from the law, till all be fulfilled." And Matthew xxiii.2f: "The scribes and the Pharisees sit in Moses' seat: all therefore

18. *CCLXI*, p. 337 & n.
19. *CVIII*, pp. 219f, 262.
20. *CXXIX*, pp. 51f, sees in the fact that the Apostles collected the donations "der erste Anfang eines kirchlichen Beamtentums" ["the first step towards ecclesiastical bureaucracy." Tr.]
21. Gal. ii.10; 1 Cor. xvi.1; 2 Cor. ix.1; Rom. xv.26. Cf. *CX*, pp. 260, 316.

whatsoever they bid you observe, that observe and do; but do not ye after their works." It is only too evident that such precepts as these are older than those which oppose them, which are the fruit of anti-Jewish polemics. They embody the first disciples' mode of thinking and acting.

Paul, it is true, opposes the Jerusalem community, the "Church of God," as he calls it,[22] to Judaism, and "the brethren" (1 Cor. xv.6) and "saints" (1 Cor. xvi.1) to the Jews. But his testimony is not of the first hour, and has no value for it.

So the brethren were Jews, along the line of the *anavim*, more spontaneously devout than versed in Pharisaic subtlety and learned religion, all of them, or nearly all, Jews of humble station, *'am ha'-aretz*.[23] But a basic trait within them differentiated them from the other Jews: they believed that this Jesus who died on the cross had been raised and glorified by God to become his Messiah, and that he would at any moment become manifest in this guise (Acts ii.36). But this singular and fundamental aspect of their faith cannot be discerned at first: its role will begin with the first attempts at propaganda, which, in my opinion—and there can be nothing but opinions on this point—is not one of the initial phenomena in this history. It was preceded, I think, by a period during which the hope, expecting imminent fulfillment, imposed its sovereign and undivided rule, a contemplative period whose exaltation was reoriented only by the delay of the *parousia*.

It is not surprising that the people thought well of the disciples so long as they knew them only by their conduct as Jews; their attitude would change radically when the disciples begin to preach. Had they wished to begin such preaching immediately, the fate meted out to their Master would no doubt have sufficed to remind them of the harsh measures against them they might provoke from the Jews or the Romans. During this first period, which was short—a few months at the most and probably only a few weeks—their numbers, undoubtedly very small, were augmented only through an individual and hidden contagion. But they became established in the City.

There is no reason to see them as separatists,[24] for their separation from Judaism was wholly *internal* and only potential. They were no more conscious of it than the outsiders. They considered themselves the *elect*, the only ones to whom the Day of Yahweh would bring joy and happiness. A not extraordinary opinion in Israel.

22. Gal. i.13; 1 Cor. xv.9.
23. *CXXII*, p. 81.
24. *CXXII*, p. 80.

But perhaps they were already scrutinizing the writings of the Prophets to find in them, not the confirmation of their faith—writings would have no part in that—but its justification. Thus they began to build the legend of Jesus, forgetting as they did so his history. Must one assume that their meetings were illuminated by stunning *charismas* of the Spirit? The story of the miracle at Pentecost (the descent of tongues of fire) would at first make us think so; I, however, am inclined to look upon the overflow of the Spirit as a phenomenon of the second hour, which occurred as compensation for the impatience and disillusion of waiting. The first enthusiasm must have been, in its certainty, more serene.

III.　Sectarian Life

Although the first community was fundamentally Jewish, we nonetheless see it as a *sect*, a Messianic Jewish sect. The members stayed close to one another, not only *physically*, in order to live, but also *spiritually*, in order to believe.

The bond that united them was *brotherhood*. In using this term I am not referring solely to the brotherly love they bore one another but also to the fact that henceforth the only thing in the world that mattered to them was the fraternal group they formed which set them apart from other men.[25] When they contemplated themselves in relation to one another, they were *the brethren* (ἀδελφοί); when they compared themselves to the rest of humanity, they were *the saints* (ἅγιοι), a nomenclature, as it were, of being separate, fenced off from others. "Thou shalt seek out every day the company of the Saints," says the Didache (iv.1), and the Apostolic Fathers would preserve for all Christians the same advantageous name. It was not necessary to invent the term; it can be found in the Scriptures, where Daniel speaks of the "saints of the Most High" (vii.18, 22).[26] Properly speaking, it did not mean that those to whom it was applied were farther advanced than others on the road of sanctification or holiness, but rather that they were *separated* from the secular world and oriented towards the works of God.[27]

One can hardly doubt the absence of real organization in the brotherhood at the beginning. Organization stems, inevitably, from the desire

25. A study of the various designations applied to Christians in Acts can be found in *XCVII*, V, pp. 375f (Cadbury).
26. Ecclesiasticus xlii.17; Tobit viii.15.
27. *XXXI*, II, p. 168.

and the hope to endure. The brethren lived only in expectation of the
end. They were assembled around a handful of people who exercised
authority by virtue of being exemplars and the moral ascendancy they
commanded through their close relations, during his life, to the Nazarene,
an ascendancy strengthened since his death by their visions. Weiss has
rightly noted [28] that Acts itself makes no mention of any true organization
of the community during its first days. The word *ecclesia*, which in itself,
at least in intent, presupposes such an organization, appears only in
Acts v.11.[29] Up to this point, the group has always been designated only
by a collective term applied to its members: *the brethren* (οἱ ἀδελφοὶ)[30]
or *the believers* (οἱ πιστεύσαντες).[31] The individual wills, inclinations, and
differences were still absorbed by, and dissolved in, the common exaltation, and this perhaps is what the writer intended us to understand when
he assured us that all were "of one heart and of one soul" (iv.32). Beyond
that, he seems to be completely incapable of understanding what this
kind of unorganized life may have been in reality.

The moral attitudes of the brethren are more easily conceived. In
this respect, commentators have quite rightly stressed the aid proffered
by the body of ethical prescriptions credited to Jesus and stabilized in the
Synoptic tradition. In particular, the small systematic catechesis known
as the Sermon on the Mount is of great help to us: it is the primitive
community's true catechism in morals.[32] The community sought the
justification of its own conduct in its more or less accurate memories,
or in the impressions which spontaneously made up for the lack of such
memories. The precepts it assembled corresponded to its practice, for
in what is ordinarily considered to be Jesus's ethic [33] we have a practical
rule of life, and not in any sense moral speculation. "Ye are the salt of
the earth" (Matt. v.13) and "Ye are the light of the world" (Matt. v.14),
but, "except your righteousness shall exceed the righteousness of the
scribes and Pharisees, ye shall in no case enter into the kingdom of
heaven" (Matt. v.20)—all these sayings apply perfectly to the brethren,
for they are in fact their sayings. Pride in being one of the restricted
number of the *elect*, of being deemed a member of *the small chosen*

28. *CXXIX*, p. 36.
29. On the origin of the word and its use in primitive Christianity, cf. *XCVII*, V,
pp. 387f (Cadbury).
30. Acts i.16; ix. 30; x.23.
31. Acts ii.44; iv.32.
32. *IX*, p. 45; *CXXIX*, pp. 56f, agrees, but exaggerates by attributing the entire
Gospel ethic to this community. There is room here for distinctions.
33. *LXXXVI*, pp. 449f.

flock,[34] is ethically intelligible only if it is related to the consciousness of being responsible for the fulfillment of a special task. The Master demanded of his own more than the legislator of Israel did of the people as a whole. He improved on the commandments of Moses.[35] The seeming paradox and inapplicability to life in an ethical society of these augmented demands dwindle, or even vanish, if we remember that they had value and meaning only for a small conventicle, divorced from the world and illumined by a supernatural hope.

I have already stated that I do not believe in the early existence of genuine propaganda, organized and methodical, because such propaganda would not have been consonant with the expectation of the momentary appearance of the *parousia,* an expectation more likely to have led the brethren into deeper withdrawal into themselves rather than to have propelled them into external activity. However, it would be inconceivable that these Jews, living in the midst of Jews—who had never been *subjectivists* in religious matters—bound to the same religion, and observing the same worship, kept a surly silence about their own special conviction and did not seek to share it with whoever was willing to listen to them. One can place no credence in the showy demonstrations Acts credits to Peter (i.15f), for if he had by chance risked them, they would instantly have drawn the little group into quite dangerous unpleasantness. But it was possible for each brother to chat privately with outsiders and convince them;[36] to evaluate the results of such individual infection is impossible. Acts v.12 (cf. iii.11) presents all the faithful assembled on Solomon's Porch,[37] implying apparently that it was their headquarters, but nothing leads us to believe that they preached there. If they had, would they have been tolerated in that spot?

History cannot retain any of the edifying assertions in the Pentecost story (ii.41–42). On that day, on a single impulse, three thousand accepted the faith and were baptized. And henceforth, they "continued steadfastly in the apostles' doctrine . . . and in breaking of bread, and in prayers." Charging it with anachronism is too lenient a judgment of this account;[38] it is pure fabrication.

Was the first "public incident" that revealed to the Jerusalem authori-

34. Matt. xxii.14: "For many are called, but few are chosen." Luke xii.32: "Fear not, little flock; for it is your Father's good pleasure to give you the kingdom."
35. Cf. Matt. v.21f, 27f, 31f, 33f, 38f, 43f.
36. *CVIII,* p. 273.
37. We know from Josephus (*Antt.* XV, 11, 3; XX, 9, 7, and *War* V, 5, 1) that the porch consisted of a double row of columns along the exterior court of the Temple, on the east side of the court.
38. *LXVII,* p. 62.

ties the presence and the heresy of the disciples the cure of the paralytic recounted in Acts iii? [39] That is quite possible. In any case, it is highly likely that the simple folk made appeals to the thaumaturgic powers of the "saints" as soon as they knew about them; that would be normal.

On the other hand, the state of withdrawn waiting could not be prolonged beyond the moment of first doubts concerning the imminence of the *parousia*. Unless they disbanded, returned to Galilee, disappeared, the disciples were forced to change their attitude, to reorient their faith by enlarging it. This salutary operation could scarcely be performed except *on the person of Jesus*, that is, by a transformation of the concept and image of his person. And if waiting and continuation of temporal existence were requisite, organization became a necessity. Irresistibly, this in turn would necessitate both *passive* propaganda, propaganda growing out of the knowledge outsiders gradually acquired of the existence of the group, and *active* propaganda, propaganda demanded by the need to justify the community's reason for being and for defending it.

Conclusion

What we know about the primitive community amounts to very little, but that little is enough to confirm the conclusions we have drawn elsewhere concerning the life, inclinations, and teaching of Jesus of Nazareth.[40] The first group of disciples sought neither to promote a new religion nor to set up an organization for conquest. They were still only a tiny group of pious Jews, living within a Jewish framework and imbued with a hope that was specifically Jewish and had meaning only for the Jews. But they invested that hope with so unique an interpretation that its strangeness soon ran the risk of angering the Jewish authorities and, equally, of disturbing and offending the Jewish community.

39. *CVIII*, p. 55.
40. *LXXXVI*, pp. 293f.

5

PROPAGANDA, PERSECUTION, AND DISPERSION OF THE HELLENISTS

PROPAGANDA, persecution, and dispersion are three interrelated consequences of the logical chain of the events to which they refer. Propaganda made the brethren intolerable to the Jews, and provoked the tribulations they suffered; the tribulations, in turn, brought about the dispersion of the Hellenists.[1] Unfortunately, the author of Acts, which is our only source, or very nearly so, made no attempt to proffer an accurate picture either of the events themselves or of their sequence. The very contrary is true, that is, he worked hard to subordinate the facts to his particular ends, to organize them in such a way as to create the impression he wanted to impose, an impression that puts the events in a false perspective.

---

1. In contemporary usage, the word Ἑλληνιστής means a *Greek*, just as Ἑβραῖος means *a Jew*. But as used by the author of Acts, the first term refers to a Jew of the Greek world. Cf. Cadbury's very thorough comment in *XCVII*, V, p. 141 and especially pp. 59f.

I. The Perspective of Acts

The author of Acts wants to convince us that the Church universal was founded by the Apostles, and that they supervised every facet of the propaganda, which, of course, they themselves had initiated, not only among the Jews, but also among the Gentiles. No contradiction, no preposterous invention, is too extravagant if it induces this happy conviction. Since he puts Peter and John, whom he converts into the leaders of this propaganda, in immediate conflict with the Jewish authorities, his account of the first trials of the faithful is drawn from a purely expedient psychological perspective, from which it is difficult to extract the true perspective. Finally, by intentionally amalgamating the propagandizing activities of the Hellenists and the Hebraizers, whom, scorning all chronological discrimination, he sets within a single Church, he creates the impression that the persecution, and consequently the dispersion (viii.1) affected the entire community, despite the fact that the rest of his own narrative contradicts his tendentious assertions. The critical labor called for by this whole construction seems both necessary and hazardous.

However, one quickly realizes that our author had at his disposal a source which indicated that the Hellenists were the instigators of propaganda and its first preachers. Eventually, converted to their methods by the testimony of the Spirit and the pressure of events, the Twelve followed them.[2] The author is anxious to compensate for every venture of the Hellenists by an undertaking of the Twelve. Thus, when Philip, one of the Seven, spreads the faith in Samaria and Caesarea (viii.5; viii.26–40), Peter quickly follows him there (xi.32f; x.7f). Hellenists plant the same faith in Antioch (xi.19f.); the Twelve send Barnabas there (xi.22f). The artifice of this scheme can hardly be denied. It emanates from the wish to retain the overall direction of the movement in the hands of the Twelve, a wish that conforms to a subsequent convention which everything belies. This is already an ecclesiastical conception.

Acts posits its theme at the very beginning of its story. "Ye shall be witnesses unto me both in Jerusalem, and in all Judaea, and in Samaria, and unto the uttermost part of the earth" (i.8). But this is pure fiction.[3]

2. *XCVII*, I, p. 309, n. 1.
3. *CVIII*, p. 159.

Had Jesus given his disciples such clear and precise instructions, what happened afterwards would appear in a better light. Or we would have to suppose that the Twelve were even more lacking in intelligence than the Gospel texts show them to have been. Everything seems to prove, in Acts itself, that the primitive community, even after the first exaltation of its Messianic expectation had passed, initiated no propaganda and did not try to extend itself beyond Jerusalem, and even less beyond the confines of Palestine.

Incidentally, this raises the question of whether the Apostles ever preached in Jerusalem. I even venture to ask whether they ever preached. In the first place, this is a problem in chronology. The entire first part of Acts contains scarcely anything more than a collection of Petrine tales.[4] Moreover, the intent of these tales is to extol and glorify, not the Galilean Apostle, but the initiator of universal evangelism and the founder of Catholic tradition.[5] That is why all the conquests of the new faith are attributed, irrespective of date, to Peter's initiative. At the most, the author acknowledges John's assistance. Whatever happens stems, apparently, from Peter's discourses or his actions. The activity of the rest of the Twelve is confined to vague statements, as in Acts v.12, which depicts them sowing "signs" and "wonders" among the people.[6]

From Pentecost onwards, when the miracle of the gift of tongues was made known, the author groups all the representatives of the Diaspora at Jerusalem around the Apostles (ii.4ff). And Peter, surrounded by the Eleven, harangues them all, expounding the truth about the person and mission of Jesus of Nazareth (ii.14ff, 22, 36). The listeners, greatly moved by his speech, naively ask him what they must do, and he tells them (ii.38): "Repent, and be baptized every one of you in the name of Jesus Christ for the remission of sins, and ye shall receive the gift of the Holy Ghost." Three thousand of them instantly obey (ii.41). "And they continued steadfastly in the apostles' doctrine and fellowship."

This account is wildly improbable, because it implies that, from the very first hour, preaching served the ends of propaganda "as regularly as the catechisms of St. Sulpice" (Loisy), and because it is impossible to conceive that so shortly after the execution of this Jesus whose *name*

4. *CXXIX*, p. 98.
5. *CVIII*, p. 117: A Roman idea, according to Loisy. *Contra: XCVII*, I, p. 330, who sees the exaltation of Peter and the *Tu es Petrus* as an Antiochene invention, designed to make fun of James, who stayed behind in Jerusalem. Who knows?
6. Cf. Acts iv.31: "They spake the word of God with boldness;" v.29: "Then Peter and the other apostles answered and said . . . ," etc.

has brought them all together more than three thousand men lived a quasi-monastic life in Jerusalem.

Acts iii.12ff has Peter preaching another sermon, after his cure of a paralytic, to the people assembled on Solomon's Porch. This time the authorities of the Temple are upset; Peter and the others who spoke with him are arrested (iv.3). But the striking miracle and the commentary explaining it lead to the conversion of some five thousand people, who are no more real than the three thousand of Pentecost.[7] Thus there is only a slight chance that the appearance of the Apostles before the Sanhedrin (iv.5ff) conforms to historical fact. In any case, the affair—if there was an affair—ends with the release of the accused because no reason is found for condemning them. It's an incoherent tale, whose anachronism is revealed by a couple of sentences concerning the Nazarene Peter supposedly addressed to the Sanhedrin: "This is the stone which was set at naught of you builders,[8] which is become the head of the corner. Neither is there salvation in any other: for there is none other name under heaven given among men, whereby we must be saved" (iv.11f). Before uttering this profound statement, Peter must surely have read the Epistle to the Philippians![9] The inconsistency of Acts on this point proves better than anything else that there was unquestionably no genuine propaganda in Jerusalem before the entry on the ledger of the Hellenists.[10]

And outside Jerusalem? Note that in Acts v.16 the writer does not dare say that the Apostles spread outside the City and went beyond the horizon.[11] It is stated only that with the spread of their thaumaturgic renown the multitude (τὸ πλῆθος) of people "round about" bring them their sick. However, in ix.31 we find: "Then had the churches rest throughout all Judaea and Galilee and Samaria . . . and in the comfort of the Holy Ghost, [they] were multiplied." Must one therefore believe that apostolic communities were already in existence in Judea, Galilee, and Samaria? The author has told us nothing of their establishment, probably because he knew nothing about it,[12] and got entangled in a

---

7. *CVIII*, p. 142. It is somewhat naive to try to save "history" by cutting the figure down, as Harnack does in *XC*, III, p. 143. He subtracts a zero, and maintains that we are here dealing with the five hundred brethren referred to by Paul in 1 Cor. xv.6—a reconstruction made to order.

8. An allusion to Ps. cxviii.22.

9. Cf. Phil. ii.9ff.

10. Loisy, *CVIII*, p. 149, agrees.

11. *CXXIX*, p. 98.

12. I can attach no importance to the alleged intervention of Peter and John in Samaria, where they are supposed to have gone to *confirm* the people who had been

maze of most dubious chronology. His "pious verbiage" can only be explained—and I do not tire of repeating this—by his desire to muster all the activities of the first Church under the authority of the Twelve.[13]

What seems to be the truth is that up to 44, the date of Herod Agrippa's persecution, the leaders of the *Hebrew* group in Jerusalem did not leave the City, where they had assembled to await the *parousia* and where they still waited. When Paul wants to see Peter (Gal. ii.1–2, 9) he goes to Jerusalem, fully confident of finding him there. If Peter ever did preach outside Jerusalem, he apparently did not do so prior to the dispersion of 44. According to Acts, the famous story of the conversion of the centurion Cornelius in Caesarea and of his baptism by Peter (Acts x.1–8; x.22–48), after a vision as instructive as it was wonderful, convinced the apostle at Joppa (Acts x.9–16) that neither *the word of God,* nor the ritual lustration, the palpable sign of repentance and faith, administered in the name of Jesus Christ (x.48), should be denied to the Gentile favored by the summons. This story, like the account of the debate which Peter's decision supposedly provoked among the Apostles and the Jerusalem brethren (xi.1–18) is an edifying and subsequent invention to justify by the direct will of God and the consent of the Apostles an extension of the faith which was at first scandalous, but which at the time the author of Acts took his pen in hand was no longer a matter for debate.[14]

However, some texts merit consideration. 1 Thess. ii.14 comforts the community of Thessalonica in its trials by citing as example the tribulations the brethren in Judea suffered at the hands of the Jews. But, since 1 Thess. is later than 44, its testimony does not carry much weight for the early period. Moreover, what does "Judea" mean? Perhaps simply Jerusalem. And of what brethren does Paul speak? Perhaps only of the Hellenists and Stephen (Acts viii.1f). Matthew x.17f puts in the mouth of Jesus a warning to the Apostles to be on guard against men, "for

---

converted by Philip, one of the Seven (viii.14–17), because it is only too obvious that the hagiographer intends to relate to the Twelve a success they did not initiate and which is foreign to them. Consequently, I don't attach any weight to the vague assurance in viii.25: "And they, when they had testified and preached the word of the Lord, returned to Jerusalem, and preached the gospel in many villages of the Samaritans."

13. *CVIII,* p. 426.

14. *CVIII, ad loc.; XVIII,* III, p. 218; *XCVII,* I, p. 340. I would say that *Aramaic* propaganda, long limited to Jerusalem, and perhaps to its environs after 44, knew no real extension until the time when the Great Revolt (66) drove (68?) the brethren out of the City and towards the Transjordan. Cf. Eusebius, *H. E.,* iii, 5, 3; *CVII,* p. 169.

they will deliver you up to the councils, and they will scourge you in their synagogues. And ye shall be brought before governors and kings for my sake, for a testimony against them." But exactly what does that mean? What is the date of the text? One would assume it refers to Paul's tribulations in the synagogues of the Diaspora, to Herod Agrippa's persecution, and perhaps even to the appearance of the Tarsiot before the governor Felix (Acts xxiii.24). There remains Luke x.1–16, which, so it seems, tells us that after the death of Jesus numerous "envoys" (ἀπέστειλεν αὐτούς), who continued to proclaim the Prophet's message about the approaching advent of the Kingdom, spread throughout the Jewish land. It is possible, as claimed, to see in the fact that their preaching was confined to the basic theme of Jesus's teaching, without in any way magnifying the person of the Master, an intimation favoring the assignment of an early date for the text. Agreed. But, aside from the fact that such an interpretation of the passage, which is that of J. Weiss,[15] remains hypothetical, we must not forget that the text concerns the *mission of the Seventy-two*. I don't doubt that in the opinion of the Evangelist these Seventy-two were "the Christian preachers who truly prepared the evangelization of the universe," [16] but neither do I doubt that his presentation is only an expression of that opinion, nor that the instructions credited to Jesus are anything more than an editorial contrivance. It would be an error to consider as a fact of the apostolic age an episode which the Evangelist presents in the perspective of Jesus's life, an episode, which even in this setting, does not in all probability transcend the confines of tendentious invention.

II. The Probabilities

It is thus quite probable that it was the Hellenists who initiated authentic propaganda, and it seems logical that such should be the case. The account Acts gives of the institution of the Seven reduces them to the role of caretakers or waiters (vi.1–6), yet it presents them only in the role of preachers. They are the ones who preach in Jerusalem, who importune their brethren of the Diaspora in the synagogues (vi.8–10), who perhaps are already beginning to carry the word outside the City, for they have no reason for confining themselves within its walls, since they are themselves outsiders. And, as a result, it is they who provoke

15. *CXXIX*, p. 99.
16. *CVIII*, p. 291.

the first resistance among the Jews, a resistance that will beget the first tribulations of the brethren—*a decisive and fecund crisis.*

As usual, our author's account of the proceedings is jumbled. He states that Stephen, one of the Seven, "did great wonders and miracles among the people" (vi.8). The next verse informs us that "certain of the synagogue, which is called the synagogue of the Libertines, and Cyrenians, and Alexandrians, and of them of Cilicia and of Asia" argued with him. I think that Stephen personifies the Seven,[17] just as Peter represents the Twelve. Thus, as is understandable, the Seven addressed themselves to men from their own countries. It was their going into the synagogues for public debating that constituted the novelty and boldness of their initiative. As far as we know, the Twelve either did not know how to, refused to, or were not able to, do as much.

What did these men say in the synagogues to which they went to give evidence of their zeal? Obviously, the pith of their remarks was that the Promises had been fulfilled in the person of Jesus of Nazareth. That alone was enough to provoke disputes, arguments, and scuffles. But they may have said something more besides. There are hints that by his bold remarks about the Temple and the Law Stephen incensed those of his hearers who remained unconvinced of the truth of his message (vi.13). He stated that Jesus of Nazareth would destroy the edifice and would replace by others the traditions that had come down from Moses. I do not, of course, place full confidence in a text that is suspect of relating, in a conventionalized manner, the substitution, realized in the author's time, of Christianity for Judaism. I do however believe that this text reflects a historical reality and is of importance: the Hellenists were beginning to leave Judaism behind, since they considered its cultic prescriptions and legal restrictions to have lost their value and meaning for the faith constituted around the person of Jesus Christ. A kind of pre-Paulinism was already making an appearance on the scene, and that pre-Paulinism could hardly have been the product of any minds except those affected by Hellenic universalism. It was based on the idea that faith as trust in the Christ was more important than legalism, its doors opened wider and were more welcoming than those of orthodox Judaism, and it held the conviction that the basis of salvation was to be found in faith, and no longer in the Law, henceforth regarded as a mere transitional discipline.[18] Such opinions or tendencies placed the Hellenists in a rather

17. Loisy (*CVIII*, p. 354) rightly remarks that the author of Acts would recognize the work of the Seven "only insofar as it could be related to the apostolic community."

18. *CVIII*, p. 462; *CXXIX*, p. 121.

equivocal position in relation to the Jews—and even to the Twelve. Amidst the confusion and weakness of the rest of the narrative of Acts we glimpse Stephen arousing in the synagogues of the Diaspora Jews violent anger against his "blasphemies." Summoned before the Sanhedrin to answer for them,[19] he reiterates and aggravates them. He is then condemned to death by stoning. *The Twelve take no part in the affair.*

After reporting the death of the arch-martyr, Acts adds: "And at that time there was a great persecution against the church which was at Jerusalem; and they were all scattered abroad throughout the regions of Judaea and Samaria, except the apostles" (viii.1). Further on, in xi.19, it is stated that some of the scattered ones went to "Phoenicia, and Cyprus, and Antioch." That is the important point. I cannot envision, as the author of Acts wants me to, "the people, and the elders, and the scribes" (vi.12) aroused against Stephen by "false witnesses" whom his adversaries, unable to find arguments with which to silence him, are said to have suborned against him. Nor can I envisage the meaning of a general persecution against the Church which did not disturb those it should have struck first, the Twelve.[20] What I do imagine is that Stephen, who had been especially compromised, was arrested and condemned by the Jewish authorities, and that following this the group of brethren under the direction of the Seven, realizing that if they stayed in Jerusalem it could only be at the price of silence or by risking Stephen's fate, decided to leave the City. Moreover, I do not think the number of people who left was in the hundreds. They returned to their homes,[21] or went to other countries they deemed hospitable.

It is quite possible that some of them did not go very far at first, and that there is a kernel of truth in Acts' picture of Philip's missionary activity in Samaria and the coastal regions between Gaza and Caesarea (viii.4f; viii.40). It is natural that these men should continue, outside the holy City, the work they had begun in its synagogues.[22]

19. *CVIII*, p. 309. Cf. Juster, *XXXVIII*, II, p. 127, on the competence of the Sanhedrin in cases of offenses against the Law.
20. *CXXIX*, p. 123. Cf. Acts viii.1: πλὴν τῶν ἀποστόλων.
21. *CVIII*, p. 354.
22. I am not confusing the episode of the Ethiopian eunuch with historical fact. It is inserted between two miracles and can be fully explained as the pseudo-fulfillment of two pseudo-prophecies: Isa. lvi.3-7, which promises an "everlasting name that shall not be cut off" to those eunuchs who are faithful to the law of Jahweh, and Ps. lxviii.31f, which seemingly reserves for Ethiopia first place in the adoption of the true faith (Αἰθιοπία προφθάσει χεῖρα αὐτῆς τῷ Θεῷ). I am inclined to view this as justification by divine approbation of the initiative of the Hellenists, who are going to grant to pagans who have *faith* in Christ Jesus the benefit of the Gospel.

The Hebraizing community was left in Jerusalem around the Twelve, who had not been disturbed (viii.1), probably because they had not yet engaged in propaganda. These Hebraizers could not, however, have failed to take into account the methods and success of the Hellenists at a time when the imminence of the *parousia* must have begun to seem less certain and when a reorientation in this life began to be necessary, since mere tranquil awaiting of the great miracle seemed in vain. Thus, when the initiators of propaganda left, the Twelve continued their work, possibly, as befitted pure Judaism, in a more conservative manner. This imitative step was soon to lead them to a momentous ordeal.

Conclusion

Reduced to its Judaizing elements, the Christian faith had no chance of survival, because the mass of the Jews would have none of it. By stubbornly staying on Jewish soil, it was being condemned to die of anemia. The Hellenists infused into it a speculative frame of mind, then a propagandizing spirit, turning it towards their own world. *The dispersion of the Hellenists insured the life of the Christian faith by carrying it to Greek soil.* In the history of primitive Christianity there is no fact more essential than this one, none which contributed more directly to the birth of the new religion.

Part II

THE BIRTH OF CHRISTIANITY

1

OUR INFORMATION

WE quit Jerusalem, where the group of the Twelve, made sterile both by its nature and its environment, remains, and follow the Hellenists who left the Holy City after the torture of Stephen, taking with them the germs of the Christian religion. Some of them may have stopped in one or another city of Palestine, but these are of only secondary interest to us. Our attention must be given to those who took refuge in the cities of the Diaspora. But can we go with them to these cities, do we have at our disposal documentary evidence of what they did there?

Everything considered, our sources come down to two: (1) the book of Acts, whose narrative, beginning with chapter ix, revolves wholly around the person and missions of Paul; (2) the collection of Epistles attributed to the Apostle himself or to his milieu. I have already tried to give some account of Acts, and will say nothing more about it. But we must consider for a moment the Pauline Epistles.

I. The Pauline Corpus

In the Canon of the New Testament there are fourteen letters attributed to Paul: Romans, 1 and 2 Corinthians, Galatians, Ephesians, Philippians, Colossians, 1 and 2 Thessalonians, 1 and 2 Timothy, Titus, Philemon, and Hebrews. If we set aside the question of their authenticity, we may divide the documents, on their own showing, into three categories, or rather three groups: [1]

1. 1 and 2 Thessalonians, which echo the missionary preaching of the apostle.

2. Galatians, 1 and 2 Corinthians, and Romans, which emanated from Paul's battles with his adversaries, especially the Judaizers.

3. Ephesians, Colossians, Philippians, Philemon, 1 and 2 Timothy, Titus, and Hebrews, which are called "epistles of the captivity" because the first six speak of the author as being in chains and the other two are classified on the basis of their relationship to these six.

There can be no doubt [2] that Paul wrote many other letters, which have been lost. Thus 1 Corinthians v.9f,[3] 2 Corinthians ii.3f [4] and vii.8f [5] presuppose that the men of Corinth received more than the two epistles which have come down to us. The statement in Philippians iii.1, "I do not tire of writing you the same things," would be difficult to understand if the Church of Philippi had not corresponded several times with the Apostle. Colossians iv.16 speaks of a letter to the Laodiceans which we do not have. How were these writings lost? Through circumstances or accidents not known to us. The Epistles that we do have survived because they were incorporated into the Canon and became Holy Scripture.

In all probability, this good fortune was theirs because, thanks to exchanges, they early went beyond the confines of the communities to which they were sent. Several of them were intended by the author to be circulars written for the instruction of a group of Churches.

We know approximately how the collection called the Apostolic Corpus was established.[6] Towards the end of the first century—probably —the author of I Clement made use of several of the letters which were

1. *CCXXXIX*, p. xiii.
2. *CC*, p. 9; *X*, II, p. 169.
3. "I wrote you in the letter . . ."
4. "I wrote this same unto you . . ."
5. "For though I made you sorry with a letter, I do not repent . . ."
6. For bibliography, see *XVIII*, IV,[1] p. 49, n. 1.

to become part of the collection and relied on their apostolic authority.[7] 2 Peter—which, it is true, is the latest writing of the New Testament and apparently postdates 150 [8]—in speaking of matters difficult to understand "in all these letters" (ἐν πάσαις ἐπιστολαῖς) and in complaining that ignorant and unstable men twist them, as they do the other Scriptures (iii.15–16), seems to attest the existence of a collection. It is also to be noted that, apart from the Johannine letters, the rest of the New Testament epistles, called "catholic," are more or less influenced by the model of the Pauline letter,[9] a fact not easily explained unless small collections of Paul's epistles were extant quite early. However, it was Marcion, who, by claiming the support of ten of the Apostle's epistles (Gal. 1 and 2 Cor., Rom., 1 and 2 Thess., Eph., Phil., Col., Philemon) for his theology, was the first (ca. 140) to find them worthy of standing alongside the Gospels.

The Church at large could not reject the authority of the man who was venerated as their founder by a number of communities and whose Epistles were, if not always well understood, at least held in high esteem by a still larger number of Churches. It had no other means of combatting Marcion than to go him one better, by snatching from him the Apostle whom he intended to make the warranty, and even initial promulgator, of his own doctrine, and claiming the authority of a better text of the Epistles than his and a more complete collection.[10] It was no doubt at this time that several writings of uncertain authorship, but more or less akin to Paul's, borrowed his name in order to slip into the Canon. At this time, too, the general principle which was to insure the ultimate future of all the Pauline tracts gained acceptance: the Apostle's purpose in writing the letters was to explain the true Catholic doctrine to all of Christendom.[11]

It even came to pass that more or less ingenious forgers later found, in their own imaginations, the lost letters mentioned in the canonical epistles. Thus we possess in Latin, but translated from the Greek, a short Epistle to the Laodiceans, and in both Greek and Latin, a 3 Corinthians and a missive from the Corinthians to Paul.[12] It is difficult to assign a date to these apocryphal writings, which are earlier than the fourth

7. *XXXIII*, I, pp. 44f.

8. *CCXXIV*, p. 137.

9. *CXC*, p. 343.

10. Apparently Marcion did alter the Pauline texts, especially by abridgment: Iraeneus, *Haer.* i, 25, 1; Tertullian, *Adv. Marc.* v, 3.

11. Muratorian Canon, l. 59: *omnibus dixit.* Cf. *CXC*, *loc. cit.*, and *XVIII*, IV,' p. 36.

12. Published by Harnack in *XLV*, no. 12, and by *CCXLIX*.

century and probably rather old, but later than the establishment of the canonical Pauline corpus, in which they would probably have found a place had they been older than they are.[13]

My chief reason for believing that these forgeries would have been admitted into the Canon is the impossibility of believing in Paul's authorship of all the fourteen letters attributed to him by the Canon. I don't believe there is a single competent critic today who admits the authenticity of Hebrews. Many exegetes—and I think they do well— reject the three Pastorals (1 and 2 Timothy, Titus).[14] Others even go so far as to declare the entire Pauline corpus apocryphal. We must first of all explain our own position on this extreme contention, for, as the authenticity of certain letters is judged by that of others, an account must be given of the greater or lesser solidity of this critical basis.

II. The Problem of Authenticity

The chief indicters of the authenticity of the Pauline epistles are the Dutch critics of Van Manen's school, the critics who call themselves "radicals," [15] and the majority of those critics who deny the historicity of Jesus. Here are their principal arguments:

1. The text of the letters is in many places unintelligible, not only to us, despite all the assistance given us by philology and exegesis, but must have been equally so even to those first readers, who were far less educated, to whom, supposedly, they were addressed. It is not possible for the real Paul to have addressed in riddles men, the majority of whom were simple, to whom he wanted to make his instructions clear.

Answer: It is certainly true that not everything in the Epistles is clear, even if we assume that extreme alteration of the text by careless copyists has made it more difficult than it was originally. Many obscure points will no doubt always remain, because we are not very well informed about the tacit assumptions of the author and his readers, the things they took

13. There is some likelihood that the Epistle to the Laodiceans was forged about the middle of the third century, probably in the West. At that time Cor. and 3 Cor. were in the canon of the Armenian churches. In the first half of the fourth century they were admitted to the canon of the Syrian churches, where they remained for a hundred years. Cf. Harnack, *loc. cit.*

14. For bibliography, see *XVIII*, IV,[1] pp. 16f.

15. *CCXLIV*, pp. 92–118; G. A. Van den Bergh van Eysinga, *Die holländische radikale Kritik des N. T. Ihre Geschichte und Bedeutung für die Erkenntnis der Entstehung des Christentums*, Jena, 1922; id., *La Littérature chrétienne primitive* (Paris, 1926), pp. 108f.

for granted. Thus, what is obscure for us may not have been obscure for them. Moreover, how would the hypothesis of pseudonymous editing in the course, I presume, of the second century make the obscure clear?

It is also true that in reading the Epistles we often wonder how the men for whom they were written were able to grasp this subtle thought or follow that tortuous chain of reasoning. But what does that prove? That Paul did not write them? Not at all. It only proves that Paul could at times think subtly, and reason without strict logic. And perhaps that he sometimes went beyond the capacity of his readers and over-estimated their intellectual abilities. Moreover, it would be very odd if a personality as indisputably remarkable and original as his, which produced the Epistles, remained anonymous, while a writer as mediocre as Justin made a reputation for himself.

2. Though several of the Epistles, notably Galatians, 2 Corinthians, and Colossians, are crammed with disputes and polemics, the author is usually content merely to allude to the men and ideas he is fighting, so that neither the opinions of his adversaries nor the replies of the pseudo-Paul are clearly understood by us. A man anxious to dissipate errors and misunderstandings in the minds of his disciples would not proceed in this manner.

Answer: The observation would be well founded if we were dealing with literary works with a tendency to generalization, works that are, in a sense, removed from their times and their date. But in the case of the Epistles the argument is not relevant; it simply reminds us that we are dealing here with letters which treat only of matters that were familiar to a given milieu. Moreover, it has been pointed out that in the letters whose certain authenticity is admitted by the great majority of critics—the four greats: Galatians, 1 and 2 Corinthians, Romans, 1 Thessalonians—allusions to details and "personalities" are abundant, creating difficulties for us, but undoubtedly not for the faithful to whom they were addressed; whereas these features disappear, or very nearly so, in Ephesians and the Pastorals—letters admitted to be inauthentic, or of doubtful authenticity—at the same time that the tendency to generalization becomes more marked.

3. Many sections of the letters are so badly linked, so poorly coordinated, and so disparate in form and substance that one suspects someone of artificially combining separate pieces of writing.[16] This aspect of the Epistles clashes with the presumption that they were composed by an

16. Loisy has recently recapitulated and developed this impression with great force. Cf. *CCXXIV*, chs. ii, iii, iv.

orderly mind writing instructions and guidance for recent converts, or for those faltering in doctrine.

Answer: Leaving aside the question of the clarity of the overall composition of each letter, we admit the validity of the criticism for many passages in which the linking together of the ideas and the logical connection of developments in the argument leave much to be desired. At several points it is indeed legitimate to ask if we are not dealing with a mosaic of disparate pieces (Rom. xvi.iff; Phil. ii.3–iii.4, which seem out of context) or of glosses inserted by mistake (Rom. ii.14–15 and ii.26–27; 1 Cor. xi.2–16; 1 Cor. x.29, where it is difficult not to see several hands at work).

The only certain conclusion that can be drawn at this time from these considerations is that the text of the Epistles has not as yet been fully sifted, and that those who transmitted it were not always very scrupulous. Antiquity offers us more than one example of faulty transmission, a fact that has not caused us to reject as apocryphal the writing which has suffered such transmission. In addition, the postulate that Paul's thinking was always orderly and his logic rigorous is certainly debatable.

4. There are evident in the Epistles considerable variations of style; we must therefore conclude that all the letters considered to be authentic cannot have come from the same pen.

Answer: I don't deny that there are differences in style, but it is difficult for me to see them as insurmountable. Assuredly, there is a certain overall unity of style in the Epistles. What is more, I do not think it prudent to draw such absolute conclusions from this kind of argument. It is fitting, too, that we should not forget that the style of one and the same author, especially if that author is impressionable, may vary sharply, depending on the circumstances of his writing and the public he is addressing.

5. The last, and by far the strongest, argument, is the one preferred by mythologists: that the portrait of Paul which emerges from the letters is improbable; even that, given the environment in which he is supposed to have appeared, and especially his affinity to the Jesus of the Synoptics, this portrait is impossible and inconceivable. One may grant that there was an apostle named Paul, but not that this historical Paul wrote the letters in question. Galatians i.11–24, for example, attests so great an attitude of independence towards the Apostles, who were the trustees of the authentic tradition, and towards the Master himself, that its existence at a date so close to the crucifixion is inconceivable. The author

of the Epistles accepts no human authority; he derives his Gospel from revelation alone, and his mission only from the heavenly Christ manifested to him. He is a mystic and a gnostic who identifies Jesus with the *Pneuma* of God (2 Cor. iii.17); he is not a disciple of Jesus.

Answer: But in the last analysis, the merit of all these objections consists only of the fact that it raises the famous question of the affinity of Paul's teaching to that of the Nazarene. In short, it may be that Paul was not much like Jesus, that he did not depend on him directly, or even not at all, and that he held himself aloof from the Galilean disciples; but all this would not prove that he did not write the Epistles. Besides, one must not forget that Galatians is by no means an objective biography, but a highly subjective polemic. The Apostle's insistence on asserting his Evangelical independence and his own function must be judged from this viewpoint. Paul knew quite well that not everything in his Gospel depended on tradition, but on more than one occasion he himself depended on it. Yet he was never a direct disciple of Jesus and his background was different. This is to be taken into consideration in explaining the differences one wishes to accentuate. Let us also keep in mind the fact that the Master and the Apostle functioned in different circumstances: Jesus remained within the strict framework of the religion of Israel and preached the coming of the Kingdom, the realization of that which the Jews had come to identify with the Promise of old. But Paul, in addition to this, preached the religion of the Christ, that is, a religion of which the Christ was already the object; he preached faith in the Christ, a faith founded on a mysticism centered in Christ's person. This is a far cry from the Sermon on the Mount, if we look upon this sermon as a résumé of Jesus's teaching. In any case, a religion whose ambition it was to win the masses could not have been founded on the Sermon alone. If a question arises in this connection, that question is: how was it possible for the religion of Paul to be born within the framework of Jesus's teaching?

It should not be forgotten that there were two intermediate consummations between the time of Jesus and that of Paul: the Judaizing community and the Hellenistic Jewish-Christian movement, which initiated the evolution that led from the religion of Jesus to that of the Christ. Thus, when Paul encountered Christianity, it was no longer the Galilean original that he saw. Since his freedom of thought and action was not restrained by personal memories, his accentuation and acceleration of the evolution already begun is understandable.

These considerations should suffice to lead us to the conclusion that it is not very reasonable to claim that the "canonical" Paul is *a historical impossibility*, nor is it reasonable to claim that his letters, written a score of years after the death of Jesus, constitute *a literary impossibility*.

The *historical impossibilities* entailed by the conjectures of the Dutch radicals are much more troubling, as an example will show. According to Van Eysinga,[17] the Epistle to the Romans, a fictitious letter, cannot be earlier than about 125, when it was composed in Rome. Now, 1 Corinthians presupposes Romans (p. 119); it, therefore, is later and likewise apocryphal. Through the same process of reasoning, 2 Corinthians is made dependent on 1 Corinthians (p. 123) and is also eliminated. Galatians does not withstand the assault, either, for "it is later than Romans and the letter to the Corinthians" (p. 128). And now that the four foundation posts have been knocked down, the whole house crumbles into a few rubbles that can easily be dislodged with one good sweep of the broom. The author's method is that of fearless assertion and peremptory inference. His temerity is frightening. But the arguments he has marshalled are demolished by a chronological impossibility. Paulinism, considered as a whole, becomes inconceivable if it is moved to the middle of the second century, for the ecclesiastical archaism it displays would make no sense at that date. The simplest comparison between its content and that of the writings which may with certainty be assigned to this period is enough to make the fact obvious. The theories of the radicals appear to be tenable only in the realm of abstract hypothesis, in which one may mistake reasoning for facts and dialectic for life. They cannot be of service to scientific progress except by being broached only to professionals and discussed only among specialists. Presented to the public at large as an expression of established Truth, they can only mislead that public and hinder its true education.

In fact, the quasi-unanimity of critics is united in admitting the authenticity of at least a certain number of the Pauline epistles. Of the ten which remain when the Pastorals and Hebrews have been excluded, seven have been accepted by practically everyone. And there are some important critics who have a good opinion of the three others—2 Thessalonians, Colossians, and Ephesians—which some would attribute rather to Paul's followers of the second generation [18]—and grant that even the Pastorals may contain authentic Pauline fragments inserted in their apocryphal text.

17. *Littérature chrétienne*, pp. 113f.
18. *CCXV*, p. 5; *CXC*, pp. 358ff; *CXXIX*, p. 108.

I have no intention of examining one by one the problems each Epistle raises—a painstaking task which has no place here.[19] I shall therefore content myself with giving a general idea of the reasoning involved in this type of critical undertaking.

Let us take Ephesians, the most disputed of the three doubtful Epistles, as an example. It is apparent that this Epistle is not aimed especially at the Ephesians, for Paul addresses himself to pagan converts and to a Church he has never seen and to which he has no particular advice to give (i.15; iii.2; iv.21).[20] The actual salutation (i.1, "to the saints who are at Ephesus") is not original, and apparently Marcion read an address to the Laodiceans. This does not prove that our Epistle is the one that, according to Colossians iv.16, Paul wrote to the people of Laodicea. The forger who wrote it, if it is false, may simply have tried to protect himself with this same text of Colossians.[21]

Its language, which employs Pauline words, but with meanings different from the ones they have in the authentic Epistles; its style; its doctrinal concerns; and its desire to broaden its instructions by generalizations—all these characteristics do indeed seem to set Ephesians far apart from the other letters, and to justify the exegetes who consider it to be a document of the post-apostolic age. The text shows an evident kinship with Colossians.[22] From this fact some critics draw the conclusion that Colossians, like Ephesians, is pseudepigraphal, others that Colossians, which undoubtedly contains a number of Pauline features, is authentic, and that the author of Ephesians had imitated it without fully understanding it.[23] And this is my opinion.

Another example is furnished by the Pastorals, so named because they are concerned with the "institution of pastors and ecclesiastical discipline." Their concern is the organization of the communities and their protection against the agitations of sectarians who want to introduce perverse teaching.[24] Comparison with the definitely authentic letters reveals in them considerable differences of style and vocabulary, a more advanced doctrine, and glimpses of a more complete ecclesiastical organization. The majority of liberal critics reject them; they are nevertheless

19. *XVIII*, IV [1]: refer to the Table of Contents for the detailed study of each Epistle.

20. *LVI*, p. 92.

21. *XLVI*, p. 161.

22. *CCXLVII*, pp. 46–53.

23. *CXXIX*, p. 108; Loisy, *XLVI*, p. 161: "The Epistle to the Ephesians *is a copy*, in another form, of the Epistle to the Colossians."

24. *XLVI*, p. 204.

"Pauline," that is, they are composed in the spirit of Paul and in accordance with the principles of his teaching [25]—and that indeed is why the orthodox critics can still maintain that they are authentic. But they were not written by Paul and date from a later period. Loisy has justly observed that had the recommendations they contain been conveyed in the time of the Apostle, Paul's closest associates, Timothy and Titus, would not have needed to receive them in writing.[26]

Each of the seven admittedly authentic Epistles has undergone rigorous and ever more thorough exegesis. This exegesis has endeavored to establish the exact circumstances of their composition, to detect the interpolations they may have suffered, and to investigate the influences various interpretations may have exercised on them and altered, more less seriously, their original text. Some of them (e.g., 1 and 2 Corinthians) have for some time been suspected of contrived editing, that is, of integrating a series of letters between Paul and the Corinthians into two Epistles. Loisy has recently stressed, very forcefully, the disparities which seem to make it difficult to reconcile some of the basic ideas at present juxtaposed in the Pauline corpus, even when these ideas occur in the same Epistle.[27] However, the conclusions, always somewhat subjective, to which a too rigorous method of analysis has led in this instance are to be accepted only with extreme caution.

Some time ago, Mr. Joseph Turmel, writing under the pseudonym of Henri Delafosse, tried to demonstrate that the great Pauline Epistles—which is as much as to say, all the Epistles—were at bottom nothing more nor less than compositions of the heresiarch Marcion (c. 140), which were later taken up, altered, and interpolated in the Catholic Church.[28] The ingenious exegete thought he could determine in this astonishing miscellany each writer's share of the Epistles. But in fact, if the fundamental hypothesis of M. Delafosse were to be found justified, we would no longer be able to apprehend in any way the fact of Paulinism, for we would be prohibited from delving back beyond the personal and tendentious interpretation of Marcion, and the assertions of the Dutch radicals would receive valuable confirmation. Most fortunately, the views of M. Delafosse are only personal, fragile assumptions, which create in their wake many more difficulties than they claim to

25. *CXC*, pp. 364f; *XLVI*, p. 204; *CCXV*, pp. 5f; *CXXIX*, pp. 108f; *CCLXIX*, pp. 264ff.

26. *XLVI*, *loc. cit.*

27. *CVII*, chs. vii and viii, especially pp. 305, 331, 335.

28. H. Delafosse, *Les Ecrits de saint Paul*, Paris, 1926–28, 4 vols., Nos. 13, 17, 23, and 28 in the collection *Christianisme* (Christianity).

dispel. The apparent simplicity of their critical basis, which appeals to the too credulous reader, is counterbalanced by insurmountable historical difficulties. These learned amusements are highly pleasing to dilettantes, but we can't waste our time with them here. Exegesis is not solely a matter of impressions, imagination, ingenuity, and dialectic; it has meaning and value only if it first plants its feet amidst positive facts, on the historical plane.

There is perhaps some exaggeration in imparting to Paul the precision and firmness of composition that as a rule modern writers impose on themselves, as well as the balanced reasoning, coherence, and consistency we demand from a good mind shaped by tested methods. I am not, I confess, greatly astonished by the fact that his letters reflect—more or less—very different ideas, since he was subjected, without his knowledge or volition, to a number of diverse influences. Accordingly, he could not attempt an amalgamation of these ideas. But I shall not labor the point here. In the use I shall make of the texts, I shall always take into account the critical observations they have elicited, and I shall not take sides without giving my reasons.

III. *Characteristics of the Pauline Epistles*

The general characteristics of the Epistles have provoked much argument, in the course of which two extreme views have emerged.[29] (1) According to a theory which is in a sense classical, and in any case canonical, a theory which prevailed for a long time, Paul's letters are true treatises of doctrinal and moral theology, parts of an organized and comprehensive system. (2) According to another theory, maintained with special vigor by Deissmann, they are simply letters, in the common meaning of the word. The first opinion has been generally discarded as excessive and false by liberal critics; the second has not prevailed because it exaggerates. The majority of critics have therefore taken a middle position.[30] But new points of view, which we shall mention later, may be developing.

One need not tarry long over the Epistles to realize that if Paul "theologized" in many cases, for the sake of both the present and the future, he did not always do so by design. He was more interested in action than in speculation, more in mysticism than in doctrine. "There can

29. For bibliography, see *XVIIII*, IV,[1] p. 38.
30. Loisy, in *Journal de Psychologie*, May 15, 1923.

be no more fatal error in the interpretation of Paulinism than that which sees it as theological treatises," says Goguel.[31] And Deissmann [32] has well demonstrated the error of considering Paul's letters to be literary treatises, and then, with the aid of these letters that have become "literary," depicting the Apostle "as a man of letters and a dogmatician." But Deissmann, in turn, forces the truth when he maintains that the basis of the error in question is to be found in the confusion between *letter* and *epistle*. The *epistle* represents a literary genre practiced by the Greeks and Romans, and even by Hellenized Jews; *it is a fictitious letter*, and both its form—the tone, the style, the language—and its content betray it as such. Now, Paul's letters are true letters; to become aware of this, one need only compare them with the letters, free of any literary pretensions, that the papyri have made available to us. In addition, study of the content of the Pauline letters reveals that every one of them corresponds to a particular situation and actual events; each one was written in one copy only and sent only to its addressees; their author did not foresee their survival across the centuries. So goes Deissmann's thesis.

There is general agreement that Paul's Epistles are true letters and not epistolary fictions,[33] and that it is precisely because they stemmed from specific and practical concerns that they are still sometimes obscure for us. The merit of this observation will become evident when we come to evaluate their documentary authority.

This, however, is no reason for denying Paul's letters any literary character and consigning them to the rank of the familiar or vulgar correspondence extracted from the papyri. Besides, it is not always easy to distinguish between letter and epistle, for it is the objective, the tone, the style, rather than the matter, that create an epistle.[34] But if Paul's letters contain a specific and precise objective, that objective is not, strictly speaking, familiar—apart from the note to Philemon. Paul was not just any individual who wrote or dictated letters; he thought and wrote as an apostle who felt himself to be in charge of souls, as guidance for the communities. This is manifest in both the tone and content of his letters. He addressed not an individual, but a collectivity (1 Thess. v.27: "I charge you by the Lord that this epistle be read unto all the holy brethren"). Even his adversaries had access to his epistles and criticized them; his letters, they said, are "weighty and powerful" (2 Cor. x.10).

31. *XVIII*, IV,[1] p. 64; cf. also pp. 37f.
32. *CC*, pp. 5f.
33. J. Weiss, *Die paulinischen Briefe*, Introduction, in *V*, II, pp. 1f.
34. Cicero, *Ad. fam.* xv. 21, 4: *Aliter scribimus quod eos solos, quibus mittimus, aliter quod multos lecturos putamus.*

They were transmitted from Church to Church; Paul knew it and, when the need arose, recommended this procedure (Col. iv.15–16). That is understandable, for what he said to one community could be useful to another, and also because he relied heavily on the authority of the Spirit, which was as valid in one place as another (1 Cor. vii.40; xiv.37; 1 Thess. iv.15). It may even be said that, in its intent, the Epistle to the Galatians is a kind of encyclical.[35]

The Epistles, then, are written instructions which confirm and continue the teaching of the Apostle, adopt its style, and follow its inspiration. Their equivalents could no doubt be found in the epistolary collection of paganism. If so, one would have to envision the letters Epicurus wrote to his disciples grouped in communities. Unfortunately, we no longer have the text of these letters. The Tarsiot did not have to invent the genre, for we know that the Jewish communities were accustomed to intercorrespondence and their reciprocal missives must have resembled, at least in intention, our Epistles.

Paul's letters are not, then, to be viewed as similar to those of a soldier to his family or steward to his master; their language brings them close to common usage, but not their style. That style, though often obscure, tortuous, chaotic, and incorrect, bears within it a fire that cannot be mistaken, especially if one reads the text aloud. And despite the incoherence of the composition, they even reveal, especially the great letters, a certain literary artistry, in no way classical, but which confers on the writing a distinction not present in an ordinary letter.[36]

A moment ago I spoke of a new point of view on the characteristics of the Epistles. This has to do with the problem of rhythm. For some time, critics have recognized that various passages—notably the instructions on the Supper in 1 Corinthians xi.17–34 [37]—show a marked rhythm which may indicate the presence of genuine strophes. Since then, some critics have wondered if the number of passages written in this manner is not much greater than it seemed at first. The question has not yet been resolved to the satisfaction of all exegetes. But the fact that it has been raised is enough to make us wonder why Paul should have adopted a rhythmic style in his epistolary instructions. Was it solely to emphasize statements designed to be read in public? Is there not, in some places at least, a liturgical influence? Or was he perhaps—and this would be most

---

35. Considerations of this kind seem to justify the opinion already found in the Muratorian Canon, l. 59: "What the Apostle says, he says for all" (*omnibus dixit*). Cf. *XVIII, IV,*[1] p. 36.

36. *CXC,* p. 353; *LXII,* p. 19.

37. Loisy, *I,* pp. 321f. Cf. *Journal de psychologie,* May 15, 1923.

important—influenced, because of his Greek education, by those stylistic processes which engendered what has become known as *die Kunstprosa* (artistic prose)? It is easy to see how important a decisive answer on these different points would be to our understanding of the true nature of the Epistles. We do not as yet have this answer; but we shall take into consideration in our study the results which those who have attempted to give it appear to have achieved.

In any event, we may conclude that the Epistles of Paul belong to a more exalted category than that of ordinary letters. It need hardly be added that each was composed as an independent work. "None was written to be part of a collection, still less to be part of a dogmatic treatise" (Goguel).[38]

IV. Historical Value of the Epistles

The qualities that make the Epistles psychologically interesting weaken their value as historical documents. They brilliantly reflect the personality of their author; are alive with the constant activity of this personality. They unfold for us his actual states of mind, his successive impressions and reactions at the time they occurred. In ancient Christian literature there is not a comparable personal document. The *Confessions* of St. Augustine are not comparable, because they confide the author's past spiritual states, attitudes and emotions removed in time from the moment when his pen intends to fix them, attitudes and emotions which that author may, therefore, have misrepresented. Conversely, every one of Paul's letters is an image of the Tarsiot, seen from a certain angle,[39] and together they present a series of pictures which combine to complete one another, even when they seem to contradict one another, or to be in conflict. This contradiction, this conflict, are but the variety and contrasts of life itself. We are far removed from the old conception of St. Paul, doctor of the Church, prophesying for eternity.

On the other hand, this highly personal character of the Epistles makes their testimony so subjective that we are forced to take serious critical precautions before making use of them. Paul is not a writer to be believed on his word alone. Another very serious inconvenience is presented by the fact that the Epistles depict their author as the center of all that went on in the Church of his day. Now, although this im-

38. *XVIII*, IV,[1] p. 49.
39. *CC*, p. 16.

pression certainly does not correspond to the facts, it is not always easy to effect a judicious scaling-down to reality. Also, the Epistles present the Apostle as the eternal polemist. It is not, however, probable, that Christian life in his time consisted only of conflicts.

Thus we must admit that the nature of both Acts and the Epistles leaves us disturbingly uncertain about a great number of points related to the days the Christian religion was born. These incomplete and imperfect documents not only do not permit us to solve all the questions they provoke, but what is more serious, they do not even let us see very well what all the questions are. They allow us to grasp only a chosen number of incidents and ideas, whose relation to the total events remains perplexing.

V. *The Apocryphal Pauline Writings*

Gleanings in the New Testament, apart from Acts and the Apostolic corpus, or in the Apostolic Fathers,[40] are insignificant, and for the moment we shall not consider them. Hope has, however, sometimes been founded on the apocryphal literature, so I want to say a word about it, at least in its relationship to Paul, since it is the Pauline milieu that is going to claim our attention now. Later, we shall try to establish whether it provides any information about the missionary career and last days of Peter.

The principal text to be considered is called the *Acts of Paul (Acta Pauli)*.[41] It consists of three apocryphal writings which were for a long time regarded as separate works: the *Acts of Paul and Thekla*, the *Letter of the Corinthians* to Paul and Paul's answer (Cor. and 3 Cor.), and the *Martyrdom of Paul*. There has been no agreement as to the place of origin or date of composition of the whole. A passage in Tertullian (*De bapt.* 17) attributes its origin to "a priest of Asia." Greater precision is hardly possible. Smyrna and Antioch of Pisidia have been mentioned, but nothing has been proved. As for the date, it oscillates between 90 and 180. If we say circa 175, give or take ten or fifteen years, we may not be far off. Ramsay and S. Reinach have maintained that the *Acts of Paul* is an elaboration of a more ancient composition dating from c. 50–70. According to this hypothesis, there is an underlying

---

40. E.g., I Clem. v.6.
41. Abundant documentation is given in *XVIII*, IV,[1] p. 65, n. 1; cf. *CXVIII*, pp. 1–49 (Bibliography, Introduction, and English translation); *XXVII*, p. 357.

stratum in this work which merits consideration, although the rest is negligible. Unfortunately, no sure means has been found to effect the indispensable discrimination. Its mention of Queen Tryphaena is cited as possible proof of the antiquity of the basic writing (*Acts of Paul and Thekla*, 27: "And a rich woman of royal descent, named Tryphaena, whose daughter was dead, took him under her protection . . .") because it has been pointed out that there did exist, about the middle of the first century, in Pontus, a Queen Tryphaena who was a second cousin of Claudius.[42] Moreover the *royal road* that Paul is supposed to have taken to go from Antioch to Iconium (*Acts Paul and Thekla*, 2) is not the route that was ordinarily taken in the second century: if the author set the Apostle on it, so we are told, it is because he was in possession of some very ancient bit of information. Finally, it is noted that the portrait of Paul traced in *Acts Paul and Thekla*, 3 seems lifelike and authentic. I don't find much merit in any of these observations.[43] The occasion presenting itself to mention a great lady, the author may have remembered this Tryphaena, and before setting Paul on his journeys, he may not have forgotten what road was used in the first century. As for the portrait, it seems to me to be only too well explained by the author's desire to contrast the Apostle's physical weakness and ugliness with his moral strength and spiritual beauty, so that its authenticity as a factual portrait is not convincing. It is probably nothing more than a gloss on some indications in the Epistles and Acts.[44] The proof that *Acta Pauli* is based on a first-century text is still to be established.

It is sometimes alleged that the work's ignorance of Paul's second captivity [45] is an indication of its great age. I, however, am more inclined to find in this fact assurance that the author had no other source at his disposal than our Acts of the Apostles.

According to Tertullian's account, this apocryphal writing brought about the deposition of its author, the Asian priest. Despite this it enjoyed so great a success in the Church that Eusebius (*H. E.*, iii. 3, 5) did not dare to reject it entirely by relegating it to the category of apocryphal writings, but put it instead in the category of "doubtful" books. The Codex Claromontanus still included it in its list of canonical books. But

42. W. Ramsay, "The Acts of Paul and Thekla," in *The Church and the Roman Empire before A.D. 170*, 4th ed. (London, 1905), pp. 375–428; S. Reinach, *Cultes, mythes et religions* (Paris, 1912), IV, p. 247.

43. *XVIII*, IV,[1] pp. 74f.

44. 2 Cor. x.10, where Paul admits that he is not an imposing person; 1 Cor. xv.8, where he seems at first glance to compare himself to a stillborn; Acts xiv.2, where he seems to be eclipsed by the more favorable appearance of Barnabas.

45. *XVIII*, IV,[1] p. 78.

neither this wavering nor this favorable treatment is enough to win our confidence in the *Acta Pauli*. It communicates nothing except inconsistent and completely unverifiable hagiographic inventions, incorporated in precisely those places where their appearance, in their own right, is not too inappropriate.

Two other apocryphal books should also be noted: the *Acts of Peter (Acta Petri)* [46] and the *Acts of Paul and Peter (Acta Petri et Pauli)*.[47] They too claim to know something about Paul. Since, however, the first does not antedate 200, nor the second 450, their authority is absolutely nil. Neither biography of the Apostle, nor study of the milieu in which he lived, can hope for any enlightenment from them.

Conclusion

M. Goguel's conclusion on what it is possible for us to know about the Tarsiot [48] may legitimately be applied to all our sources of information on the important problem we are about to approach: "The picture that we are able to form of the life of Paul resembles the maps of Africa, or of the polar regions, of fifty years ago, on which vast stretches are labeled: 'Unknown territories.'"

46. *XVIII*, IV,¹ p. 78; L. Vouaux, *Les Actes de Pierre* (Introduction, texts, translation, and commentary), Paris, 1922; *CXVIII*, p. 50; *XXVII*, p. 383.
47. *CV*, II, Pt. I, pp. 305ff, 331f.
48. *XVIII*, IV,¹ p. 80.

2

THE GREEK WORLD

A. The Jewish Diaspora

IN Acts xi.19–21 we read: "Now they which were scattered abroad upon the persecution that arose about Stephen travelled as far as Phenice, and Cyprus, and Antioch, preaching the word to none but unto the Jews only. And some of them were men of Cyprus and Cyrene, which, when they were come to Antioch, spake unto the Grecians, preaching the Lord Jesus. And the hand of the Lord was with them: and a great number believed, and turned unto the Lord." This is the text that is taken to reveal the secret of the birth of the Christian religion. It appears to be reliable, and inspires all the more confidence because it comes after the story of Cornelius the centurion, which it expressly contradicts, for that story anticipates the conversion of the Greeks; thus the text may be accepted as belonging to the early stratum of Acts.

The Hellenists would present their hope and faith to the Jews in the synagogues, just as they did in Jerusalem, but some of them in Antioch soon took the risk of going also to the Greeks. Were these *Greeks* absolute *goyim*, pagans who were strangers to the Jewish truth? I find that hard to believe. No, they were the uncircumcised, the proselytes,[1] men

---

1. There seems to have been a proselyte already among one of the Seven in Jerusalem (Acts vi.5: Νικόλαον προσήλυτον 'Αντιοχέα). But I think he must have been completely converted and a circumcised man.

whose presence and position around the synagogues on Greek soil we shall soon evaluate. Their initiative was, I think, an inevitable consequence of their disappointing results among the Jews, of the opposition they encountered in the synagogues. It was an extremely bold initiative, and of incalculable import, for it meant nothing less than acceptance of the principle that one *could become a Christian without adopting Judaism in its entirety*. Nonetheless, this approach to the Greeks followed the line of separation from legalism already manifest in Stephen and his companions. This separation, for proselyte use, of the new faith from Jewish legalism was an especially fecund contribution to the success of that faith. The Synagogue, despite the liberal tendencies of some of its members, could make no such concession. The good intentions of the uncircumcised Judaizers were superimposed on the inimical reserve or hostility of the Jews, forming, as it were, a bridge towards the indifference of the authentically pagan whom propaganda would not be long in approaching in their turn. From the moment the faith left Jewish soil, it worked only for its own ends, seeking its fortune as a separate religion.

It owed its success to the favorable religious and moral climate of the Hellenistic world. The text of Acts, in marking two stages in the propaganda—(1) among the Jews; (2) among the Gentiles—invites us to consider separately the Jewish milieu of the Dispersion and the Greco-Roman pagan milieu. In a preceding volume, I sought to describe the first;[2] let us now examine the second.

B. The Pagan World

The world of the Gentiles[3] does not concern us in its entirety, and not even all aspects of that portion of it which is under consideration will hold our attention. The Occident, with the exception of Rome (which by its ethnic, intellectual, and spiritual cosmopolitanism was related to the Hellenistic Orient) and greater Greece (one of the factors in Hellenic culture), the Occident proper, played no appreciable role in the establishment, installation, and evolution of primitive Christianity. The Hellenistic world itself has no real importance for our purposes, except as seen through the manifestations of its intellectual activity and its religious sentiment.

2. *LXXXVII*, Bk. IV, pp. 273–326.
3. Τὰ ἔθνη, in Latin *gentes* or *nationes* (from which we derive ὁ ἐθνικός, *gentilis*) is equivalent to *pagans* in the speech of the Jews of the Diaspora, and subsequently in the language of the Christians.

A first tentative analysis shows the Hellenistic world to have been the complex and confused combination of two originally distinct worlds put in direct and intimate contact by the conquests of Alexander and which through the centuries had reacted on one another by endosmosis. These worlds were the Hellenic and the Oriental. The latter was made up of rather diverse elements, for Egypt, Syria, Phrygia, Cappadocia, and the Mesopotamian lands had their own characteristics, tendencies, and originality. On more than one occasion we shall have to take these differences into account, but we are going to put them aside in the present exposition, and confine ourselves to the features that are part of the whole.

It goes without saying that the combination I have mentioned was not specifically the same everywhere, that the dosage and balance of the various elements which constituted it varied according to the regions. There were some countries, even cultural centers, where the Greek influence overcame Oriental resistance; in others, the contrary phenomenon occurred. Generally speaking, we may say that the Hellenic influence was dominant, and even determinative, in the *intellectual sphere*—cultural forms, philosophy, science; whereas the Oriental influence was vigorously affirmed in the *spiritual sphere*, the sphere of the substance and expression of religious sentiment, aspirations towards a blessed life beyond the grave, cultic organizations. Even where the two influences combined, the specialization distinctive of each remained as a rule visible.

I. Culture

a) *The School*. The Greeks had long been interested in the intellectual life in all its forms. For them, intellectual activities were not the concern and tastes of an elite alone. General attention, open to all its possibilities, was accorded to the mind. Consequently, the Greeks were in general agreement that it was fitting to prepare the child to be interested in and understand the life of the intellect, a conviction leading to the elaboration of a pedagogy, buttressed with a plan of studies and a system of instruction, that was gradually adopted in all lands of Hellenic culture. This is a fact of the greatest importance, for the identity of intentions and methods of education, acclaimed throughout the Hellenistic world, brought about a most remarkable homogeneity of mind, though there were of course nuances.[4] In this homogeneity lay a highly energetic spring for action,

4. A short bibliography is to be found in *CLXXXIX*, p. 72; *CXLI*, 6th ed., I, Bk. II, ch. i; E. Potter, "Educatio," *DA*. Cf. H. I. Marrou, *Saint Augustin et la fin de la culture antique*, Paris, 1938.

which would operate at first *against* nascent Christianity, then *within* it, and finally *for* it. The cosmological, metaphysical, and moral beliefs and postulates of the Hellenic mind's first reaction to the new religion owed a great deal more to the educational system than to the actual thinking of genuine philosophers. Eventually, Christianity would reduce these beliefs and postulates to submission, making them its own by incorporating them into its own substance. It is their propagation in the schools that explains both their widespread acceptance and their great activity.

By the word *school* I do not intend to designate only those private institutions where children were instructed under the eye of Minerva, institutions whose *cursus* covered three stages, beginning with the acquisition of the rudiments under the tutelage of the *primus magister*, and ending with the definitive instructions of the professor of rhetoric, passing on the way the grammarian's ruler. I also have in mind the establishments devoted to higher education, which we would call universities, whose approximate equivalents were to be found in Athens, as well as in the great cities of the Greek Orient, such as Alexandria, Antioch, Tarsus, Rhodes—to name only the most renowned. There the masters were chosen by the municipal authorities who paid them and placed at their disposal, often with the help of generous donors or subscribers, all the necessary tools of learning, especially books.[5]

The education provided by these schools had no doubts either of its methods or its efficacy. Wholly satisfied with itself, it was quick to scorn any individual who had remained outside its ranks: such a man was likened to a *barbarian*. Tertullian avowed that the culture of the pagans interfered with their acceptance and comprehension of the truth.[6] It was to become a commonplace in the second century to oppose *the wisdom of the barbarians*, that is, the Jews and their heirs, the Christians, to *the philosophy of the Greeks*. In fact, Christianity at first encountered vigorous antipathy from "the professorial world." On the other hand, when it began to make conquests in that world, it derived from it much benefit for its propaganda and apologetic: the conversion of a professor or a noted intellectual became a weighty argument in itself.

One can understand, however, why the first generations of Christians, who were almost entirely the products of social milieux which were strangers to intellectual concerns, were tenaciously prejudiced against the culture of the schools.[7] Its first error, in their opinion, was that *it was*

5. We know the details from inscriptions in Asia at Miletus, Ephesus, Priene, Pergamos, Teos, and Rhodes. Cf. *CLV*, pp. 306, 523, 552, 30 and 60; 619, 43, etc.
6. Apol., 21: *iam expolitos et ipsa urbanitate deceptos.*
7. *CCLXI*, pp. 447f.

pagan. And pagan it was in the sense that (1) some of its customs were religious practices derived from paganism, (2) it was wholly based on the study of ancient authors who were steeped in Olympic paganism.

What we would call "higher education" consisted chiefly of the examination of philosophical problems.[8]

b) *Philosophy.* There was at the time not *one* philosophy, but *several, schools* which claimed dependence on the great masters of times past—Pythagoras, Plato, Zeno, Aristotle, Diogenes—or else sought to combine them in a more or less coherent eclecticism.[9] The *dogmata,* that is, the basic positions attributed to the authentic old masters, served as topics for commentaries and as points of departure for the speculations of their so-called disciples. Some of these *dogmata* concerned man and his moral life, what we today call psychology and ethics. Usually, however, they soared into the realm of *metaphysics* and cosmological hypotheses. Stoicism itself, which we are wont to see as primarily a system of morals, was in that day above all else a cosmology, secondarily a theology, and last of all an ethic.

The cosmological and metaphysical views of the schools, even their opinions on theological matters, as well as certain more or less legendary *Lives* of the "Masters," especially those of Pythagoras and Plato, were to have an influence on the formation of Christian doctrine; an influence, which would finally prove pervasive, on its common philosophy; an influence on the tests and proofs to which the various dogmas would have to submit before being finally accepted as orthodox; and even an influence on the legend of the Lord. But these contaminations did not occur on first contact. The situation was different, however, in the realm of morals, which remained so important that Christianity was essentially *a way of life.* In the Pauline vocabulary, for example, a rather large number of technical terms of the Stoic ethic have been singled out, and these we shall pass in review when necessary. Does this fact mean that the Apostle sat on the benches of the University of Tarsus, where, as we know, Stoic masters were dominant? Probably not; the presence of these terms in his vocabulary can be explained by the fact that these masters were given to popular preaching.[10] They propagated the precepts of what is known

8. *CXCVI,* pp. 107–28.
9. E. Bréhier, *Histoire de la Philosophie* (Paris, 1928–1938, 6 vols.), I, chs. v and vi; bibliography, pp. 414 and 447.
10. *CXCVI, loc. cit.; CLVI,* pp. 118f; *CLXXXIX,* pp. 75f, gives a bibliography; *CLXXI,* pp. 1f (Seneca); pp. 155f (Epictetus); pp. 238f (Dion Chrysostom); *LIX,* pp. 45f; *XXVI,* II, pp. 215f; *CLXXIV.*

as the Cynico-Stoic diatribe, an eclectic amalgamation of certain Cynical and Stoic principles, which made a kind of pragmatism, an ethic for action, following the bent for practicality attributed to Diogenes. This diatribe had the appearance of a religion of morality, that is, it considered morals as a religion, a religion with its saints, the great men who were thought to have best realized its ideals in their lives, whose example was preached.[11] It was a religion based on *experience*, as was its doctrine. Diogenes and Socrates, the two pragmatists par excellence, were its great authorities. Their words and deeds, which, like their appearance, had been more or less stylized, constituted the wells from which the preachers drew. They strove for a lively style in their teaching in order not to discourage anyone. But the content of their sermons was always austere and bore a strong resemblance to that in which the *Conversations* of Epictetus were steeped. In addition, there were others besides the philosophers labelled as Stoics who preached to the people in this spirit. The general tendency of the age led professors of other schools to emulate them.[12]

All of them played the role of veritable *directors of conscience* and never tired of proclaiming their precepts in public, taking no notice of the difficulties, scorn, or even injuries they met.[13] They were not all drawn from the ranks of professors with official functions or university reputations. Some were isolated and itinerant, called to a true vocation by personal inclinations, a fact that makes us think of the Christian missionaries. For others, preaching had become a trade, which they exercised without shame, exploiting the simple, whose confidence was gained by their long beards, their stern professional cloak, and their austere appearance. The caricatures Lucian of Samosata [14] drew of these charlatans give us an idea of their unbridled cynicism and their insincerity. But if these men were able to put their confidence in outward trappings in order to earn their livelihood, it. was because these trappings went with a widespread and highly regarded profession.

We still possess a fictionalized biography of one of these preachers, written by a certain Philostratus [15] for the curious circle in Rome which gathered around the Syrian princess of the Septimius Severus family at the beginning of the third century, a circle which applied itself with great zeal to the study of the very problems which held the attention of the

---

11. *CLVI*, p. 119.
12. *CLVI*, p. 118.
13. *CLVI*, p. 93.
14. Lucian, *Hermot.*, 18; with a corrective in *Nigrinus*, 24–25.
15. Mario Meunier, *Apollonius de Tyane*, Paris, 1936; bibliography, pp. 295f.

preachers of the diatribe. This biography is the *Life of Apollonius of Tyana*.[16] The hero of the book is presented as the perfect example of the breed: he had made a vow to lead an edifying life which might serve as a model to other men.[17] He therefore imposed special obligations on himself, and went through life as if he always walked under the eyes of Truth: even in the middle of the most frightful desert, he felt himself to be under her scrutiny.[18] His bearing was enough to make his vocation known to passersby: it was that of his profession, and his stern countenance always reflected his grave inner meditation. He went about, impassive, disdainful of the gibes of the ignorant. But he knew how to speak up before the powerful of the world and point out to them their duty. This courage was not without risks, for it happened that a Nero or a Domitian did not understand, and became angry.[19] He bore the tribulations their sorry anger heaped on his head with a steadfast heart, as so many insignificant contingencies. Nothing could shake him. To Nero's decree proscribing philosophy [20] he was satisfied to reply with a line from Sophocles: [21]

Οὐ γὰρ τί μοι Ζεὺς ἦν ὁ κηρύξας τάδε.
For it was not Zeus who proclaimed that decree.

Above the practical teaching of these philosophers soared a beautiful and encouraging affirmation: beyond the city of men lies a city of philosophers where great souls find their consolation. It is entered at the price of long and painful personal effort, reflection, and separation from earthly goods and attachments. It welcomes men of all lands and all conditions who deserve its rewards. In reading Lucian's description, one cannot help recalling St. Augustine and the *City of God*.[22]

There is no need to dwell on the interest and importance such ideas have for us in relation to the beginning of Christian origins. I have already said that Christianity would first of all be *a way of life*, a rule of conduct, a road to salvation. By taking the diatribe as a model, it would find

16. Tyana is a city of Cappadocia. The chronology of Apollonius is poorly attested; it is believed that he came to Rome under Nero, and was put in prison by Domitian, but escaped by miraculous means.

17. Philostratus, *Vita*, ii, 7.

18. *Vita*, i, 35: ὑπὸ τοῖς τῆς ἀρετῆς ὀφθαλμοῖς.

19. *Vita*, iv, 35–37.

20. Nero declared that philosophers were useless and magicians in disguise; he arraigned them on the last count. Philostratus, *Vita*, vii, 6. Cf. Suetonius, *Nero*, 10: *Philosophos omnes Urbe Italiaque summovit.*

21. *Antigone*, 456.

22. Lucian, *Hermot.*, 6f; 23–24. Cf. the texts assembled in *CCLXI*, pp. 419–21.

antecedents, forms, and usages that would keep it from being thought odd. The ethic of the philosophers, valuable in its own right and not of necessity tied to a particular religion, could be transposed to the benefit of whatever cultic organization would accept its assumptions. Cynico-Stoic preaching would offer Christianity an ethical framework and a vocabulary. It would also prepare a bridge for penetrating straight to the heart of the daily life of the Hellenistic world, even as the metaphysic of the educational system prepared frameworks for Christianity's cosmology, and the forms that would welcome its dogmatics. Thus there was a veritable preparation for *the work of Christianity* to develop in the various directions that would become necessary as its strength increased, a preparation so effective that it is impossible to visualize how Christianity could have done without it, how it could have come to be if it had not already been.

c) *Science.*[23] Later, the Christian faith would be presented to the Gentiles as being in its essence *a revelation*, a gnosis of salvation, and the entire Christian catechesis would be subordinated to the desire to have this assumption accepted as verified truth. In fact, it is to the point to note that Christianity would encounter no obstacles except in the customs, and no contradictions except in the beliefs, of the same order and nature and on the same plane as its own affirmations, for in that day positive science, independent of speculation, did not exist.[24] In the era of Augustus, the scientific poem of Manilius, *The Astronomics*, reveals, in its tarrying over the most elementary notions, the ignorance it supposed its readers to be wallowing in.[25] And the author himself commits the grossest errors. Leaf through the *Natural Questions* of Seneca;[26] note in Lucian's writings the blunders made by persons who were considered to be more cultivated than the average man;[27] and you will have the proof that in the epoch of its inauguration and spread throughout the Hellenistic world, Christianity would encounter no scientific vulgarization.

But, in the proper sense of the term, neither was there any science. The Stoics claimed one, but it would be imprudent to take them at their word. I have just referred to the *Natural Questions* of Seneca. Let us put it alongside Pliny the Elder's *Natural History* and see what we find. In-

---

23. For general bibliography, see A. Rey, *La Jeunesse de la science grecque* (Paris, 1933), pp. 521f, and L. Laurand, *Manuel des études grecques et latines* (Paris, 1930), III, Appendices 1–3.
24. *CCLXI*, pp. 424f.
25. Manilius, *Astronomica*, ch. i, in its entirety.
26. *Quaestiones naturales*, vi, 3; vii, 1; etc.
27. Especially the *Liar by Inclination*, in its entirety.

teresting oddities, but disconnected and uncriticized; ill-verified facts taken from authorities who have not been checked, or checked only superficially —no sense that phenomena are related or linked to one another—; and idle reasoning that scarcely feels the need of checking its findings by experiments. This does not mean that accurate observations, which might be suggestive, are wholly lacking in all these works; it does however indicate the absence of a true scientific spirit from such compilations and, especially, of a feeling for the sovereignty of the verified fact. The impression obtains that Seneca gathered more or less accurate observations on natural phenomena for the sole purpose of providing pegs on which to hang his reasoning. Pliny assembled *mirabilia* to amuse himself and to satisfy his rambling curiosity, which had no other object. Were there no men who went beyond this rather puerile amateurism, men with a positivistic bent who were able to see more clearly? Possibly there were, as much in that age as in any other. But we do not know who these exceptions were, if they did exist, and their influence on the state of scientific knowledge of their contemporaries cannot be perceived. To draw attention to this deficiency is for us the essential point.

Lucian, for example, tells us of a certain Hippias,[28] for whom he professes boundless admiration. He states that this man had reached the limits of knowledge in all fields, so that compared to him his contemporaries were only children. But we do not know what this means. Did Hippias really know more than the scholars of his time, or did he simply know all that they knew, or thought they knew? We don't know. But what is most serious is that to all appearances his contemporaries didn't know either. We have at least part of the work of one of them, the doctor Galen,[29] who also acquired a great reputation. Observant, skilled, and sometimes ingenious and penetrating, he almost never appears in the role of a scientist, for he did not have the scientific spirit: he believed, for example, in "medical" dreams. In the realm of knowledge, the best minds were radically misguided by their faith in miracles, by their delight in, their passion for, wonders and marvels. Ordinary and quite simple phenomena neither aroused nor held their attention.

This pseudo-science, then, which was in fact an auxiliary and branch of philosophy and encumbered with morals, metaphysics, and (among the Stoics and Pythagoreans) theology, could offer no obstacle to any mani-

28. Lucian, *Hippias*, 3.
29. Born at Pergamos in 131 and died between 201 and 210. Cf. *Oeuvres physiologiques et médicales*, trans. Daremberg, Paris, 1854–1856, 2 vols.

festations of religious sentiment, no more than to the formation of any doctrinal system. The so-called scientific research—whose worth escapes us—of an Apuleius did not prevent him from being a pious soul who ran from one initiation to another. His reputation as a thaumaturge far excelled his renown as a naturalist.[30]

The positive science of that day, the one that disturbed primitive Christianity the most and ended by leaving its mark on it, was *astrology*, which must be considered in conjunction with *magic*.[31] Both, and especially the first, which was akin to gnosis, occupied in daily life a position hard for us to conceive. The importance of the second, also considerable, lies in the fact that it spread everywhere faith in the sovereign power of the ritual gesture, of the revealed form of words, which act, solely through their own efficacy, *ex opere operato*.

Astrological books, which made a large contribution to the education of the cultivated classes, were widely circulated,[32] and a host of charlatans carried, and applied, the science of sciences to all levels of society. These men were commonly called Chaldeans, a name more indicative of the birthplace of their practices than of their true origin. The weightiest minds took them seriously, or at least did not refuse to consider their claims. In fact, they scarcely distinguished between *astronomy* and *astrology*: faith in the horoscope was everywhere affirmed. What is important to note is the fact that astrological reflections and concerns had become commonplaces in the mentality of the time, paralleling the commonplaces of ethics: from commonplaces there was no escape. The more we study the texts which reflect the life of the Roman Empire at its zenith, the deeper becomes our impression of the astonishing importance of these speculations. In reality, they pertained not to science but to faith,[33] but a faith whose objective assumed the apparent rigor and reassuring aspect of scientific knowledge. Sometimes it was called "mathematics" and those who practiced it were, at least in Rome, called *mathematici*. There were skeptics and foes, but not many, and they were obviously wasting their time. Astrology bordered on religion because the stars were assimilated to

30. *CCLXVIII, Apuleius*, pp. 281f; Abt, *Die Apologie des Apuleius und die Zauberei*, Giessen, 1908.

31. For bibliography, see *CLI*, pp. 284f; *CXLIII*; Hubert, "Magia," *DA*. See also F. Cumont, *Astrology and Religion among the Greeks and Romans*, New York, 1912; E. Pfeiffer, *Studien zum antiken Sternglauben*, Leipzig and Berlin, 1916; F. Boll, "Erforschung der antiken Astrologie," in *N. Jahrb. für d. Klass. Alterthum*, XXX; *CXXXV*, ch. xv.

32. *CLI*, p. 242.

33. *CLI*, p. 251.

divinities and their courses represented a sort of cosmic drama. The great gods of Olympus themselves were finally bound to the planets.[34]

Magic appears to have been quite different:[35] it looks less respectable, and one might at first glance take it to have been nothing more than a collection of more or less bizarre recipes. But basically it was grounded on conceptions akin to those which claimed to justify astrology. It stemmed from two notions: that an indispensable relationship united all natural bodies, which are involved in an immense animism, and that nature is subject to an order and to laws. It is this order that magic claimed to know and teach, these laws it explained, along with the means of putting them into effect. On the one hand it was related to science; on the other, it appeared as "religion's bastard sister":[36] it peopled the world with spirits, on which and through which it operated. An incantation was as much a prayer as a means of constraining the cosmic spirits. As a rule, the magicians were scorned, for the means they employed were often despicable and repellent. They themselves frequently came from the world of the poor and wretched, but they were nonetheless feared and heeded. One more step, and we would have entered the domain of religion, or rather, we are there already, for magic is a constitutive element of the greatest importance in many widespread and influential cults.

II. Religion [37]

The Oriental world was very religious, that is, it was very much preoccupied with religious questions, filled with cults, practices, and superstitions of every kind, and prey to a great number of charlatans who gained a living from religion and exploited religious sentiment. The religious situation was extremely complex and confused; its currents of thought and of sentiment interconnected and combined in a manner inextricable for us, and no less so for their contemporaries. Was it not the custom of these contemporaries, which inveterate usage told them was as inevitable as it

34. *CLXXXIII*, XVI, p. 13, gives the relation between cosmic spirits and the planets; Origen, *Contra Celsus*, v, 10–11, expands on the personality and intelligence of the stars.—A. D. Nock, *Conversion: The Old and the New in Religion from Alexander the Great to Augustin of Hippo* (Oxford, 1933), pp. 99f.

35. *CLI*, 2nd ed., p. 70; *XCVII*, V, pp. 164f, assembles some interesting texts.

36. *CLI*, p. 274.

37. There is a very full Bibliographical Index in *CXXXIV*; *CLI* also gives numerous references in its notes; *CXXXV* has a very detailed Table of Contents. See also *XXIII*, I, pp. 133f; *CLXXXIX*, pp. 87f, 137f; *XXI*; *CLXXXI*, ch. iii; *CLIX*, pp. 393–481.

was natural, to syncretize beliefs and practices, and let each man have the illusion of erecting for himself, out of the enormous mass of religious materials on hand, the faith and cultus that suited him?

Initial examination of the principal constituents of these Hellenistic religions permits one to distinguish, to some extent, between the components derived from the *Hellenic background* and those that must be assigned to the *Oriental*. But detailed studies make such a distinction more difficult, and one grows more hesitant in attempting it. Nevertheless, it is quickly apparent that what is of true interest and importance for us resides in the mixtures themselves.

a) *The Hellenic Background.* To all appearances, Olympic religion was still alive.[38] Augustus restored it in its traditional forms as the religion of Rome.[39] But was there a sincere, profound, and widespread faith in the great gods? One hesitates to say. Among the higher classes, belief in the purely classical divinities must have been the exception; otherwise one could not understand how the jeers of a Lucian, for example, would have been possible. On the other hand, total skepticism was certainly a luxury for intellectuals and dilettantes, and it may very well be that the traditional gods still had influence among the lowest classes and retained their confidence. Elsewhere, attempts were apparently made to adapt Olympism to matters alien to it. One of the most commonly used means for this task was theological interpretation of the myths: Pythagorean theology, more or less revised by the Platonists,[40] and Stoic theology, whose existence I have underlined in passing, were the most widespread of these systems of adaptation, but there were others, more or less syncretistic systems. One such, for instance, is to be found in Plutarch.[41] But I am not going to dwell on this type of theological effort, because it is not this that is important for the origins of Hellenistic Christianity; only a handful of the literate, and (if one likes to put it this way) a tiny elect of religious spirits who hoped to achieve the illusion of remaining the heirs of their ancestors, were drawn to these amalgamations. It is, however, most important to note and to retain the fact that, though it seemed to respect the fact of polytheism, this interpretation of the myths actually tended toward henotheism, that is, it tended to unify the multiform plurality of the gods and divine functions into a single divine will and substance. This was not

38. On its persistence as a state religion, cf. Costa, *Religione e politica nell'impero romano*, Turin, 1923.
39. *CXLII*, I, Bk. I, chs. i-iii; *CXCI*, pp. 73f; Gardthausen, *Augustus und seine Zeit* (Leipzig, 1891, 2 vols.), I, p. 865; II, pp. 507f; Rostovtzeff, in *Römische Mitteilungen*, *XXXVIII* (1923), pp. 281f.
40. *CXLVII; CLXXXII*.
41. *CLXVII; CLXI*, ch. xiii; *CCLXIV*, I, pp. 20f.

true monotheism, but it explains why polytheism, simplified, and as it were, contradicted by this curious tendency, did not offer as great a resistance to the monotheistic affirmations of Christianity as one might have supposed.

Yet some gods, whose universal reputation rested on their reputedly indispensable specializations, still had many faithful and retained a brilliant cultus. Among them were Apollo of Delphi and Apollo of Claros, known for their oracles; Artemis of Ephesus, the inspiration and presiding deity of the Venerated Mysteries; [42] and Asclepios, the great healer.[43] Generally speaking, in the Orient as everywhere else, specializing gods, who were not always "high gods," but gods who, it was believed, would listen to requests for specific, everyday services, were not idle. They were especially revered by the masses, whose religion always lagged behind that of the educated.

By the side of the classical gods, great or small, ecumenical or local, demons loomed large at this time in the religious life. It goes without saying that no unfavorable meaning was attached to the word "demon." It designated divine beings, inferior to the gods and much more numerous, who peopled the Cosmos. Men believed that at least one of these demons watched over every human being. They were called *genies* when they were attached to men and *junones* when they protected women.[44] Servius, Virgil's commentator (*In Georg.* i, 302) defined a *genie* as follows: "The Ancients called a god of nature who was attached to a place or a thing or a man, a genie." And Censorinus wrote (iii, 1): "A genie is a god under whose tutelage every man lives from the moment of his birth." In short, a demon was a local or personal divinity who played the part of a guardian angel.

It is therefore no exaggeration to say that the old religion of Olympus survived effectively only in adaptations made to order for the men of the day, and through its exceedingly brilliant and pompous cultus which stirred many people aesthetically, even if it did not retain a hold on their emotions.[45] As we know, such long and active survival of liturgy, after its

42. *CLXXVII*, pp. 660f.

43. Ch. Michel, *La Culte d'Esculape dans la religion populaire de la Grèce ancienne; RHLR*, Jan.–Feb. 1910; Ch. Daufresne, *Epidaure. Les prêtres, les guérisons*, Paris, 1909.

44. Censorinus, *De die natali*, 3. *CLXXXIV; CLXXXVIII*, chs. vii–ix.

45. The *Didascalia*, II, lx, 2f, reproaches the Christians for their negligence compared to the zeal of the pagans for the cultus of their gods. Persius, *Sat.* 2, on the contrary, complains about the luxury of the temples: too many sacrifices, too much gold, and not enough devotion. Cf. Lucian, *On Sacrifices*, 1; *Demonax*, 27.

dogmas have virtually perished, is a common phenomenon in the evolution of religion.

Thaumaturgy is another means of prolonging a moribund religion, and the ancient Olympism is a case in point.[46] Thaumaturgy was not confined to the sanctuaries of Asclepios, but cited all the gods as its authorities. It had its own representatives (e.g., the Apollonius of Tyana of whom we have already spoken), divine men, merchants of the marvelous, who were often implicated in magical practices, or were frankly magicians.[47] It is of some importance to take note of these men and the general convictions which justified them, in order to understand why the presentation of Christian truth, founded on a miracle, seemed neither abnormal nor exceptional. Though they may have contested this or that wonder, the customs and the temper of the time did not spurn recourse to miracles as an apologetic device. Similarly, the Christian argument based on prophecies found its equivalent and its groundwork, as it were, in the prevalent faith in oracles, predictions, and divinations in all their forms.[48] It is quite remarkable that Clement of Alexandria, in his *Protreptics*, begins his refutation of paganism by a thoroughgoing attack on oracles and Mysteries.[49] I see in this fact a proof of their influence, which far surpassed that of the official religion and its conventional rites. The Christian apologists, up to and including St. Augustine, by continuing to battle against Olympism, give the impression that they always considered it to be their basic foe; and if we were not careful they would impose this illusion, which derives from their habit of enlarging conventional topics which they borrow from one another, instead of taking nothing but reality into account.

I shall not dwell on the cult of the Emperor, which became established in the Orient in the time of Augustus, and owed its success to the old Oriental custom of honoring the sovereign as a divine being.[50] Only when we study the propagation of Christianity and its advent as an organized religion on imperial soil will it become necessary for us to take note of

---

46. R. Reitzenstein, *Hellenistische Wundererzählungen*, Leipzig, 1908.

47. Leafing through Lucian's *Alexander* will give some idea of these men. It is a pamphlet directed against one Alexander of Abonotica, a Paphlagonian thaumaturge of the second century, whom the author presents as a gross charlatan. Lucian does not, however, have my entire confidence.

48. Cf. *LXXI*, ch. i for these various forms. Suetonius, *Aug.*, 31, tells us that the prince had two thousand books of predictions burned. Cf. Lucian's jokes about oracles (*Dialogue of the Dead*, 3) and soothsayers (*ibid.*, xxviii, 3).

49. *CCLIX*, p. 56.

50. *CLXXVI*, pp. 369 & n., 186f, 193; *CXXXIX*, *Introd.* and *De divinis.*

this cult. It will constitute a very formidable civic, if not religious, obstacle to the extension of the Church.

b) *The Oriental Background.*[51] The Oriental background included many old religions which, though differing in their fables and their myths, were essentially similar, in that they all rested on depictment and interpretation of the same natural phenomena. Their gods were divinities of vegetation or astral deities—which comes down to the same thing, since the growth of vegetation and the round of the seasons are governed by the course of the sun. Owing to reciprocal borrowings and the various interpretations all the myths had undergone, it had become difficult, at the beginning of our era, to establish the initial personification of each god at the origination of his cultus. It should be noted that at that time Hellenism, in the proper meaning of the term, had not as yet conquered several considerable regions of the Oriental world: [52] the Anatolian plain, the center of Syria, a part of the nomes of Egypt. In these regions indigenous cults, whose liturgy was celebrated in the idiom of the land, retained great prestige and potent power.

Some of the most widespread of these Oriental religions were centered on gods who had been men, or gods who, by one aspect of their nature, were close to men,[53] for instance, Osiris, Adonis, Attis, Tammuz. Their worshippers were naturally inclined not to regard them as inaccessible. They were, nevertheless, powerful and beneficent deities.

These Oriental religions are interesting also for their rites.[54] Springing out of a conception of life's power and its capacity for renewal, of the fecundity of nature and its need for fecundation, they often assumed obscene forms; but a profound emotion emanated from this very sensuality. And, being accessible to diverse interpretations, they also had at their disposal the means for purification. Some of these cults, of Attis and of Isis for example, had even given rise to asceticism, which in the cult of Attis was propelled to the point of sexual mutilation.

In these lands of the Orient, which had long submitted to the tyranny of absolute monarchies, the subjects did not customarily count for anything before the God-King: he and they were not forged into a people, a nation, a city. Consequently, the religion which adapted itself to these forms of political life did not resemble the one that the Greek States and the Roman people, among whom the individual disappeared before the State and was absorbed in the City, had fashioned. Occidental religion

51. *CLI* contains all the essential information.
52. *CLI*, p. 32.
53. *CLI*, Index; *CLXX*, Table of Contents; *CXLV* and *CLXIX*; *CXXXIV*.
54. *XXI*.

was concerned with preservation of the collectivity, the family, and the State; the Oriental religions with preservation of the individual. They were in the habit of practicing rites reputedly effective in aiding the work of the sun and vegetation, a work requisite for the preservation of life. These rites were gradually transposed and adapted to preparing men for the *true life*, the life expressed by the concept of *salvation*. Myths were born which broadened the scope of and, if I may say so, *humanized* the ancient rites.

c) *The Admixture.* At first glance, all these Oriental religions seem hardly to be in accord with the Greek spirit. Yet at the price of a few changes they became more or less well adapted to it. Their concord gave birth to some quite vital combinations, capable of satisfying the complex and syncretistic spirit of the Hellenistic world. The very principle of Hellenism lay in this passion for admixture and amalgamation of often wholly divergent cultural elements. And nowhere did this passion for syncretism find better ground for its manifestation and surfeit than on religious territory. Juxtaposition of men devoid at heart of religious exclusivism invariably resulted in endosmosis. In fact, the greatest infiltration of and contamination by foreign influences occurred among the Greeks, for the eastern religions were more profound, more genuinely viable, and had a much stronger hold on the sensibilities of men.

We must also take account of a few special phenomena whose influence was apparently quite potent—the intense and contagious religious life of Phrygia; the Iranian Diaspora, which brought with it Mithra into all parts of what we call the Near East; the Syrian Diaspora, which carried Adonis and his paredra, the *Syra Dea*, into all the centers of commerce on the Mediterranean; the influence of Egypt in the economic and intellectual spheres, through which Isis and Osiris, Serapis and Hermetism found favor.[55] All Oriental people who for whatever reason sought their fortune in lands other than their own, or who simply travelled, carried with them their gods and their myths. That is why the total effect of the Oriental cults appears to have been quite widespread and quite complicated.[56]

However, in some places of the Greek world, conditions were especially favorable to the confrontation of the various religions: the great cosmopolitan cities to which all the merchants of the Mediterranean flocked, Alexandria and Antioch; the junctions of the great routes of commerce, for instance Tarsus; and the great centers of Hellenic religious life, such as Claros and Ephesus, which were linked together in the devotional life

55. On Hermetism, cf. *CLXXIX*; *CXXXV*, chs. xviii-xix; *CLXXII*.
56. For the principal dates and facts, cf. *LX*, III, pp. 109f.

of the faithful, and where, as we study the successive modifications of the Ephesian Artemis and other gods, and glance at the curious struggle for influence between Greeks and barbarians around her sanctuary, we may watch syncretism in the process of formation.[57]

The multiple combinations of Hellenism and Orientalism resulted, on the religious plane, in two kinds of interdependent products, which represented two steps in, or, if one prefers, two aspects of, the same phenomenon: the *Mysteries of immortality* and *Hermetism*. If one were to try to differentiate between them, by reference to what we have already said about the distinction between the Greek spirit, more inclined to speculation and reasoning, and the Oriental, more given to mystical emotion and religious sensualism, one might say—taking care not to force the idea— that the Mysteries are more Oriental and Hermetism is more Greek. In reality, however, it was, in both cases, the Greek spirit that fructified, clarified, organized, and rationalized the old Oriental myths, even in their mystique. And Hermetism might very well have been at bottom only a philosophy, a theological explanation of the Mysteries, or of a part of them. The two termini meet Ramsay's definition very well: "An attempt of the Hellenic genius to take the spirit of Oriental religion into its service." The Greek spirit was at work on Oriental elements.[58]

III. The Mysteries

a) *Greek Dualism.* The Mysteries [59] were based on the idea of immortality, on the conviction that man can know a better life beyond the grave, happier than the life he led on earth. The Greeks had arrived at this conception independently, as a consequence of a dualist anthropology. Starting with the much more ancient idea of man's *double*, which leaves the body when he dies, they eventually concluded that man is composed of two elements: one *corporeal*, extinguished by death, the other *immaterial*, which survived and was known to the philosophers as man's *soul*. The miseries and deceits of human life fortified the hope in an immortal life of the soul in a blessed realm. Understandably, in the terrible times which preceded and immediately followed the beginnings of the Christian

57. *CLXXVII*, chs. vii, v and viii, iv.
58. *XCII*, I, pp. 21f., enumerates these elements.
59. Sources: *CLXXXVII*. Explanation: *CLXX; CL; CLI; CLXXXVI; CXXXIV; CXXXV; CLXXVI; CLXIV; CLXII*. Depiction on monuments: *XXI*. Hellenistic antecedents: *CLXV*, II, pp. 168f.

era men dwelt on the expectation of this future, which seemed to be just compensation for the tribulations of the present.

The ancient national religions had not been favorable to, or rather had not been interested in, this hope of a beyond: they were no more concerned with the future destiny of the individual than they were with his spiritual and moral perfection as religious ends. We know that they were able to achieve a constant marshalling of energies and sentiments in the service of the city or the nation, whose prosperity and continuation constituted their real aim. Their indifference to any future life takes a very curious form in the Jewish Bible, where it is formulated several times: the dead are of no concern to Yahweh; [60] Sheol, into which they have descended, is not properly a part of his domain.[61] Whether it is Sheol and the *Rephaim* who dwell in it, or Hades and the shades which people it according to the Homeric conception, it cannot be said there was any true life in these realms. In these underground habitations, men knew only a kind of larval prolongation of their earthly existence, and for the Jews the state of the *Rephaim* seems to have been even lower than that of the shades was for the Greeks.[62]

The conceptions of Minos, Aeacus, and Rhadamanthus, influenced probably by the Egyptian belief in the judgment of the dead, were more advanced, at least in the moral sense, since these mythological characters introduced the notion of the responsibility of the living before the superior Powers. Unfortunately, this notion was never defined in a satisfactory manner, and was tied to an affabulation difficult to maintain for long. I have in mind Juvenal's verse (*Sat.* II, 149f.): "'That there are somewhere Manes and an underground Kingdom, and Charon's oar and dark frogs in the abyss of the Styx, and that a single barque can suffice to take so many thousands of the dead across the water, even children no longer believe, except those who have yet to pay for their bath." The same impression is found also in Plutarch, and, of course, even more in the Epicureans, whose influence is seen in the well-known saying often used as an inscription on tombstones: "I was not, I have been, I no longer am, little does it matter to me!" [63]

It would be a great mistake to suppose that the pagan consciousness of

60. Ps. cxv.17; lxxxviii.11; Isa. xxxviii.18.
61. Amos ix.5.
62. A. Lods, *La Croyance à la vie future et le culte des morts dans l'Antiquité israélite*, Paris, Pt. II, ch. iii and Index, at the word *refaïm*.
63. The saying is found with several variants: non fui. non sum; non curo; non fui, non sum, non curo; and, in Greek, ἤμην, οὐχ εἰμι. τοσαῦτα. Cf. J. Carcopino, "Le Tombeau de Lamoiridi et l'hermétisme africain," *Rev. archéologique*, XV (1922), 130.

the first century of the Roman Empire is adequately summed up in such statements. I mention them only to make clear how inadequate were the presentations of life beyond the grave in classical Greco-Roman religion. Logically, this inadequacy led to Epicurean skepticism.

However, the Greek world had long been conscious of this inadequacy, and religious sentiment had long sought to overcome it. The Mysteries antedated, by far, the conquest of the Persian Empire by Alexander, and if possible Oriental influences were already hidden under some of their Greek forms, they are very difficult, if not to uncover, at least to define. The cults of Dionysus and of Orpheus, of Demeter and Kore at Eleusis, of the Cabeiri at Samothrace, of Artemis at Ephesus, of Apollo at Claros had become, fundamentally, Mysteries, that is, they claimed to initiate one into a divine secret, the revelation and guarantee of a future life of blessedness, and into a method for assuring oneself its benefits. The origins, the stages in the evolution of these cults, the external influences that may have enriched or modified them, are all so many questions that still remain quite obscure for us, not only because the facts are remote and the texts rare, but also because the essential thing, that is, the transformation and adaptation, often escaped the Ancients, as it does us, since every one of the various revelations claimed to possess the complete and definitive truth and to have preserved it without any alteration. Orphism, for example, which started with rude and bloody rites in which the animal, a substitute for the god, was torn apart by the teeth of the initiates, ended by becoming a kind of theology and ethical doctrine, with both expounded in an abundant literature.

All the Greek Mysteries had, apparently, several general traits in common.[64] (1) They thought that the human soul, weighed down by the body, was incapable of finding unaided the road to salvation and that this was why instruction in the Mystery (μύησις) was necessary. (2) They practiced an initiation of several stages, which led from the status of child in the Mystery (νήπιος) to that of perfect one (τέλειος). (3) The initiates usually passed from one stage to another by means of some liturgical rite. It may well be that Orphism was an exception, in that it was more a *doctrine* of salvation than a *story* of salvation. The difference is clearly seen in Pausanias's remark (i, 37, 4): "He who has *seen* the Eleusinian Mysteries or who has *read* the books called Orphic knows what I mean." (4) Ordinarily they had no dogmas, they told a sacred story; they gave no lessons in metaphysics, they presented a spectacle and revealed

64. *CXXXIV*, ch. ii.

the efficacy of suitable liturgical gestures.[65] Nor did they give instruction in morals, they demanded purification rites. The initiate's own merits, his qualities or his virtues, were not taken into consideration: he derived his salvation from the fact of his initiation alone.

These old Mysteries, which had existed in their successive forms throughout all of Greek antiquity, still maintained a considerable influence in the century which surrounds the beginning of the Christian era. This was especially true of the Mysteries at Eleusis and Claros. It is not quite certain whether Orphism still existed as an organization, as (let us say) a Church,[66] but it certainly still subsisted as a combining element in religions whose specifically non-Orphic elements were derived from the Eleusinian Mysteries, from theories rightly or wrongly attributed to Pythagoras, or from obscure developments and interpretations of Dionysiac myths. Archaeological discoveries, whether very recent or quite ancient, but whose meaning has really been understood only in our day, have revealed the existence of a complete syncretistic religion, based on Pythagoreanism and Orphism, in the Graeco-Roman world, especially at Rome and in Italy. It seems to have attracted a great number of distinguished minds.

The archaeological discoveries I have in mind are principally[67] the frescoes of the Farnesina in Rome; the stucco decorations of the tombs on the Latin Way and those of the Basilica of Porta Maggiore, which together present a sort of history of the initiation and the destiny of the soul; and the eloquent decorations of the Villa Item and of the Homeric House at Pompeii. Of course, there still remain uncertainties concerning the interpretation of all these pictures and symbols. But the total impression that emerges from the ensemble leaves nothing to be desired. The wealthy men who adorned their dwellings with all these costly decorations intended them to express their urgent spiritual concern, which turned them towards the immortal destiny of the soul, at the same time that they affirmed the certainty of their hopes and their confidence in the rites their Mystery revealed to them. It seems certain that the liturgy by which their initiation was effected and their devotion sustained was interpreted with the aid of a metaphysic and a cosmology which were based on the so-called Pythagorean doctrine.

The Roman world knew a renaissance of Pythagoreanism in the last days of the Republic, but it did not restore the authentic teaching of the

65. *XXI*, nos. 53, 54, 168, 169, 170, 171.
66. *CXLIV*, ch. ii.
67. *CXLVII*; *CLXXXI*, Pt. III.

philosopher of Crotona. It gathered together under his name a potpourri of secret doctrines, definitive *dogmata,* and magical practices, where borrowings from Orphism and the Oriental religions existed side by side with the stale remains of Etruscan rites and the speculative elements derived from the Pythagoreans and the Stoics. The whole was more or less harmonized and interpreted symbolically.[68] What seemed to be distinctively Pythagorean in this mixture was its overall orientation towards the future life, with a tendency to asceticism and mysticism, the latter meditating on the purity requisite for the soul, and the former struggling to maintain it. For the believers in this doctrine thought that this life, being only the preparation for the one to come, ought to free itself, from the baseness in which matter involved it, by moral discipline and ascesis. It is perhaps not too great an exaggeration to say that this Neo-Pythagoreanism, which found expression on the walls of buildings that are haunted by the imagery of the Mystery, attracted from all points of the intellectual horizon those men who were eager for the certainty of salvation and uncomfortable in either the official religion or in Epicurean skepticism. Was there a uniform doctrine, a detailed catechism, a teaching balanced and coherent in all its parts? Of course not. But there were manifestations of an ardent religious feeling and of an indefectible eschatological aspiration. This doctrine was widespread at Rome in the time of Cicero and Varro, who wanted to be buried according to the Pythagorean rite,[69] and in the circle of Nigidius Figulus, *Pythagoricus et Magus,*[70] who had no doubt sought it out in the Orient. It was influential in Alexandria,[71] and in the second century Lucian was to echo its nearly general unpopularity, an unpopularity occasioned in all probability by the sect's seemingly aristocratic and exclusive character.[72]

As I have said, Orphism no longer existed as an independent religion. Its ideas, however, survived to so great an extent in the religious thought of the time that it was still singularly fruitful. It should not be forgotten that the notion that the world is delivered to evil and that the body is a burden and a hindrance for the soul, whose destiny is to escape its bonds and arrive at eternal and blessed life, was spread by Orphism, which also implanted the conviction that man's efforts to win salvation were power-

---

68. Stobeus, *Flor.,* V, 72: Καὶ μὴν οὐδὲν ἐστιν οὕτω τῆς Πυθαγορικῆς Φιλο-σοφίας ἴδιον ὡς τὸ συμβολικόν...

69. Pliny, *Hist. nat.* xxxv, 160: . . . *Pythagorico modo in myrti et oleae atque populi nigrae foliis.*

70. Hieronymus, *Chron.,* ad ann. *45;* CXLVII, pp. 196f.

71. Ed. Zeller, *Die Philosophie der Griechen in ihrer geschichtlichen Entwicklung,* 5th ed. (Leipzig, 1920–1923), III,² pp. 113f.

72. Cf. Lucian, *The Cock* and *True Stories.*

less without divine assistance. These two ideas were put into circulation by what I would call the dislocation of Orphism. The importance of this fact lies in its having given independent value to these conceptions, so that one could accept them and be open to their suggestions without explicit affiliation to any Mystery.

What was missing in these old Mysteries was not so much emotion (which, for example, was very strong at Eleusis), as the intensity of mysticism, the practical realization in asceticism of the idea of reparation, precise comprehension of the ways and means of salvation. If, as our era draws near, the Mysteries, especially in the syncretistic combinations which had developed outside the regular organizations, still had many adherents among the wealthy classes, they apparently no longer wielded much influence among the people, although they were, in principle, quite egalitarian. We know that the initiation at Eleusis took no heed of the age, sex, social condition, or way of life of the *mystoi*. In this the Eleusinian Mysteries resembled the individualism of the Oriental Mysteries, and although the Eleusinian differed from the Oriental, they were in no way opposed to submitting to the latter's influence.

b) *The Wave from the Orient at the Inception of the Christian Era.* At the time we are considering, a veritable wave from the Orient combed the shores of the Greco-Roman world: [73] Egypt with Isis, Osiris, and Serapis; Syria, with Adonis-Tammuz, Atargatis, and the Baalim; Phrygia, with Cybele, Attis, and Sabazius; Iran and Mesopotamia with Mithra, Ishtar, and the astrologists, etc.—all were manifesting their influence simultaneously. In fact, the whole of Asia Minor, imbued with the same general ideas and stirred by the same aspirations, was filling up with unequally developed and organized cults and initiations, all tending towards mystical exaltation and hope for salvation.

The origins of this religious effervescence are of course very obscure. We can see, however, that it is related to those myths which, as we have already mentioned, originally dealt with the life of the sun and of vegetation. Transposed to man and interpreted in relation to his destiny, they ended with a common doctrine, a doctrine practically invariant from one sect to another, whose general characteristics were as follows:

1. Man is a fallen being, incapable of working out by himself his salvation, which is the gift of divine grace. Some receive it, they are the elect; others do not, they are the damned.

2. There is an element in man that endures and matter that perishes. Opinions differed however on the nature of the bond that united these

73. *CLI*, ch. ii and notes.

two aspects of man and on the essential distinction that separated them. Consequently, the survival of the human being was presented in two quite dissimilar forms: sometimes it was conceived as the installation of the immortal soul in the abode of the blessed; at other times as a reconstitution of the entire human being, his corporeal nature having been purified. Thus there was on the one hand belief in the immortality of the soul; and on the other, expectation of the resurrection of the flesh.

3. To help man in his struggle for salvation, one relies on the example, intercession, and assistance of a divine being whose office it is to save. In Greek this being was called "Soter." The Orientals had for a long time considered their sovereigns to be terrestrial divinities and saviors; adapting this notion to serve the ends of a life beyond the grave was therefore easy. Most frequently, this intervention of a Savior took the form of a divine experience: the divine being had lived, suffered, died, and then been resurrected. The man who shared in this experience through mystical identification with the god found therein both a model and surety for his own life.

4. It was enough to discover the efficacious precepts and mystical acts which assimilated the initiate to his Savior. Each salvation Mystery had its own method, allegedly effective, for bringing about this assimilation to the sufferings, the fate, and finally the glorification of the Soter. The method was based on all-powerful rites, both realistic and mystical, which were valuable in themselves. The principal ones were related to the two most striking forms of communion among men: the bed and the table.

5. The concept was born, and growing, that a holy life, a life purified by constraint of the desires of the flesh, was a requisite, in order to prepare for the indefectible election and to merit the grace of a perfect initiation which "divinized" the *mystos*.

6. As for their initiation, men were divided into two categories: children (νήπιοι) and perfects (τέλειοι), with stages between the two. The perfects formed a fraternity, made one in their god and bound to his service, which was conceived as absolute freedom.

7. The elect could come from any world, any social condition, any nation. That is why these various sectarian fraternities, which were practically closed corporations, were all based on universalism, since each aspired to contain the whole of humanity. And each was administered by a specialized priesthood, because correctness in its liturgical life was thought to be paramount.

Recruitment was guaranteed by private propaganda: each initiate considered himself to be a missionary, and was encouraged and sustained by his pride in being one of the elect. What strikes us as most odd is the fact that there was no hostility among these rival organizations. The conviction each had of possessing the truth didn't cause it to excommunicate all the others. Thus, one and the same man could seek several initiations, and could simultaneously be a member of several Churches, and theoretically, of all. I have already recalled the example of Apuleius. The common background whose principal features we have just summed up favored this syncretism, of which the vast Hermetic literature [74] is such a curious example: it seems to be the incorporation into theories and doctrines of the empirical salvationism of the Mysteries.

As a footnote to this résumé, I add one remark, a rubric of paramount importance, in order to warn the reader not to lose sight of it: the death of the god in the Mystery was for the faithful a requisite example and an indispensable lesson, which instructed them in the conditions and forms of their salvation, but *it was not in itself their redemption*. By this I mean that the god did not give *his* life as compensation for the lack of merit in *theirs*, that *he did not really sacrifice himself for them*, but only *before them* and for their edification. The study of Pauline soteriology, which we shall soon establish, holds an instructive comparison.

Conclusion

It would be an egregious error to imagine that this Hellenistic world, in which the apostolic faith sought to find its place after the dislocation of the Church of Jerusalem, was dried up by skepticism. To picture it as flung into complete moral and religious decadence is to draw a caricature. If the old forms of the classical religion were indeed largely emptied of any living substance, by their side a number of new categories were available to the religious sentiment and mystical anxiety of men, categories in which they could find something to satisfy the exigencies of their spiritual life. For too long credence was given solely to literary documents and the declamations of moralists. Today the impressions they fostered have been duly corrected by inscriptions, papyri, ostraca, and carved monuments. The tares of this society are not to be denied, but it is fitting not to neglect the wheat, which is evident as soon as one takes the trouble to look at it. Does not Paul himself invite us not to overlook it when he says (Rom. ii.14–15) that the Gentiles, who have not the Law, nonetheless do by nature what it prescribes and show its work written in their hearts?

74. Published in *CLXXXIII*. Cf. *CLXXII* and *CLXXIX*.

We have insufficient information, for the first century, on the true extension of the Mysteries in all their forms, but we may rest assured that from this time onward the extension was very great and that it fed on a widespread religious feeling, manifest in different forms in all classes of society; a religious feeling that was intensely alive, favored both by the evident retreat of Greek rationalism and the lack of positive science. How otherwise could Christianity have been born and how could it have been established as a religion of salvation if it encountered nothing but indifference to religious emotion and concerns, and incredulity concerning the expectation of a future life? On the contrary, if one takes into account the ideas and facts we have just assembled, the success and prodigious evolution of the Christian hope, which the Hellenists of Jerusalem had just transported to Greek soil, are not inexplicable. As the composite elements of this living religious matter on which it will feed are determined, it is easy to perceive the favorable conditions which prepared its paths.

3

THE CHURCH
OF ANTIOCH [1]

**Origins, Life,
Organization, and Faith**

THERE is no serious reason to doubt the veracity of the brief narrative in Acts xi.19–21, our only source for the beginnings of the Church of the Gentiles.[2] According to its account, it was the Hellenistic Jews who took the Good News with them when they left Jerusalem, where they could live no longer after the execution of Stephen, and successfully sought to acclimatize it in their adopted countries, in the heart of the Diaspora, in Syria, Phoenicia, and Cyprus. As Jews, they began by addressing themselves to the Jews only, and no doubt to their total proselytes; then "some of them," who came from Cyprus and Cyrene, arrived in Antioch and spoke also to the Greeks—that is, I presume, to the "God-fearers" who were attracted to the synagogue.[3] It is not surprising that this fruitful undertaking was initiated in Antioch, where, as we know (Gal. ii.11–13), the Jewish community was in large part com-

---

1. *CXXIX*, pp. 124f; *CVIII*, pp. 65, 96, 460–71; Gillis Wetter, "Das älteste hellenistische Christentum nach der Apostelgeschichte," *Archiv für Religionswissenschaft*, XXI (1922), 397–429; *CVII*, ch. iv.

2. Cf. above, p. 132.

3. It is permissible to believe that the narrative is basically dependent at this point on a document of Antiochene origin. (Cf. *LXXVII*, p. 178; *XVIII*, III, pp. 229f.) It is unfortunate that the account of Acts does not reproduce it in its entirety, and does not even give us the assurance that it reproduces at least a part of it.

posed of pagan converts. But it is a pity that we do not know what happened at the same time in Cyprus and Phoenicia. What's more, we are not even able to get a very close view of what took place in Antioch. The continuation of the story in Acts was probably contrived to make it conform, with no great care for history, to the ideas and intentions of the author. And that is even more regrettable. But the fact itself remains, and it is valuable.

If we were to take quite seriously Paul's title, claimed by himself, as Apostle of the Gentiles, we might think that the foundation of the first community on pagan soil dates back to his efforts. But it does nothing of the sort. In his letters he never said that he was the first to preach to the Gentiles. In Galatians i.16, where he presents this preaching as his special mission, he does not claim it as being something new.[4] And he does well, for it is in Antioch that we first perceive that essential resolve, which led to the Christian religion, to offer the Christian hope to the uncircumcised. Renan's judgment was quite right, and hardly forced the meaning of the words, when he wrote: [5] "The point of departure for the Church of the Gentiles, the original home of Christian missions, was really Antioch. There for the first time was established a Christian Church free from ties with Judaism; there the great propaganda of the Apostolic age was founded; there St. Paul received his definitive formation."

We know nothing of the personality of the founders of the Church of Antioch. I am inclined to believe, however, that we find their names, or at least some of them, in Acts xiii.1: "Now there were in the church that was at Antioch certain prophets and teachers; as Barnabas, and Simeon that was called Niger, and Lucius of Cyrene, and Manaen, which had been brought up with Herod the tetrarch." The text adds, "and Saul," because it speaks of all these men only after having admitted Paul into their number and having begun to show him in action. We feel certain that the Tarsiot was not a worker of the first hour in Antioch. The only one of the four names which means anything to us is Barnabas, whom Acts xi.22 presents as a kind of delegate of the Church of Jerusalem, charged by it to conduct an inquiry at Antioch and to sanction, in the name of the Apostles, whatever favorable action may have been taking place there. There is reason to fear that this is nothing more than a wholly contrived account conforming to the author's set purpose of subordinating everything in the primitive Church to the authority of the

4. *XCII*, I, p. 41, n. 2.
5. *LV*, p. 226.

Apostles.[6] I don't even think it unlikely that in Acts iv.36 "Joses, who by the apostles was surnamed Barnabas . . . a Levite of Cyprus," was brought into the narrative for the sole purpose of preparing the future mission of this distinguished brother.[7] To our author, it did not seem possible, or at least not acceptable, for the community of Antioch not to be directly dependent on the Apostolic Church. But it may very well be that Barnabas was one of the first founders, I would even go so far as to say the first founder, of the Antiochene community, and that it was he who really *planted* the Good News in the Syrian milieu. When one reads in Galatians ii.lf.; "Then fourteen years after I went up again to Jerusalem with Barnabas," and in ii.9; "And when James, Cephas, and John, who seemed to be pillars, perceived the grace that was given unto me, they gave to me and Barnabas the right hands of fellowship," one does not have the impression that Barnabas was especially dependent on the Apostles, nor that he is their delegate. On the contrary, one feels that, in relation to them, Barnabas put himself on the same footing as Paul himself. Again, one notes with Loisy that the writer of Acts xi.22 refrains from stating the precise object of Barnabas's mission in Antioch, and that he is careful not to have him return to Jerusalem. That, to say the least, is surprising, if this envoy of the Apostles was charged with informing them in person about what he had seen. And that is why I am inclined to see Barnabas, who was aided in his work by Hellenists—Acts xiii.1 gives us the names of the chief ones—as the real founder of the Church in Antioch. This hypothesis assigns him an eminent place in the history of the birth of the Christian religion. Paul was unjust to him, and I believe it was correct to say that "his eyes were opened to the great road that lay ahead of the Church," before Paul's.[8]

The Antiochene milieu was favorable to the enterprise of these men. The population of the city, the third most numerous in the Empire, was very mixed. Antioch was the crossroads where all the beliefs and all the superstitions of the Orient met. Its large Jewish colony,[9] surrounded by proselytes,[10]—at whose side there was certain to be an imposing flock of "God-fearers"—and participating in the intellectual and material life of the Greeks, was, a priori, much more disposed, as I have already tried to show, to listen to the new preaching than the Galilean synagogues could

6. *CVIII*, pp. 466f.
7. *CVIII*, pp. 263f.
8. *CCLIII*, p. 14.
9. Josephus, *Antt.* XII, 3:1; XIV; 12:6; *Jewish War* II, 18:5.
10. Josephus, *Jewish War* VII, 3:2.

have been. We can imagine without temerity that the spirit and tendencies of this preaching stemmed from the tendencies and spirit of Stephen, since in Jerusalem our Hellenists followed the line taken by the deacon-martyr. In short, they accentuated faith in Jesus's mission and subordinated the requirements of Judaism to it.

In all probability they won few pure Jews, for Acts leaves the impression that they expended most of their effort elsewhere. They must have reaped their principal gains from among the proselytes and especially the "God-fearers." [11] Even pagans, who were more or less interested in the synagogue but not especially attracted to it, may have been reached and won by individual propaganda. Did the founders deliberately address themselves to them? [12] I doubt it, for that would have been an act of singular boldness on their part and a most astonishing display of foresight. But, under the prompting of their hearts, they accepted good will and faith in Christ Jesus no matter where they were manifested.[13] That was already a very important step.

However that may be, it is in any case certain that those who were strangers to pure Israel, the "God-fearers" and Gentiles, were not long in forming a large majority in the Christian community of Antioch, and that even the name "Christian," which the brethren received there for the first time, from outsiders,[14] clearly proves that, because of its recruitment, their group was soon distinguished from Jewry. Nor was it possible for it not to set itself up apart from the Jewish synagogue, as soon as it gained self-consciousness.

If there were in Antioch two kinds, if not two groups, of converts, the Jewish-Christian and the Helleno-Christian—which is quite possible, and when one reads the account of the conflict between Paul and Peter in Galatians ii.11f, almost believable—there was not, to our knowledge, any rupture between them. They ate together (Gal. ii), indicating that the Jews who had accepted the Good News raised no objections, through scruples of legal purity, to communion with the Gentiles.[15] Trouble and discord came about only because of the intervention of men from Jerusalem.[16] This laxity may be attributed to the broad-mindedness of the

11. XCII, I, pp. 46f.
12. On this much—and rather sterilely—disputed question, cf. CVIII, p. 465.
13. LXXVII, p. 180; CXXIX, p. 124.
14. Acts xi.26; Loisy, CVIII, p. 470, on the pagan origin and formation of the word. The Jews continued to refer to them as Nazarenes. For detailed study and bibliography, see XCVII, V, 383f (Cadbury). Cf. P. de Labriolle, in Bulletin du Cange, V (1930), 69f.
15. XCII, I, p. 46, n. 1; CXXIX, p. 125.
16. Acts xv.1f.; Gal. ii.11–13.

Hellenists, and to the probable fact that the majority of the brethren came neither from the ranks of pure Jews nor from those of total prose-lytes. But I believe that one must attach especially great importance in this instance to the role that was attributed to baptism in the Antiochene community, and to the use made of it.[17]

I shall add no more to what I have already said about the obscure origins of this rite, except to recall that it signified purification of sins and was as well a sign of consecration. It was natural that the Christians, faced with converts who came from semi, or wholly, heathen backgrounds, tended to accentuate the second of these two aspects, the one that was to distinguish the faithful from the unbeliever. Baptism was thought to bestow upon its recipient sanctification along with purification: the bap-tized became the property of God; he was marked for his Kingdom by the name of Christ Jesus.[18] Thus understood, the Christian rite took precedence over every other practice, every preliminary observance. It estab-lished between those who had received it a bond which surpassed the com-munion in legalism and rendered negligible all considerations of impurity of contacts according to the Law. Very soon, if not from the start, it was understood that baptism created the bond of brotherhood between the ini-tiates in the Christian revelation—we may already say the *Christian Mystery*—and effected their communion (κοινωνία) in the Christ.

The lack of texts unfortunately prevents us from having a clear or ac-curate understanding of the spirit, life, and doctrine of the Church of Antioch.[19] We do not even know how the material separation from the Synagogue was accomplished. However, one hypothesis doesn't seem too rash; one can believe it likely that in this milieu, where perhaps none of the brethren had known Jesus personally, but all nonetheless put their fervent hope in him, the ascension of the Christ towards God and his divinization were accentuated and accelerated. Or at least that his glorifica-tion acquired definite form. In other words, the Antioch brethren's notions of his person and his role tended to set aside everything that might still relate it to Jewish Messianism in favor of a broader and more elevated conception, a conception that corresponded to the title *Kyrios = Lord.*[20] On reading forms of words such as the following in 1 Corinthians v.4— "In the name of our Lord Jesus Christ, when ye are gathered together,

17. *CXXIX*, p. 125.
18. I Cor. vi.11. For the specific power of the name of Christ Jesus and its various primitive uses, cf. the interesting study in *XCVII*, V, 121–40.
19. *LXXVII*, pp. 181f., tried to arrive at such an understanding, but he only strung together a series of generous presuppositions and deductions founded on contestable premises.
20. On the use of this term in Acts, cf. *XCVII*, V, 359f (Cadbury).

and my spirit, with the power of our Lord Jesus Christ (σὺν τῇ δυνάμει)"—
one can understand, without scrutinizing their content, that for the man
who used them, the name of the Lord (or better, the name of *Lord*) was
a powerful cultic factor, that uttering it was to assure oneself the presence
of the person, the cultic action of the *dynamis* of Christ Jesus.

It is clear from even a superficial reading of the Pauline epistles that
the person of the *Kyrios* dominated the whole life of the Christian community the Apostle frequented. He was the head of the body this community formed; his name expressed the interrelationship of the faithful
with one another and with him.[21] They knew that "God also hath highly
exalted him, and given him a name which is above every name: that at
the name of Jesus [i.e., the name Jesus received from God] every knee
should bow, of things in heaven, and things in earth, and things under
the earth" (Phil. ii.9f). *Kyrios* was the sacred cultic name: the place the
name *Yahweh* occupied in the Jewish religion was filled by *Kyrios* in the
young Christian cultus, if we take Paul's word for it. It was Yahweh who
said in Isaiah xlv.23, "unto me every knee shall bow;" does he not seem
to abdicate his might in favor of the *Lord* Jesus? But this title of glory
cannot have been invented by Paul, for there is something here that
transcends the will of a single man; we are in the presence of a manifestation of the collective consciousness of a community, realized in a living
cultus.[22] Hence, the Tarsiot received the name and the notion of *Kyrios*
from the Hellenistic community where he himself was formed. The question then is to know how this consciousness grew and whence it derived
the fruitful notion in question.[23]

In the knowledge that in the Septuagint, "Yahweh" is always transcribed
by "Kyrios," [24] some have thought that the term was simply transferred to
the benefit of Christ Jesus. But as the brethren certainly did not at first
assimilate Christ Jesus to Yahweh and since the Messiah was never designated by the name "Lord" in Judeo-Hellenic literature, one must look
elsewhere. Others have found the basis of the attribution of the title
"Kyrios" to Christ Jesus in Psalm cx.1 (Ps. cix in the Septuagint), which
soon attracted the attention of Christians (e.g., Mark xii.35–37): "The
Lord said to my Lord," interpreted as "God said to the Christ." But how
can one believe that this exegesis of so slim a text—an exegesis which is,
to say the least, a misinterpretation—was sufficient to give birth to the

21. *IX*, p. 105.
22. *IX*, p. 107.
23. For literature on the subject, see *IV*, *ad verbum*, col. 722f.
24. W. Baudissin, *Kyrios als Gottesname im Judentum und seine Stelle in der
Religionsgeschichte*, Giessen, 1926–1929.

concept of Kyrios, so rich in meaning, in the guise in which it appears in Paul? At the most, one may view the verse from Psalm cx as a witness after the fact, for faith in the Lord Jesus preceded its justification by texts from Scripture.

Moreover, the fundamental relationship between the terms "Kyrios" and "Christos"—the expression "Kyrios-Christos" seems quite natural—appears to point to the fact that a close link was established from the first between "Christos" and "Kyrios." The application of the title *Lord* to Christ was, in other words, something direct and *technical*. In contemporary usage the word "Kyrios" denoted the relation of the slave to the master; in Christian usage it denoted the essential and specific relation of the slaves of Christ to Christ himself (1 Cor. vii.22). That is why there is no reason for lingering over the hypothesis that the word *theos* (= god) was a bridge between "Christos" and "Kyrios," that is, the thesis that once he had been made the center of the Christian cultus, Christ would have been called *god*, and as *God* was *Lord*, he would also have become *Lord*. This supposition seems to me to be inconsistent. If it is, the origin of the title in question must be sought in the idea of protection and salvation. In the beliefs and practices of the Orient, this idea belongs to: (1) the cult of sovereigns and especially of the Emperor; (2) the cult of the Soter gods. Of the two elements, it was the second that exercised great influence, for at that time the cult of local sovereigns was no longer anything but a memory in Syria and the cult of the Emperor, still in its infancy, had not yet acquired the dominating importance that would later in the Orient make the prince an Epiphanes God and Savior of the world. *Kyrios* was the current title of the savior gods of Egypt, Syria, and Asia Minor. The Artemis of Ephesus was *Kyria*, and so was the *Magna Mater* of Phrygia. Also *Kyrioi* were Zeus-Sabazius, Dionysus, and the Syrian Baalim, as well as Atargatis, Marduk, Isis, and Hermes-Tot. And the same name was bestowed on Osiris and Serapis, and many other divinities of lesser stature and patronage, whereas the great gods bearing this title were rare exceptions. Besides, the title was, apparently, bestowed on these latter gods precisely and only when they were considered to be beneficent and salvation deities, or when, by grace of syncretism, they lent their names to some local divinity. Thus, East of the Jordan, *Kyria Athena* is *Allat* and *Kyrios Dionysos* is *Dusares*, both Arabian divinities. It sometimes happened, however, that the title was applied to quite illustrious gods. But in such cases the gods were alien, as Zeus was in Syria, Apollo in Cappadocia, and Helios in Galatia. Finally, the title is sometimes found in conjunction with the name of divinities who achieved a widespread cultus at a late date, such as Asclepios and Hecate. It would seem that in all cases it was bestowed on divinities who were central to a cultus which united members of a community or religious order.

Thus the adoption by the Christians of Antioch of the title *Kyrios* to designate Christ Jesus is in fact an infiltration into their faith of a basic notion from the Syrian salvationist milieu. Because the brethren gradually installed Jesus Christ at the center of their cultus, they bestowed on him a title suggested to them by the customs of their milieu as appropriately representing the function their faith would attribute to him with greater and greater precision, that is, the function of Savior. When the Hellenized Jews made Yahweh the Kyrios, they were unconsciously moved by a similar influence towards a most analogous conclusion. The same would be true of the Simonians, who also considered their Master to be a Kyrios.[25]

Faith in the Lord and the cultus of the Lord were the foundations of the belief and piety of the Hellenistic Christians, which grew strong as they became more fully separated from the Jewish Synagogue. When they recognized in Christ Jesus the Lord, a decisive step was taken towards his inevitable divinization, and the transcription of the Septuagint, Yahweh-Kyrios, favored the Christ's transition to God, a transition the Septuagint could not have effected alone. The confusion between the Lord Jesus and the Lord Yahweh is already discernible in Paul.[26] On the other hand, the Tarsiot was quite right in comparing the God and Lord of the Christians (ὁ θεὸς καὶ ὁ κύριος) to the gods (πολλοὶ θεοί) and Lords (πολλοὶ κύριοι) of pagan religions (1 Cor. viii.5–6). The attribution to Christ of a title so widespread, a title whose current meaning corresponded so well to the needs and trends of the Hellenic community, seems, if one takes the trouble to think about it, to have satisfied a pressing want of the religious milieu of Antioch.

The adoption of the title *Kyrios* to designate the Christ Jesus had important consequences, because it meant that the initial trust in Jesus, in what he had said, commanded, and done, was irresistibly and wholly transformed into faith, belief in Jesus, in his mission, and in the wonderful uniqueness of his person. In the end one will believe in him as in God. It is not possible to compare the value of the *Kyrios* of the Antiochene Hellenists with that of the *Son of Man* of the Judaizers. The magnitude of the latter was of an *eschatological* order, that is, it had meaning only for the future of the age, provided that future continued to be viewed with the eyes of the Messianists of Israel; whereas *the Lord* was a title of

25. *IX*, pp. 118f.
26. Rom. x.13, xi.34, xiv.11; 1 Cor. ii.16; 2 Cor. x.17; etc.

present greatness whose presence and action was felt by the assembled community when it invoked *his* name.[27] Even if we didn't know what actually happened, it would not be difficult to predict that the Hellenistic conception would prevail over the other. It is, in the first place, pregnant with the whole Pauline Christology.

It is permissible to wonder whether our Antiochenes did not go farther; if, for example, they had not already sought to explain the troubling death of the Lord Jesus (which, according to the Jerusalem brethren, made him Christ) by the notion, common in their midst, of the God who dies and is resurrected in order to provide an example for his worshippers and a guaranty for their own lives, to guide them on the road of salvation, and to help them by his intercession; there can be no question as yet of redemption. No answer is possible except that of a personal impression. Mine is that this notion may have arisen because, (1) the whole atmosphere drove the brethren in that direction; (2) it was a decisive means of shedding the scandal of the Cross by converting it into the most requisite and priceless deed; (3) it was a most valuable means of transforming for the use of the Greeks the Jewish notion of Messiah = Christ, a notion overly narrow, nationalistic, and materialistic, and by so doing universalize the faith; (4) endowing the death and resurrection of Jesus with the notion of a model, *example*, and *guaranty* was a counterweight to the main advantage offered by the Mysteries to their adherents. Pauline soteriology undoubtedly developed from the basic notion to which these various elements led and in the direction they determined. There can be no possible doubt that that soteriology did not come to Paul from the Church of Jerusalem. I am inclined to believe that the Tarsiot received it from the Hellenistic community, which I identify, substantially, with the Church of Antioch.[28]

Conclusion

The community the Hellenists founded, by dissidence, by heresy, and in opposition to the Synagogue of the Syrian capital, was therefore the true cradle of Christianity. Under the unconscious pressure of the religious milieu in which it lived, it effected, without being aware of it, one or two syncretistic operations, which infused in the fragile hope brought from Palestine a power of life and a capacity for radiation which determined the entire destiny of the Christian religion.

27. *CVII*, pp. 174f.
28. *CXCIII*, pp. 53f.

4

PAUL OF TARSUS:
PROLEGOMENA [1]

> We know very well that Biblical criticism does not an-
> swer all our questions, but we also know that its investiga-
> tions cannot have, ought not to have, and in fact, do not
> have any limits except those imposed by its own nature;
> for no authority is qualified to impose its conclusions on
> criticism in any matter subject to critical investigation, i.e.
> anything susceptible of methodic observation in the order
> of universal reality.   —Loisy, *Les Origines du N.T.*, pp. 5f.

ACCORDING to Acts xi.22f the
Church of Jerusalem apparently got wind of unusual happenings in
Antioch, and sent Barnabas to investigate. He realized that the "grace of
God" was being manifested there, and, since "he was a good man, and
full of the Holy Spirit and of faith," he charged the brethren who were
laboring in that place to persevere in their attachment to the Lord. Hence,
he sided with this group of Hellenists and without further deliberation
set to work beside them. But—we don't know why or when—he wanted
to assure himself a collaborator, whose merits, so we must believe, he
knew, since he had already worked for the Lord at his side in Jerusalem—
this information comes from our disturbing author [2]—and so he "departed
to Tarsus, for to seek Saul."

---

1. The bibliography is formidable. For all pre-1911 material, cf. *CCXLIV*; post-
1911, *XVIII*, IV.[1] All known facts are assembled and organized from different points
of view in *CCII*, I; *CCIII*; *CCXXIX*; *CCXLI*; *CCL*.

2. Acts ix.28. This verse is incoherent and seems to be inconsistent; I shall come
back to it.

I. *Paul's Self-Presentation; Our Information About Him*

Here, then, is the man who, insofar as we are acquainted with the first age of Christianity, appears as its star figure. His strong personality, his energetic activity, the extent and depth of his influence, make him appear as "the great spiritual force of the apostolic age; he not only worked more, but also"—so we were told—"founded more than all the others"; that is, more than the other moving spirits of the new religion.[3]

So great is his pre-eminence that some have even accorded him all the glory for having created Christianity. Actually, however, closer examination of the texts and the events they relate leads to a less advantageous appraisal of the Tarsiot. Nonetheless, this short-tempered man, who was so apt to put himself forward that one begins to find him somewhat in the way, presents a type of religious worker of exceptional interest to both the historian and the psychologist.

His thought, as manifested *in Paul himself and in his successors*, appears to be inseparable from the later evolution of Christian theology, especially in what concerns the origin and development of the understanding of the *Christ* (Christology), the definition of the notion and conditions of *salvation* (soteriology and ethics), and the conception of the nature and forms of the *Church* (ecclesiology).

For the moment, by his thought, I mean the form it took in his letters, which were soon to be elevated to the rank of Holy Scripture, and I reserve judgment on the question of its fundamental originality.

Finally, in the development of its activity—which must be credited for the initiatives it engendered—we catch on the wing, at least in one of its aspects, the inauguration of the Christian faith in the pagan world and its transformation into an autonomous religion of salvation. And this phenomenon is of interest not only for the consequences it entailed, but also for the forms in which it was clothed and its decisive contribution to the solution of the great problem: *how is a religion born?*

We are far from having adequate information about Paul's life and his role in the early Church. Our sources of information, in the last analysis, come down to two, neither of which, as we already know, is satisfactory: the Acts of the Apostles and the Epistles. I mention Acts first, because it is in intention a narrative that claims to give us the essential information on the life of Paul, essential that is for a Christian of the post-

3. *CC*, p. 1.

apostolic age who is also, and primarily, an apologist more anxious to have his opinions prevail than to set down actual memories of the apostle. Our concerns and interests happen not to be in accord with those of such a man, and that's too bad for us. The Epistles are only incidentally narrative, but they contain the most convincing testimony to the thought of the Apostle—which does not mean that they contain all of his thought, any more than Acts gives a complete biography. This thought cannot, however, take us beyond Paul's own horizon, which certainly did not embrace all the Christian life of his time. Moreover, in several extremely critical places the text of the Epistles arouses anxiety and is legitimately suspect of interpolations and rearrangement, which may even go so far as to introduce highly important ideas that are not Paul's. Such doubts become annoyingly obsessive. Absolute respect for the letter of a work of the mind, as I do not tire of repeating, was not one of the scruples of the Ancients, least of all of the theologians and polemists of Christianity.

Another difficulty is presented by the easily perceived fact that the Paul who appears in the various episodes of Acts and the Paul revealed behind the Epistles are rather dissimilar.[4] If we had nothing but Acts, it would be impossible for us to have any inkling of what Paulinism was, or of the substance of his Gospel. But that's not the worst of it: to the despair of exegetes, the two witnesses contradict each other on simple facts, which, it seems to us, could have been easily ascertained. It has been said [5] that Acts rendered Paul the service of making him known to the communities in which he had not labored, by furnishing a biographical background to his Epistles, which are often difficult to understand and do not spontaneously yield the personality of their author. Maybe. But I am not convinced that the Tarsiot would have happily and unhesitatingly recognized himself in the image Acts has propagated. Is it an image more acceptable to the Judaizers and the general run of Christians than the authentic portrait of the grim Apostle? I don't doubt it. Moreover, it is an image that errs by blurring and smoothing over his distinctive traits.

On the whole, we are a very long way from knowing what would be needed to give us a sure picture of Paul and to situate him accurately in the progress of apostolic Christianity. On a number of points inevitable questions arise, which we can eliminate only by more or less likely, and

4. *XCVII*, II, Pt. II, ch. ii.
5. *CXXVII*, p. 159.

therefore always contestable, conjectures. It is only honest not to attempt to endow them with more consistency than they possess.[6]

II. Pauline Chronology [7]

If we only knew with certainty the setting of Paul's life in time! But who will tell us exactly when he was born? When he embraced the Christian hope? The dates of his missions? When he died? We are reduced to risky deductions founded on supposedly definite indications in the Epistles and Acts—none of them dated—and on a small number of other texts more apt perhaps to confuse our vision than to clear it. This problem is a striking example of the difficulties which slow the course of historical research.

The terminal and necessary dates, the birth and death of the Apostle, escape us. If we resign ourselves to approximations—which is wise—we can say that the birth occurred near the beginning of the Christian era and the death circa 64, with a margin of at least twelve to fifteen years for the first date, and ten years for the second. Then, with this framework set up and collating, come what may, the sporadic data of the texts, we may reason as follows: Paul, after his conversion, spent seventeen years in Damascus, Antioch, and Tarsus (Gal. i.18 and ii.1); the great missions (Acts xiii.4–xxi.15) seem to take up six or seven years; the captivity at Caesarea (Acts xxiii.23–xxvi.32) and the journey to Rome, with a stop-over at Malta (Acts xxvii.1–xxviii.14), may have taken two years; his captivity in the City (Acts xxviii.15–31) may have been of like duration; thus we have a total of some twenty-eight years. If 63–64 is accepted as the final date, the conversion would be placed circa 35; it only remains to cut the interval into slices according to the computations I have just summarized and put the principal facts in place. With a little good will, we may reach general agreement as to the probability of this little outline, which is both vague and elastic.

But as soon as one becomes more demanding and aspires to examine the problem more closely, doubts and hesitations multiply and become entangled.

It is first of all necessary to find a fixed point around which the data

6. For an inventory of these questions, see *CCXV* and *CXCV*.
7. *CCV*; *XVIII*, IV,[1] ch. ii; *CCXXVII*, pp. xiiif; Harnack, "Chronologische Berechnung des Tags von Damascus," *Sitzungsberichte der Kön. preus. Akad.*, 1912, pp. 673–80.

of the texts may be organized. For a long time this point was thought to be the change in the procuratorship of Judea, from Felix to Festus. According to Acts xxiv.27, this must have occurred two years after Paul's arrest. Unfortunately, the accounts of Josephus, Tacitus, and Eusebius are difficult to reconcile on this point, so we really do not know when the change occurred.[8] And the authority of Acts cannot remove this difficulty. Consequently, we hesitate between the years 58 and 61. This means that there is a four-year fluctuation in the chronological framework, which, naturally, obtains throughout the computations based on this pseudo-exact date. Some present-day critics think that they have found a better point of departure, or pivotal date. An inscription found at Delphi, which is given by Emile Bourget (it's a copy of a letter of Claudius to the Delphinians), names Gallio as proconsul of Achaia. Now, we read in Acts xviii.11f.: "He [Paul] continued there [in Corinth] a year and six months, teaching the word of God among them. And when Gallio was the deputy of Achaia, the Jews made insurrection with one accord against Paul, and brought him to the judgment seat." Consequently, the Apostle's stay in Corinth (Acts xviii.1–18) occurred during the proconsulate of this Gallio.

The inscription at Delphi,[9] although greatly mutilated, does permit us to know that Gallio was in office at the time Claudius received his twenty-sixth imperial acclamation, which took place in August 52, the twenty-second, twenty-third, twenty-fourth, and perhaps the twenty-fifth having occurred intermittently during 51. Hence, Gallio was proconsul in the first six months of 52. If the customary practice was followed, he may even have taken office as early as the summer of 51. By this reckoning, Paul would have arrived in Corinth in 50 or 51, and left in 51 or 52.

A really fixed date, however, still escapes us. First, because even on the basis of the most favorable hypothesis we come only within a year of it: the inscription does not state whether it corresponds to the beginning or the end of the proconsulate of Gallio, and the dates of the proconsulate itself are somewhat uncertain. Secondly, because Acts establishes no relationship between the time Paul is supposed to have appeared before Gallio and the time that magistrate took office. It does not even tell us at what point in Paul's sojourn at Corinth his trial took place. According to Acts xviii.18, after the dismissal of his case, Paul

8. *LX*, I, p. 577, n. 38 gives an extensive bibliography.
9. For literature, see *CC*, p. 162.

remained in the city "yet a good while" (ἡμέρας ἱκανάς); thus, we are still at approximations.

Help has been sought from another allegation of Acts (xviii.1–2), according to which Paul, on his arrival in Corinth, found there Aquila and Priscilla, who had but lately (προσφάτως) come from Italy, whence they had been expelled by an edict of Claudius against the Jews. Now, Paul Orosius (beginning of the fifth century) wrote (*Hist.* vi. 6, 15) that the edict was promulgated in the ninth year of Claudius's reign, viz., 49–50. If one assumes that the two exiles landed in Corinth at the beginning of 50, and that Paul followed soon after—in the springtime— and then adds a year and a half to that date, the Apostle's departure would have taken place in the autumn of 51, and his stay in Corinth would therefore correspond to one of the possible dates of the procon- sulate of Gallio (from the spring of 51 to May 52).[10] But what is the testimony of Orosius worth? It is true that he depends on a text of Josephus (*Josephus refert*), but he does not, unfortunately, quote it, and we do not know what it was. In this instance, the credibility of this late chronicler is not the best attested.[11]

The worst is yet to come: the historicity of Paul's appearance before Gallio is not affirmed on any other grounds than the word of Acts.[12] The entire section could very well be fictitious, and my fear that it is prevents me from placing my confidence in all the argumentation based on the inscription at Delphi. Even if one were to overcome his uncer- tainties and doubts, and persuade himself that he has found *the* fixed date, it would still be necessary to have the means of easily classifying the other facts related to it. I shall confine myself to two examples of what I mean.

1. In Galatians i.18 Paul tells us that he made a first trip to Jerusalem three years after his conversion (μετὰ τρία ἔτη). Does this mean after three years had passed, or in the third year, or in the third year including the one which serves as point of departure?[13] The result to which any one of these interpretations leads is quite different from those derived from the other two. Moreover, a complication arises from the fact that Acts ix.23–30, which places the journey in question as taking place quite soon after the conversion of the Tarsiot (ὡς δὲ ἐπληροῦντο ἡμέραι ἱκαναί), seems to contradict Galatians i.18.

10. *CC*, p. 174.
11. *LXVIII*, II,[2] p. 637.
12. Loisy, *RHLR* (1913), p. 487.
13. Hypothesis of *CCXLIII*, p. 274.

2. In Galatians ii.1 Paul wrote: "Then fourteen years after I went up again to Jerusalem." Fourteen years after what? After his conversion? Or after the first trip? Critics are divided between the two opinions, which proves that no decisive argument has been produced which could bring them to agreement. Now, according to the first opinion, the conversion took place fourteen years prior to the second trip; according to the second, seventeen years (14 plus 3). Moreover, since the date of this second journey can itself be established only in relation to one of the two so-called fixed points—the procuratorship of Festus or the proconsulate of Gallio—and since the chronological relationship between a number of facts which took place in the interim and serve as links remains uncertain, it is understandable why the date of the second trip to Jerusalem oscillates, in the proposed calculations, between 43 and 52, and the conversion between 29 and 40, with, in both cases, every intermediate year finding its partisans.

I have just said that the linking facts are hard to date. Here is proof: Acts xiii and xiv place the missionary journey of Paul and Barnabas to Cyprus, Pamphylia, and Galatia before the second journey to Jerusalem and the so-called Apostolic Council. But some critics believe that the author was mistaken, and inverted the order of events: this belief of course changes their point of view concerning the dates involved. How long did the mission last? Exegetes are not all of one opinion. Some say two years (Ramsay); others, three, though without much confidence (Clemen); [14] four or five, say still others (Renan); nobody knows anything about it. It may be wise to admit, along with Loisy, that it falls "outside the limits of true chronology," and that it is based on supposition anyway. Then too, the stages of the various journeys are often rather poorly indicated to permit us to make sure of the order of events. [15] I have said enough to make it clear that prudence recommends that we should not claim to have attained more than rather loose approximations of the Pauline chronology. We shall re-encounter the difficulties it raises as we continue our study of Paul.

III.   Paul's Appearance, Temperament, Character

We should very much like to have at our disposal at least a presumption of accuracy concerning the image, both physical and intellectual,

14. *CXCIX*, I, 351.
15. *XLVI*, pp. 488f.

we draw of Paul. But if it is true that the Epistles and Acts yield some traits which seem to deserve our confidence, they are far from forming a spontaneous and coherent whole that can satisfy us.

The contrast between the weakness of Paul's body and the strong force of his character has for a long time been the subject of more or less successful literary expositions,[16] but they do no more than take up again the antithesis set up by the Apostle himself in 2 Corinthians x.10 where he has his adversaries say: "His letters . . . are weighty and powerful; but his bodily presence is weak (ἀσθενής), and his speech contemptible."

In fact, no certain tradition has come down to us which tells us what we need to know about his physical appearance, and the "portraits" that have sometimes been hazarded remain inconsistent and artificial.[17] We are in the same position as the Colossians and Laodiceans who had not seen his "face in the flesh" (Col. ii.1). The Apocryphal writings and the various legendary sources do not present him in a very favorable guise. See, for example, the picture the *Acta Pauli et Theclae*, 3, draws of him: "He saw Paul coming, a short, bald, bowlegged man, with a noble countenance, full of grace, and a long nose." At first one believes that the hagiographer derived his work from a tradition, which he tried to ameliorate by compensating for its piteous impression of Paul with references to his noble and gracious countenance. But on second thought, one comes to believe that he quite simply glossed and concretized a few intimations found in the Epistles.

There are two passages in the Epistles which do apparently allude to serious physical afflictions, probably the same in both cases, and a third passage contains a word which gives the impression of being a final, or overall, judgment, on a pitiful creature: (1) 2 Corinthians xii.7ff: "And lest I should be exalted above measure through the abundance of the revelations, there was given to me a thorn in the flesh, the messenger of Satan to buffet me, lest I should be exalted above measure. For this thing I besought the Lord thrice, that it might depart from me. And he said unto me, My grace is sufficient for thee: for my strength is made perfect in weakness." [18] (2) Galatians iv.13–14: "Ye know how through infirmity of the flesh I preached the gospel unto you at the first. And

16. *CC*, pp. 42f.

17. Ramsay's efforts, for example, cause one to smile; in *CCXXXVI*, pp. 37f, he attempts to assemble and co-ordinate the traits scattered in the texts.

18. The word ἀσθένεια, used here as the equivalent of "weakness," could, if need be, apply to a passing ailment; but that is not the impression given by the text as a whole.

my temptation which was in my flesh ye despised not, nor rejected; but received me as an angel of God, even as Christ Jesus." For centuries commentators have wondered what infirmity, what illness, is at issue here, and have given, at times with the collaboration of medical men, the most divergent answers.[19] It would no doubt be the better part of wisdom to admit that the texts do not allow us to give any answer at all and only authorize us to believe that Paul was not well, that he was suffering from some painful chronic ailment. Most frequently this ailment is thought to have been *epilepsy*, the *sacred* illness of the Ancients,[20] but *leprosy* has also been mentioned,[21] as well as *purulent ophthalmia*, and even rheumatism and hemorrhoids; but all these guesses are based on indices too insubstantial for the weight they are made to carry.[22]

Several attacks of his "malady" have left their traces in the Epistles. Thus, when we read in 1 Thessalonians iii.1 that Paul, who was most anxious for news from Macedonia, sent Timothy to Thessalonica, but preferred "to be left at Athens alone," (καταλειφθῆναι ἐν Ἀθήναις μόνοι), it is permissible to believe that he was ill at the time; καταλειφθῆναι seems to indicate that he was, and this impression is confirmed by 1 Corinthians ii.3: "And I was with you in weakness, and in fear, and in much trembling." And 2 Corinthians i.8–11 mentions an attack the Apostle suffered in Asia, an attack so serious "that we were pressed out of measure, above strength, insomuch that we despaired even of life." It seems likely that these texts all refer to the same affliction. But what was it? We don't know, more's the pity, for it would in some respects make a difference in our exegesis if we knew that the Tarsiot was, for instance, an epileptic. It is certain that his health was poor, but we do not know why. We have said everything there is to say when we add to this very general statement the observation that Paul's very sharp reactions manifest in the Epistles gives us the impression that he was a nervous man who was easily exasperated.[23]

19. *CCX*, in *EB*, par. 32, n. 2; *CC*, p. 43; *CLXXXIX*, p. 218, n. 1; all commentaries *ad loc.* and *XVIII*, IV,[1] pp. 129f.

20. *CCXV*, p. 14; *CCX*, par. 32; *CLXXXIX*, p. 218; *CCLVIII*, p. 4.

21. Preuschen, "Paulus als Antichrist," *ZNTW*, IV (1901).

22. Creichton, "Eye (Diseases of the)," § 4, in *EB*, bases his comments on Gal. iv.12 and 15: "Ye would have plucked out your own eyes, and have given them to me." Feine, *XV*, p. 231, suggests the aftereffects of malaria, migraine, or some kind of neurosis. Imagination costs nothing.

23. There have been endeavors to extract from Paul himself general proof of his sickly appearance. In 1 Cor. xv.8, at the end of an enumeration of the appearances of the Lord, we read: "And last of all he was seen of me also, as of one born out of due time (ὡσπερεὶ τῷ ἐκτρώματι)." But no one would have attempted to read into this verse more than it contains had he taken the trouble to read the

This observation is, however, important, and it will be well to keep it in mind when we are called upon to explain the presence in some parts of the Epistles of ideas and doctrines not in accord with those contained in other passages. I have already said that in its entirety the Pauline corpus is composed of writings dictated by circumstances. I would add that their author seems to be a man who had few defenses against the influences of the various environments with which he was in contact. These influences can at times be observed in the employment of words and phrases which make one letter markedly different from another, and I believe that they are also to be found in divergent views that seem at first more or less surprising. The vehemence of Paul's pen would easily incline one to believe that his character was all of a piece and that his personality was as stable as it was original. The reality was, I think, quite different. An ever susceptible sensitivity, coupled with a highly emotional nature; an awareness of the concrete situation which instinctively accepts all the adaptations, and even all the transpositions, that seem useful; a mind with a few fixed ideas that are never more than provisionally definitive, but which, as long as they last, serve as principles; a mind, however, sufficiently discursive not to confine itself to its *dogmata*, as well as sufficiently realistic and supple to adapt itself to the conclusions of actual experience; finally, a passionate man, given to extremes and probably hard to live with—such I imagine was the psychological mold in which nature cast the Tarsiot.

---

one that follows: "For I am the least of the apostles (ὁ ἐλάχιστος τῶν ἀποστόλων), that am not meet to be called an apostle, because I persecuted the church of God." From which it follows that it was not Paul's intent in xv.8 to refer to his physical appearance, or state of health, but that he merely wished to make, in passing, a minor act of humility—a rather prideful act, in fact—by recalling his past error: that *he is only an abortive apostle*, born too late to know Jesus in the flesh, and it was only by a special grace that the Lord appeared to him.

5

PAUL BEFORE
HIS CONVERSION

I. Biographical Problems: Country, Family, Social Status

IN what we know of his Epistles, Paul does not name his place of birth; Acts tells us (ix.11; xxi.39; xxii.3) that it was Tarsus in Cilicia. This fact has sometimes been questioned,[1] and even rejected,[2]—wrongly, I think. There was no reason for the writer to invent it, and it must have been public knowledge in the area. Moreover, it is confirmed in the Judeo-Christian tradition represented by the Ebionites, the Essenes, and the Elkasaites.[3] In these hostile milieux Paul was known as "the Tarsiot" and opposed, to his disadvantage, to the Palestinian Apostles; it was even said that he came from paganism.[4] The pseudo-Clementine literature also testifies in favor of the observation of Acts.[5]

No text gives us any indication of the date of birth. The only two

---

1. *CXCV*, I, p. 12.
2. By those who follow a tradition related by St. Jerome (*De viris*, 5; Ad Philem., 23), which claimed that Paul was born at Gischala in Galilee.
3. *CCXLVIII*, p. 189. Cf. Epiph., *Haer.*, 30, 15–16 and 25.
4. Epiphanius, *Haer.*, 30, 16: "They claimed that he was Greek, son of a Greek mother and father." According to this version he became a proselyte and accepted circumcision for love of a daughter of the High Priest (τοῦ ἱερέως); then, offended by her father's rejection of him, he began to write against circumcision and against the Law. Cf. *XCII*, I, p. 49, n. 1.
5. *Hom.* 2 (Letter from Peter to James); *Recogn.*, 1, 70, 71, 73; 4, 35; *Hom.* 11, 35.

approximations that we have are very vague: in Acts vii.58, Paul, at the time of Stephen's torture, is described as a "young man" (νεανίας); and in Philemon 9—which must have been between 57 and 62—he calls himself an "old man" (πρεσβύτης). Unfortunately, the two designations were at the time used very loosely, and the date of Stephen's death is uncertain.[6] If one accepts 30 as the date of Jesus's death and 32 or 33 as the date of the Deacon's stoning, one could estimate that Paul at the time was probably between sixteen and twenty-five years of age. This would make him ten, twelve, or perhaps fifteen years younger than Jesus. For lack of a better one we shall be content with this supposition, which seems credible.

In Acts he is first called Saul; then, when he begins his apostolic career, he is named Paul (xiii.7). He seems to have used both names (Acts xiii.9: Σαῦλος ὁ καὶ Παῦλος), in accordance with a custom still observed by pious Jews: in a sense, one of the two is *sacred*, the other *profane*. Specifically, the sacred name is *Saul*, Σαῦλος, the Grecized name of the first Jewish king, who came from the tribe of Benjamin, as did the Apostle himself (Phil. iii.5); the profane name is *Paul*, Παῦλος, the Grecized form of the well-known Latin *Paulus*.[7] There have been lengthy discussions on the origin and meaning of this *Paulos*: they are of course unknown, and I will not go into them here.[8] It is probable that *Paul* is the Roman citizen's name of the Tarsiot. To judge from his letters, he bears it with pride in his relations with the Greco-Romans.[9] It has been pointed out that *Paulus* is a *cognomen*; we know neither the *nomen* nor the *praenomen* which accompanied it, provided the Apostle had the Roman *tria nomina*; but there were numerous exceptions to the rule in the Orient.[10] Paul must also have been attached to a Roman tribe and to have indicated it by adding its name to his;[11] but this is a detail that still escapes us and which, moreover, the Jewish Roman citizens commonly omitted.[12]

As for his family, we know only what he said about it, and he said very little. He emphasized the purity of his Jewish blood, probably because his adversaries contested it: "Circumcized the eighth day, of the stock of Israel, of the tribe of Benjamin, an Hebrew, of the Hebrews"

6. *CCV*, pp. 2f; *CCXV*, p. 10.
7. *CC*, pp. 63f. One can draw no conclusions about the person of Paul from this *Paulus=Petit* (small), which is not a nickname.
8. On the various hypotheses, cf. *CCX*, par. 4.
9. *CXXIX*, p. 133; *CCX*, *loc. cit.*
10. *CCXXXVIII*, pp. 208f.
11. *CCXXXVI*, p. 31; *CCXV*, p. 16.
12. *XXXVIII*, II, p. 235.

(Phil. iii.5).[13] This insistence on the term *Hebrew* has been reasonably interpreted as intended to mark the difference between a man who knew and fluently spoke Aramaic and a Hellenistic Jew who knew only Greek.[14] Such a detail would lead one to believe that Paul's family had not been long established at Tarsus.

However, his father was not a newcomer there, since he seems to have possessed the freedom of the city (Acts xxi.39) and the rank of Roman citizen (xxii.28). It is hardly probable that he could have acquired the latter privilege on Jewish soil.

In view of the tradition I have noted which considers Gischala in Galilee to have been Paul's birthplace, one should perhaps infer that his family was, or believed that it was, originally from that small city; this family may have fled from it in the year 4, when Varus repressed the uprising of John of Gamala in that country.[15] Hypotheses! We do not know how long the parents of the Apostle had been established at Tarsus. The large Tarsiot Jewish community was not new, and probably dated from the times of the Seleucids.[16]

In any case, it is more important to us to know the social status of these people; but on this point, as on so many others, we have only the hazardous deductions that we can draw from some of the details in Acts. The writer has Paul say, "I am a Jew, a citizen of Tarsus in Cilicia" (xxi.39); and when Paul claims his status as a Roman citizen in order to avoid flagellation, he affirms that he possesses it "by right of birth" (xxii.28). He derives this citizenship, as well as his freedom of the city at Tarsus, from his father. Such honors were not as a rule conferred on the common immigrant Jews; there is therefore reason to believe that we are not dealing here with people of base extraction and small estate.[17] One thinks rather of *petit bourgeois* or of well-stationed artisans, on the order, for instance, of tradesmen in such fabrics as were commercially important in Tarsus.[18] It would be an exaggeration to say, with Deiss-mann, that Paul came from "a background of illiterate manual laborers." [19] The Epistles in no way support this impression—and from where else could it come? We know that he learned a trade and lived by it in the

13. 2 Cor. xi.22: "Are they Hebrews? So am I."
14. *CXXIX*, p. 131; *CVIII*, p. 84.
15. *CC*, p. 61, n. 1; *CXXIX*, p. 131, n. 1.
16. On the controversial issue (which interests us only incidentally) of the acquisition of the right of the freedom of the city by the Jews of Tarsus, cf. *CCXXXVIII*, pp. 177, 180f.
17. *CXIV*, p. 114; *CCXV*, p. 9.
18. *CXCVI*, p. 133.
19. *CC*, p. 34.

course of his missionary wanderings (Acts xviii.3; 1 Cor. ix.12, 14); there is no reason to draw very firm conclusions from this fact. Paul's parents could have occupied a comfortable position and destined their son to become a Doctor of Law without, at the same time, neglecting to teach him a trade: such a precaution was customary, and practically a requirement, in the education of a rabbi.[20] It is not impossible that later, when this boy upon whom so many hopes had been founded had failed to fulfill them and had displeased his parents by taking another direction, they stopped supporting him, in which case he could have made very practical use of his worker's skills. Ramsay, who proposes this explanation of Paul's need to live by his hands, justly remarks [21] that it would give a most interesting meaning to the text of Philippians iii.8, where Paul says that all that he has lost for Christ Jesus his Lord were *ordures* (σκύβαλα). There would also seem to be an echo of the debates between the Apostle and his father in Colossians iii.21: "Fathers, provoke not your children to anger, lest they be discouraged." [22]

Ingenious, but overly pretentious, conjectures. We do not even know the name of this allegedly intractable father, and Paul's only known definite allusion to his family is in a passage of Acts xxiii.16, where we read that a son of the Apostle's sister comes to Jerusalem to warn him of the homicidal designs upon him of a handful of fanatical Jews. This nephew arrives at a very opportune moment, and I am not convinced that he was not born of the writer's imagination.[23] In any case, he returns to the shadows immediately after his unexpected arrival, having left us no useful information.

As for Paul's trade in question, we are not sure what it was: *skenopoios* = *tabernacularius* = *tentmaker*, what exactly does that mean? It has been interpreted arbitrarily as *tapestry-worker*; as *weaver of tent materials*, because Cilicia produced goat-hair tissues which were sought for the manufacture of tents; [24] as *sewer of tents*; and numerous equally uncertain suppositions. Had Paul worked continuously at this modest profession, it would have confined him to the lower classes and the jobbing workers. I doubt that that was his entire world before his conversion.

In any case, the true problem for us is that of his intellectual formation.

20. *CXXIX*, p. 135.
21. *CCXXXVI*, p. 34.
22. [Above transcription follows King James Version of Bible; literal translation of the French would be: "Fathers, do not mistreat your children, lest they lose heart." Tr.]
23. *CVIII*, p. 841.
24. *CCX*, par. 5; *XXXVIII*, II, p. 306.

II. Intellectual Formation

The only positive information we have about the place where Paul grew up and about his studies is in Acts; but I find this information inconsistent.[25]

In Acts xxii.3, in a discourse attributed to Paul himself, we read that he was born at Tarsus in Cilicia, but that he was "raised in this city" (at Jerusalem, where he was at the time) "at the feet of Gamaliel." [26] This famous master was the grandson of Hillel and directed the "moderate school" (*l'école modérée*) in the Holy City. It is impossible to prove definitively that the assertion in Acts is false; but for the following reasons I am convinced, with Loisy, that it is not true: the writer habitually invents circumstances needed to justify attitudes or reactions attributed by him to his characters but which, in reality, are much more in accord with his own intent than with the probabilities. It is disconcerting enough to find this affirmation in a discourse ascribed to Paul, that is, to find it in the composition of the writer of Acts. It is even more disconcerting to try to note the connection between this affirmation and various incidents of the book, all of which are suspected of being forgeries. Thus Acts vii.58 depicts the executioners of Stephen as leaving their mantles with the young Saul, who approves the torture (viii.1); but the fact is that the writer, wishing to persuade us that Paul began by being a ferocious persecutor of the name Jesus Christ, believed it proper to lead him to Jerusalem and to associate him, at least in intent, with the first crime committed against the Church. And he did so without taking into account the fact that he was refuted by Galatians i.22, where Paul himself states clearly that prior to his conversion he was "unknown by face in the communities of Judea." Again, in order to magnify the miracle which turns the malevolent passion of an ill-natured Jew towards the service of the Lord, the writer wishes to convince us that Paul was a remarkable person. To this end he endows him with the best of academic educations and consigns him to Gamaliel, because Gamaliel was a name and a guarantee; yet he does this without troubling to ascertain

25. Among the most recent critics, this is not the opinion of J. Weiss, *CXXIX*, p. 135, nor of Omodeo, *CCXXXII*, p. 105, n. 3, Bacon, *CXCIII*, p. 63, Goguel, *XVIII*, IV,[1] p. 146, or Lietzmann, *CIII*, p. 103. *Contra*: *XCVII*, IV, p. 279, and Montefiore, *CCXXVIII*.

26. [King James Version: "I am verily a man which am a Jew, born in Tarsus, a city in Cilicia, yet brought up in this city at the feet of Gamaliel . . ." Tr.]

whether what he says of Saul's intractable Pharisaism would not be more in conformity with the school of Shammai, the rigorist. Now, he has already made Gamaliel intervene once (v.34–39) by attributing to him a short conciliatory discourse in favor of the Apostles summoned before the Sanhedrin. Unfortunately, "this Doctor of Law honored by all the people" is rather maltreated by the pseudo-Luke: he has the latter recall the adventure of Theudas, a Messianic agitator who appeared about a dozen years after the time Gamaliel supposedly spoke, as well as the adventure of Judas the Galilean "in the days of the census," which he places *after* that of Theudas but which in fact antedates it by at least forty years.[27] These gross discrepancies prove, I think, that in this case the intervention of Gamaliel is imaginary. I am even more strongly inclined to believe that the same is true of the passage which concerns us,[28] since Gamaliel's name does not appear anywhere in the Epistles, where it would naturally be invoked when Paul emphasizes his fundamental Judaism. Since Paul himself admitted that he had persecuted the Church, [29] the author of Acts assumed that this persecution must have taken place at Jerusalem, and that is why he associated Paul with the torture of Stephen; hence he instantly aged the adolescent who could only look on and approve (viii.1) and made him, three verses later (viii.3), the principal leader of the tribulation imposed upon the adherents of Christ. Similarly, thinking it requisite for the Apostle to have received a basically excellent Jewish education, he believed that this could best be guaranteed by studies conducted at Jerusalem "at the feet of Gamaliel." Both here and there, one finds the same procedure and the same fiction; or so it seems.

I add [30] that if Paul was raised in Jerusalem, he must have been present at the Passion of Jesus. But in his letters he says nothing of what should have been for him the basic memory of his youth; and I believe that one can reasonably affirm that all that he says of the Master proves that he did not see him suffer or die. Finally, these same letters do not give the slightest impression of having been written by a Palestinian; nowhere do they reflect such an education as one presumably acquired under the direction of Gamaliel or of a Judean rabbi. Rather they reflect the spirit of a *Septuaginta-Jude*,[31] of a Jew of the Diaspora nourished on the *Septuagint* and fundamentally a stranger in the Palestinian world. If Paul

27. *CVIII*, pp. 246f.
28. *CVIII*, pp. 813f.
29. *Phil.* iii.6: κατὰ ζῆλος διώκων τὴν ἐκκλησίαν.
30. *CCX*, par. 5; *CXCVI*, p. 151.
31. *CC*, p. 63.

knew this world, if he came from it, how was it possible for him not to dream of winning it over after he had changed sides? And from where did he get the idea of immediately attacking the Diaspora? [32] Why should he at first have avoided Jerusalem and then only passed through the city, if not because he did not feel in harmony with the Judean milieu, did not feel at home there?

It seems to me most likely that Paul was raised at Tarsus. We should like to have positive assurance of this from some reliable witness; but at least the contents of all the Epistles favor this hypothesis. Furthermore, he lived at Tarsus before the beginning of the great missions (Acts ix.29–30); we believe that Tarsus is his city.

III. *Tarsus*

Today ancient Tarsus lies under a layer of six or seven meters of sediment collected by its river, the Cydnus; the modern city was constructed on this debris.[33] There has been no excavation; all our information comes from a collection of coins of uncertain meaning and a meager assemblage of inscriptions and texts.[34] We are often reduced to quite tenuous deductions and inductions; but what we do know is of profound interest.

Modern Tarsus is twenty kilometers from the sea, which has been pushed back by the alluvia of the Cydnus; in antiquity it was a maritime city, connected to its port Rhegma (a kilometer away) by the river, deeper at the time,[35] and accessible to large ships.[36] Located at the opening of the Cilician ports and of the Syrian channel, open to the maritime routes of the entire Mediterranean, the city had wide commercial and industrial activity; the merchants brought with them the ideas of their various countries. More particularly, Tarsus was a meeting point, a bridge between two worlds. Today, Tarsus is at the borders of the Turkish and Arab world; in those days it lay between the Asiatic

---

32. *CCXLVIII*, p. 191.

33. For bibliography, see *CXCVI; CCXXXVIII*, pp. 85–244; *CLVIII*, I, ch. vi, par. 3.

34. The most fully expounded are a passage of Strabo (d. 20?), ch. xiv of his *Geography*, and several discourses of Dion of Prusa who is called Chrysostom (30–117). Edition J. von Arnim, Berlin, 2 vols., 1893 and 1896. The principal types of coins are in E. Babelon, *Les Monnaies grecques et romaines* (Paris, 1901–26; Pt. II, plates, 1907–1916), Vol. II, nos. 575, 577, 579–82.

35. Dion Chrysostom, *Or.* 33, 1 (called *Tarsica prior*): . . . τοῦδε τοῦ Κύδνου ὅς δεξιώτατος ἀπάντων ποταμῶν καὶ κάλλιστος.

36. Plutarch, *Anton.*, 26, on the luxurious ascent of Cleopatra and of the triumvir to Tarsus.

Hellenistic world, which began behind the Taurus to the north, and the Semitic world, which extended behind the Amanus to the southeast.

At first sight, Tarsus had the appearance of a Greek city: the Seleucids had labored to Hellenize it, and, practically at the time of Paul's birth, the philosopher Athenodorus (around 10 B.C.), commissioned by Augustus, reorganized it by, in fact, placing it under the government of his university. Unfortunately, we know nothing of the functioning of this surprising rule. The base of the population probably consisted of a mixture of Ionians and Assyro-Persians; but the active element was represented by recently arrived immigrants of the Hellenistic epoch—Greeks and Jews. The pressure of the Orient influenced the whole. It is remarkable that about a century after Strabo had shown Tarsus as a Hellenic city Dion Chrysostom saw it as an Oriental city which had lost all of its Greek characteristics and to which he attributed only one virtue: the wholly Oriental rigor with which the women were veiled. Ramsay strongly admired the fact that at Tarsus the Greek spirit did not turn towards anti-Semitism,[37] and he saw the cause of this surprising phenomenon in the balance and harmony of the Hellenic and Oriental elements which the Tarsian cosmopolitanism had achieved. I see it rather in the predominance of the Semitic component: the population was fundamentally Oriental and the institutions of the city, under their Greek appearance, did not override this basic reality.

It seems to me that what we know of the religion of the city confirms my impression; Oriental divinities dominated it under Greek names; the Greek arrivals identified the Tarsian gods with their own as well as they could, but they did not essentially transform them.[38] In actuality, Tarsus was an Oriental city behind a Greek façade.

According to Strabo, however, Tarsus enjoyed the reputation of an intellectual city in the Greco-Roman world. It maintained the famous schools whose ensemble formed a sort of university. It is unfortunate that we cannot know the organization and the functioning of this large corpus;[39] we only assume that it flourished, since Strabo compared it with analogous institutions of Athens and of Alexandria, and praised the philosophic zeal of the Tarsiots. Because this university was the predominant influence in municipal affairs[40] since Athenodorus's reform of the *politeia* of Tarsus, the pursuits and concerns of its masters had a general importance for all of the inhabitants.

37. *CCXXXVIII*, pp. 88f.
38. *CCXXXVIII*, p. 139.
39. *CXCVI*, p. 113; *CCXXXVIII*, p. 231.
40. *CCXXXVIII*, p. 235.

Now, these masters seem to have been mostly philosophers, and Stoic philosophers. It is probable that the cycle of general studies was considered as preparatory to the acquisition of the doctrine of the Porch. This priority is not surprising. Stoicism was a product of the Greek Orient: [41] Zeno was born at Cyprus, Aratus and Athenodorus in Cilicia, as was also Chrysippus, whose father, Apollonius, was from Tarsus; also from Tarsus were Zeno, pupil of Chrysippus, and Antipater, whom Cicero ranks among the *principes dialecticorum*, and several other important figures. We know the thinking of Athenodorus and of his colleagues only from a few sentences in Plutarch and in Seneca; [42] but we are not so much interested in placing these men in the history of philosophy as in ascertaining the influence they may have had on Paul's mind.

Nothing leads me to believe that the young Jew frequented the university, or that he actually pursued the Greek studies; but the simple fact of being a citizen in the "philosophical" city must have drawn his attention to the basic themes, the *dogmata*, of the Stoics, and made him familiar with the most frequently used technical words. Without actually going to them, he could hear them, because they preached to the people; they proffered him the teaching of the *diatribe*, already defined by us.[43] It contained a small number of basic truths and essential formulas, presented to the audience from different points of view and urged upon their attention by ceaseless reiteration, so that they became permeated with them. The aim was to supply them with a faith and to impel them to a moral effort that would make them better and purer.[44]

But there was not only a philosophical life at Tarsus; there was also profound religious activity. Although our general knowledge of this activity is imperfect, we do know several very important aspects of it.

Two divinities, which, under various names, traverse the whole pagan history of Tarsus, dominated the variety of gods serving the city: one was supreme, somewhat passive, and placed well above those who adored him; the other was active and more accessible. The first, Baal Tars, was identified with Zeus by the Greeks; the second, Sandan, with Hercules.

The Lord of Tarsus (Baal Tars)[45] was an old Anatolian rural god,

41. *CXCVI*, p. 108.
42. *CXCVI*, p. 114.
43. Cf. above, pp. 136–37.
44. *CXXXVII*, p. 626.
45. *CCXXXVIII*, p. 139; *CXCVI*, p. 19.

protector and probably promoter of the earth's fertility.[46] During the Roman epoch he appeared in Greek dress, holding in his left hand a long scepter and in his right hand various objects: ears of grain, grapes, a Victory, an eagle. He had become a celestial king, master of the gods and of men.

Sandan,[47] according to Dion Chrysostom, was the ruler (ἀρχηγὸς) of Tarsus;[48] his name, in different forms, was fairly widespread in all of Asia Minor and has no intelligible meaning for us. We know neither the country of his origin[49] nor the source of his legend. The Hellenistic coins of Tarsus represent him in an Oriental manner: draped in a long talaric tunic and wearing a tiari, he stands on a winged and horned lion; he carries a sword at his side and a quiver passes under his left arm; in the raised right hand he holds a flower or a branch; in the left, a double-edged axe and sometimes also a crown. These symbolic attributes are easy to interpret, but it is only the branch, which signifies purification, that interests us specifically: for this god teaches the rites that efface sin and lead to purity. Various remarkable details appear on the coins of the Roman epoch.[50] The depiction of Sandan is in the main similar, except when his identification with Hercules presents him in the nude; but his lion stands on a platform decorated with garlands and the god is framed by a sort of pyramid which appears to be made of billets of wood; on the summit perches an eagle with outspread wings. Sometimes a rounded canopy, an arch of wood or of fabrics enhanced by seven florets (?), or perhaps an arch of foliage, bends over this pyramid and descends on each side, where two beardless figures in short tunics support it.

There are many hypotheses to explain this: fortunately the major ones are not irreconcilable. One view claims that the representation is of a processional machine used every year by the city in the festival of the god; another speaks of symbols directly related to the myths betokened in the festival. An allusion in Dion gives us a glimpse of this festival:[51] the principal ceremony consisted of lighting a stake erected for the occasion. I think that the god himself, represented by his image or by

---

46. He is on the bas-relief of Ivriz, on the north side of the Taurus; cf. Perrot and Chipiez, *Histoire de l'art dans l'Antiquité*, IV, p. 725; CXCVI, p. 21.

47. CXCVI, pp. 26f., cites ancient references to this god.

48. Dion Chrysostom, *Or.* pp. 33, 47.

49. CXCVI, pp. 33, 37f; on his probable relation with the Hittite god Teshup, see CLVIII, I, pp. 128f.

50. CCXXXVIII, p. 148.

51. *Or.* 33, 47.

some other substitute, was burned, as a sign of his ascension to heaven.[52] Dion tells us that it was Hercules; but we know that at Tarsus Hercules was Sandan, and it is possible that the characteristic feature of death at the stake engendered an assimilation that must certainly be very ancient, for Hercules was depicted on the coins of the city even prior to the fourth century.[53]

At first one is tempted to believe that the stake is derived from the legend of Hercules, from which it was borrowed by Sandan; but according to all appearances, the feature in question is secondary in the Greek legend of Hercules. In its most ancient form this legend does not include the stake, and it has for a long time been suspected that it is Oriental in origin.[54] If this is the case, Sandan's death was peculiar to him; it was, I repeat, his means of ascending to heaven. The eagle at the summit of the pyramid confirms this interpretation, for in ancient Oriental symbolism the bird signified an ascension; the cult of the Hellenistic sovereigns and the Roman apotheosis adopted it together with its meaning. The eagle was presumed to carry to the heavens the immortal principle —let us call it the soul—of the being whose perishable parts had just vanished in the fire.[55]

The arch probably represents the sky, and the seven florets are the seven planets. *Thus Sandan is a god who is presumed to die each year and ascend to heaven;* he must then be resurrected every year on earth. The various hypotheses—that he was a sun god, or a god of the year and of the originally lunar time, or a god of war and of victorious heroes —are not important to us. It is the annual renascence followed by an annual death by fire that concerns us, for this conception connects Sandan with the Babylonian Tammuz and the Syrian Adonis, whose death festival was celebrated in the summer (June–July) at the moment when the sun burned the vegetation, with the Phrygian Attis and the Egyptian Osiris. Thus, in the times of Augustus he became a god of vegetation and of fertility like these other gods, a god whose death and resurrection signified the annual withering and renewal of nature. This aspect of Sandan, in connecting him with the divinities I have just mentioned, favored the transpositions between him and them that it had become customary for them to accept.

It would be of great interest for us to know if the cult of Sandan

52. *CLVIII,* I, p. 126.
53. *CXCVI,* pp. 40f.
54. A. Maury, *Religions de la Grèce antique* (Paris, 1857–1859, 3 vols.), III, p. 152 and n. 7. Cf. Durrbach, "Hercules," *DA,* p. 106.
55. *CXCVI,* p. 32; *CLVIII,* I, p. 126.

at Tarsus constituted a *Mystery*, if his public festival marked the first stage towards initiation, or if it was accompanied by a partially developed Hermetism. Since we do not know this, we can at best propose only a hypothesis based on analogies.[56] In general, gods of vegetation who died and were resurrected brought a revelation to the initiated; the essential feature of this revelation was its being the means of permitting the *mystos* to become one with the god, in order to participate in the salvation which the god has won.[57] On the other hand, at the beginning of the first century Hercules was one of the *savior gods* (θεοὶ σωτῆρες),[58] whereas the coins of Tarsus do not apply this epithet of "Soter" to Sandan. Its absence does not constitute a decisive argument, since we do not have all the monetary species of the city; but at least it proves that the epithet in question was not commonly regarded as characteristic of the god.

Hence, we cannot affirm that at the time of Paul the Mysteries of Sandan existed at Tarsus, or that the periodic death and resurrection of the god contained salutary virtualities for those faithful to him. And yet it seems likely that such was the case, and that the *active* god played the role of a *savior* god, an efficacious intermediary between his worshippers and the supreme lord. For that matter, it would be important for us even if Sandan merely revealed to the young Paul the spectacle of the apotheosis of the dying god.

Of the other Tarsian divinities I will say only that there existed between them and Sandan a transposition of attributes and symbols which at first strongly marked the syncretistic tendencies of the city, and later proclaimed the growing predominance of Sandan.[59] There have been most divergent opinions concerning the date of Mithra's installation at Tarsus. However, it seems probable that this occurred at the time of the defeat of Mithridates,[60] for he was the god of the pirates whom Pompey destroyed in 67; but we know absolutely nothing of the importance which the Mysteries attached to his cult may have had in the city in the first century. We are just as ignorant about the cult of the other Oriental or Greek divinities with whom a Mysterious discipline is usually associated.

56. *CXCVI*, pp. 46f., which connects the festival Dion speaks of with that of the Syrian goddess described by Lucian; there are, unfortunately, many shaky suppositions in his construction.

57. Firm. Maternus, *De errore prof. rel.*, 22, 1; *CLIV*, p. 179: "das Heil der Mysten hängt an der Rettung des Gottes."

58. Dion Chrysostom, *De regno*, 1f.; *CXCVI*, pp. 50f.

59. *CXCVI*, pp. 58–61, 67f.

60. *CL*, p. 28. Cf. *CXCVI*, p. 77; *XCIII*, pp. 25, 73f; *CLXXXIX*, p. 181, n. 1; *CXLVIII*, p. 11; *CCXXXVIII*, p. 156.

We know of their existence in cities, such as Rhodes, which had business relations with Tarsus; but one can only conjecture that they were also installed in the Cilician metropolis, at least Demeter, Dionysus, and Triptolemus.[61]

In any case, it seems reasonable to believe that a crossroads city which entertained merchants worshipping Adonis, Attis, Tammuz, Melkarth, and Osiris, as well as initiates of Eleusis and of Samothrace, knew the principal mythic themes and basic assurances of the Mysteries of immortality, and did not escape their influence. Besides, it seems to me hardly contestable that there prevailed at Tarsus that spiritual disposition, that mode of envisaging religious and conceptual problems, which is called *mystic*, and whose country of origin was Syria.[62] We shall soon know to what extent this tendency influenced Paul's doctrine; it is noteworthy that, with an immediate and cogent grip, it seized and guided the thinking of many of his compatriots.

Finally, a *syncretism* rich in teachings had been growing in Tarsus for a long time, and it made possible the coexistence and amalgamation of divinities of such diverse origins. Every people who had passed through the country had left there something of its legends and its gods, from the Hittites to the Greeks. Ahura-Mazda and Baal Tars dwelt in propinquity to each other and to Zeus, as did Sandan to Hercules; and through transpositions and adaptations Zeus Semantikos, Zeus Karpodotes, Zeus Kalokagathos, Zeus Boreios, Zeus Heliopolites, Apollo, Helios, Mithra, and others had been installed in the midst of the two great Tarsian divinities.[63] And this fact provides another argument in favor of the existence of Mysteries at Tarsus, for syncretism nourishes Mysteries. Syncretism is also the authentic father of *universalism* in religion, because it tends to treat diverse organizations of belief and of cult as variable and fragmentary forms of an immutable Whole whose sovereign dominion extends over the entire Cosmos, containing and contained; and also because it is interested in the *individual per se* and apart from the social distinctions and categories to which the religions of the ancient City attached such great importance. Now, all religions concerned with the individual tend naturally to universalism, by the fact that they have freed themselves from the bonds of State or Nation; the universality of men is in fact nothing more than the sum total of individuals.

It is likely that Paul frequented Antioch. Here he found a culture

61. *CXCVI*, pp. 77f.
62. *CXCVI*, pp. 80f.
63. *CXCVI*, p. 15.

analogous to that of his country, the same religious spirit, the same tendencies and the same aspirations, realized by the same means. I find it no
more necessary to suppose, as has been done, that the young Saul studied
the Mysteries and strained his eyes deciphering the Hermetic writings,
than I found it necessary to assume that he regularly attended the university at Tarsus. It is enough to have listened to, and talked with, the
pagans for him to become familiar with the fundamental myths and
essential hopes which nourished their religious life and be cognizant of
the principal speculations which sustained it. These widespread notions
explain the influences which penetrated him without his knowledge; he
inhaled them without analyzing or perceiving them, and they enveloped
him throughout his life. Even when he assumed a defensive attitude
against them, the state of mind and conscience they had imbued in him
intermingled with his own spiritual nature.

It has been asked if all of Paul's syncretistic acquisitions were derived
by him from immediate personal influences, or if the Jews of Tarsus
were already so imbued with these tendencies that they transmitted their
essence to him, as if they were their own beliefs. I am in agreement with
the second alternative.

There was at Tarsus a considerable Jewish community,[64] of which a
portion at least had the freedom of the city and therefore held offices
there and participated in the various aspects of its municipal and public
life. That is, the community was not simply a closed and tolerated ghetto
marginal to the normal existence of the city. We would very much
like to examine closely the religion of these Jews; unfortunately, we are
unable to do so. I think that the substance and form of their beliefs
varied according to their social conditions and their culture. On the
whole, they must have welcomed the relaxing of legalistic rigor demanded
by their coexistence with the *goyim*, a relaxing that grew even more
flexible as in his daily life the Jew came into greater contact with cultivated and socially distinguished pagans. And some of these *Hebrews*
must have individually *syncretized* or collectively formed groups which
resembled the sects. At no point is the absence of documents more
trying. Paul knew several of these sects and he later regarded them as
powerful enemies. One glimpses them in Galatians iv.8–11 and even
more fully in Colossians ii.8f., where the Apostle combats them by
counterposing a doctrine which resembles theirs in spirit and in tendency,
if not in form and mythology. I have wondered if the words of Galatians

64. *XXXVIII*, I, p. 193, n. 2; *CCXXXVIII*, p. 173; *LX*, III,³ p. 17; III,⁴ p. 123,
n. 18; *VII*, pp. 74, 104f.

iv.12, "Be then as I am, for I too have been as you are, brethren," do not imply the admission of having formerly belonged to one of these sects, and I am still strongly tempted to believe it. If this was the case, the hypothesis that the syncretistic elements of his thinking were transmitted to the young Saul by his Jewish teachers would be fully verified. It remains infinitely likely, for it explains better than any other hypothesis the context and the working of the Apostle's mind, and the assimilation of ideas and basic impressions that he seems to have experienced before his conversion.

IV.　The Greek, the Jew, the Roman in Paul

It has been said that it is by effect rather than by chance that Tarsus gave birth to the Apostle of the Gentiles.[65] The city was predestined[66] to conceive and to form the man who was to reunite the Orient and the Occident under the banner of a religion, and recapitulate Alexander's campaign in an inverse direction. It is added[67] that it is logical for Paul to have come from one of the ancient centers of worldwide commerce; his country was for him a microcosm where, under his eyes and for his example, the forces active in the great Mediterranean world met and amalgamated. We should, however, be wary of deductions which, vouched for only by a certain appearance of logic, correspond in the end to no reality. Actually, one must go to the Epistles for true details on the intellectual formation of the Apostle; examination of them does more than engender uncertainty, for these writings are witness to the successive influences, besides those of his youth, undergone by their author; and here it seems to be no easier to analyze them than it is to apportion their components. Assuredly, Paul's culture was not so firmly grounded as to withstand the adventitious actions of the diverse milieux through which he passed. This is evident in the vocabulary changes of his letters.[68] To varying degrees three series of influences, or three personalities, merged in him: the Greek, the Jew, and the Roman.

a) *What Paul Received from Tarsus.* First and fundamentally his language. Even if this were all, as has been claimed,[69] it would still be

65. *CCXXXVIII*, p. 88; *CXIV*, p. 113.
66. *CXCVI*, p. 4.
67. *CC*, p. 23.
68. See, for example, the number of characteristic *hapax* which runs through Colossians, as for instance: αἷμα τοῦ σταυροῦ, αὔξησις τοῦ Θεοῦ, δόξα τοῦ μυστηρίου, ἐλπὶς τῆς δόξης, etc.
69. *CCLIII*, p. 7.

a great deal, for the knowledge of Greek not only furnished him with an incomparable means of action, but also endowed him with something of the spirit and soul of the wandering Hellenism. Words convey ideas, and such terms as *God, Spirit, Lord, reason, soul, conscience* denote so many ways open to the concepts attached to them in Greek thought and to the types of reasoning, discussion, demonstration, the rhetoric which is as a rule inherent in the language of every people.

Formerly it was claimed that Paul's language was simply bad Greek, full of Aramaisms [70] and alien to the true spirit of the Hellenic idiom. This is no longer said, not since close study of the ordinary [Greek] speech revealed reliable bases of comparison and a precise analysis of the Pauline vocabulary permitted an objective appraisal of its content.[71] In it were found many expressions derived from the classic language, an equal number of words of the *koine* used by Polybius, Diodorus of Sicily, and Epictetus, and later, a large number of vocables and popular phrasings found in the papyri, familiar inscriptions, and ostraca. Finally, there is a small group of terms whose usage is thought to have a meaning different from that encountered elsewhere, or for which correspondences have not yet been found in other texts. In sum, Paul's language is a common Greek, resembling, for example, that of Epictetus, but containing more popular, or even coarse, touches. The syntax confirms the indices of the vocabulary.

This language does not reflect a true literary education. When Paul is not transported by an idea, he writes very badly. His propositions are not linked; instead, they are aligned in parallel construction by interminable strings of καί ... καί (both ... and) and sustained, for better or for worse, by ponderous colonnades of participles. The sentences are endless, laborious, crude, and give the impression of constricting and retarding the thought. Even though the writer employs some elementary rhetorical devices resembling those of the diatribe, from which they are probably derived, he is not a master of the art of composition.[72] He succeeds in irresistibly gripping his reader, but this élan emanates from his ardent desire to convince and from his impetuous character, rather than from his craft; the same is true of his highly original stylistic contrivances, which may be said to have made the Greek tongue resound in new tonalities.[73]

70. *LV*, p. 166. On the discussions and divergences relative to this problem, cf. *CCXLVIII*, pp. 193f., 265f., and *XVIII*, IV,[1] pp. 158f.

71. Th. Naegeli, *Der Wortschatz des Apostels Paulus*, Basel, 1904–05.

72. Ed. Norden, *Die antike Kunst-Prosa*, Leipzig, 1898, pp. 492f. (2nd ed., 1909).

73. *CXC*, p. 358; *CCLIII*, p. 7.

The scholars are not in agreement concerning Paul's Greek education. Some hold that he did not go beyond primary school;[74] they emphasize the difference between his style of writing and that, for example, of Philo. Others believe it impossible for him to have gone no further;[75] a rhetorician, they say, influenced his formation and he was sufficiently familiar with the modalities of the Greek mind for "all aspects of Hellenism" to leave an imprint on his style.[76] At any rate, it seems certain that he remained ignorant of the highest Greek culture and thought ill of it.[77] It is useless to base a supposition that he was a man of letters on 1 Corinthians xv.33, which cites a sentence from Menander (Fragment 211: "Bad company ruins good morals" (RSV); the whole corpus of the Epistles seems strongly to prove the contrary.[78] How many verses of La Fontaine, for example, which have become proverbial, are cited today by people who do not know whence they come! Remembering a sentence from Menander which expresses only a banality proves nothing. Incontestably, true rhetorical "tricks," such as antitheses, resonant words, verbal harmonies, etc., are employed in many passages of the Epistles;[79] but these do not go very deep, even if one assumes that they were borrowed from scholastic devices, although they could just as well derive from the habitual banalities that had for a long time been used by the Jewish teachers of the Diaspora.

It is perhaps a little too harsh to say that Paul's "literary knowledge hardly goes beyond the Scriptures (that is, the Septuagint), which is probably the only book he ever studied,"[80] but the word "hardly" leaves a small margin: let us put in that margin Enoch, Wisdom, and several other modest manuals. However, I would not go so far as to think, with Toussaint, that he may have read Aratus or Cleanthes.[81] It should be remembered that many of the various Greek acquisitions were already

74. CXIV, pp. 113f.; CCX, par. 5.
75. CXXIX, p. 133.
76. CCXLVIII, p. 269.
77. CLXXXIX, p. 244.
78. CLXXXVIII, p. 356; CCXV, p. 17.
79. Cf. Rom. i.29: μεστοὺς φθόνου φόνου; i.32: ἀσυνέτους ἀσυνθέτους; 2 Cor. ix.8, marivaudage on πᾶς: δυνατεῖ δὲ ὁ θεὸς πᾶσαν χάριν περισσεῦσαι εἰς ὑμᾶς, ἵνα ἐν παντὶ πάντοτε πᾶσαν αὐτάρκειαν ἔχοντες ... κ.τ.λ. Analogous examples are fairly frequent. Cf. list in CXC, p. 355.
80. CLXX, p. 322.
81. Let us remember that the famous "Some of your poets have said: we are of his race"(τοῦ [Διὸς] γὰρ καὶ γένος ἐσμέν), ascribed to Aratus, Phaenom. 5 and to Cleanthes, Hymn to Zeus 4, is reputed to have been cited by Paul only by Acts xvii.28. And "The Cretans are always liars, evil beasts, slow bellies," is to be found only in Titus, i.12.

used in the Jewish Apocrypha, where Paul could have gone in all confidence to look for them.

I would say the same thing of the Stoic contaminations evident in the Epistles; they remain superficial and imply no direct contact with the philosophical writings. The influence of the atmosphere created at Tarsus by the *preaching* of Athenodorus and his colleagues is a satisfactory explanation of their origin, especially if one adds to it the always possible influence of Jewish syncretism.[82] I do not believe that Paul as a Jew felt more sympathy for the "wisdom of this century" than did Paul as a Christian. Qualms would no doubt have stopped him from even starting such study; for the same reason it appears to me equally improbable that he would ever have opened a Hermetic book or become deliberately interested in a Mystery.[83] Certain passages of the Epistles remain unintelligible to us if we do not compare them with Hermetic texts.[84] However, I believe that this circumstance proves nothing more than an environmental action unconsciously received, and perhaps the penetration of some primary and characteristic images of the Hellenistic religiosity in the Judaism from which Paul came.

It is certainly inexact to see in Paul simply a Jew who spoke Greek and read the Septuagint;[85] he carries the stamp of more profound Hellenistic influences, whether he experienced them directly or not.

The very fact that he came from the Hellenized Diaspora had one important consequence: In comparison to strict legalism, Paul was very open-minded.[86] Moreover, it is highly interesting that he was not intellectually attracted by the Greek culture, for if he had been so attracted, the Christian hope would not in all likelihood have conquered him and he would merely have been another Philo. Comparison between the Tarsiot and the Alexandrian seems to me particularly instructive.[87] They were contemporaries; both came from the Diaspora; both were born in large

82. *CXIV*, p. 115; Loisy, *RHLR*, Sept.–Oct. 1913, p. 489. For a detailed study of the question, see *CXCVI*, pp. 115–28, 168.

83. *CLXX*, p. 323; *contra*: *CLXXVIII*, pp. 59, 209.

84. Examples: Col. i.17: καὶ αὐτός ἐστιν πρὸ πάντων, καὶ τὰ πάντα ἐν αὐτῷ συνέστηκεν ("And he is before all and in him all subsists"). Cf. Poimandres, 5, 10: πάντα δὲ ἐν σοί, πάντα ἀπὸ σοῦ ("All is in you, all comes from you"). Col. i.19: "For it pleased the Father that in him should all fullness dwell." Cf. Poimandres, 12, 15, where the πλήρωμα is God. The central idea expressed in the entire passage of Col. i.15–23, i.e., that the Cosmos is potentially included in Christ, is found in Poimandres 8, 9 and 10, 14, where the Cosmos is presented as the Son of God and engenderer of creation. Besides, in Philo, the *Cosmos noetos* is the *Logos*.

85. *CXXII*, p. 104; *CCXXXIX*, pp. 28f.

86. *CXXIX*, p. 132. Cf. *LXXX*, ch. ii.

87. *CC*, pp. 76f.

cosmopolitan cities; both nourished by the Septuagint; both capable of mystico-ecstatic experiences; and both alike in many particulars. And yet, how different they are! As different, if you like, as an Erasmus and a Luther: Philo writes and Paul speaks; the works of Philo are literary; Paul's stress action, and when we read in Galatians vi.11. "Ye see how large a letter I have written unto you with mine own hand," we are inclined to believe that it was difficult for him to write at length; ordinarily he probably dictated his letters, perhaps without interrupting his manual work.[88] Philo is a philosopher and an intellectual: Paul scorns philosophy and intellectualism; Philo is a seeker who expects everything of reflection and ends with a theologian's system: Paul is a prophet and herald of a revelation; it is only in a manner of speaking that a theology is attributed to him. In one sense, Philo marks an ending, a conclusion: Paul represents a beginning, an inauguration; finally, Paul might have known Philo by name: Philo certainly knew nothing of Paul.

As one first examines the texts, it is evident that the Tarsiot is the more Jewish of the two; when closer study reveals the real syncretism of the Epistles, one perceives that he uses *practical* presentations and not speculation. Paul thinks only in order to act, or rather, thinks only in acting, as a function of his action; Philo speculates with an intention whose aim is determined in advance: to reconcile and harmonize two cultures to which he was equally attached and both of which he succeeded in falsifying. The work with which Paul was concerned has been more decisive and fertile; but it was determined by the workings of sensibility, a profound sense of reality, which owed nothing to literature or to pure thought.

b) *Paul's Pharisaism.* Modern Jewish scholars refuse[89] to see in the renegade a member of the Orthodoxy, a true Pharisee, an authentic *rabbi*; and they are right. However, even without fully accepting the assurances of Acts (xxii.3) and of Paul himself (Phil. iii.5), which depict him as a Pharisee and an irreproachable legalist before his conversion, we must admit that the Epistles rather strongly support the hypothesis that he came from a truly Jewish family, that he received an approximately rabbinical education, and that he knew something of the Pharisaic spirit.[90] Assuredly, his Christian vocation meant for him a break with his Jewish past, and some maintain that, when writing some twenty years later, he even became incapable of understanding and appreciating the Pharisaism

88. *CC*, pp. 36f.
89. *CCXXVIII*.
90. *CCVII*, p. 371, which emphasizes this a little too strongly, in my opinion. In contrast: *CCXLVIII*, pp. 207f.

he had cast off.[91] However, it seems reasonable to say that "without his Jewish past, his religious genius would be incomprehensible" (Wendland).

His mind always manifests itself in Jewish and even Pharisaic guises: he is a subtle debater and caviller, skilled in polemic, harsh and tenacious. He combats the Law by the very procedures it had formerly instilled in him,[92] and his ingenious and arbitrary exegesis reflects his school. It is not simply a question of form: his dialectic, if I may say so, rests on a foundation of rabbinical concepts concerning human nature, sin, the relation of sin and death, and the like. Similarly, the Jew in him speaks through his theory of the Torah, his presentation of Satan and his demons, his apocalyptic usages, the aspects of his piety, the nature of his morals, and the role he assigns to history.[93]

We must, however, be careful not to exaggerate. Paul bases his Jewish piety on the Septuagint; at least in his letters, he adjudges the Book through the Septuagint,[94] and that Greek Bible had an obvious influence on his religious and moral vocabulary. This alone is enough to persuade us that the Tarsiot did not have a very advanced Jewish education. A Jew? Certainly; but a Jew brought up in the spirit of the Diaspora, which was already largely contaminated by Hellenism.

When he comes into contact with pure Palestinians, even if they are Christians, there is mutual misunderstanding and lack of comprehension; this also is significant. My overall impression of his Jewish culture is ultimately the same as that which seems to me to stand out in the study of his Greek culture: Paul's rabbinism is superficial and did not even inculcate him with that respect for the *sacred science* which was its very reason for being. One might say that he sees the true rabbis, the pure Pharisees, only through a prism which deforms them; and it would not surprise me to learn that this was, in fact, the way in which one would view them from the perspective of a Jewish school in Tarsus, an average school of the sort that Paul must have frequented. When his studies were finished, he perfected himself in the synagogue discourses. On the whole he is, within the Jewish context, *more a man of the synagogue than a man of the school.*

c) *The Roman Citizen.* I do not believe there can be any legitimate doubt that Paul was a Roman citizen; several important consequences spring from this distinction.

91. J. Weill, "L'Essence du pharisaisme," *REJ*, Jan. 1913, p. 14.
92. Rom. ix.11. Cf. *CC*, pp. 67f, 73.
93. *CCXV*, p. 31.
94. It has been conjectured that he might have used a text revised by a Jew. It is possible. Cf. *CC*, p. 71.

First of all, and *ipso facto*, he was a free man, socially superior to the slaves and proletariat who peopled the communities.[95] Secondly, his view of the Empire was wholly different from that of a Palestinian Jew, who saw the Roman domination as a passing but insupportable trial imposed upon the chosen people. For Paul the Empire was a truly great power, an organization willed by God and not an obstacle to the installation of the Kingdom. Reread the good counsels of loyalty in Romans xiii.[96] Next, he did not manifest the resentful attitude of a disinherited proletarian towards the established order. In the provincial milieu where he lived, his distinction of citizenship put him, before the law and public opinion, within the ranks of a sort of aristocracy.[97] He had the interests of a Roman citizen: the Roman world—the Roman concept of οἰκουμένη—had for him a meaning that must have contributed to determining in his mind the concept of the unity of the human race, whose corollary was the universalism of the religion of the Lord Jesus Christ.[98]

Conclusion

Thus numerous and quite diverse elements entered into the spiritual and intellectual formation of Paul; none of them is unimportant. Their very variety left open in him a faculty of adaptation which played an important role in the orientation of his activity, as it did in the enriching of his spirit, to the point of creating a disturbing complexity of contrasts. This role was decisive, for through it he became a Christian, through it collaborated so energetically in transposing the Galilean hope into a true religion.

In the analysis of the Tarsiot's personality it is naturally fitting to take note of the imponderable elements: the original religious temperament and unique dispositions that were part of his *genius* and were not, no more then than today, the lot of an ordinary man. But neither was the combination of influences which fashioned his mind banal. Without it, his aptitude for grasping situations so ostensibly singular and acting in conformity with his experience would remain inexplicable. A pure Jew (supposing that he would at any time have dared to venture into the midst of such intricacies, which is hardly conceivable) would in similar

95. *CC*, pp. 36f.
96. *CLXXXIX*, p. 243.
97. *CCXXXVI*, p. 30; *CXXIX*, p. 132.
98. *CLXXXIX*, p. 244.

circumstances inevitably have been lost because the whole seemed unintelligible. Paul's horizon extended to the very limits of the Greco-Roman world and the Apostle perceived himself, successively, as being a Jew unto the Jews, a Greek unto the Greeks, and a Roman unto the Romans (cf. 1 Cor. ix.19f) as his activity, or at least his designs, transferred from one milieu into another.

His instinct and taste for action seem to us the most striking of all his talents. Paul's astonishing "virtuosity of the inner sense," [99] his profound mysticism, could cast him into the desert; but far from prevailing over his need to act, these *charismata* exalted and nourished him, and his Christian vocation drove him to ardent propaganda and struggle without rest. Nothing discouraged his rugged sowing.

I willingly believe that the primary formation of his childhood and youth was, in *intention*, completely Jewish; but he came neither from the same social background, nor from the same Jewish milieu, nor, properly speaking, from the same Judaism as Jesus. And between the spirit of the *anavim* of Israel and that of the Jews of Tarsus a whole world of impressions, perceptions, ideas, aspirations, and tendencies had arisen, a world that turned towards syncretism the legalistic exclusivism which the ancestors of these immigrants had undoubtedly brought from their country of origin.

This syncretism is the primary component of Paul's education. It prepared him for absorption of the influence of Helleno-Oriental mysticism and the salvationism of the Mysteries, which continued to surround and to overtake him in various forms throughout his life.

This is why, if one epitomizes by the name of Tarsus all the extra-Jewish influences exerted on Paul, it is correct to say that it was not simply by chance that in this city was born a man who saw his vocation in the evangelization of the Gentiles, as a result of which *Paulinism* was born.

99. *CCLIII*, p. 8.

6

PAUL'S CONVERSION [1]

I. The Problem

AUL'S conversion to the Christian faith poses a delicate problem of religious psychology; it would be an exaggeration to say that it has been perfectly resolved at the end of the innumerable studies and debates it has provoked.[2] According to the hero himself, it was the simplest event imaginable: one day the irresistible grace of God moved him and from persecutor of the Church that he had been he was transformed into an apostle of the Truth by the will of the Lord Jesus. He had no choice (Gal. i.12–17); he was seized by Christ (Phil. iii.12) and belonged to him: "For though I preach the gospel," he states (1 Cor. xi.16), "I have nothing to glory of: for necessity is laid upon me; yea, woe is unto me, if I preach not the gospel!" Viewing the event as a miraculous and sudden transformation, he was not conscious of the mysterious preparation which made it possible, and he does not help us to divine that preparation. Acts is of no greater help; for this text too the conversion is a miracle that happened on the road to

1. [This chapter was published in the *Revue historique*, CLXXXII (1938), 7–23. M. B.]

2. For bibliography, see *VXIII, IV*,[1] p. 195; *LXXXIII*, p. 495. B. W. Robinson, "Influences Leading towards the Conversion of Paul," *XVII*, p. 108; *CXXIV*, pp. 34–45; interesting especially for the relations he establishes between Acts (ix.22f., esp.) and the more or less analogous cases we know from ancient texts.

Damascus (ix.1–9; xxii.1–16; xxvi.4–20). And the variants tolerated by the writer in his three successive versions prove that he was more interested in exemplifying the hagiographic theme of vocation by irresistible conversion than in analyzing the basic phenomenon and giving some explanation of it. He did not even pose the question. We are therefore reduced to basing our reasoning on a few interpretive hypotheses, which is why the exegetes find it so difficult to agree.

We do not gain much by declaring that we are dealing here with an abrupt conversion of impressions dimly acquired by Paul's subconscious. But from where did these impressions come? What was their nature? And what action had blocked them to produce the effect by which the spiritual life of the Tarsiot seems to have been overturned? It is easier to ask these questions than to answer them, and one can't blame Alfred Loisy for writing: "The inner workings which culminated in his [Paul's] conversion can be grasped neither in the Epistles nor in the Acts."

II. *The Period of Unconscious Preparation*

It would be of great advantage to us to know precisely what the relations were between Paul and Jesus's disciples before the crisis we wish to explain; but we are far from this ideal.

It has been asked if Paul knew, or at least saw, Jesus. If he was present at Stephen's martyrdom, especially if he studied at the feet of Gamaliel, it would be likely that he lived in Jerusalem at the time of the Passion; but I repeat that I do not find credible the allegations of Acts concerning either the first of these points (vii.58) or the second (xxii.3). It seems obvious to me that nothing in the overall impression obtained from close study of the Epistles suggests that their author had the occasion, even in passing, to see the Lord. Had he had such an occasion, he could not have remained so completely indifferent to the details of Jesus's human life, nor would he have attached so little value to the historical prerogative of the immediate disciples (Gal. i.15–17). There exists however a text that has been debated at length and which seems to a number of critics [3] to testify against what I believe to be the truth: "*Though we have known Christ after the flesh, yet now henceforth* (ἀλλά)

3. For example, Keim, Sabatier, Wabnitz, Clemen, J. Weiss, Moulton, etc.; *contra:* Renan, Wellhausen, Jülicher, Brückner, Feine, Deissmann, etc. Cf. *XVIII, IV,*[1] p. 177, n. 2; *CCXI, ad loc.; CCLIV, ad. loc.; CCXLV,* pp. 11f and *LXXXII,* pp. 100f. Practically, one can oppose *CXXIX,* p. 137 and *CCLI,* pp. 16f. to *CC,* p. 83, n. 2.

know we him no more" (2 Cor. v.16). Note that this declaration is inserted in a reasoning which runs as follows: *The flesh no longer counts for me; I no longer know anyone after the flesh; if I had so known the Christ himself, thus I should no longer know him.* It is quite likely that the controversial verse is outside the realm of facts. But whether Paul *saw* Jesus or not, he certainly did not *know* him; and if he received from the spectacle of the Passion an impression destined to be of service to him,[4] he did not realize it immediately and it remained in the depths of his subconscious, even more inaccessible to us than it was to him.

The most reliable texts present the first meeting of the future apostle and the disciples as a violent conflict: "I am not worthy to be called an apostle, because I persecuted the Church of God" (1 Cor. xv.9); "For you have heard of my conduct in time past in the Jews' religion, how that beyond measure I persecuted the Church of God, and wasted it" (Gal. i.13). But what exactly did he do? We are not sure, and get the impression that the bewailing of his error tends to enlarge it. Only in a discourse ascribed to him in Acts (xxii.4) does he give specific details: "And I persecuted this sect (ταύτην τὴν ὁδόν) unto death, binding and delivering into prisons both men and women, as the high priest doth bear me witness, and all the estate of the elders." Speaking in his own name, the author of Acts has already said: "As for Saul, he made havoc of the Church, entering into every house, and haling men and women committed them to prison" (viii.3).

Obviously the two passages are closely related, and xxii.4 is derived from viii.3. As the latter is woven out of enormous improbabilities,[5] the pseudo-precisions collapse when one tries to grasp them. The entire conclusion of the story of Stephen (vii.58–viii.3) is incoherent and it is difficult to believe that the *young man* (νεανίας) who reputedly guarded the clothes of the Deacon's executioners (vii.58) was so quickly transformed into the animator and omnipotent agent (viii.3)—by virtue of what authority?—of a persecution which ravages and disperses the community while respecting the Apostles (viii.1). In his desire to aggrandize Paul's character and to contrive a striking contrast between Persecutor and Convert, the writer surpassed himself. He perseveres to the point of being ridiculous in his exaggeration and inconsistency,[6] up to the moment when he shows us (ix.1–2) Saul "still breathing menace and slaughter against the disciples of the Lord," and going to the High

---

4. *CCXV*, p. 21.
5. *CVIII*, pp. 357, 816; *XVIII*, III, pp. 195f.
6. *CVIII*, pp. 387f; Heitmüller, "Das Problem Paulus und Jesus," *ZNTW*, IV (1912), 328; *IX*, p. 92.

Priest to request the mission of pursuing the Disciples even into the synagogues of Damascus in order to lead them back in chains to Jerusalem.

Apparently the writer dramatized the very simple confession of Galatians i.13 that I have just recalled, calling on his imagination to supply all the details.[7] With regard particularly to the alleged commission bestowed on the young fanatic by the High Priest, there is every reason to believe that it conforms to no juridical possibility, for the High Priest himself did not possess the right which he allegedly delegated.[8] But since it was incumbent for the writer to lead Paul to Damascus, he must have found it very interesting to have him proceed to that city for a purpose that would enhance the marvel that we were going to be told about. (ix.3f).

The most divergent opinions and the most crushing arguments have been advanced to support the historicity of the episodes in question. It is best to leave all subjective assurances alone and to hold on only to what Paul himself told us, without seeking to know what he did not tell us. He admits that initially he inflicted as much harm on the Christians as he could. We do not know in what manner he was able to exercise his ill will; but we envision tribulations similar to those he himself suffered in the synagogues in the course of his missionary journeys: insults and blows which stopped his preaching.[9] In view of his known temperament, it is unlikely that he would have listened quietly to the Nazarene propagandists proclaiming their hope and expounding their affirmations; both were dangerous blasphemies for the good Jew he believed himself to be (Phil. iii.5f).[10] We can very well imagine him inveighing furiously against the intolerable innovators, throwing himself upon them, urging the bystanders to abuse them. "It would be surprising," as Loisy justly remarks, [11] "if the Christianity of James, Peter, and John would have seemed to him to be so subversive of Judaism. But it was not this Christianity that he first encountered." It was the Hellenizing Christianity.

7. His two characteristic words—διωγμός or *persecution* (viii.1) and ὁ πορθήσας or *he who destroys*—are borrowed from this text of Gal. i.13: ἐδίωκον τὴν ἐκκλησίαν τοῦ Θεοῦ καὶ ἐπόρθουν αὐτήν.

8. *CVIII*, p. 390. Cf. Juster, *XXXVIII*, II, p. 145 and n., on the correct scope of the texts and facts that have been invoked to justify the author of Acts; none works; *LX*, II, pp. 187, 206. *Contra: CXIX*, p. 55, and *CXXIX*, p. 135, who are inclined to concede to the Sanhedrin a competence virtually accepted by the Romans, in cases of disputes concerning one's way of life. In itself, this concession does not lead very far in this case.

9. 2 Cor. xi.23–25.

10. *CCVII*, p. 16; *CXXIX*, p. 135; *CC*, p. 77.

11. *CLXX*, p. 307.

Where then did he encounter it? Probably in the synagogues peopled with Hellenists, where the boldness of the adherents of the Messiah Jesus could be more insistent than that of the pure-blooded Judeans. But despite assertions to the contrary,[12] I do not believe that this tumultuous encounter took place at Jerusalem. My disbelief is based on two main considerations. The first is the fact that in Galatians i.17 Paul writes that immediately after his conversion he did not go up (οὐδὲ ἀνῆλθον) to Jerusalem, whereas if had come down from the City, expressly led by God on the road to Damascus to receive the great revelation, he would have written, I think, *I did not go up again* or *I did not come back*; the second, the fact that in Galatians i.22 he states that he was "unknown by face to the churches of Judea which were in Christ," a statement that ill accords with the copious manifestations of hostility he allegedly conducted against the members of these communities three years earlier (i.18).[13] Moreover, it seems likely that had he vented his rage against the [Christian] community of the Holy City, he would have felt himself to be responsible for reparations to that community and would have served it instead of consecrating himself to the Gentiles, as he did. Putting aside Jerusalem, Damascus too has been suggested, and it could just as well have been Antioch; let us prudently say that the question involves one, or several, of the communities installed on Greek land by the Hellenists after their dispersion (Acts xi.19).

The interest and importance of Saul's campaign against the brethren resides in the fact that it put him in contact with them, compelled him to hear Jesus spoken of by those who believed in him and to learn from them the reasons on which they based their faith. He could judge the faith absurd and its justifications weak at the same time that two vague and unconscious currents were already being engendered in him: first, a rapprochement between the revolting affirmations of the Galilean heretics and the equally detestable assertions of the pagan syncretists of Tarsus; then, a mysterious adaptation of the certitudes of these enthusiasts to the transpositions that pure Judaism had undergone in the religious consciousness of the Jew of the Diaspora, which he was himself. The "light" came to him in an abrupt consciousness of the spiritual reality engendered by these two profound phenomena.[14]

Paul entered what he calls "the Church of God" as one entered a

12. *CXXIX*, p. 136; *CXIV*, p. 119.
13. The neutralization of this text attempted by J. Weiss, who wishes to understand it as *unknown as a Christian*, is rather ridicuous (*CXXIX*, p. 136, n. 1).
14. *CVIII*, p. 399, and *CLXX*, ch. x; *XVIII*, IV,[1] pp. 195f; *LXXXIII*, ch. xxi, is especially suggestive.

Mystery religion, not as a calculated effect or a reasoned conclusion, but by an irresistible impulsion: [15] he acted in conformity with a command given him by the Lord Jesus. Thus did the hero of Apuleius, Lucius, favored by a vision of Isis, conform in haste to the commands he received from the ever-triumphant goddess (*invicta*).[16] "Among the spiritual qualities one must attribute to Paul and to the great initiates of the Christian faith in the heroic period of its foundation, first rank should be accorded to the singular aptitude to appropriate the ideas which they combatted" (Loisy). True; but the observation can be enlarged. On the plane of religion, extreme sentiments are apparently capable of being reversed with an astonishing facility in men whose conduct is completely ruled by emotions and the impulses of the heart. The history of contemporary mysticism offers curious examples of this reversal, which illuminate the case of the Tarsiot. I shall confine myself to two particularly striking instances: that of Sadhu Sungar Singh and that of the Jew Ratisbonne.[17]

The "Sadhu," or the "Saint," was born in 1889 in the religion of the Sikhs, a Hindu sect influenced by Islam which dates from the end of the fifteenth century. He was passionately devoted to the sect and when he came in contact with Christianity in the school of a Presbyterian mission he conceived a fierce hatred of the foreign religion which sought to sap his own beliefs. When a Bible fell into his hands he tore it to bits; he pursued the missionaries with insults, threw stones or dung at them, and planned to write a revengeful book against them and their faith. Yet he could not abstain from reading the Christian Scriptures he hated and found in them ideas that seduced him, formulas that enchanted him, because they responded to his own aspirations, which tended towards peace and. joy of the soul. However, he was so little conscious of his inner workings that he once more concluded that since Christ could not save himself, he could not save anyone; he thought to assure this certitude by publicly burning his Bible on December 16, 1904. The day after this *auto-da-fé*, when he had reached the depths of despair and was ready to commit suicide, he cast a last lost cry to God. A great light suddenly dazzled him and a voice said:"Why do you persecute me? Reflect that I gave my life for you on the Cross." *And he*

15. *CLXXVIII*, pp. 25, 95.

16. *Metamorphoses* XI, 7. Ananias's revelation (Acts ix.10–18), which prepares him to receive Paul after the miracle, is similar to the one in which the High Priest of Isis is given instructions corresponding to the commands communicated to Lucius (*ibid.* XI, 13).

17. For details and bibliography, cf. *LXXXIII*, pp. 407, 413.

saw the Crucified One. That did it, he became a Christian. Assuredly, the history of Paul's conversion, which he knew, determined the form of his own crisis; but the striking feature is the parallelism of the two emotional evolutions throughout the two similar actions, the striking similarity in both cases of the modalities and of the psychological mechanism of this reversal of faith.

The conversion of Maria Alphonse Ratisbonne, an Alsatian Jew born in 1814, is just as instructive. He was far from being a zealot, but he was devoted enough to Judaism to be scandalized and angered by his brother Theodore's conversion to Christianity in 1824. Because of this conversion he conceived a violent animosity towards convertors. Nevertheless, he did not avoid them, and had already seen three of his brother's friends, authentic Israelites, receive baptism. Moreover, he unconsciously carried within himself a religious soul, tending towards mystical emotion. Returning from a voyage in the Orient, he passed through Rome, where he first felt a profound disturbance in the church of Ara Coeli. He confided this to an ardent Catholic propagandist, the Baron de Bussière, who persuaded him to accept a holy medallion and the text of a prayer to the Virgin. He believed that he had yielded in order not to be uncivil to a courteous man; besides, in acceding to the baron's persuasions, he had reiterated that he was born a Jew and intended to die one. However, he read and reread the prayer to the point of knowing it by heart and unconsciously repeating it; and M. de Bussière became more pressing. Several days later, on January 20, 1842, Ratisbonne, who had by chance entered the church of St. Andrea, saw a vision of the Virgin Mary as she was depicted on the medallion. The preceding night, caught in insomnia, he had been pursued by a persistent vision of a large cross of singular form; in the morning, he noticed that the reverse side of the medallion carried the exact image of this cross. He left the church an enthusiastic Christian: his conversion marked the logical end of a long inner struggle and of an obsession whose progress we can easily follow.[18]

III. The Road to Damascus

What happened to Paul was readied and realized according to the same process as that which turned the two ardent adversaries of the Church, of whom I have just spoken, into two ardent Christians. The Tarsiot did

18. For all conversions in the Christian Church, cf. Arnold Meyer, *Die Auferstehung Christi* (Tübingen, 1905), pp. 217–72.

not leave in the Epistles a description of the decisive phenomenon which made him conscious of his conversion. Not, as Renan says,[19] because his memories were confused or because he had failed to observe the physical circumstances of the miracle, but rather because he doubtless had no occasion to write the story which he must often have recounted to his flock. Was not the marvel of this irresistible *metanoia* his true claim to glory and the very guarantee of his office as Apostle?

However, he alludes to his marvellous vocation in three places: in Galatians i.12–17,where he asserts that his Gospel comes not from man, but was received by him from a revelation of Jesus Christ (δι᾿ ἀποκαλύψεως ᾿Ιησοῦ Χριστοῦ), and that it was the grace of God which, in revealing his Son to him (ἀποκαλύψαι τὸν υἱὸν αὐτοῦ ἐν ἐμοί), had instantaneously transformed him from a persecutor into the Apostle of the Gentiles; in 1 Corinthians ix.1, where he writes: "Am I not free? Am I not an apostle? Have I not seen Jesus Christ, our Lord?" (οὐχὶ ᾿Ιησοῦν τὸν κύριον ἡμῶν ἑόρακα); in 1 Corinthians xv.8, where, after having enumerated the various appearances of the Resurrected One, he adds: "And last of all he was seen of me also, as of one born out of due time." There is nothing more, and the three texts, even when juxtaposed, leave us in ignorance of the essential. It is not certain that in these various allusions Paul was referring to only one appearance and that he was speaking only of the one which, according to Acts, we usually situate on the road to Damascus;[20] and, in any case, he gives us no hints about the modalities of this sovereign revelation.

That it was for Paul something *real*, that he believed truly to have *seen* Christ (with all due reservations concerning the *form* taken by the Glorified One), is most evident in the third of the texts I mentioned, where the words: "he was seen of me also" (ὤφθη κἀμοί) doubtless refer to a phenomenon similar to the one expressed by the words, "he showed himself to Cephas" (ὤφθη Κηφᾷ), which affirm that the Resurrected One was *seen* by Cephas (xv.5). I say *similar* and not *identical* because, though the reality of Christ's presence held no doubts for either Peter or Paul, it is possible that the two apostles did not *see* the Lord in the same guise. Christ also *spoke* on the occasion of these appearances, or on one of these occasions, and, lacking his exact words, Paul gives us their sense: they bestowed upon the converted one an apostolic function in relation to the Gentiles and communicated to him the fundamental themes of the

19. *LV*, p. 182.
20. G. P. Wetter, "Die Damaskusvision und das Paulinische Evangelium," in *Festgabe für Adolf Jülicher*, Tübingen, 1927.

Gospel, as assumed in our first two texts. It is quite possible that the words
"God judged it right to reveal his Son in me" (ἐν ἐμοὶ) contain impressions from several visions, such as the ones dealt with in Galatians ii.2 and
in 2 Corinthians xii.1–9. In any case, the Christ must have made known
to Paul from the start the intentions he had for him; for the Tarsiot to
know what he henceforth had to do, it would not have sufficed for him
simply to have contemplated the "radiance of the glory of God" in the
countenance of the Lord (2 Cor. iv.6).

Only Acts is precise about the place and the circumstances of this
first vision. The triple narration of this event (ix.3f.; xxii.1f.; xxvi.12f.) has
caused almost as much ink to flow as the texts concerning Jesus's resurrection.[21] Despite the divergences of detail in the three passages, there
is no doubt that they represent three versions, three more or less perfected
revisions, of the same story; the basis of this story is guaranteed by
nothing more than the assurance of the writer, which does not carry
much weight. It seems to be a free interpretation, an amplification—
which borrows its components from the theophanies of the Septuagint
—of the affirmations in the Epistles that we have cited. The writer
knows nothing more than what he has learned from the Apostle: he
explicates and enlarges according to what he believes to be likely within
the framework he has invented (Paul's mission of persecution in Damascus), because he has the point of view of a hagiographer.[22] It is a waste
of time to try to weigh the historical elements in all this. To make up
for this, he echoes all the ancient narrators of visions or appearances,
common currency of the classic marvels. There is nothing in his story,
even in the fundamental theme (the notion that the epiphany on the
road to Damascus completely reversed Paul's destiny), that does not
conform to the thinking of the Ancients concerning the effects of these
celestial manifestations.[23] Our writer is thoroughly in tune with the
hagiographic conventions of his time.[24]

It was probably Galatians i.15–17 that furnished him with the very
likely setting for the miracle. Here is the text: "But when it pleased

21. *XVIII*, III, pp. 204f.
22. *CLXX*, p. 318, n. 1.; *CVIII*, pp. 394f.; *CC*, p. 81; *CCXLII*, p. 110. The Christ
speaks from the midst of his dazzling *glory* as did Yahweh from the center of the
burning bush. The writer has not only the hagiographer's attitude, he also knows
and largely uses all the clichés of pagan hagiography. *CXXIV*, pp. 34f., 39.
23. The concept of an individual altering his way of life and giving a new
orientation and direction to it at the injunction of a dream or a vision is, if one may
say so, banal in Antiquity. *CXXIV*, pp. 34f., gives the essential references.
24. *CXXIV*, p. 39. It is common for a god to communicate with someone by
speech without showing himself, and to speak without being heard by the witnesses.

God, who separated me from my mother's womb, and called me by his grace, to reveal his son in me . . . immediately . . . I went into Arabia and returned again (πάλιν) unto Damascus." If he is *returning* to Damascus, it is because he left from there or from near there, and it is there that he heard the decisive call. It remains to be known in what form and manner.

In the first (ix.3f) account Acts tells us that as he approached Damascus Saul, pondering his evil designs against the brethren, suddenly feels surrounded by a radiance coming from the heavens, as by a flash of lightning, which throws him to the ground. He hears a voice which says to him: "Saul, Saul, why do you persecute me?" He asks: "Who are you, Lord?" And the voice replies: "I am Jesus, whom you persecute; . . . arise and enter into the city and you will be told what you must do." The divine light has left him blinded; his companions are terrified, because they *heard* the voice but *saw* nothing. He himself regains his sight only after three days, after a disciple named Ananias comes to lay his hands on him as ordered to do by the Lord in a vision (ix.10–16); he baptizes Paul (ix.18).

The second account (xxii.6f.) asserts that the miracle happened at noon and that Paul's companions *saw* the light but did not *hear* the voice which spoke. Aside from that, it resembles the first.

The third (xxvi.12f.) differs in that the Lord allegedly spoke briefly to Paul, telling him that he had manifested himself in order to make him "his minister and his witness" (ὑπηρέτην καὶ μάρτυρα). There is no mention of the blindness, nor of Ananias, nor of what is supposed to happen at Damascus, as related in the other two accounts.

All evidence points to the conclusion that the writer of Acts treated the hagiographic theme he imposed upon himself—*the apostolic institution of Paul*—with the same unscrupulous liberty as did his contemporaries in similar cases.[25] The Epistles sufficed to furnish the theme itself, and there is no reason to believe that the imagination of our hagiographer was supported by an authentic tradition, except, at the most, the one contained in the simple information that the Lord converted Saul at Damascus. Luke could have known this and must have said it. His adaptor liberally added details he judged to be suitable and convincing, save for slight contradictions, taking little notice of the fact that they disagreed with Paul's own testimony.

Ultimately, it is this alone that is important for us. And it is this that

25. On the internal relations of the three accounts, cf. *XVIII*, III, pp. 204f; on their criticism, *CVIII*, p. 384, and *XVIII*, III, pp. 208f.

prevents a close enough approach to the vision, or visions, which converted the witness for us to grasp their true nature. We are, to be sure, unable to arrive at a satisfactory psychological analysis of the *event;* [26] but not because the *event* was in itself especially mysterious, but because of the dearth of texts. We do not doubt that Paul contemplated the majesty and radiant glory of the Christ [27] in a guise that definitely excluded all hesitation. But not everyone who longs for visions has them; for their materialization a predisposed temperament and circumstances appropriate to the phenomenon are incumbent. Paul was a *visionary,* that is, the vision was for him the usual form of the manifestation and operation of the Spirit within him (2 Cor. xii.1–4) or, if you prefer, the habitual reaction of his disturbances, his perplexities, or his mystic exaltation. All the spiritual difficulties which for a relatively long time struggled within him, and which he believed could be resolved only by the intervention of Yahweh or the Lord (who were the same for him), led him to this *materialization,* which his fundamental realism demanded.

IV. Attempt at an Explanation

If we were to envisage a pure Judean, student of an illustrious master of the School, such as Gamaliel, and nourished on the strict Pharisaic orthodoxy, who one day abjures himself in order to echo the inconsistent assurances of some obscure Galileans, we would have to despair of understanding anything at all about so remarkable a reversal, and nothing short of a stunning miracle would make us believe it. But this is not the case. We already know that Paul's education familiarized him with the impressions and ideas that readied his conversion to the Nazarene heresy.

In his homeland of Tarsus,[28] and doubtless later at Antioch, he lived in constant contact with men who anticipated a blessed life, after their earthly existence, through the intervention and the discipline of a Soter. They believed in their mystical assimilation to a god who died as they had to die and was resurrected for them by virtue of giving them, through his example, the certitude and formula of resurrection.

In the Pharisaic milieu which he tells us he frequented, he became attached to the Messianic expectation which was apparently so cherished

---

26. *CC,* p. 81.
27. *CXCV,* p. 20: "Die Herrlichkeit, den Strahlenglanz des Herrn Christus."
28. *CXCVI.*

by Pharisaism.[29] In the Greek territory, where he had encountered it, this expectation may already have been influenced by soteriological presentations of the Mysteries; in any case, it was not impossible for it to assimilate with the hope conveyed by these presentations. The practical exigencies of life in the Diaspora inculcated in Paul the habit of not being immutably closed to outside ideas. It is likely that, born with the apostolic vocation, he engaged in Jewish proselytism among the pagans and in doing so learned "that Judaism does not conform to the requirements of universal salvation."[30] It follows that he would be converted as soon as he became convinced that the Christians were right in attributing to Jesus of Nazareth the accomplishment of the salutary work whose need the pagans had suspected and which in their blindness they attributed to their demons, but which the Scriptures had long since promised to Israel. In other words, his conversion was provoked by the violent encounter, and simultaneous climactic perception, of familiar notions, buried deep in his subconscious, and the Christian affirmation presented by the Hellenists in a form acceptable to a Jew in Greek realms. The Tarsiot came to a Mystery, a religion of salvation by the Christ Jesus. Afterwards, his rabbinism spontaneously operated to elaborate, explain, and organize "that which he received" (1 Cor. xv.3). But how and where did he receive it, and why did he accept it?

At first he received it, without wanting or knowing it, through his passionate debates and furious disputations with the Nazarenes of Tarsus, Antioch, or Damascus. He fought with all his strength and all his power; but slowly their conviction and their faith penetrated him. He was unaware of it until the day they pervaded his whole being, and his *metanoia* is to be conceived not as the logical conclusion of reasoned observations but as "a sort of revolution, a mystic leap of faith."[31] The event occurred because the subject's own inclinations enabled it to occur, and there are a number of subjective elements in this occurrence that escape our investigation. In the main, it is more necessary to authenticate the fact *per se* and at its phase of exteriorization than to explain it.

It has been believed, and often still is, that the predominant emotion that effected the conversion was a profound disturbance, a malaise engendered by man's impotence to truly observe and realize in practical

---

29. It has even been conjectured that even before the vision which made him conscious of his conversion he carried within him a pre-existent abstract conception of the Christ, more or less analogous to that of the Son of Man of Enoch. Cf. *CCLV*, pp. 84f.; *CCXXXII*, p. 35; and *CXVII*, p. 431. I shall refrain from this type of assertion.
30. *CLXX*, p. 326.
31. *CVIII*, p. 399.

life the prescriptions of the Torah. This conclusion is based on the famous passage of Romans vii.7f:

> What shall we say then? Is the law sin? God forbid. Nay, I had not known sin, but by the law: for I had not known lust, except the law had said, Thou shalt not covet. But sin, taking occasion by the commandment, wrought in me all manner of concupiscence. For without the law sin was dead. For I was alive without the law once: but when the commandment came, sin revived, and I died. And the commandment, which was ordained to life, I found to be unto death . . . For we know that the law is spiritual: but I am carnal, sold under sin. For that which I do I allow not: for what I would, that do I not; but what I hate, that do I. If then I do that which I would not, I consent unto the law that it is good. Now then it is no more I that do it, but sin that dwelleth in me . . .

And Paul continues to stress the torments of the bitter struggle in his moral life between the Law of God, which preaches good to him, and the law of sin, which dominates his body and impels it to evil. He ends with the cry (vii.24): "O wretched man that I am! Who shall deliver me from the body of this death?"

Clarification of, and commentary on, this difficult text would entail too much.[32] Moreover, its general meaning is obvious: it expresses a feeling of anguished insecurity with regard to the Torah. It has certainly been abused by those who thought to find in it the key to Paul's conversion; first, because they paid no attention to the fact that it emanated from the progress of an emotion rather than from a conscious conclusion;[33] secondly, because they forgot that if the passage claims to describe the state of the author's spirit *before* the crisis that transformed him, he wrote it *afterwards*, in the language of a convert and at a moment when, no doubt, he was no longer able to remember exactly his pre-Christian mentality. The text of Romans vii, "a classic expression of the anguish of a soul which aspires to an ideal that it does not succeed in realizing" (Goguel), corresponds in the main to a subjective experience produced by Paul's conversion and to a secondary reaction of his consciousness.[34]

I believe, however, that there is something to grasp at in the emotion underlying the obscure words. It is not, certainly, a question of claiming that the Tarsiot's conversion is nothing more than a psychological drama,

32. Cf. the commentaries of Sanday-Headlam, Lietzmann, Jülicher, Lagrange, *ad. loc.*
33. *CVIII*, p. 399; *CLXX*, p. 324.
34. *LXXXIII*, p. 426.

the conclusion of a series of moral and mystical experiences under the yoke of the Torah, a crisis similar to Luther's, but rather a question of grasping the emotion so strongly projected in the text: the Law taught Paul that sin was everywhere. And the perception of the frailty of his flesh, of his own inability to hold fast to the means of salvation—was this not a common feeling all about him?—convinced him, chiefly perhaps after his contact with the Christians, that he could not avoid the fatal fall; from this came the anguish of his spiritual life.[35]

I see nothing that would have made him invent this anguish after becoming a Christian, and I think that he simply exaggerated it, as do St. Augustine and Luther when they recall their past. He is not the only mystic to reveal to us this painful torment; it is an easily understandable emotion in a man whose imagination and sensitivity transcended reason, a man in whom Pharisaism, even—and especially—if it was elementary, had developed a feeling of doubt. After his conversion, Paul viewed the Law as an introduction, a preparation for faith: "But before faith came, we were kept under the law, shut up unto the faith which should afterwards be revealed" (Gal. iii.23). I think it reasonable to see in the conception which sustains this text a confirmation of the idea I am trying to draw from Romans vii.7f.: that of an interrelationship between Paul's reactions when he was still ruled by the Torah and his conversion.

As judged by a true rabbi, the Torah radiated certainty and joy; but for the Tarsiot, whose pure Judaism had already been complicated by so many foreign influences, it could hardly have been the same. If this hypothesis is well founded, Paul must have been deeply impressed by the contrast between the Christians' feeling of confident bliss and enthusiastic certainty and his own state of anxiety. The simple affirmations of the Galileans, especially the one that transformed the Crucified One into the Messiah, would not have affected him, haunted as he was by the terrible words of Deuteronomy xxi.23: "Cursed is every one that hangeth on a tree" (Gal. iii.13). But he was confronted by a Hellenized Christology [36] which, in order to remove the malediction, endowed Jesus's death with the meaning of an expiation for the sins of men, "according to the Scriptures"; it transposed the traditional Messianism, henceforth affixed to the Crucified One, into a universal salvationism. It is conceivable that

---

35. *LXV*, p. 278; *CC*, pp. 64f.; *CCXV*, p. 20: *CXCIII*, p. 79, which stress the notion that Paul finds the endeavor to be at peace with God merely through obedience insupportable when he sees the Christians participating in this peace by the grace of the Lord.

36. Cf. above, pp. 159f.

he had been ready to succumb to similar presentations, and that, even while he verbally contradicted them, and before he had clearly understood them in the light of his revelation, he dimly sensed in them the satisfactory solution to the problem which had for so long tormented him. Moreover, it is not impossible that he unconsciously found potent comfort in the Christian transformation of the notion of submission to the Law, a transformation traced back to Jesus himself, and in the substitution of "the idea of the morality of the self for that of the morality of actions alone." [37]

Undoubtedly, this preparatory work was hidden and subconscious, with the consummation of each aspect of the future synthesis ripening autonomously and apart from the others throughout the course of the polemic conducted against the Nazarene heretics. The synthesis itself was effected in a decisive vision. For great mystics to *turn* at a moment of crucial crisis by encountering a supposedly miraculous incident or accident is a frequent occurrence. St. Francis of Assisi and Ignatius Loyola also *realized* themselves in visions which culminated and in some way recapitulated a whole series of antecedent impressions. The immediate and tangible cause that triggered Paul's crisis remains unknown to us, which is not surprising; but its effect is clear and intelligible.

That falling a persecutor Paul rose an apostle is most natural and we remain within the logic of the phenomenon; *mutatis mutandis*, it is what happened to St. Francis and to St. Ignatius. Actually, it is simply a matter of transposition. After his decisive vision, the Tarsiot changed neither in temperament nor in spirit, but only in fanaticism and direction.[38]

In all likelihood he acquired fuller knowledge of the Christ and of Christianity from the brethren at Damascus and, unceasingly, began to ponder that which he had *received,* to subject it to familiar processes, to examine and enlarge it. His apostolic experiences were added to this initial foundation to form *his Gospel,* which he was always to consider as a sort of personal charisma: "For I neither received it of man, neither was I taught it, but by the revelation of Jesus Christ" (Gal. i.12). He felt no need to go and speak with the Apostles of Jerusalem. What could they teach him? He had surpassed them from the start. Interested only in the Crucified One, he already knew much more about him than they did. Moreover, was it not sufficient for him to be assured that the Lord died

---

37. *LXXXIII*, pp. 428–29, attaches a primary importance to this impression. Cf. *CXCIII*, pp. 53f.

38. *CC*, p. 67; *CCLVIII*, p. 5; *LV*, p. 183.

for the sins of the world and that his resurrection guaranteed that of mortals? It was not necessary for him to ask Peter, John, and the directors of the old community for a confirmation of his apostolic mandate, for he held it from Christ himself.

Conclusion

A pure Jew, a Pharisee reared in the study of the Torah and shut up in the atmosphere and spirit of the rabbinical schools, would probably never have come to Christianity by the roads followed by Paul. Conversely, Paul's religious evolution and conversion seem natural and understandable phenomena if we are dealing with a Jew of the Diaspora, a Hellenized and *syncretized* Pharisee, ardent and mystical, for whom the Christian affirmations, progressively and unconsciously assimilated by him prior to the affirmation of his own faith in the full light of revelation, could be the means of harmonizing and reconciling his unconscious aspirations as an Asiatic and his Jewish hopes. Accentuating the tendencies already present in the new religion when he encountered it, he quite naturally conceived it as a Mystery of salvation, justified by a *gnosis* more or less analogous to the ones he later combatted as obstructions. In so doing, he put himself within the general current of the religious world in which he lived, where he is by no means an isolated and inexplicable figure. As for the still unknown elements in the phenomenon of his conversion, they are no greater than the ones encountered in parallel evolutions of other great mystics; they leave us with the normal aspects of the case.

7

PAUL'S APOSTOLIC
ACTIVITY [1]

I. Paul's Apostolic Sense AFTER his conversion, Paul felt
that he was an apostle, Christ's servant and ambassador. Herein lay his
personal charisma, and he knew well that he could not dismiss the
obligations which followed from it. But at the same time he would permit
no questioning of it, and if one dared do so, grew angry: "Am I not free?
Am I not an apostle? have I not seen Jesus Christ our Lord? are not ye
my work in the Lord? (1 Cor. ix.1). When he began a letter, he summarized, so to speak, his essential qualifications in the first lines: "Paul,
called to be an apostle of Jesus Christ through the will of God . . ."
(1 Cor. i.1); "Paul, a servant of Jesus Christ, called to be an apostle,
separated unto the gospel of God . . ." (Rom. i.1).[2] The farther he
went, the more vigorous became his affirmations; facts and new visions
strengthened even more his initial conviction, if that is possible. In
Col. i.24f., he ended by proclaiming that his apostolic sufferings completed Christ's Passion, and that it was God's design that he be the one
to spread everywhere the knowledge of the Mystery of salvation, hidden

1. For bibliography, see Goguel, *XVIII*, III, ch. vii, and IV,[1] chs. v, vi, viii. All
of the biographical works on Paul study the question to some extent. See especially
CC, ch. vii; *CCXXXVI; CCLIII; CXV*, III, chs. ii, iii, viii, ix; *CXXIX*, Bk. II,
chs. viii, ix, xi, xii; *CCXVI*, Table and Index; *CCXXI*,[1] pp. 449f; and *CVII*, ch. v.
2. Cf. Gal. i.1; 2 Cor. i.1; Col. i.1, which give analogous formulas, imitated
besides by the Deutero-Paulinians, Eph., 1 Tim., 2 Tim., Titus.

for so long from "aeons" and from men, and presently being manifested to the "saints."

His mission was his reason for being and he went where he believed the Lord directed him to go; nothing could stop him, except a command from the Spirit, and he ran many considerable risks and perils.[3] "Christ sent me not to baptize, but to preach the gospel . . ." (1 Cor. i.17) he affirmed, and one can appreciate the weight of such a declaration when one remembers the importance he attached to baptism, the rite of entering into the Mystery and the act of saving union with the Lord.

In truth, he was born an apostle, and it is precisely this that explains why, before his conversion, he was so active a foe of the Christians; one can see him quite clearly even earlier, in the guise of the sort of Pharisee Matthew xxiii.15 speaks of, a man who roams the world in order to make a proselyte. He must have been active in the Jewish propaganda among the *Goyim*. He was one of those men who live for a single idea; he knew neither family nor friends, unless they took second place to his work, and he had no true country or home. His aim was to win souls over to his Gospel and he tried to adapt himself to the diverse spiritual outlooks he encountered: "Greek with the Greeks, Jew with the Jews" (1 Cor. ix.19f.). However, it is probable that he was not as successful in this as he apparently believed, for we do not get from him the impression that he knew much of the real world and of the infinite variety of its inhabitants. He classified men summarily, usually on the grounds of religious distinctions alone: Jews and Gentiles,[4] or Jews and Greeks;[5] which is ultimately the same for him because, among the *Goyim*, he was actually interested only in the Greeks. At times he used the classical expressions, "the Greeks and the Barbarians," [6] but only in order to signify *all the Gentiles*.[7] All of this is based on the most elementary anthropology; evidently, Paul knew well only the Jews—he was one himself. The rest of the people were a single mass, *the mass of perdition;* those who were part of it "became vain in their imaginations, and their foolish heart was darkened" (Rom. i.21).

The list of pagan vices, which were intended to characterize the Gentiles and to which he constantly returned,[8] he drew from any con-

---

3. 2 Cor. xi.24; cf. *CVIII*, pp. 744–47.
4. Gal. iii.28; 2 Cor. xi.26; Rom. iii.29; xi.13.
5. Rom. i.16; ii.9–10; iii.9; I Cor. i.22–24; xii.13; Col. iii.11.
6. Rom. i.14.
7. Rom. xi.25; xv.9f.
8. Cf. the great verses of Rom. i.18–32; Gal. v.19–21; Rom. xiii.13; 1 Cor. v.10 13; vi.9–11; 2 Cor. xii.20; Col. iii.5–8, etc.

venient Jewish manual of morals or of propaganda.[9] If we had only his Epistles from which to form some idea of the culture of the world in which he was raised and where he lived, it would remain completely closed to us. Was his unawareness due to indifference, to the deliberate aloofness of a sectarian, rather than to fundamental ignorance? It is possible, for it is difficult to understand how a Jew of the Diaspora could know so very little of his environment. However that may be, from the point of view of what the Tarsiot wanted to accomplish in his contemporary world his insufficient awareness of its complexity was undoubtedly a defect.

On the other hand, he gives the impression of an overwhelming *individualism*; this is the reverse side of his personality. I have already conjectured that he must have been rather difficult to live with, and in fact, it does not seem to have been easy for his collaborators [10] to put up with him. They apparently left him, one after the other, beginning with Barnabas, and only Timothy remained faithful to him until the end (Phil. ii.20).[11] Paul, to be sure, never attributed the responsibility for this desertion to himself, and consoled himself in his isolation by considering himself to be the only missionary worthy of pursuing the task begun, the only true Apostle of the Gentiles—which is untenable—and by accusing all the others of Judaizing—which is certainly false.[12] To be afflicted with a difficult nature is also a defect. Hence, Paul was not a perfect missionary,[13] but, pursuant to his temperament and his nature, he manifested, in order to realize his apostolate, an admirable activity.

II. Paul's Apostolic Field

The field of this activity was Greek Asia, Thrace, Macedonia, Greece, all the countries accessible to him through his education. He hardly ever wandered far from the coastal region, and the area in which he most usefully circulated was the one enclosed by the Aegean circle: Troas, Philippi, Thessalonica, Corinth, Ephesus.[14] He seems to have been interested only in the cities: as soon as he succeeded in "planting" within

9. *CCLIII*, pp. 6f., and *CCXX, ad. loc.*, on Stoic parallels.
10. Fr. X. Pölzl, *Die Mitarbeiter des Weltapostels Paulus*. Ratisbon, 1911.
11. *CCXXI*,[2] p. 457, and *CVIII*, p. 609, on Barnabas; pp. 499, 510f, 520f, 612, on John–Mark; p. 705, on Silas. Cf. *CXCIX*, II, p. 132.
12. *CVIII*, p. 607.
13. *CCLIII*, pp. 6f., 11.
14. *CC*, pp. 25f., who stresses the cultural, spiritual, and social unity of this world.

the city walls a community of converted people, he was impelled by an urge to push on farther, to begin again elsewhere.

It is not evident that he had seriously thought of struggling with Jerusalem: his insistence on his status of Apostle *for the Gentiles* [15] confirms this abstention, which is instructive. A text of Acts ix.26f, which we have already encountered, gives a different impression: the neophyte Apostle presumably went to the City and, after Barnabas had testified for him to the Twelve, was "coming and going in Jerusalem, preaching with assurance in the name of the Lord" (ix.28). But this is most certainly an invention of the writer. Just as, in telling us of the miracle on the road to Damascus, he took care to say nothing of a direct revelation of the Gospel of Jesus Christ by the Glorified One himself (Gal. i.11–12), because he did not want to admit that Paul's Gospel was not precisely that of Peter, so he now means to have the newly elected one begin his apostolic role "under the auspices of the Apostles," in order to make it clearly understood that from the very beginning a most fraternal bond was established between the Tarsiot and the Twelve. It is the view of a harmonizing apologist, indifferent to history. [16]

However, Paul himself does not fail to assert that the Apostles of Jerusalem recognized his mission (Gal. i.24) and accepted his collaboration (Gal. ii.9), perhaps not at their first contact and not without reservation, for it is definitely not a question of an accord reached at the time of Paul's first journey to Jerusalem, three years after his return to Damascus (Gal. i.18), but of one established no earlier at least than after the success of his missionary tours in Syria and Asia Minor, and during his second stay in the City, fourteen years after the first (Gal. ii.1f).

According to his account, the accord was based on the principle of a division or sharing of the evangelization of the world; the Jews were allotted to Peter, the *Goyim* to him: "For he that wrought effectually in Peter to the apostleship of the circumcision, the same was mighty in me toward the Gentiles" (Gal. ii.8). *Apostle of the Gentiles* is the distinctive title he gives himself and the function he attributes to himself: "Never-

---

15. Gal. i.16: . . . ἵνα εὐαγγελίζωμαι αὐτὸν ἐν τοῖς ἔθνεσιν = ". . . that I might preach his Gospel to the Gentiles." Gal. ii.7: . . . ὅτι πεπίστευμαι τὸ εὐαγγέλιον τῆς ἀκροβυστίας = ". . . that the gospel of the uncircumcision was committed unto me."

16. *CVIII*, p. 424. Our writer exaggerates his thesis to the point of absurdity when he adds (ix.29): "And he spoke thus and disputed with the Hellenists; but these sought to kill him." No doubt he forgot that he has just told us (ix.22–25) that at Damascus Paul "confounded the Jews" and that he had to flee because they "gathered to kill him." If Paul exasperated one group, he must have pleased the others.

theless, I have written unto you . . . because of the grace that is given
to me of God, that I should be the minister of Jesus Christ to the nations
ministering the gospel of God, that the offering up of the nations might
be acceptable, being sanctified by the Holy Ghost" (Rom. xv.15–16).

Audacious assurances, or assurances that reveal in him who risks them
a capacity for singular illusions. First he simplifies, against all truth, by
attributing to Peter alone the preaching to the Jews: it is a name he
attaches to his own. He designates Judeo-Christianism as *Petrinism*, as
opposed to his own conception of Christianity, as opposed to *Paulinism*.
Then he forgets that at a time when the initiative of each apostle
depended only on his own inspiration and his spontaneous impulses,
others besides himself believed themselves qualified to spread the Christian
faith among the Gentiles. Insofar as they were not his collaborators, participating in the derivative power of the *exclusiveness* of his *charisma*, he
ignores or reduces to secondary importance the roles of Barnabas,
Apollos,[17] and many others whose activity we glimpse in the same areas
as the ones where Paul is active, and who seem to have no suspicions
that they are trespassing (1 Cor. iii.6f). However, the Tarsiot is not
ignorant of their existence when he states, in Romans xv.20, that he
has been careful not to build "upon the foundations of another"
(ἐπ' ἀλλότριον θεμέλιον). Finally, in excluding Peter and the Judeo-
Christians grouped around James from the evangelization of the Gentiles,
he forgets the indignation aroused in him, at Antioch, by the attitude
of the first and the intervention of the second. Yet this incident in his
conflict with the Judaizers is proof that the people of Jerusalem did not
feel in the least bound to confine their efforts only to the Jews, and
that they had not the slightest notion of dividing the world between
themselves and the Tarsiot. An analogous impression is conveyed clearly
in the famous passage of 1 Corinthians i.10–12, which reveals the divisions
of the Church at Corinth:

> Now I beseech you, brethren, by the name of our Lord Jesus Christ,
> that ye all speak the same thing, and that there be no divisions among
> you; but that ye be perfectly joined together in the same mind and in
> the same judgment. For it hath been declared unto me of you, brethren
> . . . that there are contentions among you. Now this I say, that every
> one of you saith, I am of Paul; and I of Apollos; and I of Cephas; and
> I of Christ.

Do we not also know, from Paul himself (Rom. i.10–13), that
unknown men planted the Roman community?

17. Cf. P. Schmiedel, "Apollos" and "Barnabas," *EB*.

Moreover, to go back to the probably Antiochene source used by Acts in narrating the beginnings of the mission into pagan land, Paul was at first and for several years—from 11 to 14—a companion and assistant of Barnabas (Acts xi.25; xiii.lf; xv.12); [18] he worked only in the latter's shadow, and did not acquire importance for the writer in his own right, or complete independence, until after his break with the Cypriot (xv.38), [19] shortly before his second great missionary journey.

It is, moreover, remarkable that this so striking depiction of the division of the world between the authority of the two missionary heads did not initially occur even to the Tarsiot, but came to him only after his second journey to Jerusalem. Did he misunderstand the assurances of the heads of the mother-community which, since it accepted his initiatives concerning the Gentiles, could only commit it to pursuing them from the same point of view? We do not know. But we observe that little by little he quarrels with most of the other apostles. Thus it might be that his solitude and his singularity, which seem to him justified by the Lord and in conformity with the designs of God, impelled him to the conviction that he was, by divine right, the only authentically qualified missionary for the Gentiles. This mystical idea fits in well with the rest of his character; but it is nonetheless inexact.[20] Failure to perceive this completely distorts one's perspective of the inauguration of Christianity on pagan soil.

If we knew the activity of Barnabas, Apollos, and the other Gospel workers, whose competition or collaboration we barely catch sight of in the Epistles and Acts, we would probably have to largely reappraise the importance Paul attributed to himself which has for so long been accepted solely on the basis of his own testimony. Actually, it would be better to say, *on the basis of one of his testimonies*, for in passing he contradicts this testimony by writing (1 Cor. iv.15): "For though ye have ten thousand instructors in Christ, yet have ye not many fathers." Naturally, he alone is the true father of the Corinthian brethren; but it is difficult to believe that the deferential collaboration of so imposing a number of preachers was accorded to him alone. Besides, Paul overstresses his assurances that only his Gospel is the true one, in order to put an end to the circulation around him of other, more or less different, versions, which exasperated him, for, according to him, they could only propagate error and yet be received by some people: "As we

18. *CXXIX*, p. 130. In Gal. ii.1 and 9, the only places where Barnabas is named by Paul, he is clearly relegated to the second plane, against all likelihood.
19. Acts iv. 36: . . . Λευείτης, Κύπριος τῷ γένει.
20. *CVIII*, pp. 463, 577, 608f.

said before, so say I now again, If any man preach any other gospel
unto you than that ye have received, let him be accursed" (Gal. i.9).
Nor did he exempt from this curse even "an angel from heaven" who
dared to contradict that Gospel (Gal. i.8; cf. 2 Cor. xi.4) and to convey
fundamental affirmations about Christ and the Christian Mystery different from his own.

III.   The Religious and Social Milieu of Paul's Activity

a) *The Religious Milieu.* Undoubtedly, the religious milieu in which
Paul expanded his effort was not the same throughout his career. His
original idea seems to have been to preach in the synagogues to the
Jews, who would, he believed, be prepared to receive the truth, because
"God has not rejected his people whom he foreknew" (Rom. xi.2; RSV).
Romans xi in its entirety illustrates the following theme (xi.17): The
Gentiles are a wild olive that has been grafted onto the trunk of Israel;
they owe their salvation only to this adaptation. The whole of Israel
will be saved when all the Gentiles have thus been grafted upon it (xi.25).

During the Sabbath assemblies in the synagogues of the Diaspora, it
was easy for a visiting preacher (if the *archisynagogos* gave his consent)
to speak after the regular reading of the Scripture (cf. the scene Acts
xiii.14–16 places at Antioch of Pisidia) and to be heard, on the presumption that he had some profitable teaching to communicate. Everything
seems to point to the fact that the Jewish propagandists had notebooks
and manuals in which they had assembled the Scriptural texts related to
the Promises; it was easy enough to take these texts as the point of
departure for Christian catechesis and apologetic, for it was precisely
a question of convincing the Jews that these Promises had been fulfilled
and realized in Jesus.[21] The reading in the synagogues and commenting
upon the Scriptures related to the Messiah, and drawing from them the
appropriate deductions, is what Acts calls "preaching the word of God"
(xiii.5).

Accordingly, Paul first preached the word of God in the synagogues;
but, by God's design, Israel was at that time afflicted with partial
"hardening" (πώρωσις) (Rom. xi.25), and resisted the Truth. Certainly
the Apostle attained only a very limited, and dearly bought, success in
this milieu ill-disposed to believe that the Blessed One of Yahweh could

21. On the use of these compilations of excerpts in the initial Christian propagandizing, cf. *CXX*, Pt. II.

be confounded with a Galilean whose unimportant life had ended miserably on a Roman cross. Even though they had adjusted to the pagan atmosphere in everyday life, in matters of religion the Jews remained intolerant and reacted forcefully, with denial and with violence, to everything that offended them. Paul had painful experiences with this frame of mind, which he shared when he himself had fought the Nazarenes. "Of the Jews five times," he says, "received I forty [stripes] save one. Thrice was I beaten with rods, once was I stoned" (2 Cor. xi.24).[22] The writer of Acts probably exaggerated somewhat in steering Paul, wherever he went, first into the synagogue, from which the Jews quickly and violently expelled him. It is more likely that upon realizing that he could not gain much from this side he deliberately turned away from it. Acts xiii.46f is right to ascribe to him the following declaration: "It was necessary that the word of God should first have been spoken to you; but seeing ye put it from you . . . we turn to the Gentiles. For so hath the Lord commanded us: I have set thee to be a light of the Gentiles, that thou shouldest be for salvation unto the ends of the earth" (Isa. xlix.6). The Tarsiot did indeed view the hardening of the Jews as effected by God's will; but his characterization of them at the end is sufficient proof of his failure in their synagogues.[23]

However, since, apparently, he labored in no city which did not have a Jewish community, however small it may have been,[24] I believe it probable that, from the pure Jews, he turned to the proselytes. As we already know, they were much readier to listen to him than the others and it is they who must have been his chief conquests, for they turned Christian in much greater numbers than the Jews. They were tied neither to circumcision nor to legalistic restrictions; or, in other words, they were more accustomed to regarding these orthodox demands as obstacles to their full adherence to Judaism. For the same reason, the fundamental nationalism of Jewish Messianism could not have been very congenial to them. Hence the Pauline Gospel must have seemed to them a simpler

22. The Jewish penal law, practiced in the communities of the Diaspora as well as in Palestine, punished by flogging a great number of transgressions (Maimonides, *Mishneh Torah, Hilkhot Sanhedrin XIX*, gives 207). Deut. xxv.3 recommended only forty blows "lest, if one greatly exceed this number . . . thy brother should seem vile unto thee." It was probably known from experience that the culprit's life was endangered when this total was exceeded; hence usage fixed the authorized number at thirty-nine. The punishment was inflicted in the synagogue. The Roman authorities must have known of the practice, but we have no juridic text that authorizes it. Cf. *XXXVIII*, II, p. 161.

23. Phil. iii.2: "Beware of dogs, beware of evil workers, beware of the concision" (βλέπετε τὴν κατατομήν).

24. *CCLIII*, p. 3.

faith, more flexible, more encouraging, and more oriented in the direction of their own aspirations. Moreover, in addressing them, Paul remained within the tradition adopted by the founders of the first Hellenic community (Acts xi.20).

It has been asked whether the Pauline preaching extended to the true pagans; there is no certain answer, for, as used by the Apostle, the term *Gentiles* (τὰ ἔθνη) can refer to Jewish converts or even to Christians of Gentile origin (Rom. xi.13; xv.27; xvi.4) as well as to pagans as opposed to Jews or to Christians (Gal. ii.8; Rom. iii.29; ix.24; xv.10). However, logic calls for an affirmative reply. How could Paul have believed himself to be the Apostle of the Gentiles if he avoided the task of evangelizing them directly? And how could he possibly have dreamt, the moment he himself turned away from the Jews and from the Torah, of imposing the stage of Jewish proselytism between their original paganism and the Christian faith? All of the evidence proves that he did not do so, if only by his own outright assertion that the incredulity of the Jews was the basis of salvation for the Gentiles (Rom. xi.11–12, 27).

Thus the problem becomes one of knowing if Paul had the means of reaching true pagans. He could no doubt reach isolated individuals, then win them over. His Gospel was made for them, at least for those among them who had already been penetrated by the concerns and the spirit of the Mysteries; they instantly recognized themselves in him. It has been said that his biblicism, or the importance that, in his preaching, he apparently attributed to the allegation of the Scriptural texts, must have troubled and repulsed listeners wholly alien to Judaism, and consequently must have greatly circumscribed his success among them. I am not too sure of this, first of all because I believe that his Bible was, in practice, reduced to a summary of *Testimonia*; secondly, because what mattered most to the pagans were the sacred history and the mutually guaranteed affirmations of redemption which formed the base of the Pauline catechism: all this depended only indirectly on the Scriptures. Fragments of the Scriptures, presented as prophetic guarantees of what had happened and transposed out of the Jewish context, could in no way surprise a pagan. The typical conversion of an intellectual such as Justin, a century later, furnishes the proof of this.[25]

Apropos of this subject, I can't refrain from saying a few words about the famous incident, described in Acts xvii.19–34, of Paul's preaching at

25. Justin, *Dial. with Tryphon*, ch. vii; *1 Apol.*, chs. xxxf, on the Christian use of prophecies.

Athens before the Areopagus.[26] The passage is surrounded with difficulties. First, what was this "Areopagus"? The rock situated to the west of the Acropolis, or the tribunal which held a session there? Obviously, the writer wants us to believe that the reference is to the tribunal, that is, to an assembly qualified to hear the imposing discourse the Apostle is going to deliver: the philosophers are the ones who, judging Paul's propositions to be in contempt of the city's gods, seize him and drag him to the Areopagus (ἐπὶ τὸν ᾿Άρειον πάγον) (Acts xvii.19). But did the philosophers have the authority to introduce, by this expeditious process, an action before the tribunal? Moreover, it is astonishing that, having done so, they (1) are exceedingly courteous to the culprit, asking him, with the utmost civility, for the explanations they are interested in; (2) the affair had no consequences, everyone going his own way when the short sermon was finished. It is obvious, on the other hand, that the preliminary disputes between the Apostle and the philosophers are nothing more than a presumption deemed suitable to initiate the discourse, to which the writer attaches considerable importance. He endows it with the importance and scope of a Christian apologetic proffered to all pagans of rank, to prove to them that the essence of the new religion is to be found in the deepest aspirations of their own hearts.

The body of the discourse has been scrutinized with the most painstaking attention, ever since Norden renewed its study.[27] Independent critics are generally of the opinion that it is derived from an oratorical pastiche, and that in ideas and the formulas used to express these ideas it conforms so closely to a classical—one may say Attic—oration that to attribute it to Paul is to transcend the realm of probability. Its spuriousness betrays itself in the following verse: "For as I passed by, and beheld your devotions, I found an altar with this inscription: To The Unknown God" (xvii.23). Such an altar could certainly never have been found at Athens. We know from various Christian writers, for instance Tertullian, Origen, and St. Jerome, that altars dedicated to "unknown gods" [28] existed here and there, and that such an altar found at Pergamus does indeed carry the inscription cited.[29] It need hardly be demonstrated

26. Commentaries *ad. loc.*; *CVIII*, pp. 660f.; *XVIII*, III, p. 267, which lists recent literature on this subject.

27. *CCXXXI*.

28. *CXIX*, p. 109. Tertullian, *Ad Nationes*, 2, 9: "Nam et Athenis ara est inscripta: 'Ignotis deis.'" Hieronymus, *In Tit.*, 1, 12: "Inscriptio autem arae non ita erat, ut Paulus asseruit: ignoto deo, sed: Diis Asiae et Europae et Africae, diis ignotis et peregrinis."

29. *CC*, pp. 178f, which contains a photograph of the altar.

that the meaning of this inscription is completely different from the one the writer of Acts found so expedient; it simply represents the very ancient feeling that there are divinities whose names are unknown but whom it is wise to placate.[30] It may be conjectured that Paul, having, in passing, seen from afar the inscription he allegedly invoked, committed an error of the type we impute to Justin when, after perceiving and misreading the dedication of a statue at the point of the Tiberine island, he confused *Simo Sanctus* with *Semo Sanctus*—the magician of Samaria with the old Sabine god, guardian of good faith.[31] But so wrote the apologist, and we do not know what reaction his oversight provoked in his readers: how could the Apostle, who was addressing an elite audience, have introduced so lame an allegation without arousing quick protests? The writer hazarded as much as Justin; moreover, as we have seen, even the Christians have contradicted him. The "discourse at the Areopagus" is, then, simply a rhetorical fantasy which we cannot retain as documentary evidence of Paul's activity among the pagans.

b) *The Social Milieu.* We should certainly like to know in what social milieu Paul expanded his apostolic activity; but on this point we are still vague. It was probably not the intellectual milieu, although it is prudent to reserve the possibility of several mystics who had already been won over to the neo-Pythagorean salvationism. But must we believe, with Deissmann,[32] that Paul belonged to a world of jobbing workers, which he did not leave because he was held there by a trade at once highly engrossing and very modest?[33] I do not think so, for proselytes were not recruited solely from among the lower class. However, it is quite likely that the number of converts from the upper classes was never very large; had this not been the case, Acts would not have so obligingly recorded the missionaries' relations with one or another famous person.[34] It is careful to note, for example, that at Cyprus the proconsul Sergius Paulus took the initiative in a conversation with Paul and Barnabas (xiii.7), as did the procurator Felix at Caesarea (xxiv.24), and that Festus, another procurator, as well as King Agrippa and Queen Berenice, showed personal consideration for the Tarsiot (xxvi.24–32). It is wise to believe only half of our author's allegations, so felicitously "advantageous" for his hero. It seems more likely then that, in general, Paul's activity was confined to the

---

30. J. Marquardt, *Le Culte chez les romains*, I, pp. 39f (of the Brissaud translation, Paris, 1890).

31. Justin, *1 Apol.*, 26, 2.

32. *CC*, pp. 34f.

33. 1 Thess. ii.9; 1 Cor. iv.12; ix. *in toto.* Cf. 2 Thess. iii.8.

34. *XI*, p. 37.

lower and middle classes.[35] Such is the conclusion apparently to be derived from 1 Corinthians i.26–28: "For ye see your calling, brethren, how that not many wise men after the flesh, not many mighty (δυνατοί), not many noble (εὐγενεῖς) are called," [36] as well as from the recommendations of 1 Thessalonians iv.10–11: "But we beseech you, brethren, that ye increase more and more; And that ye study to be quiet, and to do your own business, and to work with your own hands, as we commanded you; That ye may walk honestly toward them that are without, and that ye may have lack of nothing." It is not thus that one ordinarily addresses those favored by fortune. Besides, it does not seem that Paul ever sought to rise socially; consequently, he never sought to leave his original milieu.[37]

IV. The Forms of the Apostle's Activity and the Obstacles He Encountered

a) *His Speech.* Paul's missionary activity took two main forms: he spoke and he wrote. His adversaries were apparently of the opinion that he spoke badly, but knew how to write correctly: "For my letters [say they] are weighty and powerful; but my bodily presence is weak, and my speech contemptibile" (2 Cor. x.10). Such an opinion should not surprise us, for the defects of his style of writing are a good enough index to those of his manner of speaking. The ideas in his sentences, which are so often overlong and badly articulated, hurry, jostle each other, and become entangled: they give the impression of a crowd pressing towards a door that is too narrow. Some of them are crushed. Transitions collapse, connections linking the various aspects of the reasoning are broken. In return, digressions hurl themselves into the openings; no sooner does the author conceive a striking word, than he's tempted to drain it of all its potentialities, even at the expense of well-ordered discourse. There is no evidence of true care for clarity, or the difficulties of the reader. The whole says what he wants to say, often with an irresistible intensity; but the harsh and grating particulars by means of which he arrives at the whole discourage and rebuff.[38] I believe that many passages of the Epistles, over which commentators continue to ponder, must have already seemed rather unintelligible to his first readers, even though they had at the time been clari-

35. *CC*, p. 143.
36. [Again, for nearly all the biblical passages quoted, I have used the King James version of the Bible. Tr.]
37. *CC*, p. 38: "Er ist kein Emporkömmling."
38. Reread, for example, 2 Cor. i., *in toto*, and Rom. i.16–32.

fied for them by the Apostle's previous teachings. Now, all these faults must have been aggravated in his preaching. No doubt he always preached more or less the same thing, and the fundamental ideas of his catechesis are few; but he had to contend with interruptions, reply to objections, improvise, and it is quite possible that he did not always extricate himself with ease from these contingencies—which his combative ardor certainly did not fear. If we also take into account the probable mediocrity of his oratorical skill, ill served by the physical means at his disposal, it is understandable that the preacher may have seemed somewhat feeble. There dwelt within him the force of persuasion, derived from his apostolic zeal and his invincible conviction; I am willing to believe that in personal conversations and in small groups, gathered around his worker's bench, it was more efficacious than in actual preaching before a fairly large audience.[39]

b) *His Letters.* We owe Paul's letters first of all to the desire to maintain contact with his communities and to continue to direct them, by confirming them, advising them, and, if necessary, reprimanding them; [40] next, and above all, to the determination to defend himself against adversaries or detractors, to warn of the true or imagined evil designs of enemies from without and from within. They create the impression of a perpetual battle, dominated by unceasing self-vindication.[41]

On the first reading of the Epistles and of Acts, one might believe that nearly everywhere the obstacles to the Pauline propaganda were erected by the Jews. This impression is probably untrue, except when applied to the initial endeavors of Paul's apostolic career, when he preached in the synagogues. After he renounced this enterprise, which was as barren as it was dangerous, he most likely no longer encountered these "dogs" whom he counselled his sheep to beware of,[42] even when they had become Judeo-Christians. But if he spoke frequently of the hostility of the Jews, it is because their ill-treatment of him had always been his most dazzling claim to glory.[43] Moreover, in depicting his trials, especially in 2 Corinthians, he no longer distinguishes their sources and juxtaposes weariness, imprisonments, mortal dangers, blows,[44] vigils, fasts, afflictions submitted to and

39. *CCLIII*, pp. 18f.
40. Cf. 1 Cor. i.10f; Col. i.2f; Gal. i.6f.
41. The words καυχῶμαι, καύχημα, καύχησις, all of them related to the concept of self-glorification, of stating and believing something complimentary, occur frequently in his writing (cf. the Dictionaries of Bauer-Preuschen, Thayer, etc. *ad verba*). He applies them to himself, especially in 1 Cor. i.31; 2 Cor. xi.16 and 18; xii.1 and 6; etc.
42. Phil. iii.2.
43. *CC*, pp. 44f, stressed Paul's ordeals as missionary.
44. 2 Cor. i.9; xi.23.

outrages endured,[45] all of them accepted in imitation of the sufferings of Christ, in his service, and for the benefit of his faithful.[46] He believes that to die for his work would for him be an enviable destiny, and of service to his disciples. In Philippians ii.17 he writes: "Yea, and if I be offered upon the sacrifice and service of your faith, I joy, and rejoice with you all."

When he turned away from the synagogues, he directed his endeavor toward the "household Churches" (ἐκκλησίαι κατ᾽ οἶκον), that is, to meetings of the faithful or of proselytes who assembled in some particular dwelling, to "invoke the name of the Lord" and sit down at his table (1 Cor. i.14; Rom. xvi.23; Acts xx.7). In the cities where "the word" had not yet been carried, the Apostle first endeavored to contact people sympathetic to him, in order to find the quarters needed for his work. Acts xvi.13–15 shows him at Philippi, seated near a spring he believes to be a "place of prayer" (προσευχή) [47] frequented by the proselytes of Judaism; and, in fact, women come whom he approaches and catechizes. One of them is won over, receives baptism, and offers her home to the Apostle. Nothing is more likely. If, in some places, he did not meet this type of reception, he passed on: this, I think, is the meaning of Acts xvi.6, which states that the Holy Spirit prevented Paul and Barnabas "from announcing the word in Asia."

Even though he as a rule no longer had anything to do with the Jews, he continued to encounter in the Church itself opposition from the Judaizers, who had probably been ill-disposed towards him from the start. He saw them, imagined them, suspected them everywhere, even perhaps where they were non-existent; he exaggerated their hostility, and also, no doubt, his own animosity towards them. However, this is not to say that the first did not exist and that the second was wholly groundless.

In reality, the conflict transcended him: it was a conflict between two tendencies in Christianity determined by force of circumstances ever since the faith began to grow on Hellenic soil. Two tendencies, not two schools: we too must not exaggerate. These two tendencies were as follows: (1) Since it had been the Master's wish to remain strictly within the realm of Judaism, there was no reason for his disciples, become his Apostles, to leave this realm. They had, it is true, displaced the core of the Nazarene's teaching and said "He will return" rather than "The Kingdom will come," but they remained within the perspective of the Jewish Messianic

45. 2 Cor. vi.4f.
46. 2 Cor. iv.8f.
47. On the προσευχή, cf. *XLIX, ad verbum.*

hope; Acts was probably right to depict them as very correct Jews. However, the brethren of Israel had not followed them and it would have meant death by quick extinction for the Christian faith if only authentic Jews were accepted into the community. And this death would have come before the inevitable interpretation of the death, and then the life of Jesus, could impose upon the disciples the obligation to separate themselves from Israel. (2) But the transposition of their hope onto Greek soil precipitated the evolution of their faith in a direction that insured its duration and made of it a true religion which progressively developed its own pattern. Soon it was no longer concerned with the Judaism of its adherents; it no longer imposed upon them Jewish obligations before admitting them to baptism.

The question then arose of the need for these obligations and, concurrently, of the universalization of the faith. The Judeo-Christians were caught between their customs, their prejudices, their fears, and the manifest concerns of the propaganda. As soon as they lost their numerical advantage, which had to happen soon, they found themselves obliged to yield, to renounce the imposition of legalism upon the proselytes of Gentile origin, while they maintained it for themselves. This is what is called the *compromise of Jerusalem*. We shall soon have to relocate it within the context of the historical circumstances which determined it. For the moment, let us be content with defining it as an illusory attempt to reconcile the conservative Judaizing tendency and the Hellenists' strong need for religious freedom. In a milieu indifferent or even hostile to Jewish legalism, the Hellenists rapidly reached the point of no longer recognizing it, and Paul himself ended with doctrinal propositions which rejected the Law as henceforth useless, for if one were still to attribute saving value to it, one would have to believe that Jesus Christ died in vain (Gal. iii.11; v.1–2).

Under the circumstances it is understandable that the Judeo-Christians should have vowed hate for the Tarsiot, a hate that pursued him in all his endeavors and resounded even beyond the apostolic age in writings wherein the Judeo-Christian spirit persisted. It must, however, be admitted that Paul was inclined to imagine that no one, except a Judeo-Christian, would oppose him in whatever guise (for example, by accusing him of arrogating to himself a centrifugal or too presumptuous a task in the fraternity).[48] This is no doubt an exaggeration,[49] for in fact we cannot actually perceive the element of Judaism in the opposition to the Apostle

48. Cf. especially Gal. ii.3–5; 2 Cor. xi.1–4f.
49. *CCXXI*,² pp. 467f.

at Corinth: we sense there much more strongly the influence of Apollos, whose more learned preaching probably showed to ill advantage the simplicity of Paul's teaching.[50] It is not even impossible that the difficulties Paul encountered with the Galatians derived from a syncretism for which the people from Jerusalem could not have been responsible; the Epistle to the Galatians does not permit us to "conclude with certainty that rigorous pressure was exerted on the Galatians to make them accept circumcision and other legal observances" (Loisy).[51] The adversaries against whom the Epistle to the Colossians battles may have had some ties with Judaism (ii.16), but they were probably adherents of an astrological gnosis,[52] which apparently also claimed to be a Gospel.

It may well be said that the most redoubtable obstacles of all that Paul encountered were the ones presented by other apostles whose vocation was more or less similar to his, who believed themselves authorized equally, by the call of the Lord, to preach a Gospel that was not only independent, but also more or less different from his. Let us remember that there was at the time no final rule of faith; by what recognized authority could it have been established? The prestige of the Mother Church at Jerusalem was not strong enough to confer upon it the right or the means to determine doctrine. Paul himself is the living proof of this; we know how greatly he prided himself on his independence and the originality of his Gospel (Gal. i.12). It is quite natural that such varied and personal speculations should have developed around the basic notion represented by the person of the Lord Jesus. When, for example, in the Epistle to the Colossians, Paul erected upon his Christological pre sentation a whole organization of the Cosmos wherein the Kyrios is everywhere the head and the beginning (κεφαλή, ἀρχή), the complete expression of the Whole, the realization of the Pleroma (Col. i. and ii.), he did not, I imagine, *receive* this from his first Christian initiators, but was in all likelihood led to it by the need to combat an astrological gnosis. Others availed themselves of the same liberty that he permitted himself, by setting forth other points of view; but he never acknowledged that they had the right to do so.[53] He was extremely intolerant, because he was always certain that he held the incontestable Truth from Christ himself. And that is why he lived in the middle of an endless and ruthless polemic.

---

50. *XLVI*, p. 44.
51. *XLVI*, p. 31.
52. Col. ii.8, 10, 15, 20. Cf. *CCXLVII*, *ad loc.*
53. Loisy, *CVII*, p. 229, is perfectly right in saying that Paul's career was only a *sample* of the extraordinary propaganda which sowed Christianity in the world of that time.

We have every reason to be convinced that he has not let us see this polemic in its true light. Its determining cause was, in the majority of cases, the resistance and hostility provoked by the pretensions, the temperament, and the manners of the Tarsiot; but he himself wanted to persuade us, and perhaps he first persuaded himself, that it emanated from his resolution to maintain a Truth which the others contested, and that in the last analysis it expressed a conflict of principles. His word has been credited for far too long a time, at least concerning his opposition to the Judeo-Christians, which has been depicted as a sort of division between two schools or a schism in the Church of Christ. Matters had not reached such a point in Paul's time—his temporary accord with Peter and, conversely, his break with Barnabas testify to this—and when they did reach such a point, after 70, Judeo-Christianity was no longer important in the life and evolution of Christianity.[54]

EXCURSUS

Apollos

Quite a problem is presented by the mention of this individual in 1 Corinthians 12; but I do not intend to examine it at the moment. I shall merely try to approximate the particular type of apostle that this man seems to represent.

His name is not certain; it seems to be a contraction, or rather an abbreviation, of "Apollonios," a form given, besides, by the Codex D.[55] Paul really tells us nothing of him, but Acts devotes a brief note to him in xviii, 24–28. There we read that he is a Jew born at Alexandria and that he is "eloquent [ἀνὴρ λόγιος], mighty in the Scriptures [δυνατὸς ἐν ταῖς γραφαῖς]," and "instructed in the way of the Lord"; he "speaks fervently in [or by] spirit [ζέων τῷ πνεύματι]"[56] and he preaches with zeal "the things of the Lord" [τὰ περὶ τοῦ Ἰησοῦ]," but he knows only the

54. *CVIII*, p. 21.
55. *XCVII*, III, p. 179.
56. The reference is not, I think, to the Holy Spirit, and I understand it to mean: *he spoke with fervor of spirit*. Cf. *XCVI*, I, p. 118.

"baptism of John." [57] He comes to Ephesus and begins to speak boldly in the synagogue, where Aquila and Priscilla hear him; they become interested in him and teach him "the way of God more perfectly" (ἀκριβέστερον τὴν ὁδὸν τοῦ Θεοῦ). He then goes into Achaia, where he renders great services in arguing against the Jews with singular force and in proving by the Scriptures that Jesus is the Christ.

As if often the case in Acts, the seeming precision of this passage hides an incoherence that leaves us confused.[58] Let us note first of all that it is an aside in the narration of Paul's journey that the writer is recounting; it thus becomes a question of the use made of a particular source. By itself this passage does not appear in too bad a light, with due reservations concerning the use the author made of it. We accept without difficulty that Apollos is an Alexandrian Jew instructed in Greek letters and well versed in the scriptural exegesis prevalent in his region; we accept his eloquence and the ardor of his conviction. But how can we explain that he can *at one and the same time* be *"instructed in the way of the Lord"* (κατηχημένος τὴν ὁδὸν τοῦ κυρίου), teach *"diligently"* (ἀκριβῶς)—that is, I think, "precisely"—*"the things concerning Jesus"*—which no doubt means: the realization of Jesus's promises; the miracles and "virtues" of Jesus—*and* know only the baptism of John; especially, how could he be in need of the Christian teaching given him by Aquila and Priscilla? The principal difficulty disappears if one follows Benjamin Smith, who made a special study of this text; his notion is that Apollos, totally ignorant of the evangelical pseudo-Jesus, preaches *the Lord, the Savior, the Jesus* whose pre-Christian cult existed before the advent of the Christian Christ. If this were the case, it would be reasonable that Apollos should know only John's baptism. Unfortunately, I do not believe that this hypothesis is acceptable.[59] One could, it is true, retain some aspects of it by saying that Apollos, before meeting the Aquila-Priscilla couple, preached with zeal, exactitude, and erudition only on the principal theme of the Baptist: *He who must come is approaching;* that consequently he developed, illustrated, and exalted the Messianic hope of Israel, in addressing himself especially to the Jews, as was proper. In fact, it is not unlikely that the writer of Acts, convinced that the Messianic Promises were realized by the Lord Jesus, was naively led to write "the things concerning Jesus" for "the things concerning the Messiah." I would not reject this explana-

57. Cf. *CX*, p. 44.
58. *CVIII*, pp. 710–17; *CVII*, pp. 198f.
59. Ch. Guignebert, *Le Problème de Jésus*, Paris, 1914, pp. 138f.

tion as resolutely as some have;[60] however, it is not the one ordinarily favored by liberal exegetes, or at least by those who have refused to solve the problem by arbitrary and vain interpretations. They prefer the hypothesis that the original text was more or less distorted in rearrangement.[61] The question then becomes: exactly what arrangement? On this point there are naturally different opinions, which proves that no single one of them is self-evident. Some scholars, Schmiedel for instance, have emphasized the writer's desire to make Apollos subordinate to Paul, and they present the relation between the original and the rewriting as follows:

> xviii.24: *And a certain Jew named Apollos, born at Alexandria, an eloquent man, and mighty in the scriptures, came to Ephesus.*
> 25a: *This man was instructed in the way of the Lord;* b: *and being fervent in the spirit, he spake and taught diligently the things of the Lord;* c: *knowing only the baptism of John.*
> 26a: *And he began to speak boldly in the synagogue;* b: *whom when Aquila and Priscilla had heard, they took him unto them;* c: *and expounded unto him the way of God more perfectly.*

In itself, this arrangement is plausible; for it is not easy to reconcile xviii.28, "For he mightily convinced the Jews, and that publicly, showing by the Scriptures that Jesus was Christ," with 1 Corinthians iii.6, "I planted; Apollos watered," which assumes that Apollos is addressing the same converts, the same category of believers as Paul himself, former pagans and not Jews. One concludes that xviii.28 was written by the same author who wrote 26a, and perhaps 25c and 26b and c as well. Again, the beginning of Acts xix, where it is stated that Paul lays on his hands and transmits the Spirit to John's disciples at Ephesus, seems to exclude the likelihood that, according to the source, Apollos was a disciple of John, because no tie is noted between him and the alleged disciples of the Baptist *consummated* by Paul.

Unfortunately, one can just as well claim, as does McGiffert, the converse hypothesis, according to which Apollos originally simply called himself a disciple of John and aligned himself with the disciples of the Forerunner mentioned at the beginning of chapter xix. If such was the case, 25a would have to be considered as an addition by the second writer, probably because it was impossible for him to conceive that this Alexandrian would come to proclaim in the synagogue of Ephesus anything other than the Gospel of the Christ Jesus. On the other hand, it has also

---

60. *XCVI*, I, pp. 119.
61. *XCVI*, *loc. cit;* Schmiedel, "Apollos," *EB; CXIV*, p. 290; *CVIII*, pp. 710f.

been conjectured that Apollos was actually a Johannist preaching repentance in view of the imminent arrival of the Kingdom, a Johannist converted after that by the Jewish couple won over at Corinth by Paul himself. This would not be impossible.

However, I wonder if still another hypothesis would not be more acceptable, in that it would not contradict the letter of our text: this Alexandrian Jew, who is well versed in the "things concerning Jesus" and yet knows only John's baptism, was perhaps an authentic Christian who was still ignorant of the baptism of initiation practiced in the Hellenic communities. If so, it would mean, not that Apollos was John's disciple— which the text does not say—but that he was converted by a Judeo-Christian and had seen only the practice of immersion, the symbol of repentance, and not the Pauline Sacrament. This explanation could, it seems, turn to good account the "Johannic" conception of baptism, which appears also in Acts ii.38: "Then Peter said unto them, Repent [μετανοήσατε] and be baptized every one of you in the name of Jesus Christ for the remission of sins [εἰς ἄφεσιν τῶν ἁμαρτιῶν ὑμῶν] and ye shall receive the gift of the Holy Ghost." It is, perhaps, important to note that we are not told that Aquila had judged it expedient to baptize him at the time when, according to Acts xix.5, Paul supposedly baptized "in the name of the Lord Jesus" the dozen disciples of John whom, it seems, he encountered at Ephesus. The writer of Acts is, apparently, putting us on guard against the quite tempting conviction that Apollos introduced the Christian faith to Ephesus. Actually, his warnings do not prove much; but we cannot positively contradict them. The only impression that has some consistency is the one we derive from what seems to be a sort of flight the Alexandrian executes prior to Paul's arrival. When the Tarsiot comes to Ephesus, he departs; ditto at Corinth. It may well be said that he is not eager to meet Paul, for the reason, no doubt, that he too had *his Gospel,* which was not exactly the same as Paul's, or that his notion of the proper approach to the Judaizers differed from Paul's. We do not know.

The Apollos problem is to be found in two more places: 1 Corinthians i.12, where Paul reproaches the Corinthians for their divisiveness; some say, "I am of Paul!" others, "And I of Apollos!" or, "And I of Cephas!— And I of Christ!" Was there then a group of Christians at Corinth guided to the faith by Apollos, a group distinct from Paul's? And yet, we read in the second text, iii.4–7: "For while one saith, I am of Paul; and another, I am of Apollos; are ye not carnal?[62] Who then is Paul, and who is Apol-

62. That is to say: you have the human passion of divisiveness and discord.

los, but ministers by whom ye believed, even as the Lord gave to every man? I have planted, Apollos watered; but God gave the increase." Hence, one must believe that Apollos came to Corinth after the Tarsiot, that he followed in his steps, expanding and strengthening the results already obtained, so that the converts of the worker of the second hour, forgetting the true founder, were able to say: "We are of Apollos; it is his teaching that we follow." But in what did this teaching differ from that of Paul? Let us read the following, in Corinthians iii.8: "Now he that planteth and he that watereth are one: and every man shall receive his own reward according to his labor. For we are laborers together with God: [63] ye are God's husbandry, ye are God's building." Thus, in the work of God, one must not counterpose Paul and Apollos: they are inseparable and God reserves for each the reward he has merited. All that follows—about which the commentators are hardly in agreement—seems to establish the fact that the two masters did not diverge in the essence of their teaching,[64] but differed more or less in the forms they employed, and it was not for their flock to judge them; the latter were only to look upon them "as ministers of Christ, and stewards of the mysteries of God" (1 Cor. iv.1).

We have no other acceptable information on Apollos. We encounter the name in Titus iii.13, but we do not know whether it refers to the same person; in any case, one can learn nothing from that mention. The list of the seventy disciples (Luke x.1) drawn up in the fifth and sixth centuries includes Apollos and assigns to him the diocese of Caesarea; [65] that only proves that a name encountered in the New Testament has always been of service to the pious falsifiers who "perfected" the Christian traditions on the threshhold of the Middle Ages.

I believe that Apollos is to be viewed as a proper apostle, independent of the Tarsiot but led, by an analogous make-up, as well as by the influence of the milieu in which he labored, to pose the same postulates. He came from the Jewry of Alexandria, whose thinking was more or less similar to that of Tarsus or Antioch; he was converted, perhaps in his own land, by a Judeo-Christian, and he believed that he was called to proclaim the Good News of the Lord Jesus; in other words, he adopted and assimilated the Gospel of the Hellenists in the guise which, it seems to us,

63. Meaning, *the instruments of God.* Cf. 1 Cor. xv.10: χάριτι Θεοῦ εἰμι ὅ εἰμι = "it is by the grace of God that I am what I am."
64. Confirmed by 1 Cor. xvi.12, where Apollos is called "brother" (ἀδελφός) and appears to be on an intimate footing with Paul; however, he acts as he will and the importuning counsels of the Tarsiot do not change his resolution one whit.
65. Cf. *Chron. pascale,* ed. Bonn. 1, 442; 2, 126; Schmiedel, "Apollos," *EB,* par. 3.

it assumed at Antioch; then he left, voluntarily, as Paul did.[66] And when their paths crossed, they knew that they preached the same Lord, each in his own way. A simple fact that suffices to enable us to assess the extent of Paul's originality and to appraise how well-founded was his claim —hazarded in an hour of polemic—to exclusive investiture as Apostle to the Gentiles by the Lord Jesus.

66. Perhaps because of his doctrine he remained, if not closer, at least on better terms with the Judaizers than Paul. Cf. *CVII*, p. 200.

8

PAUL'S APOSTOLIC
JOURNEYS [1]

I. The Beginnings BECAUSE of frequent uncertainty about the veracity of Acts, it is impossible for us to render a satisfactory account of the exact itinerary of Paul's voyages. Hence the report I am going to present remains hypothetical on many points. This, obviously, is always the case when one tries to extract coherent information from the unfortunate text in question.

We left Paul on the road to Damascus, his conversion accomplished. From Acts ix.8f. we know that he then settled in Damascus (supposing, of course, that he had not come from there). This stay can be confirmed by Galatians i.17, where we read that after his voyage to Arabia, he *returned* to Damascus (καὶ πάλιν ὑπέστρεψα εἰς Δαμασκόν).[2] He probably received baptism there (Acts ix.18) and strengthened his new convictions by speaking "with the disciples at Damascus" (Acts ix.19). But what did he do after this? Acts (ix.20f) tells us that, animated with the greatest zeal, he went immediately into the synagogues to proclaim that Jesus was the Son of God. The Jews were at first surprised by this new attitude, since he had until then been known as the great enemy of the Christians;

1. For all bibliographical and critical information, see *XVIII*, IV,[1] pp. 215f, and *XVIII*, III, ch. vii. See also *CC*, ch. viii; *CXXIX*, Bk. II, chs. viiif; *CCXXVII*, chs. ivf; *CXV*, III, ch. ix; *CVIII* and *CVII*, ch. 1.
2. *CXXIX*, p. 144.

then they became angry and contemplated killing him. He would not have escaped them but for the devotion of some friends who aided his flight by lowering him in a basket from the top of the wall.

In itself Paul's zeal is quite acceptable, and a passage of 2 Corinthians (xi.32) confirms the fact of the flight, if not the circumstances; but the recital of Acts, which is coordinated with a voyage to Jerusalem (ix.26), which the Apostle himself contradicts (Gal. i.17: ". . . without going up to Jerusalem"), is not in good repute.[3] The best that can be said of the account in Acts is that this episode is out of place, since it fits in better with the return from Arabia.[4]

Paul himself (Gal. i.16–17) assures us that he *"immediately* [εὐθέως] *without conferring with flesh and blood, without going up to Jerusalem to them which were apostles before me,"* went to Arabia, then returned to Damascus, and "then, after three years" (ἔπειτα μετὰ τρία ἔτη), went to Jerusalem. It is therefore probable that he left Damascus immediately after his conversion. Acts also contradicts itself about the duration of his first stay at Damascus, for in ix.10 it confines it to several days (ἡμέρας τινάς), whereas in ix.23 the Jews allegedly become angry only after having endured Paul's propaganda for many days (ὡς δὲ ἐπληροῦντο ἡμέραι ἱκαναί).

We have no details and actually no information on this expedition into Arabia; we even wonder what Arabia the writer is referring to. It is not the desert; it is rather, in conformity with the terminology of Josephus, the kingdom of the Nabataeans,[5] to the south of Palestine, between the Euphrates region and the Red Sea, whose capital was Petra. Aretas IV (9 B.C.–40 A.D.) reigned there.

What was Paul going to do there? We do not know. It has been suggested that he was going into retreat, to a sort of meditation in solitude.[6] Concerning what he calls Sinai in Galatians iv.25, Lightfoot is even inclined to believe that he wanted a solemn season of communion with God, at the site where Yahweh had given the Law to Moses.[7] This is of course simply a hypothesis. I would be more inclined to believe that Paul began to preach in this land of Arabia, and I think that, if he went there, it was doubtless because, with contemporary Damascus under the influ-

3. *CVIII*, pp. 144f; *XVIII*, III, p. 217.
4. *CCXXVII*, p. 18.
5. Idumea, Upper Syria to the outskirts of Damascus could equally well be taken for Arabia. Cf. Strabo, 16, 4.
6. This is still the opinion of Ed. Meyer, *CXV*, III, p. 339. On the other conjectures, cf. *XVIII*, III, p. 216, n. 2; *CXXIX*, p. 144.
7. *St. Paul's Epistle to the Galatians*[7] (London, 1881), p. 88; cf. *CCXXVII*, p. 18.

ence of Aretas, the attention of the neophyte Apostle could quite naturally have been drawn towards Petra. But he may also have gone there because it seemed to him that the sites in Palestine and in Antioch had already been pre-empted, and he preferred, for his start, a land that, most likely, had not yet been broached by Christian propaganda. No text informs us about what he did there, or how long he stayed, or what success he had. Perhaps the text of 2 Corinthians xi.32, to which I have just alluded ("In Damascus the governor under Aretas the king kept the city of the Damascenes with a garrison, desirous to apprehend me") permits the conjecture that he had to some extent disturbed the Nabataeans, that he was obliged to depart rather hastily in order to take refuge at Damascus, and that the animosity of Aretas pursued him there, so that he soon had to flee again.

Then (ἔπειτα), *at the end of three years*, he went to Jerusalem (Gal. i.18). For what purpose? Three years after what? After his conversion, or after his return to Damascus? Ingenious exegetes have devoted their careers to the resolution of these minor problems.[8] I am inclined to interpret the statement as meaning three years after his conversion, for throughout the passage of Galatians which includes our text Paul's purpose is to prove that his mission owes nothing to the Apostles of Jerusalem.

Why did he resolve to go to the Holy City? He tells us in Galatians i.18: "to meet Peter" (ἱστορῆσαι Κηφᾶν). Was this simple curiosity? This is improbable; but we are again reduced to hypotheses about the true reason for his visit. I reject all those which assume that the Tarsiot desired to obtain apostolic confirmation of his mission: he never doubted himself nor his Lord on this point. He stayed only fifteen days (δεκαπέντε) with Peter and saw no other Apostle, except perhaps James, the brother of the Lord (Gal. i.18–19). Verse 18 suggests that he wished to make contact with the companions of Jesus; but why? Was he interrogated? Did he come up against the foreseeable questions: but who are you? Who knows you? Who guarantees you? Did he think that he had to be authenticated and accepted by the witnesses of the Resurrection? We cannot answer any of these questions. When he wrote to the Galatians, he was preoccupied with proving that his mission depended only upon Christ, and that the witnesses of Jerusalem had not doubted it. He did not deem it necessary to tell us about what happened and was said between him, Peter, and James during those fifteen days.

I believe it likely that he wanted to become attached to the mother-

8. [Cf. above, pp. 212f].

community. This appears to be the conclusion of Acts ix.26f., whose additions and commentaries are at the same time disturbing: they introduce Barnabas as a go-between between Paul and the Apostles, and take him with his protegé into the synagogues of Jerusalem. All one is able to gather from these more or less tendentious confusions is—again!—an impression of the Judeo-Christians' mistrust of this man, yesterday the enemy of Christ Jesus, today apparently the Lord's most favored among them. At least, so he says. From our point of view, what matters is the meeting of the Tarsiot with Peter and James. Henceforth, they accept him in the apostolic realm.

After this first voyage to Jerusalem, so obscure to us, what did he do? He tell us in Galatians i.21: "Then I went into the regions of Syria and of Cilicia." Nothing more, and we are inclined to believe that he went to Antioch and to Tarsus; perhaps to Tarsus first, and then to Antioch.[9] It is not at all likely that it was Barnabas who called him to Antioch, as Acts xi.25 [10] claims, because Barnabas, one of the founders of this large community, had no need of his aid. It seems probable that the two met at Antioch and worked there together in a milieu that Paul knew well. The writer of Acts confused everything in his desire to make the Church of Antioch, even its founding, dependent on the Church of Jerusalem. In any case, this period of Paul's activity at Antioch and at Tarsus proves that at that moment in his career he did not object to preaching where a considerable apostolic work had already been realized.

Paul tells us (Gal. ii.1) that he stayed in these regions of Syria and Cilicia for fourteen years. This period of his life is completely hidden from us, because, in his subsequent letters, he never speaks of the communities of Cilicia or Syria. I think that this circumspection is due to the fact that he worked there only in collaboration with Barnabas, if not even under his orders, and that he could never recognize this as his own work. I would willingly ascribe to the same cause his silence concerning the first large missionary voyage attributed to him by Acts xiii.4–14, 26, which he also made in the company of Barnabas. I would assume, however, that this important trip took place in the fourteen-year period of which Galatians speaks, and that the formula "the regions of Syria and of Cilicia" easily implies a hook in Pamphylia, Lycaonia, and Pisidia.

9. *XVIII*, IV,[1] p. 221.
10. *CVIII*, p. 468.

II. The First Missionary Journey

A short, unembellished [11] note at the beginning of chapter xiii of Acts lets us glimpse why and how Paul and Barnabas left Antioch to expand their propaganda. The Spirit, it seems, revealed to the *notables* of Antioch that he had reserved Paul and Barnabas for a special task: for this reason, these eminent men, having apprehended the designs of the Almighty, and having prayed and fasted properly, gave their blessing to the two apostles and sped them on their way. It should be understood that the Spirit urged the heads of the Antioch community to send the two companions to do elsewhere that which they had already done well in Syria, so that Paul's first great apostolic journey is presented as *a mission willed by the brethren of the Church where Christianity was born.*

It has been asked if, before leaving, the Tarsiot had—more or less together with Barnabas—conceived a plan of evangelization, if he had determined in advance the field he was going to cover. Several noted critics have replied affirmatively.[12] In fact, when one recalls in Paul's letters the names of Antioch, Ephesus, Thessalonica, Corinth, and even Rome, the impression is created that he mapped out the bases of operations which logic as well as geography imposed upon him, provided he planned to propagandize in the Greco-Asiatic regions of the North Mediterranean world; because otherwise, he would have gone to Alexandria, Cyrenia, and Carthage. In fact, if he had ecumenical evangelization in mind, it would be difficult to understand why he did neglect these three cities. But I am afraid that the imagination of the exegetes is no substitute for Paul's own uncertainty, for there seems to be no evidence in the Epistles of a general itinerary determined in advance. The intentions hinted at in the Epistles appear to be always limited in extent, and concern only the near future. At the most it is possible to believe—without being sure—that at the end of his final stay at Corinth, Paul expanded his plans and thought of returning to Jerusalem, then going from there to Rome and to Spain.[13] But such a resolution would still be far removed from a prearranged and precise plan.

On the contrary, these texts emphasize the uncertain and precarious character of the Tarsiot's projects, always subservient to the sovereign and

11. *CVIII*, pp. 499f.
12. *CC*, pp. 130f.
13. *XVIII*, IV,[1] p. 240.

arbitrary action of God. He writes to the Corinthians (1 Cor. iv.19) that he will soon come to them "if the Lord wills it," and reiterates the statement at the end of his letter (xvi.7). He says to the Romans that he is continually asking in his prayers (i.10) that he be granted "by the will of God" the time to come to them, a declaration he repeats in xv.32. The same note is sounded in Philippians ii.24. Here Acts confirms our impression by showing us Paul being guided on his way by inspirations or by visions. He crosses Phrygia and Galatia, but is prevented by the Holy Spirit from announcing "the word" in Asia (xvi.6); and, immediately afterwards (xvi.7), as he plans to go to Bithynia, "the Spirit of Jesus prevented him." He then descends towards Troas, where (xvi.9) a vision appears to him in the night: "There stood a man of Macedonia, and prayed him, saying, Come over into Macedonia, and help us." He went there, because it was his conviction that it was the will of God. Thus he followed the inspiration of the moment, a frame of mind that would have worked havoc with any plan.

Obviously, the detail of his itinerary, his choosing to stop in one city rather than another, the length of his stays, must have been determined by special circumstances, which often escape us; besides, he sometimes accommodated himself to practical wonts, to the traffic facilities which connected two cities.[14]

In the company of Barnabas and John-Mark, he went first to Cyprus, probably in the spring of 44.[15] They converted the proconsul Sergius Paulus, who already *feared God*, or was at least a Judaizer (Acts xiii.6f.). The incident is disturbing, for it may well have been contrived in order to ascribe to Paul a role analogous to that played by Peter when he confronted Simon the Magician (Acts viii.18–24), who is here represented by a Jewish prophet, also a magician, who is struck blind by Paul, in order to offer the Roman an irresistible *sign*. This is naive thaumaturgy, but it masks a profound truth: it may be that Sergius Paulus has no historical reality, but he is a *type*: that is, he typifies the intelligent proselyte (συνετός) (Acts xiii.7) who understands the superiority, for a man like himself, of this new Judaism, so welcoming and so receptive compared to the old, which so frequently opened its gates to proselytes only reluctantly and was inclined to impose upon them so many burdensome obligations. Paul's victory has symbolic value, and prophesies the victory of Christianity over the Jewish proselytism and the magicians.

14. *XVIII*, IV,[1] pp. 243f.
15. Nothing in the Epistles confirms this mission. On its disturbing effects, cf. *CVII*, pp. 171f.

From Paphos, Paul and Barnabas evidently went to Pamphylia, then pushed to the north, towards Pisidia. At this point John-Mark left them, whether because he did not approve of their methods and their liberality— it is noted that he returned to Jerusalem (Acts xiii.13) [16]—or because their itinerary displeased him. From Pisidia they went to Lycaonia, to the northeast, stopping at Iconium (Acts xiv.1), Lystra, and Derbe (xiv.6). Acts abounds in brief anecdotes about this journey: disputes in the synagogues (xiii.14–15), violent demonstrations against the Apostles, for example at Lystra (xiv.19), where the people stone Paul and throw him out of the city, "supposing him dead"; or, conversely, manifestations of enthusiasm: even at Lystra, before the crowd is swayed by Jews who had come from Antioch, Pisidia, and Iconium, the Apostles, it seems, found it difficult to keep the people from worshipping them (xiv.18).

Actually, all of the details of these stories in Acts are highly suspect— if only because of the introductions to the discourses—of contrivance in their arrangement and even of being fabrications of the writer; but it is almost impossible for us to separate the true from the false. However, it is not likely that the writer imagined the hostility of the pure Jews and their resistance to the Christian propaganda, or the compensatory good will of those who "feared God." And, except for some vague approximations, the likelihood of the general outline of the itinerary being exact is equally small.

The apostolic voyage ended on the coast of Pamphylia, to which the missionaries returned, perhaps by the same route; from there they came back to Antioch by sea. I would not risk saying for how long they were gone.

What they accomplished there differed so greatly from the practice and the spirit of the brethren of Jerusalem, gathered around their Elders and the Twelve, that such an initiative could not pass without an explanation of its basis. The explanation did indeed take place; but the version given by Paul and that of the writer of Acts do not quite correspond. The Tarsiot, as usual, tells the whole story only as it relates to himself, whereas Acts treats it more generally, which, on the whole, probably enables us to realize more accurately what really happened.

16. *CXXIX*, p. 159; *CXV*, III, p. 174.

III. *The Accord with Jerusalem*

Here is Paul's version: "Then [after his first great missionary journey] fourteen years after I went up again to Jerusalem with Barnabas, and took Titus with me also." [17] He asserts that a revelation imposed this voyage on him: of himself, he would perhaps have drawn back before such a step, despite the fact that it was so important for the future of his missions; but he could not oppose the will of God. I imagine that in fact the will of God served to corroborate some rather urgent manifestation of anxiety on the part of the "saints" of Jerusalem. Thus Paul appeared before the Mother Church, whose heads alone knew his face (i.22): "And I went up by revelation and communicated unto them [18] that gospel which I preach among the Gentiles . . . lest by any means I should run, or had run, in vain" (Gal. ii.2). Which means that his *gospel* had met with opposition in the Mother Church and was in danger of disavowal by it. And by gospel I do not mean simply, or even especially, the substance of his faith, but also the practice and the discipline of his preaching.

The account in Acts (xv.lf) [19] differs a little at first but comes down to the same thing in the end: "And certain men which came down from Judaea taught the brethren [at Antioch], and said, Except ye be circumcised after the manner of Moses, ye cannot be saved." The converts were greatly troubled by this assertion; Paul and Barnabas opposed as best they could these zealots of the Law; finally, the community at Antioch decided to send them both to Jerusalem for an explanation with the Apostles. Note that Galatians ii.4 declares that "false brethren unawares brought in, who came in privily to spy out our liberty which we have in Christ Jesus." We are not far removed from Acts. Besides, the objections that the Jewish converts must have opposed to Paul and Barnabas were probably couched in practically the same terms as those adopted by the writer of Acts. They led to this conclusion: "It is not thus that one proceeds at Jerusalem; you are not in communion with the Apostles." From whence the need for a meeting.

This meeting has been given the somewhat ambitious and misleading

17. Gal. ii.1. Fourteen years after his first voyage to Jerusalem or fourteen years after his conversion? This has been debated at length, with strong arguments on both sides. The first interpretation appears to be more in accord with current notions.
18. Αὐτοῖς = those of Jerusalem.
19. *CVIII*, pp. 564f.

name of the "Apostolic Conference of Jerusalem," or the "Council of Jerusalem." As usual, we are badly informed about what really happened.[20] Acts (xv.1–33) proffers us a long story: but it is difficult to accept it, first because it differs greatly from what Paul says in Galatians ii, secondly, because it presents matters in such a fashion that, if true, nothing in the Pauline account that follows would be comprehensible. Indeed, if the issue had been resolved by a clear and positive apostolic decision, how could the difficulties described in Galatians ii.11—called the *conflict of Antioch*—have arisen? Prudence counsels that basically we abide by Paul's testimony on this point (Gal. ii.2–10). Here it is, in its entirety:

And I went up [to Jerusalem] by revelation, and communicated unto them [αὐτοῖς = the brethren of the City] that gospel which I preach among the Gentiles, but privately to them which were of reputation [οἱ δοκοῦντες],[21] lest by any means I should run, or had run, in vain.[22] But neither Titus, who was with me, being a Greek, was compelled to be circumcised [*the matter at issue*]: And that because of false brethren unawares brought in, who came in privily to spy out our liberty which we have in Christ Jesus, that they might bring us into bondage: To whom we gave place by subjection, no, not for an hour; that the truth of the gospel might continue with you. But of these who seemed to be somewhat (whatsoever they were, it maketh no matter to me: God accepteth no man's person:) for they who seemed to be somewhat in conference added nothing to me:[23] But contrariwise, when they saw that the gospel of the uncircumcision was committed unto me, as the gospel of the circumcision was unto Peter . . . and when James, Cephas, and John, who seemed to be pillars [οἱ δοκοῦντες στῦλοι εἶναι] perceived the grace that was given unto me,[24] they gave to me and Barnabas the right hands of fellowship; that we should go unto the heathen and they unto the circumcision. Only they would that we should remember the poor; the same which I also was forward to do.

It is perfectly clear that the question posed here is that of Jewish legalism, whose observance the Judeo-Christians regarded as indispensable to the faithful, whereas Paul and Barnabas found it useless and perhaps already inconvenient, at least for the Gentile converts. The two apostles from Antioch fought the "false brethren," that is, those who doubted that Jesus freed his own from the bondage of the Law, hence those who

20. *XVIII*, III, pp. 245f; IV,[1] p. 223; *CVIII*, pp. 564f.
21. I understand this to mean that the Tarsiot reserved for "them which were of reputation" some additional explanations.
22. I.e., to see all of the results of his missions ruined.
23. I.e., imposed on him no instructions restricting his apostolic freedom.
24. They judged it by its results.

remained in the authentic line of the first tradition. They *"ceded nothing"* to them; by which we understand that they rejected their demands and, especially, refused to have Titus circumcised. They knew that to remain within the confines of legalism was equivalent to rejecting all the pagan converts and this, for Paul, would have been a denial of his gospel and its ruin. Those whom they considered to be "men of repute" that is, those men whose personal influence more or less guided the community, did not support the rigorists; they were already acting like men of authority. They did not seek to impose their usages, nor, perhaps, their opinions; they admitted that there could be two ways, equally blessed by Christ, of reaching him. Assuredly, Paul simplified matters in imagining a sort of division of the work of conversion between himself and Peter; the Apostles of Jerusalem merely had the wisdom to say: "You are successful; do not change your method; and, since your affairs go so well, remember that ours are less prosperous." Thus, the apostolic "pillars" maintained the communion (κοινωνία) in Christ of the workers on both sides; they assuredly did not issue any decree, in the sense of the law—I was going to say, canon law—ruling on the problem. That is why difficulties reappear concerning special points: for instance, the meal with its legally impure food, which the Christians partook with the pagans, and the consumption of the *idolothytes*, that is to say, the meats sacrificed and offered to the gods.

What is especially interesting to us, from Paul's point of view, is that this accord with the "heads" of the Mother community left him complete freedom of movement in his propaganda, and perhaps confirmed his certainty that he was on the right path. Moreover, the field of his activity, after the meeting as before it, appears to have been determined much more by geography than by any distinction between Jews and non-Jews; for, in the Asiatic world where he carried his message, he always began by preaching in the synagogues to the Jews, as though he himself was an apostle of circumcision.[25] A strong impression is created that he does not feel in any way confirmed in his apostolate by the fellowship of Jerusalem: in writing to the Galatians about what happened in the Holy City, he takes care to remind them that he holds his apostolate not from men but from Jesus Christ and from God the Father (i.1: οὐκ ἀπ' ἀνθρώπων οὐδὲ δι' ἀνθρώπου, ἀλλὰ διὰ 'Ιησοῦ Χριστοῦ καὶ θεοῦ πατρός). Indeed, this remained his conviction up to the end of his career.

25. *CLIII*,[2] pp. 18f; *XVIII, IV*,[1] p. 234.

IV.   The Conflict of Antioch;
Expansion of the Pauline Mission;
The Second and Third Journeys

a) *The Conflict of Antioch.* After the explanation at Jerusalem, whose date remains uncertain, Paul and Barnabas returned to Antioch and, undoubtedly, remained there for a while.[26] Peter went there to join them, we do not know when or why, and there was renewed conflict between him and them, invariably on the issue of legalistic observances. The Galilean apostle was at first very broad-minded; but the people who had come from James would have rejected him (Gal. ii.12). And Paul apparently reproached him for this recanting. We do not know how the incident ended. We must neither exaggerate nor dramatize it, as was done by the "Tübingen school"; but at least it proves that the alleged apostolic decree found in Acts is a fabrication. For the moment, I shall go no further than this conclusion.

What is of greatest interest to us in this conflict is the fact that it probably consummated the separation, if not the break, between Paul and Barnabas. The latter who, in our opinion, was the protagonist of the first missionary journey, was, apparently, enticed by the Jews to follow Peter (Gal. ii.13); that is to say that, though disinclined to impose the observance of legalistic prescriptions on the Gentile converts, he did not think that he himself was authorized to dispense with them. And he went his way (Acts xv.38). Our writer explains this schism between Paul and Barnabas by ascribing it to a disagreement concerning John-Mark, whom Barnabas wished to take along but whom Paul wanted to leave at Antioch as punishment for his desertion during the course of the first journey (xiii.13).[27] At the most this is a pretext and, more likely, a soothing invention of Acts.

Did Paul's stand against Peter and against Barnabas in this quarrel more or less estrange him from the entire Church of Antioch? It is certainly possible.[28] Then, more isolated in his apostolic labor, he also became more inclined to systematize his preaching, to dispense with the Law, and to deserve the increasing hostility of the Jews. Thus we arrive at

26. Acts xv.30–35, confirmed, it seems, by Gal. ii.11.

27. Was he beset by the doubts of a Judaizer? I believe so, if it is true that he immediately returned to Jerusalem: ἀποχωρήσας ἀπ’ αὐτῶν ἐπέστρεψεν εἰς ’Ιεροσόλυμα.

28. *XVIII*, IV,[1] p. 271; *CXXIX*, p. 207.

the conviction that if he ever really believed in the division of propaganda between him and Peter he had great illusions. Assuredly, his accord with the "pillars" of Jerusalem did not stem from any radical interpretation of doctrine.

b) *The Second Voyage*. Leaving Antioch with Silas, whom he had brought back from Jerusalem, the Tarsiot then went to Cilicia. When? And what are the chronological relations of the first and second journeys? [29] Two questions that we can answer only by hypotheses. The period of time was probably short, a year or so at the most.

As a start, Paul visited the Churches he had established during his first journey (Acts xv.36); then, guided by the Spirit (xvi.6, 7, 9) and accompanied by Silas and Timothy, who joined him at Lystra, he went across Phrygia and Galatia to Mysia, into ancient Troas, and from there, obeying a vision, he went to Macedonia (Acts xvi.11–12). We observe him at Philippi, then at Thessalonica, beaten and chased from the one (xvi. 21f), accused of evil political designs by the Jews of the other (xvii.5–8); [30] pursued to Berea by the hate of the same adversaries; and finally obliged to flee hastily from Berea to Athens under the escort of several devoted brethren, leaving on the way Silas and Timothy.[31] From Athens he went to Corinth (xviii.1f.) where, in a more cosmopolitan milieu, he encountered more favorable conditions for his preaching. Yet it was there that he had one of his most dangerous collisions with the Jews. They arraigned him before the proconsul Gallio, accusing him of teaching men to worship God in a way contrary to the Law (xviii.13); but the Roman, unable to find in the charge against the accused any violation of common law, ended the proceedings by letting the bystanders beat the *archisynagogos* Sosthenes (xviii.17).

We must of course relinquish any close examination of the incidents reported by Acts, as well as any attempt to establish between them a firm chronological link.[32] Moreover, our version of these incidents has obvious gaps; it says nothing, for example, about what Paul did in Galatia and in Phrygia, and since the pronoun "we" that is supposed to inspire confidence appears for the first time only in xvi.9–11, it is likely that the vagueness and lacunae of our text are to be imputed to the second writer, who tampered with the original.

Though it had perhaps been Paul's intention to merely pause at Cor-

29. *XVIII*, IV,[1] p. 81: "Les Points fixes de la chronologie paulinienne."
30. 1 Thess. i.6; ii.2; ii.14 speak also of the Apostle's difficulties at Thessalonica. These were not the same as those described in Acts.
31. He could have arrived at Athens in the spring of 50. Cf. *XVIII*, IV,[1] p. 287.
32. *CVIII, ad loc., XVIII*, III, pp. 258f; IV,[1] pp. 272f.

inth while awaiting an occasion to return to Macedonia, he stayed there a year and a half (Acts xiii.19). Now, Corinth was destined to become *his city* and he was apparently especially attached to it. The city he saw [33] had been founded by Julius Caesar (*Colonia Laus Julia Corinthiis*), on the site of the Greek city destroyed in 146 B.C. Located between two ports, Cenchreae to the east and Lechaion to the west, it was the center of considerable commercial traffic. Re-established as the capital of the province of Achaia, it was inhabited by men from all corners of the Mediterranean who had made of it a crossroads of beliefs and cults, one of the most active centers of Greco-Oriental syncretism. Its morals were loose, and there was much talk about a temple to Aphrodite which, according to Strabo, had formerly housed in Corinth an imposing body of one thousand sacred prostitutes; [34] it is not known how many there were in the new Corinth. However, the current expression, "to live like a Corinthian," was full of promises. Such dissoluteness, not usual in the Greek cities, indicated a predominance of the Oriental element. Corinth harbored a large Jewish colony, and did not enjoy an intellectual reputation.

Paul prolonged his stay at Corinth because Silas and Timothy soon came back from Macedonia and convinced him that he would have no success there. Then he looked for work and took up his trade again, together with a certain Aquila and his wife Priscilla, already won over to the faith, according to all appearances.[35] They were people of leisure,[36] natives of Pontus, who came from Rome, from where they may have fled under an edict of Claudius.[37] The Lord himself, by means of a nocturnal vision (Acts xviii.9), had encouraged Paul in his conduct. Exactly what did he do in the city? We are far removed from clear knowledge of the answer. The short recital of Acts (xviii.1–18) is badly presented and evidently does not retain much of its original information: the conflicts between the Jews and the Apostle must have continued. They are, as it were, assembled and typified in the incident of the trial before Gallio. What is the truth in this affair? This has been debated at length,[38] and one can keep on debating without arriving at any satisfactory conclusion. The most reliable information comes from some verses of 1 Corinthians. There we learn that Paul considered himself to be the true and sole founder of the Church at Corinth (1 Cor. iii.6, 10), its father (iv.14),

33. *LVI,*[2] pp. 211f; *XVIII,* IV,[1] pp. 338f; *CVII,* pp. 203f.
34. Strabo, 8, 6, 20.
35. *XII,* I, p. 54; *CXV,* III, p. 111.
36. 2 Cor. xvi.19 speaks of a house they had at Ephesus, and Rom. xvi.5 of another at Rome.
37. Suetonius, *Claudius,* 25.
38. *XVIII,* III, pp. 271f.

and that he regarded the very existence of this Church as the seal of his apostolate (ix.2). He sowed and reaped among the former pagans, whether or not they had passed through the stage of Jewish proselytism (xii.2: "you know that when you were pagans . . ."). Practically all these converts came from the lower classes (i.26) or from the slave element (vii.21). However, there were in the community a few wealthier men; they humiliated their poorer brothers by eating and drinking according to their means at the fraternal meals (xi.22).

Towards the end of the fall of 51, Paul apparently left Corinth for Ephesus, where in passing he left Aquila and Priscilla. From there, Acts (xviii.22) leads him to Caesarea in Palestine and into Jerusalem to "salute the Church"; but there are grounds for believing that this is an invention of the writer, who is once again anxious to stress the perfect accord between the Tarsiot and the other Apostles.[39] It is more likely that he returned to Antioch from Ephesus, and there ended his second missionary journey.

c) *The Third Journey.* According to all appearances, the third journey must have begun shortly afterwards, in the spring of 52.[40] Paul apparently first revisited his communities in Galatia and Phrygia (Acts xviii.23); at the end of several months (summer of 53?) he was in Ephesus. He probably stayed there over two years (xix.8–10), in a very mixed religious milieu where the most diverse tendencies were juxtaposed. Acts names the Jews (xviii.19), Apollos (xviii.24–28), the disciples of the Baptist (xix. 1–7), and magicians (xix.13–20). It may well be said that the Tarsiot encountered great difficulties. In 1 Corinthians, written at Ephesus, he speaks of numerous collisions with adversaries (xvi.8–9); in 2 Corinthians i.8, he tells us that at Ephesus he almost lost his life; in 2 Corinthians xi.23 he speaks of a prison with which he has become much more familiar than all the other heralds of the Gospel. An obscure text (1 Cor. xv.32) tells of his battle with "beasts at Ephesus" (ἐθηριομάχησα ἐν Ἐφέσῳ); we do not know exactly what he meant by these words, but it is clear that in writing them he wished to convey a strong idea of the dangers he had endured.[41]

From Asia he returned to Macedonia, then went to Corinth (Acts xx.1–2), came again to Macedonia, and went from there to Troas, then

39. The text says: "And when he had landed at Caesarea, and gone up, and saluted the church, he went down to Antioch." It has been said that the greeting was addressed only to the Church at Caesarea. This is hardly likely: ἀναβαίνω is a term generally used to indicate the voyage to Jerusalem. *CXIX*, p. 114; *CVIII*, p. 707; *XVIII*, III, p. 278.

40. XVIII, IV,[1] p. 361.

41. On the various interpretations proposed, cf. *XVIII*, IV,[1] pp. 364f.

to Mytilene, Samos, and Miletus. Acts, which deals very briefly with the first part of this itinerary, dwells on the details from the moment Paul leaves Corinth to his arrival at Caesarea in Palestine (xxi.8). There ends the third missionary journey. It ends at Caesarea only because the Tarsiot decided to go from there to Jerusalem, in the company of several men who probably carried the collections gathered in the communities of Berea, Thessalonica, Corinth, and Ephesus and apparently represented their Churches (Acts xx.4). What was he going to do in the City? We do not know. Acts (xx.16) says that he was going to the feast of Pentecost; but we find it difficult to believe this. The brethren of Caesarea were not too certain that he would be well received in the Holy City, for after having tried to dissuade him from going there, they had him escorted and took care to find him lodgings with a certain Mnason (xxi.16) in whom they undoubtedly had confidence. He was an "old disciple," a Cypriot by origin, and therefore a Hellenist.

V. The Last Phase: From Jerusalem to Rome

We have only one document concerning this last phase of the Tarsiot's life: the account which fills the last chapters of Acts (xxi–xxviii) and to which it is certainly impossible to accord full confidence.[42] The methods of emending it at our disposal, internal criticism and criticism of probability, seem at first to be more appropriate to asking questions than to resolving them, to filling the margins of the text with question marks rather than to extracting the total or partial truth it may contain. However, we may perhaps not wander too far from the truth if we adhere to the fundamental affirmations of the account.

A doublet (xxi.18–25) which contrasts with the writer's familiar harmonizing themes, and which therefore inspires some confidence in us, relates that when Paul arrived at Jerusalem there was a meeting between him and James, at which all the Elders were present. These brethren approved the Apostle's work among the pagans, but warned him that the faithful who still adhered to the Law considered him an apostate, and counselled him to make a public demonstration that would absolve him of so onerous a suspicion; i.e., to join four Judaist Christians who had made "a vow" (xxi.23) and accompany them to the Temple. It has been conjectured that Paul himself had also made a vow, at Corinth or elsewhere,[43]

42. CVIII, ad loc.; CVII, pp. 210f.; CXXIX, pp. 280f.; XXXVIII, II, pp. 143f.
43. CVIII, p. 802; XVIII, III, p. 298.

and that he wanted to carry it out (xviii.18). But it is rather surprising to see him in the posture of a *nazir*, that is to say, for him to submit to rites of penitence that were in such ill accord with the spirit of his Gospel, and to mingle besides with a group of men bound by the same obligations. Desire not to attract the attention of the Jews, who had no better opinion of him than the Judaizing Christians, does not, it seems to us, suffice to warrant such curious behavior. Must we believe that, although he did not impose the yoke of the Law on his Gentile converts, he did not feel authorized to reject it for himself? [44] We may as well say that the motives for his decision escape us.

Moreover, if he thought that by these means he would escape the attention of his enemies, he was mistaken (Acts xxi.27f.): some Jews from Asia recognized him and incited the multitude against him by identifying him as the man who held the Jewish nation and the Torah in contempt— an accusation not wholly false. They claimed, perhaps in good faith, that he had brought into the Temple, from beyond the court of the Gentiles, one of his uncircumcised companions, a Greek named Trophimus. Instantly a vast tumult ensued: the Jews threw themselves upon him, pushed him out of the Temple, and were about to kill him when a commanding officer from the tower of Antonia came running with a company of soldiers. Although the officer could gather nothing from the furious outcry, he suspected that he had caught an agitator who should be imprisoned, perhaps the Egyptian who had recently disturbed the country (xxi.38); he led his captive to the fortress and was about to scourge him in order to elicit some information, when Paul claimed his right as a Roman citizen (xxii.25). The issue instantly assumed another aspect, and Paul was sent under escort to Caesarea, to defend himself before the procurator Felix. Such is the brief summary I think it possible to draw, with some accuracy, from the obviously dramatized and incredibly embellished account of Acts. It would be difficult to imagine, for example, the enraged crowd listening to the discourse the Tarsiot presumably addressed to them from the steps of the Temple (xxii.1–21); one wonders, too, how the Roman authority could have permitted a Roman citizen to appear before the Sanhedrin to answer possible charges (xxii.30–xxiii.9).

Moreover, it has correctly been remarked [45] that in claiming the privilege of his status as a Roman citizen, Paul placed himself, and Christianity with him, *outside Judaism*, for by this act he rejected the competence of the Sanhedrin in a case which so obviously appeared to be

44. *CVII*, p. 208; *CVIII*, p. 801.
45. *CVIII*, p. 834.

within the jurisdiction of this tribunal. There is no reason to believe that the Tarsiot foresaw this consequence of his action; even less to suppose that he sought it.[46]

Felix continued to keep Paul under arrest while awaiting the accusers (xxiii.35); but from this moment on it becomes difficult to see clearly through the allegations of Acts. There was supposedly a trial before the procurator; but it evidently resolved nothing, because the absence of the tribune Lysias, who had arrested Paul, left Felix in the dark about the substance of the affair. Paul allegedly remained in captivity, which was not too rigorous, two years (xxiv.23), in the course of which Felix was replaced by Festus. The latter was in no greater hurry to reach a verdict. Finally, at the insistence of the Jews, there was a second trial; Paul, believing that the Roman was hostile to him and wanted to compel him to accept the jurisdiction of the Sanhedrin, appealed his case to Caesar (xxv.11). Whereupon Festus, delighted to be freed of so embarrassing a prisoner, said to him: "You have appealed to Caesar, to Caesar you shall go." (RSV).

It is a waste of time to demand any juridical precision from Acts. What valid legal ground was there behind Paul's arrest? Of what was he accused? Why did the procurator keep him in captivity? We do not know. According to Acts xxi.28–29 and xxv.8, the Tarsiot's crime consisted of an attempt to bring a pagan into the Temple; but, according to xxvi.21, this crime was his adherence to the Christian hope and his preaching in its favor. The two complaints are quite different. Actually, our writer is interested not in the legal point involved but in expanding his thesis of the systematic and ruthless hostility of the Jews.[47] Moreover, did it not occur to the procurator, when questioning his prisoner, that there was something more in this affair than a Jewish quarrel; that Paul's preaching belonged in the category of illicit teachings; that it held propositions dangerous to the public order or, at least, disturbing to a magistrate? I would gladly believe that this is what happened. And there is no evidence to prove that the charge proffered by the Jews was not linked to some other complaint likely to arrest Festus's attention. It is alleged that the lawyer Tertullus, whom the people of Jerusalem had apparently hired to present the charge, accused Paul (xxiv.5) of being a "pestilence"—a public plague —of having excited dissension among all the Jews of the world, of having acted like the ringleader of the Nazarene sect. If something of the sort was really said, it is understandable why the procurator did not release

46. CCXXX, p. 36. This is also Ramsay's opinion.
47. XXXVIII, II, p. 143, n. 1. For bibliography, see pp. 144–45 and n.

the accused. Another indication of the Roman's possible view of the affair is perhaps to be found in Acts xxiv.25: "And as he reasoned of righteousness, temperance, and judgment to come, Felix trembled, and answered, Go thy way for this time." Whether or not he already had some precise notions of the Christian propaganda,[48] Felix could not but distrust a man who engendered such redoubtable ideas in the Jewish world.

Thus Paul was sent to Caesarea. His voyage, as related in Acts (xxvii. 1–28, 31), lasted a long time, perhaps six months; there were many incidents and accidents—the shipwreck before Melita (Malta), for instance. If Acts xxviii.15 is to be believed, when the prisoner, who had landed at Puteoli, approached Rome, the brethren of the city came to meet him as far as the Forum of Appius and up to the Three Taverns; a strange meeting, since the first of the two sites is on the Appian Way, a day's trip from Rome, the second only sixteen kilometers away. Moreover, the fact itself is even more surprising than its setting, for, according to Acts itself, once he is in Rome, the Apostle is completely isolated; to say nothing of the fact that it is difficult to conceive such a manifestation around a prisoner and several guards. It is also to be noted that the "we" disappears from the account in xxviii.16, as if the original source had stopped there. The following section, which describes an interview with the eminent Jews of Rome, appears to be an unlikely invention. Nothing in the text leads us to believe that Paul was in contact with the Christian community at Rome, which is not mentioned in the Epistle to the Philippians, which has so often been dated as written from the capital and traced back to this period. It is vain to seek an explanation for this apparent singularity, but it may be said that the more or less accurate mention of Paul's active preaching in Rome (xxviii.31) favors the hypothesis of his acting independently of the brethren already grouped there.[49] The haste to meet Paul that our writer obligingly attributes to them is a very good argument for persuading us of their indifference.[50]

Paul, henceforth at the disposal of the prefect of the praetorium, who judged in the name of the Prince, was allegedly kept in very easy captivity, as he waited to appear before the imperial tribunal; he was lodged in the city, under the surveillance and escort of a soldier: this form of detention, very commonly practiced in the Empire, was called *custodia militum* or *custodia libera*.[51] Then Paul allegedly rented a house, where he stayed two whole years (xxviii.30–31), receiving whom he wished and "preach-

48. *CVIII*, p. 862.
49. *CVIII*, p. 948.
50. *CVII*, p. 222.
51. "Custodia," *DA*.

ing the kingdom of God, and teaching those things which concern the Lord Jesus Christ, with all confidence, no man forbidding him."

These are the last words of Acts, and the abrupt termination has given the exegetes much trouble.[52] In fact, it is thus that Paul leaves history, and the numerous hypotheses offered to clarify the end of his life are founded only on conjectures devoid of authority.

VI. Hypotheses Concerning Paul's End

We are confronted by two traditions juxtaposed by legend:

a) *The Acquittal and the Voyage to Spain.* Paul appeared before the imperial tribunal, which acquitted him. He then went to Spain,[53] in accordance with a plan expressly testified to by Romans xv.24. Two later texts allegedly confirm this fact: (1) The *First Epistle of Clement*, 5, 7, where it is stated that the Apostle "teaches justice to the whole universe" and that he has gone "to the extremities of the Occident" (ἐπὶ τὸ τέρμα τῆς δύσεως ἐλθών); this is interpreted to be Spain; (2) The *Muratorian Canon*, which speaks of *Paul's departure from the City for Spain* (*profectionem Pauli ab Urbe ad Spanium* . . .). The journey was probably short, for Paul supposedly came back to Rome in time to die with Peter under Nero's persecution in 64.[54] If one accepts the authenticity of the Pastorals, the question becomes even more complicated, for one would have to admit two captivities, separated by a period of preaching in Crete (Titus i.5) and in Nicopolis (iii.12).

b) *The Decapitation at Rome.* Paul did not go to Spain, but perished at Rome, decapitated on the Ostian Way, at the site called the Three Fountains, where they still show the three springs that spouted when his head rebounded three times.[55]

If one notes that the text of Clement of Rome is supported by nothing more than the intent specified in Romans xv.24 and 28 ("From you, I will go to Spain") and that actually the authority of the *Muratorian Canon* is rather weak, then it must be admitted that the voyage to Spain

52. *XVIII*, III, pp. 326f.

53. Texts assembled and discussed in Dom Leclerq, *L'Espagne chrétienne* (Paris, 1906), pp. 25f.

54. *CXXIX*, p. 299. For discussion of details, cf. *CCLX*, pp. 141f.

55. It was Gregory the Great who set aside for the maintenance of Paul's tomb the ground called *ad Aquas Salvias*, the site of the Apostle's execution according to the tradition. Cf. Duchesne, *Le Liber pontificalis* (text, introduction, and commentary, Paris, 1886, 2 vols. in-4), I, p. 196.

is rather dubious.[56] Our main problem is to explain the abrupt ending of Acts: obviously neither the author of the book nor its reviser could have been ignorant of what happened to the Apostle; then why their silence? It is difficult to conceive what would have prevented them from telling us about a trial that ended with an acquittal, since their thesis concerning the Roman authorities' good-will towards the Christian brethren could have exploited this fact to its advantage; if, on the other hand, the Imperial tribunal condemned Paul, their apologetic would have been somewhat embarrassed and hampered by this outcome of the trial.[57] To confess that Paul was condemned by Nero would have been an even graver admission than acknowledging that Jesus was condemned by Pilate.[58]

But what could have been the basis for such a condemnation, since, judging it from the Roman point of view, the accusation hardly seems consistent? We do not know. It has been suggested that there was Jewish intrigue, with Poppaea as the go-between; [59] this is not an unlikely supposition, but it is nothing more than a supposition. Undoubtedly, Nero would not have hesitated over legal scruples; actually however, it was probably Burrhus, the prefect of the Praetorium, who passed sentence. Moreover, if the hypothesis I advanced above is correct, and if the account given by Festus, which evidently accompanied the accused, emphasized unlawful and dangerous teachings; if it denounced Paul as *molitor rerum novarum*, or *instigator of alarming innovations*; and if, rejected by the Jews and no longer protected by the Jewish charter, he had been goaded into taking a stand against the imperial religion, a condemnation would no longer be surprising.[60]

My conviction—for it is nothing else—is that the Apostle was executed at the end of his trial, the first and only one, because, if the affair had another conclusion, it is unlikely that Acts would say nothing about it. It is true that one can still claim that the pseudo-Luke's logic was not perhaps the same as ours. Nevertheless, when I read, in chapter xx of Acts, Paul's alleged discourse at Miletus before the Elders of the Church of Ephesus (xx.18–35), I cannot escape the impression that it is the Tarsiot's final farewell to his listeners, a conclusion to the end of his career, and consequently that the author of the speech (the pseudo-Luke) knows

56. *CCXV*, pp. 12, 47f.; *CXXIX*, pp. 298f.
57. Let us note that the writer has consistently tried to persuade us that in the trial at Caesarea the Roman authorities did not find the slightest reason for condemnation. *CVIII*, pp. 833f.
58. Loisy, *RHLR*, July–August 1913, p. 362.
59. *XI*, p. 80.
60. *CCXXI*,[2] p. 471, and *CVIII*, pp. 953f.

that his hero will not return from the voyage upon which he is starting (xx.25): "And now, behold, I know that ye all . . . shall see my face no more; (xx.37): "And they all wept sore, and fell on Paul's neck, and kissed him, Sorrowing most of all for the words which he spake, that they should see his face no more." I am convinced that the author would not have written this testimonial scene if he had not known that, in going to Jerusalem "bound in the spirit" (xx.22) and facing the "bonds and afflictions" which awaited him there (xx.23), Paul took his first step towards martyrdom.

Finally, one of the writer's declarations merits attention: it is placed in the mouth of Agrippa II in xxvi.32: "This man might have been set at liberty, if he had not appealed unto Caesar." I interpret this passage as meaning that liberty was not to be Paul's fate at the conclusion of the judiciary action started by such an appeal. Acquittal by the imperial tribunal would have been the best justification of the Apostle and of Christianity; there is no mention of it, therefore it must not have happened. I believe that this point is sufficiently established.[61]

The acquittal hypothesis—an acquittal followed, of course, by an equally obscure second trial and condemnation—still has partisans. They stress two texts: (1) Philippians i.12–13: "But I would ye should understand, brethren, that the things which happened unto me have fallen out rather unto the furtherance of the gospel; So that my bonds in Christ are manifest to all the Praetorium [ἐν ὅλῳ τῷ Πραιτωρίῳ] and to all the others." Actually, this is a very obscure formulation; it would be a great mistake to think that its first reference applies only to the headquarters, and more particularly to the vestibule of the prefect of the praetorium. The word "praetorium" may also signify the camp of the praetorians or the entire dwelling reserved for the public authorities.[62] And the term "the others" (τοῖς λοιποῖς πᾶσιν), I interpret simply as meaning "all the others who saw my trials." Because the text is so vague, it would be rash to cite it as supporting the acquittal hypothesis. (2) 2 Timothy iv.16f, where Paul speaks of his *first defense* when none helped him except the Lord who "strengthened" him, so that he was rescued from the "mouth of the lion" (a reminder of Ps. xxii.22). Unfortunately, the Pastorals are inauthentic and cannot reasonably maintain their claim to having been written by Paul except by leaning on the fiction of the double trial. They doubtless represent nothing more than a secondary tradition, en-

61. CVIII, pp. 774f, 907; CVII, pp. 220, 223f.
62. Cagnat, "Praetorium," DA, p. 642.

gendered by the silence of Acts. I do not believe this tradition merits the slightest confidence.

Conclusion

Thus Paul perished, martyr to the Christian faith and to his gospel, in virtue of a judgment pronounced in the name of Nero. The great problem of the date remains: even the historians who connect the deaths of Peter and the Tarsiot [63] separate them in fact: neither the place, nor the day, nor the type of execution is the same for the two Apostles. I regard their association in death as a simple apologetic construction, representing their reconciliation, or, even more, their perfect union. If, however, it is admitted that there is some truth in this contention, the date of their deaths must be designated as 64; if the contention is not accepted, this date no longer holds and one is tempted to advance somewhat the time of Paul's execution. Without attempting to discuss the precise dates that have been suggested, I would say that the Apostle was decapitated on the Ostian Way around the spring of 62, give or take a year or two.

Such was the end of an active and full career, in the course of which he assuredly developed great personal virtues. It is impossible to appraise its positive results merely through the impressions acquired by a reading of the Epistles; throughout his life Paul had been too constantly and too harshly contested and contradicted for us not to have the greatest reservations about his own favorable claims. We shall be able to form a reasonable opinion only after we have studied the substance and the spirit of the Pauline Gospel.

63. *XXII*,² I, p. 240; *CXV*, III, p. 500.

Part III

PAULINISM

DEFINITION OF
PAULINISM

That if thou shalt confess with thy mouth the Lord
Jesus, and shalt believe in thine heart that God hath
raised him from the dead, thou shalt be saved.—(Rom. x.9)

I CONSIDER Paulinism to be fundamentally Pauline, but distinguish it from what must have been the Tarsiot's authentic teachings because I doubt the complete veracity of the Epistles. At the time they began to circulate, no one respected texts sufficiently to refrain from making use of a venerated name as surety for the acceptance of an idea considered advantageous to the brethren, or to resist the temptation of interpolating into an authentic exposition the additions developed here and there by the evolution of the doctrine. Had there been no genuine letters of the Apostle, neither of the two actions I just noted would have taken place. They do not have much meaning today, and their only interest has always been that of an explanatory gloss or of a finishing touch deemed necessary to an encounter with the Pauline Gospel and of a type of speculation accepted by Paul's immediate posterity.

I therefore call Paulinism that body of doctrines which is affirmed in the Epistles and which contains the thought of their first author, with possible retouches *along his line* of speculation by his closest disciples. Neither the incoherence of the exposition, nor even the occasional contradictions of its contents, seems to me to be sufficient to expose these retouches. In considering, for example, the Epistle to the Ephesians or the Epistle to the Hebrews and the Pastorals, which affirm views that are assuredly secondary and which diverge more violently from the assemblage of theses included in the Pauline Corpus than they ever do from each other, I am inclined not to confuse the probable interpolations with the basic modifications.

THE PROBLEM

I. The Viewpoint of Paulinism

IT is a moot question, to which there is no answer, whether Paul had built a system of doctrines, a logical and coherent body of concepts that he proffered to his flock.[1] However that may be, the Epistles tell us nothing of this. This should not surprise us; Paul did not believe that he preached a new religion; he only claimed to give the true interpretation of the old, namely the Jewish;[2] and he maintained this illusion even in the face of the obstinate opposition of the Jews. We must eschew the suppositions prompted by an indiscreet zeal which seeks to fathom what he did not say, or to build upon what he did say, through more or less logical deductions. This is the passion of theologians who have, in effect, drawn from, or rather imposed upon, the Epistles a well-ordered *theology*. I think that the true Paul would be astonished about more than one point in the exclusively intellectual conception that some have of him.[3] This kind of

1. Bibliography: the essential materials for a study of Paulinism, dispersed in the texts, are assembled in sizable books devoted to the theology of the New Testament, especially in *XXXI*, II, pp. 1–262; *LXV*; *XV*, pp. 190–513. All these works provide abundant bibliographies. One should especially add *CCL; CCLV; CC; CXXIX; IX; CCXLV*. There is a good summary in *LXXXII*, ch. vi.
2. *CCXLIV*, p. 177.
3. Wernle's small book, *CCLIII*, opposes "das intellektualistische Missverständnis des Paulus."

interpretation is excused as being necessary to the service of dogmatics, but it only harms history. If we want to understand the Apostle of Tarsus, let us leave him in his time, which is antiquity, and in his milieu, which is Asiatic; let us neither modernize nor Europeanize him.[4]

We are thus confronted by a certain number of assertions that are often peremptory, but isolated and usually advanced without any explanation; and even more often by allusions which those who received the letter understood, since they corresponded to what the Apostle had said to them earlier, but which are often incomprehensible to us. *Thus the Epistles are not a course of doctrine, but circumstantial instructions, founded on oral teachings which we do not know;* let us never forget this.

Fortunately, Paul did not write to say nothing, or, at least, the letters that we have say something, and it is for this that they have been preserved. They deal with questions of faith or morals, of discipline or cult, matters the Apostle considered essential, especially when they involved his apostolic responsibility and his authority. It follows that he puts these questions before us, even if only indirectly, and answers them, even if only by appeals to his former instructions; hence our field of research contains a certain number of points of reference which at least permit us to form some idea of the scope of the tracts themselves and of their content. It is clear that Paul, without being "a stiff doctrinarian or a cold systematic dogmatician," [5] was a man driven by a need to impart his religious experience in teaching and in a doctrine which was, if not a system, at least a synthesis.[6]

When we read the Epistles for the first time, we get an impression of the nature of the author's mind, of the character of his reflections and inspirations.[7] His mind seems to be full of contradictions, to say nothing of its many flaws. The reason is perhaps to be sought more in the diversity of influences exerted upon him than in the contradictions of his own nature: he is both mystic and rabbi; the mystic lifts him above all reality, while the cavilling dialectic of the synagogue impedes him with its argumentation, and the import of the polemic restores him to the most immediate contingencies. He fights, he lectures, he edifies, he exhorts, he grows indignant, he prophesies, sometimes in so jumbled and chaotic a manner that it is practically impossible for us to extract a meaning from his clumsy style and weak logic.

However, in his most aberrant ramblings, in the midst of parenthetical

4. *CC*, p. 50, rightly insisted on this idea.
5. *CXC*, p. 352.
6. *CXXVIII*, p. 211.
7. Leisegang, *Der Apostel Paulus als Denker*, Leipzig, 1923.

digressions marked by his disjointed and deficient reasoning, he never forgets *his Gospel*. The *raison d'être* and the justification of his mission are to expand, propagate, sow, and work for the good of his Gospel. But our difficulty begins when we have to define this Gospel, to determine the scheme of the Apostle's teaching and the source of his preaching.

To begin with, it is difficult to learn from what source and by what means he derived its substance. Sometimes he tells us, without specifying the means of transmission, that he *received* it from a tradition, sometimes he attributes it to the Holy Spirit, or discovers it in the Old Testament, or derives it from a vision (Gal. i.16; 11–12). His personal conclusions, based on his apostolic experience, coordinate its disparate elements with the needs of propaganda and of action. In reality, his visions and inspirations are realizations of influences of which he himself was not fully conscious, but which we are able to grasp.[8] It was apparently his impression and conviction that he perceived at one fell swoop the essential content of his Gospel; but nothing is less certain than the accuracy of his conviction, and one wonders if the principal discrepancies between his Epistles are not due to an expansion and evolution of his thinking.

II.   The Great Pauline Themes

The central themes of this Gospel are immediately perceptible. They do not seem to be many.[9]

First comes the *Truth*, then immediately, in an indissoluble and obvious union with it, *God*, his sovereignty, the history of his relations with mankind, man's need to please him and to receive his grace, which is indispensable to the fulfillment of his saving commandments (i.e., indispensable to *salvation*).

Then follows *the Lord Jesus*, whose very name is apparently already charged with many powers and whose being, constituting in itself alone a veritable order of creation, reveals itself as polymorphous. What Paul said about the nature of the Lord and its relation to that of God on the one hand and to that of man on the other, as well as what he said about the essential gifts of that nature and the forms of its manifestation —of its *doxa*—is properly speaking Pauline *Christology*.[10]

It is complemented by a *cosmology* which determines the Lord's role

8. I have in mind especially Paul's relationship with the religiosity of the Mysteries. Cf. *CCXXXII*, App. II; *CCXVI*, ch. iv., Apps. I and II.
9. *CCLIII*, p. 21.
10. *CCXXXII*, ch. vi: "Il mito di Christo."

before the world, then in the creation and in the world, and especially his relation to the cosmic powers, which the speculations of the Hellenistic milieu had armed with active power over the *Elements* (στοιχεῖα) and the design of the universe.

But the Lord, according to Paul, exercises sovereign authority not only over cosmic matter and the essence of things, but also over all mankind. He alone can raise mankind to God, he alone reconcile man and God, and only through the mysterious and irresistible operation to which he consented in assuming the body of a man and in accepting ignominious death on the cross can mankind expect salvation. Thus Pauline *anthropology* is coordinated with his *soteriology*: because man is what he is, the world needed the redeeming work and intercession of the Lord Jesus, pursuant to God's design.

For the Lord's role transcends mankind and the span of men's normal life on earth; it is prolonged beyond this, in the great crisis which will transform the cosmos by purifying it.[11] This is Paul's *eschatology*, the true conclusion to his Christology, for he conceives the advent of a day when Christ, having completely fulfilled his mission, will remit all his powers to the Father (1 Cor. xv.27–28). Henceforth, God will reign over the regenerated universe, and over a mankind spiritualized in those aspects which God has judged worthy of being saved from perdition.

All these religious ideas, which are combined with metaphysical and mystical conceptions of a very high order (although not all of them are very original or even personal), are never presented as pure speculations or as themes for meditation. Whatever at bottom is their true nature, they always tend towards actualization,[12] towards adaptation to pragmatic ends, they are organized into a practical system for an edifying life aiming at the application of a true precept of individual salvation rather than at a logically constituted body of doctrines to satisfy the mind. Above all, the Apostle sought to conduct all his listeners along the road to Damascus which had led him to the Truth.[13] He claimed to reveal not God himself,[14] but the sure way that, through *confidence* and *belief*, led to God, that is to say, to the Lord Jesus, and the requisite faith in him.

To assure for oneself the benefit of Christ's saving initiative, Paul taught, it is indispensable to achieve union, *koinônia*, with him. A mystic

11. Texts grouped in *CXCVII*, ch. v, par. 1.
12. To spiritualize Paul, as do Pfleiderer or Holsten, is to travesty him and make him unintelligible. The essence of his preaching, as perceived by the author of Acts xx–xxi (discourse at Miletus) is τὴν εἰς Θεὸν μετάνοιαν καὶ πίστιν εἰς τὸν κύριον ἡμῶν ᾽Ιησοῦν. Cf. *CCXXVI*, pp. 77f.
13. *CCLIII*, p. 27.
14. *CCXV*, p. 26.

union of course, but—if I may say so, since the coupling of these words has not much meaning for us—it is not a mysticism lost in the clouds, it is *positive* and demands expression in fully consummated actions. For Paul the phrase *to be united with the Lord* is no more merely a way of speaking than *to be united with Attis* is a simple verbal formula for an initiate in the Mystery of the Great Mother. And herein lies the substance of a true *Christian Mystery*: it is not as fully conditioned as the other Mysteries of immortality (we shall see why), but this small difference does not change its fundamental nature.

The key that opens the secret door is *faith*, and Paul has his own conceptions and ideas about the nature of faith and the means of acquiring it,[15] as he has about the place faith occupies in religious life in its relation to the other forms of union with God which may have existed before the coming of Christ, especially in its relation to the Jewish Law, and about the special state of grace, peace, and security in which the possession of this unique and requisite faith places the Christian *mystos*.

But he is also too much a man of his time to confine faith wholly to the spiritual plane, to deprive it of complementary rites—rites that are certainly less necessary than faith itself, which have meaning only in it, and which could even become very dangerous without faith, as is a sacrilege, but which are nevertheless very powerful in themselves. There are two principal rites: *baptism*, fundamentally a rite of association with the death of the Lord, and the *Eucharist*, the sacramental meal at the *table of the Lord*. The underlying realism of these ritual gestures seems patent from the start: they are sacraments which not only symbolize the attainment of positive grace but also procure it. The *prayer* consolidates the grace. Here we are at the very heart of Paulinism, which is a powerful religious actuality—I cannot repeat this too often—rather than a theological edifice.

Although in the last analysis Paul's concern is individual salvation, he does not view individual man as a solitary being, does not in fact teach for the sake of the isolated man. The believer is a *brother*, and therefore a member of a fraternity: this is the *Ecclesia*, the Lord's assembly, the body of which the Lord is the head, and each specific community is only one of the components of this great whole. Indeed, it is in this *Ecclesia* that the Lord really lives, in a continuous and palpable presence; through it he manifests himself by the invincible operation of the Holy Spirit, through it receives the worship due to him. For this Church is not only a spiritual union in Jesus Christ; she is, within the confines

15. *CCIX*.

of a particular community, a center of intense communal religious life, a place of prayer, edification, and supernatural manifestations. And she is also a body which presupposes organization, and practically administration: through this fact she readies the future of the Christian religion, which, without her, would promptly become dispersed in individual pseudo-pneumatism. The Church is the human face, the material framework of faith. She is also the guardian and director of the Mystery, from which she cannot be separated. In fact, as formulated in Paulinism the Church is as essential to true faith as the Mystery itself.

But the Church is not yet a body independent of the faithful; she is the whole and the assembly of the faithful. Above all, she is created for them, as the auxiliary of their own efforts, and as the common means of salvation. Obviously, she can assume this role only if every believer brings to her a correct frame of mind, that is, a frame of mind compatible with the commandments of the Lord. In making this particular point Paul is careful to address himself to the individual, to apprise him of his obligation towards the Lord, the brethren, and himself, as well as of his duty to use all these instructions for the attainment of salvation.

It is these teachings that comprise what may be called the religious and moral catechesis of Paulinism, the compendium of the most immediate and most practical precepts it prescribes, and, in a sense, its point of departure.

By point of departure I mean the basis of Paulinism's religious activity and of its pragmatism, for the point of departure and basis of its doctrine must be sought elsewhere. The ecclesiastical structure of Paulinism, its cult, discipline, and ethic, are in the main *evolved from experience*: the religious experience of the Christian named Paul of Tarsus, conjointly with his apostolic experience. His doctrine, on the other hand, is *a gnosis*, a revelation, which can find its justification and its reason for being only in mysticism. And it is a matter of no little astonishment to us to note the existence of this extraordinary assemblage of realism and ideas, which were established outside the control not only of reason, by definition, but of the reasoning process as well.

Conclusion

It should be clearly understood that the synthesis I have just presented is based strictly on material taken from the contents of the Epistles. But no synthesis is given there, and I offer mine only as a succinct summary of Paulinism. We must also be careful not to confuse this expression of the Hellenistic faith in the Lord Jesus with that which from that time onwards one is tempted to call Christianity. At that time, Christianity was more expansive, it included other forms, and when, in the course of its slow evolution, it made the choice among them, it did not retain all of the forms of Paulinism; [16] we shall perhaps have some difficulty in weighing the present importance and future influence of a mode of thinking, which, if one listened to it alone, would seem to have dominated its entire age and to have definitively determined the directions of Christian life.[17]

16. H. Bulcock, *The Passing and the Permanent in St. Paul*, London, 1925; "Paul," in *EB*, pars. 44 and 48.

17. [*Important note:* Here the manuscript left by Charles Guignebert stops; the author did not have the time to develop the theory noted above. He wrote only the chapter on the Pauline mystery (which would have been Chapter IV), for a conference. It follows below. M. B.]

THE PAULINE MYSTERY[1]

I. The Problem

IT is not my intention here to study the doctrine of the Apostle Paul, nor to analyze it, nor to sort out the components of the whole and *of its essence*; I intend only to describe and to explain *the form* it assumed and the aspect under which it is presented to us. A mere glance at the great Epistles that I consider to be substantially authentic (Gal., 1 and 2 Cor., Rom., Col., Phil., 1 Thess.) is enough to show that in following the Apostle of Tarsus we enter a realm wholly different from the one in which the *synoptic* tradition, which nurtured the first three Gospels, evolved. It is the realm of Hellenistic religiosity on which many religious systems had already developed and prospered before Paulinism sought its place there.[2] Why didn't Paul leave this environment? Was it not because deep-seated affinities and an impulsion, perhaps secret and unsuspected by him, prohibited him, if not from repudiating it, at least from avoiding it? This I believe is the truth, and my thesis may be formulated as follows: *In the form it assumed, Paulinism is a Christian adaptation of the point of view of the Hellenistic Mysteries*; and this very adaptation was one of the fundamental factors in Christianity's becoming a new religion.

1. [Presented at the Conference of *l'Union Rationaliste*, May 16, 1933, and published by *Les Cahiers rationalistes*, No. 24, June 1933. M. B.]
2. [See above, Pt. II, ch. ii., sections II and III. M. B.]

I know that this proposition has already aroused numerous and lively objections. The Catholic exegetes have made great efforts to free Paul from any "charge of Mystery," from any suspicion that he ever owed anything to the religious organizations believed to be contemporary to his Gospel and which we call the *Mysteries of immortality* or *the religions of salvation.*[3]

Recently, Father Lagrange's polemic against Loisy's book, *Les Mystères païens et le Mystère chrétien*, assumed the aspects of a crusade.[4] Indeed, the large *bibliography*[5] on this question demonstrates chiefly how greatly men's passion and their partisanship can confuse and lead astray their critical sense. Arguments have been exchanged like pugilistic blows; for the moment, I shall confine myself only to the one which continues to disturb several good minds, and which at first sight gives the impression of being completely objective, namely, the chronological argument.

According to this argument, the Mysteries had not yet been organized and the Hermetic books not yet written at the time of Paul; hence, the Apostle could not have been influenced by either; he could not have conformed to a model which did not exist. Now, after the revelations in the frescoes and stuccoes of the Farnesina and of the Basilica of the Porta Maggiore in Rome, in the Item Villa and the Homeric Villa in Pompeii, and after the importance of Attis in the City in the first century has been made clear to us through a close study of Claudius's religious policy,[6] I find it impossible to still doubt the existence—which has been denied— and the organization of Mysteries in the century which overlaps the beginning of the Christian era. As for the treatises assembled in the *Corpus hermeticum*, one need only read them carefully to recognize that they develop a small number of basic themes that are most likely older than the writings. If, at the time of the Antonines, in the middle of the second century, a Christian text in Rome—the *Shepherd* of Hermas—thought it appropriate to assume the guise and conventions of a sort of Hermetic revelation, it is doubtless because this genre had been known for a fairly long time in the milieu in which the author lived. I think it not unreasonable to assume that a characteristic product of Helleno-Egyptian syncretism, such as Hermetism, was known in the Orient before coming to the capital of the Empire.

---

3. [See above, pp. 146–53.]
4. In *Revue biblique*, 1919.
5. On fairly old publications, cf. *CCLIV*, the Table of Contents and the Index; on the more recent ones, *CCXXVI*, the first pages. See also Jacquier, "Les Mystères païens et S. Paul," in *Dict. d'apologétique* (1920), III, cols. 964f; *CXXXIV*, pp. 315f.
6. *CXLVII; CXLVI; CLXXXI.* On the Asiatic milieu, see *CXCVI.*

As for other contentions, the details of our study will provide several opportunities for taking a stand on the basis of concrete facts.

II. The Presentation of the Pauline Gospel

a) *Terminology.* Let us start with a fact: at the end of the second century and the beginning of the third, Clement of Alexandria still presented Christianity to the pagans as the *true Mystery*, as opposed to the other Mysteries, which he regarded as being only demoniacal counterfeits.[7] He was well aware that the new religion contained teachings which it was expedient to transmit only by warily labeling them a Mystery.[8] Thus the ancient apologist did not reject a rapprochement, or even a comparison, between Christianity and the Mysteries, both equally shocking to his modern successors.

Now, Paul himself did not reject a rapprochement—as a first reading of his Epistles shows—for he was especially addicted to using the word *mystery* to designate the contents of his Gospel, the substance of his own revelation. We read in 1 Corinthians ii.7: "But we speak the wisdom of God, in a mystery, even the hidden wisdom, which God ordained before the world unto our glory." And the same idea, expressed in similar words, is to be found in the final doxology of Romans xvi.25f. This fragment is in general of dubious authenticity, but the sentence I cite stems substantially from Paul's thinking and presents it in instructive form: "Now to him that is of power to stablish you according to my gospel, and the preaching of Jesus Christ [i.e., the preaching which has Jesus Christ as its object], according to the revelation of the mystery which was kept secret since the world began, But now is made manifest . . ." Let us add the testimony of Colossians i.25f: ". . . the church whereof I am made a minister, according to the dispensation of God which is given to me for you, to fulfil the word of God; Even the mystery which hath been hid from ages and from generations,[9] but now is made manifest to his saints: To whom God would make known what is the riches of the glory of this mystery among the Gentiles; which is

7. *Protrepticus,* 12, 120.
8. *Stromateis,* 1, 2, 23.
9. I interpret this as a reference to *Aeons,* in the gnostic sense, to beings who govern the *Cosmos:* thus the Mystery was hidden from the world of cosmic spirits and from that of men. I base my interpretation on 1 Cor. ii.8, "the princes of this world," and Eph. ii.2: "according to the aeon [τὸν αἰῶνα] of this world, according to the prince of the power of the air."

Christ in you, the hope of glory" (i.e., the hope he brings that you shall one day be glorified like him).

Here, then, is the primary meaning: *Paul's Gospel holds a Mystery and he derives revelation from it.* This Mystery *is Jesus Christ,* or the way of salvation. The Apostle's affirmation refers simultaneously to the person, the coming, and the role of Christ the Savior, but also to the method to be followed by the faithful in order to derive positive benefit from all this.[10] This is, in fact, the *substance of a Mystery.* It is most remarkable that the Paulinians, the authors of Ephesians and of the Pastorals, insistently applied the word *mystery* not only to the Gospel,[11] but also to the faith [12] and to *eusebeia,*[13] or "the operative, cultive piety." [14] This proves, according to all appearances, that they considered this term characteristic of their master's customary language.

Whatever the manner in which Paul conceived this *Mystery,* I think it important that he deliberately used, as label for his doctrine, a word whose current usage endowed it with so precise and special a meaning.

Moreover, whenever he's especially anxious to emphasize the importance of some particular aspect of his teaching, especially when it is a question of eschatology, he labels that aspect too a *mystery* (1 Cor. xv.51: "Behold, I show you a mystery"; Rom. xi.25: "For I would not, brethren, that ye should be ignorant of this mystery." Cf. Eph. v.32: "This is a great mystery"). And the aggregate of all the revealed teachings, of all that it is requisite to know in order to enter into the saving faith, is "all mysteries and all knowledge" (1 Cor. xiii.2). No doubt the word "mystery" is used here in a popular and banal sense, a sense that has persisted and is still maintained by orthodoxy when it speaks of the mysteries of the Trinity or the Incarnation. In any case, these μυστήρια themselves are revelations; access to them is strictly guarded by an initiation; thus they are easily linked to a *mysterious* whole.

Moreover, it is significant that we find in Paul's writings two terms customarily linked in pagan mysticism: *mystery* and *gnosis;* the former refers to the liturgical form of revealed knowledge, the science of *essential things,* which is signified by the latter.

Our first impression is one of *undeniable similarity of terminology* between the Pauline presentation and teaching and that of the revelation

10. This idea is made evident by the development of 2 Tim. i.8f.; cf. Col. ii.3; iv.3.
11. Eph. vi.19.
12. 1 Tim. iii.9.
13. 1 Tim. iii.16.
14. *XLIX, ad verbum.*

of the Mysteries. And, I may add, of Hermetism. Here we are then, ready to ask if it was not the Apostle's intent to oppose his doctrine, as the authentic Mystery of truth and of salvation, to the abomination of the Mysteries of error and perdition.

b) *The Content.* Examination of the rather redoubtable passage of 1 Corinthians iii.1–3 raises the problem of content and opens the way to several instructive remarks.

Let us read it: "And I, brethren, could not speak unto you as unto spiritual, but as unto carnal, even as unto babes in Christ. I have fed you with milk, and not with meat; for hitherto ye were not able to bear it, neither yet now are ye able. For ye are yet carnal . . ." Now, these verses, establishing a clear distinction between the terms *carnal,* assimilated to *babes* (νήπιοι) and *spiritual,* regarded as *perfect* (τέλειοι),[15] are addressed to the faithful of Corinth, that is, to men who had been called to the faith by the grace of God and of the Lord, who had been united to Christ by baptism, and who were in the habit of strengthening that union by the Eucharistic repast taken at the *Lord's table.* How then could they still have been only νήπιοι?

The distinction between *babes* and the *perfect* could evidently relate wholly to an *intellectual order,* with Paul separating those who understood with difficulty and whom it was necessary to lead from those who understood well and to whom one could tell everything. But the Apostle himself diverts us from this interpretation by clearly placing the wisdom he attributes to the *perfect* beyond the plane of *the spirit of this world* and by presenting it as the fruit of a revelation of the divine Spirit.[16] And yet, it is certainly the Spirit who worked among the converts of Corinth, the Spirit and the divine *dynamis:* Paul says it positively in 1 Corinthians ii.4–5. Nevertheless, they are not *perfect,* they do not merit the name of *pneumatics,* they are still *psychic* and *carnal.* What does this strange discrepancy mean? There seem to be only two explanations: either the Corinthians have lost *their gift* or they have not wholly received it. Not a word in the text favors the first explanation and it clearly leans towards the second. It does so by its tenor as well as by *its context, which is strewn with expressions that evoke the Mysteries and the gnosis.*[17] Most of the broad-minded critics have no difficulty in recognizing that, in the

15. The term occurs in 1 Cor. ii.6.

16. 1 Cor. ii.13: "Which things also we speak, not in the words which man's wisdom teacheth, but which the Holy Spirit teaches; comparing spiritual things with spiritual."

17. ii.6, 7, 10, 13; cf. the counterposing of the *psychical man* in ii.14 to the *pneumatic* of ii.15 and the affirmation of iii.2,¹: "I have fed you with milk, and not with meat, as unto carnals, as unto babes in Christ."

whole development in question, Paul speaks *the language of the Mysteries,* that the term "perfect" (τέλειοι) especially is to be understood in the sense of "initiated" (μεμυημένοι) and that λαλεῖν ἐν μυστηρίῳ means "to speak as they do in the Mysteries."

Some scholars [18] have taken the trouble to establish either that the expressions we have just examined are found also in contemporary usage outside the Mysteries, or that they are not used by Paul in the same sense as the one they have in the Mysteries. It has been noted, for example, that in ordinary speech the two terms νήπιος and τέλειος mark the beginning or the ending of anything whatever. This is debatable; the question, however, is not whether these Greek words are found in the common usage of the Greek language, but to learn *from what context* Paul took the words he chose and assembled in order to formulate his essential affirmations—*whether they were or were not derived from the context of the Mysteries, where they can incontestably be found.*

A moment of attention and reflection will give us the answer. We read in verse ii.16 of 1 Corinthians: "But we have the 'Nous' [νοῦς] [i.e., the mind] of Christ." The Apostle used the word *Nous,* which designates the faculty of thought and understanding, hence reflection and intelligence, rather than *Pneuma,* the exact equivalent of *mind,* because he is referring to a text of Isaiah x.1.13 ("who hath known the 'Nous' of the Lord?"). The classical Greek language did not confuse the two terms, but Greek mysticism had already altered the meaning of the first.[19] It was used to designate a god Nous (Νοῦς),[20] who favored his elect with a celestial gift also called "nous," which immediately endowed them with the absolute knowledge of the All (τὰ πάντα γνωρίζειν) and also conferred immortality. He who had received this gift was called Ennous (ἔννους or the Intelligent). Now, in a Hermetic writing [21] I find this: "Thus those who have been baptized by the Spirit [or "in the Spirit"] have participated in Knowledge and have become perfect [as] men who have received the gift of the Spirit [Mind]." It should be understood that the divinity sent the *Nous* to earth in a great crater, which served in the purification (baptism) of those initiated into the Greek Mysteries, and that this was the baptism that rendered man τέλειος. He who had not participated in this salutary operation remained reduced to the sensations (αἰσθήσεις)

18. Lietzmann, *XLIV,* IX, *An die Korinther,* I,² p. 15; Clemen, Feine.
19. *CLXXVIII,* pp. 164f.
20. Cf. *CLXXXIII,* Bk. XI, p. 210: Νοῦς πρὸς Ἑρμῆν.
21. Κρατὴρ ἢ Μονάς, *CLXXXIII,* Bk. IV, p. 4. No doubt the title means *Water and Fire;* κρατήρ= "vase, crater" properly; μονάς is "unity," but also "fire" for the Pythagoreans.

and the teachings of the senses; γνῶσις (absolute Knowledge) was closed to him and, in sum, he did not rise above the level of the ἄλογα ζῶα (those deprived of reason).

Let us encompass our Hermetic text with two sentences borrowed from syncretistic philosophy—one from Philo,[22] who defines the *perfect one* as "He who is on the border of uncreated nature and the corruptible, thus neither god nor man"; the other from Iamblichus,[23] stating that τέλειος is he who knows "the divine transport and how it is produced"— and conclude that, according to the thinking reflected in these different but essentially similar passages, the τέλειος is the man who, by the gift of *Nous* or of *Pneuma,* has penetrated to the heart of the Mystery, who possesses the faculty of intelligence (νοεῖν) and the fullness of knowledge (γνῶσις). This is precisely the meaning of *perfect* in Paul's writings.

Furthermore, the image of milk, the sustenance of the νήπιος, occurs, not only in the technical language of the Mysteries but seems also to refer to a rite of initiation (?) practiced in their ceremonies, which we do not, however, know.[24]

We may consider it as certain that *perfection* (τελείωσις) *according to Paul,* and thus *the entire mystical presentation which accompanies it, can be situated within the realm of the Mysteries and of Hermetism.*

However, there is not a trace of *esoterism* in Paulinism, nor of *stages in initiation.* It is impossible to tell where the *nepios* ends and the *teleios* begins, and it is very easy to observe that the Mysteries could not tolerate such indecision, that for them the distinction between the stages of initiation is of fundamental importance. We read in 1 Corinthians xii.13: "*For by one Spirit are we all baptized into one body . . . and have all been made to drink into one Spirit.*" Thus there are not two Spirits, one for the *babes,* the other for the *perfect,* nor two halves of the same Spirit that one must acquire successively in order to pass from one rank to the other. He who believes receives the Spirit [25] immediately and becomes a Christian *in fact* instead of being one only *in intent,* as he had been before. He henceforth possesses the prerequisites of salvation, if he pleases God. The ἰδιώτης mentioned in I Corinthians xiv.16 and 25 is he who does not yet know and wishes to know; later he is called the *catechumen.* To preach Christ to the Gentiles is to *reveal the Mystery* to

22. *De Somniis,* II, 234.
23. *De Myster. Aegypt.,* 3, 7.
24. *CLXXVIII,*[1] p. 157; *CCXXIII,* p. 163, n. 2.
25. Gal. iii.2–5 states explicitly that the Galatians received the Spirit by the "hearing of faith."

them, a Mystery that has no stages but is simply *an attainment* (an *assimilation*) of greater or lesser perfection. Man is *perfect* in Christ, or he remains at various distances from perfection, according to his own strength. But in fact all Wisdom (σοφία), all Knowledge (γνῶσις) have been proffered him from the beginning. A very clear Deutero-Pauline text in Ephesians iv.4–5 confirms and clarifies this conclusion: "There is one body (σῶμα) [the body of Christ, which is represented by the Church] and one Spirit (πνεῦμα) even as ye are called in one hope of your calling. One Lord, one faith, one baptism." Had Paul taught the contrary, his disciples would not so insistently stress this *unicity*.

However, from here on I believe it incontestable that it was Paul's intent to present his Gospel as the revelation of a Mystery; an *essentially Christological and soteriological* Mystery, which God had kept from the beginning, carefully hiding it from the world and its princes. It is summarized in two words: *Christ and his Cross*.

III. The Nature of the Pauline Mystery

The other Mysteries, especially the Oriental Mysteries to which Paulinism is more visibly connected than to the Greek Mysteries,[26] are also based on *the story of a divine being and of his passion*, on the interpretation of both as teaching the way to salvation, as a warranty of salvation, and thus of the blessed immortality of the initiated. But the *essence* of their Gospel lies, if I may say so, in the transmission of rites and of formulas which tend to unite the *mystos* with the god, to join his destiny with that of the god in order to assure for himself the radiant survival of which the god has given an example and which he supposedly renews each year, *mystically*, in the presentation of a liturgy at once symbolic and realistic, the living, immediate encouragement. Instruction in a doctrine is to be found in the Hermetic books; in the Mysteries, there are only the hope and the example.[27] Let us note this well: *none of them, as far as we know, presents the passion of its god as an expiation for the sins of men, a redemption*; not even, properly speaking, as a compensation for the infirmities of their nature that prevent them from following by themselves the way to salvation and to follow it alone. However, in all

26. With the exception, perhaps, of Orphism, which unfortunately, is not clear to us.

27. A sentence from Pausanias (I, 37, 4) marks the difference between the two teachings that of the Mysteries and that of Hermetism: "He who has *seen* the Mysteries of Eleusis or who has *read* the Orphic books . . ."

cases, *it is the secret that constitutes the Mystery*, that is to say, *the way itself to salvation;* these are not the modalities of its revelation. This is why it is wrong to deny that Paulinism is a Mystery under the pretext that it proffers its *secret* to anyone who will accept it and that the secret itself rests not on a divine story but on the twofold doctrine of the Incarnation and the Redemption, both of which are alien to the Mysteries, *for it is the very substance of the Pauline Gospel that is expressed in the language of a Mystery.*

The theory of salvation presented by Paul is, in reality, a myth, which on the whole, though not in its central point, resembles the myths of Osiris or Attis: it is no more founded on reason and experience than they are. Its main theme is that of a celestial being who descended to earth from heaven, where he existed since before the birth of the Cosmos, *in the form of a god* (ἐν μορφῇ θεοῦ) ; he became incarnate in the man Jesus, and died on the cross *first of all* in order to *mysteriously* effect the reconciliation of the Cosmos, contained and containing, with the heavenly Father, by a sacrifice accepted by and conforming to the eternal will of God, in crucifying sin with his own body and in having it die with him; *then,* to open to all men the true way of salvation. I presume that no one who has read the synoptic Gospels would claim that this is a teaching of the Nazarene; no one should confuse the pseudo-predictions put here and there into Jesus's mouth, which are simply adaptations of the writer to the faith of his time, with the assurances of the Pauline gnosis. No one will find the myth of the Cosmos, modified in the way I have just shown, in the realm of Jewish piety. Israel knew the theme of the moral value of expiation, but it is not a question of this value in the event with which we are concerned; here, rather, is the *"mystic value inherent in the death of a being who is both divinity and man"* (Loisy), a death which signifies the death of sin and, consequently, the redemption and eventual glorification of man. We are in the presence of a presentation which could have been formed only on Hellenistic soil, in the atmosphere of the Mysteries and, as it were, the function of the myth of an immolated god, a god who dies and is resurrected.

As for the theory of Redemption which constitutes its center, it is analogous to Orphism, but springs primarily from a fundamental need that is worth examining.

Paul is careful to warn us several times that he preaches only *"Jesus crucified,"* [28] that he knows no other, and that his entire preaching is only a *"word of the cross"* (λόφος τοῦ σταυροῦ) which is *"folly to those*

---

28. I Cor. ii.2.

that are perishing, folly and scandal; scandal for the Jews and folly for the Gentiles." [29] Scandal *for the Jews;* for how could the Blessed One of Yahweh, the Messiah, he in whom God existed even before time, how could he have perished by the hand of the evil whom it would have been his function to reduce to impotence or to exterminate? How could one understand his terrible torture when Yahweh himself had said (Deut. xxi.23): "He that is hanged is accursed"? Folly *to the pagans* because there was nothing, *absolutely nothing,* in their myths of salvation nor in the symbols of their Mysteries that resembled the fundamental Christian theme of redemption and of the saving cross. We even ask ourselves from where did all these notions derive and how was this new religion able to encompass, not the concept of redemption itself, whose mystic grandeur and moving profundity affected even the Greek philosophers, though it did disconcert the Jews, but the dramatic realization of the redemption by and on the cross? We would keep wondering, or rather would have to keep wondering, about this without arriving at any satisfactory answer, were we to disbelieve the historical reality of the Crucifixion.

We have arrived at the *fundamental need* of which I spoke a moment ago. The Galilean prophet who announced the imminent coming of the Kingdom of God and awaited the realization of a Great Miracle, which he had come to seek on the hill of Zion, had seen his dream brutally demolished by the intervention of Roman power; his disciples, seized with fear, had dispersed, abandoning him to his destiny, and he had perished. It seemed to be the total end of his illusion. But those who had believed in him and had loved him revived, shortly afterwards, the hope that he had put into their hearts: their love and their faith restored him to life, and soon they were ready to testify that they had seen him, that he had been resurrected. Henceforth, it was necessary to explain why he had died, why he had endured the terrible trial. The disciples then conceived the notion that it all happened according to the design of God, who had, by the resurrection, consecrated Jesus as his Messiah: *the death determined the resurrection* and the infamous cross prepared the glorification of the Nazarene. Moreover, this explanation corresponds rather well to habitual Jewish piety, which always willingly saw in the greatest evil the herald and precursor of the greatest good.

But when the apostolic hope was transposed into Greek territory, when it became necessary to effect a new transformation of the person Jesus Christ because the Jewish Messiah participated in a Jewish nationalism to

29. 1 Cor. i.18, 23, 24: Gal. v.11.

which the Gentiles, and even the proselytes of the Diaspora, were indifferent, and to enlarge his role of restorer of Israel to the realm of universal salvation by making him the absolute Savior, it became at the same time imperative to coordinate the drama of Golgatha with this new presentation. Thus was born, probably at Antioch, the explanation which Paul certainly did not invent but which we know from him: *the Lord died because he willed to die,* in conformity with the plan God had for him from all eternity; he desired this not only because his torture exalted him, but because it was an operation inextricable from the redemption of humanity and of the world, and he accepted the cross, the abominable punishment of slaves, because he wished to assume the most humble of all the *forms* and conditions of man—the form of slavery (μορφὴν δούλου)[30] *"in the likeness of sinful flesh,"* [31] in order to gather unto himself at least all of the appearance of sin which filled the world and to annihilate it on the cross.[32] By so doing he prepared "the transformation of our vile body that it may be fashioned like unto his glorious body," [33] and deserved as well to receive from God, together with the supreme exaltation, the triumphant name before which the whole of creation kneels: *the name of Lord.*[34]

Obviously, I have at this point only scratched the surface of the great Pauline myth of the Redemption. I only wished to show its source. In connecting the myth's point of departure to the first speculation about the resurrection and the cross,[35] it is easy to see how it lines up with the Mysteries and why it retains its originality. This originality does not proceed from the inspiration of a mystical genius but from the mythical interpretation of *a fact,* troubling and shocking in itself, that of the death of the Nazarene. It is by this detour that Pauline speculation bears witness to the historicity of Jesus, which I personally find incontrovertible.[36]

If one considers the adaptation apart from the *Pauline revelation,* it is inexplicable and even inconceivable that Paul should have been its prin-

30. Phil. ii.7.
31. Rom. viii.3; 2 Cor. v.21.
32. Rom. vi.9–10: "For in that he died, he died unto sin." Cf. 2 Cor. v.21; also 1 Peter, iii.18.
33. Phil. iii.21.
34. Phil. ii.9–11. He is the *Lord of glory* in 1 Cor. ii.8.
35. Read the instructive verses of Phil. ii.2–11. [Cf., for the meaning of this text, the report presented by the author to the Congress of the History of Religions at Paris, Oct. 12, 1923, entitled "Quelques Remarques d'exégèse sur Philippiens," ii.6–11, in *Actes du Congrès* . . . (Paris,) II (1925), 290–316. M. B.]
36. [On the historicity of Jesus, cf. Ch. Guignebert, *Le Problème de Jésus,* Paris, 1914, and his review of *Mystère de Jésus* by P. L. Couchoud, in *RHR,* XCIV (1926), 215–44. M. B.]

cipal artisan, or even only its principal theoretician. The adaptation in question is presented as the work of a *gnosis*, which must in itself be taken as the special gift of the Spirit to the Apostle. In 1 Corinthians xii.8, after having enumerated the various *charismata* dispensed by the Spirit, Paul concludes: *For to one is given by the Spirit the word of wisdom* (σοφία) ; *to another the word of knowledge* (γνῶσις), *by the same Spirit."* He's certain that he possesses both, and it is only for the sake of rhetorical modesty that he puts the following affirmation in the conditional (1 Cor. xiii.2) : "And if I have the gift of prophecy, and understand all Mysteries and all Knowledge." We may be certain that he *understands* them, that he *knows* the world and life, man and God; he has sounded *"the depth of the riches both of the Wisdom and Knowledge of God"* (Rom. xi.33).

But then, from the point of view of the attainment of this *gnosis*, it is conceivable that Paul had some notion of stages: at the lowest level, the stage to which the elected one ordinarily raises himself; at the highest, the stage to which he is raised by the Spirit himself.

In other words: on the lowest rung, the Knowledge he has *received* with faith; on the topmost, the Knowledge he owes, as a splendid complement and radiant explanation, to the grace of the Spirit, the Knowledge that enables him to scrutinize all depths. Those of the faithful who have attained this stage may be called *perfect* (τέλειοι) in Wisdom (σοφία) and in Knowledge (γνῶσις).

However, let us note that Paul does not say that his Corinthians become *perfect* by communication of this supreme *Wisdom*, but that he communicates it *only to the perfect*, for they alone can understand it. Consequently, their perfection comes from elsewhere.

I believe that I was wrong to speak of *stages*, although the apparently very precise counterposing of *babes* and *perfect* seems to presuppose them. Actually, the first of the two terms refers to the minimum of faith and Christian virtue necessary to salvation, and it marks the point of departure of the *continued progress* that can raise the faithful to *perfection*. Paul is not so naive as to think that all those who believe attain this perfection or are capable of doing so. He writes in 1 Corinthians viii.7: "there is not in every man that Knowledge." He knows that the baptismal purification is not enough to endow all with the means to overcome their carnal instincts.[37] The Christian's own dignity, he declares, and his aptitude to receive and to understand more and more completely the revealed Wis-

37. On this point, read the entire chapter of Rom. viii., especially viii.9: "But ye are not in the flesh [since you are Christians], but in the Spirit, if so be that the Spirit of God dwell in you."

dom lie precisely in the intensity of his life in the Spirit; *in other words, in his religious and moral effort and the positive results which he obtains from it.*

Two Deutero-Pauline texts—which are naturally more explicit or more systematic than the allusions in the authentic Epistles, because they have a catechetical air—two texts of the Epistle to the Ephesians [38] will at once clarify the meaning of this fundamental distinction between *babes* and *perfect*, and the nature of the Pauline Mystery.

The first forms the end of a tirade in which the pseudo-Paul tells the Ephesians that he prays that God may grant them "by the riches of his glory to be strengthened with might (δύναμις) by his Spirit in the inner man," so that they might grasp, with all the saints, "what is the breadth, and length, and depth, and height [i.e., the world and life] and to know the love of Christ which passeth all knowledge," in order that they may be "filled with all the fulness of God." [Eph. iii.16–19.] I understand this to mean: in order that they may attain to the *pleroma* of God, to the comprehension of that which God contains,[39] after having realized, through total love of Christ, the mystic fusion with him that is presupposed by the following formula: "It is no longer I that live, but Christ liveth in me." [40] The man who has reached this point knows *All*, and possesses, in the Mysteries, all the revelation necessary, he is the initiate whom the sovereign rites have assimilated to the Soter. I think that in both cases, the Christian and the pagan, the feelings of the elect who had arrived at this point of *perfection* must have been oddly similar.

Here is the second text: "I therefore, the prisoner of the Lord [or for the Lord?] beseech you that ye walk worthy of the vocation wherewith ye are called." There is but a single body, a single Spirit, a single Lord, a single hope, a single faith, a single baptism, but to each man Christ has granted a measure of grace, that is, his charisma; and "the edification of the body of Christ" (the Church) is pursued by common efforts, "Till we all come in the unity of the faith, and of the knowledge of the Son of God, unto a perfect man, unto the measure of the stature of the fulness of Christ; That we henceforth be no more children, tossed to and fro, and carried about with every wind of [all sorts of] doctrine . . . But realizing the Truth in love [= being concerned only with the Truth] may grow up into him in all things, which is the head, even Christ." Thus the body,

38. Eph. iii.17 and iv.1f.
39. The same in *CLXXXIII*, Bk. XI, p. 1. *Nous*, speaking to Hermes, says: "Listen, my son, to what is God and the All;" and he urges him to contemplate the Cosmos *through himself.*
40. Gal. ii.20. Cf. Phil. i.21: "For to me to live is Christ."

which is the Church, is built by the effort of all the faithful. Hence they must not behave as do the Gentiles; Christ has taught them not to live any longer according to seducing lusts alone, "to put off the old man, And be renewed in the spirit of *Nous*, And that ye put on the new man, which after God is created in righteousness and true holiness." [Eph. iv.1ff.] Then follow precepts of practical morality.

There are in fact two ways to attain this perfection in Knowledge, a conception that haunts Paul and his spiritual descendants: that of *the love of Christ* and that of *moral effort*; both can be followed only with the aid of the Spirit or, in theological language, the aid of Grace, which is not the same for all of the faithful. And, as the "old man" defends himself, most people remain all of their lives "imperfect members of the body of Christ." So long as they are in this state, they cannot be regarded as *pneumatic*, because they are not guided solely by the *Pneuma*; human nature, the flesh (σῶμα-ψυχή), still carries a counterbalance in them. Hence these people are *psychical, carnal*; the divine *Nous* within them still exists only as in the babe, in a latent and quasi-vegetative state, the *nous* of the created man. Paul envisages the Corinthians as being in this state of imperfection when he writes to them.[41]

Thus the distinction between *perfect* and *babes* does not, in reality, conform to a classification recognized in the Pauline Church, is not applicable to two different believers or to two stages of an initiation to the Mystery. *It is of a wholly practical order* and affirms only the truth that there are among the elect many men who do not make the Spirit bear fruit and do not go beyond the knowledge of those elements of the Mystery which are indispensable to salvation, whereas there are others who have deserved to "*probe all the depths*." It is not a matter of two doctrines, but of two aspects of the same doctrine: that of the common catechesis and that of the great Pauline gnosis. Obviously, *the language of the Apostle corresponds only to a more or less accurate analogy*, since in his writing the words νήπιοι and τέλειοι are far removed from the precision they have in the Mysteries, or, to better express it, have a meaning different from Paul's.

However, I do not think that one can see in these terms only a metaphor.[42] It should be remembered that they were currently used in the Stoic ethic, where they indicated not determined stages of philosophic initiation and attained wisdom, but, as in Paul, *the progression* which any assiduous man can pursue from a life governed by instincts to one directed

41. 1 Cor. iii.1–2.
42. Thus J. Weiss, *Der erste Korintherbrief*, Göttingen, 1911, p. 74.

by pure reason. Thus Philo distinguishes between *the beginner, the progressor,* and *the perfect one.*[43] In Paul's time, the language of the Mysteries had absorbed the Stoic or Cynico-Stoic terminology; it is from this language that the Apostle borrowed the two words in question, for he uses them concurrently with a number of the terms employed in the Mysteries but not by the Stoics.

Furthermore, I hold it to be certain that, even though the Pauline distinction of terms does not correspond to an esoterism, it nevertheless carried within it a seed of it. Its failure to engender esoterism was due primarily to the fact that ultimately Christianity's organization in the Greek realm did not conform to the mystic representations of the Tarsiot.

The above analysis of the two terms, νήπιος and τέλειος, in Paul's thinking leads us to the conclusion that the Mystery, whose existence they at first seemed to attest, is, like their very distinction, reduced to an inexact way of speaking; and, like this distinction, evaporates. A quick look at the content and the substance of the Mystery will enlighten us.

IV. *The Content and the Substance of the Mystery*

Essentially, the substance of the Mystery is the revelation of Jesus Christ, of his being, his nature, and his cosmological and soteriological role: "For it pleased the Pleroma [Father] that in him should all fullness dwell . . .[44] and by him to reconcile all things unto himself, having made peace through the blood of his cross, by him, whether they be things on earth, or things in heaven." The fact of the death and resurrection of the Lord takes its meaning only from the revelation which explains it. In the Synoptics, *the mystery,* or the substance of the Messianic announcement, is the coming of the *Kingdom* or *the Reign of God,*[45] because the Synoptic tradition is still within the Jewish perspective. Thus the *mystery* is the fact of the realization of the hope of Israel in a manner and form which Israel neither expected nor knew, and which it was unable to fathom and to apprehend all alone. For Paul, installed within the Hellenistic perspective, the substance of the mystery is transposed; it is concerned more with *personal salvation* than with the Kingdom. A similar differentiation existed between the pagan Mysteries and the national religions.

43. *Leg. alleg.,* 1, 94; 3, 150. Cf. Seneca, *De beneficiis,* 2, 18, 4, and the numerous related texts assembled in J. Weiss, *loc. cit.*

44. Col. i.19–20. Read especially i.15–18.

45. Mark, iv.11: "Unto you is given the mystery of the Kingdom of God." Here the word "mystery" is used in the ordinary rather than the mystical sense.

We already see proof of the fact that the Pauline revelation contains the substance of an authentic Mystery in the affirmation that it is a *gnosis,* a knowledge acquired only by the *Pneuma;* there is even clearer proof in the complementary affirmation that this *gnosis,* fatal to the *princes of this world,* artisans of perdition and sources of sin in the world ruled by Satan,[46] constitutes a secret inexorably hidden from them since eternity. Had they suspected the meaning of the Mystery, they would have refrained from collaborating in their own ruin by crucifying the Lord, that is, by helping him to realize the sacrifice of salvation.[47] It is not difficult to recognize in this myth of a secret hidden from the princes a gnostic presentation according to which the inferior aeons are incapable of penetrating the secrets of the Pleroma.[48] Furthermore, what is the *Mystery,* properly speaking, in a *mysterious* religion, if not a certain presentation of the story of the Soter in his relation to salvation, that is, within the framework of the saving work? And what is the *secret of the Mystery,* if not the revelation of this life and its meaning, together with those ways which efficaciously associate the believer with the benefit of the god's work?

Thus the revelation of Jesus Christ as Savior, and of the forms of his work of salvation, concerns the *principles* of the Mystery. Along with them go the revelation of their realization in man by *communion* (κοινωνία) with the Lord, and that of the proper ways to obtain it. For "he that is joined unto the Lord is one spirit" [49] and "if the Spirit of him that raised up Jesus from the dead dwell in you, he that raised up Christ from the dead shall also quicken your mortal bodies by his Spirit that dwelleth in you." [50] The communion with the Lord is the mystic substitution in the believer of the being of Christ for that of the Christian.[51]

The realization of this mystically effected but *real communion* between the *mystos* and the Soter is essentially the operation of Mystery.

Paul calls the full knowledge of the Mystery *epignosis.*[52] The word seems to have been borrowed from the current philosophical language. The matter concerns the communication of all that a privileged human being is able to apprehend of God's secrets, total communication being possible only on the Day of the Lord. This communication practically

---

46. 2 Cor. iv.4. Cf. John xii.31. Moreover, this was also current Jewish opinion.
47. Fundamental text: 1 Cor. ii.6–8. Note that in the Synoptics demons are more clairvoyant and clearly recognize the Lord; there we are not in the context of the Pauline salvation myth.
48. *CCLVI,* pp. 242, 260.
49. 1 Cor. vi.17.
50. Rom. viii.11.
51. Gal. ii.20: "It is no longer I who live, but Christ who lives in me."
52. Col. ii.2: "In the epignosis of the Mystery of God."

engenders *the new man* in making him like the image of his Creator, the
Christ himself.[53] "To put on the new man" is to "put on the Lord Jesus." [54]
It has justly been remarked that, in the context of the Pauline Mystery,
"epignosis . . . is a form of epoptia, the act and supreme end of initiation
into the Mysteries." [55] Assuredly, there is, apparently, no connection between the proper natures of the one and the other, since the *epoptia* is a
presentation and a contemplation, while the *epignosis* is *illumination* by
the Spirit; but it is the character of *perfection* in the initiation to the Mystery that one must emphasize here, and then the profound relation between the two operations becomes clearly apparent. The *epignosis* then
reveals itself as Paul conceived it, as the supreme expression of the *substance* of the Mystery.

"To be in Christ" or "in the Lord" (ἐν Χριστῷ), (ἐν Κυρίῳ), or from
another point of view "to carry Christ within one," "to be clothed with
him," [56] is what Colossians i.27 strongly calls "the riches of the glory
of this Mystery"; it is through this that the Mystery radiates and fructi-
fies. All saving operations are accomplished ἐν Χριστῷ; for example, "the
circumcision made without hands, in putting off the body of the sins of
the flesh," [57] "the circumcision of the heart" by which the carnal instincts
are overcome; [58] also, for example, the redemption and remission of sins,[59]
the reconciliation,[60] the resurrection,[61] the acquisition of all the homely
and familiar virtues,[62] and the guarantee of perseverance against temptations.[63] This is the lot of the *perfect*.[64]

It is remarkable to see how strongly the Deutero-Paulinians insist upon
this mystic operation which unites the true believer with Christ; I see in
this the proof that this was the central theme of Paulinism. Even in a
rapid reading of Ephesians and of the Pastorals one is struck by what I
would call the haunting memory of this mystic union and of its effects.
The Second Epistle to Timothy offers the most striking of all the formulas
setting forth the practical benefit of the communion with Christ and the

53. Col. iii.9–10.
54. Rom. xiii.14.
55. *CCXLVII*, p. 180, n. 1.
56. Gal. iii.27: to "put on Christ."
57. Col. ii.11.
58. Rom. ii.29.
59. Col. i.14.
60. Col. i.22.
61. 2 Cor. i.10.
62. Col. iii.9f; iii.18f.
63. Col. ii.6f.
64. Phil. iv.13; 2 Cor. xiii.4.

annihilation of the old man in him. Here it is: [65] "Therefore I endure all things for the elect's sake,[66] that they may also obtain the salvation which is in Christ Jesus with eternal glory. It is a faithful saying: For if we be dead with him, we shall also live with him." [67]

The union between the *perfect* and the Lord is so intimate, and realizes so great a symbiosis, that the sufferings of the *perfect* for his faith are added to those of Christ and, somehow, complete the merits of the Passion for the good of the Church.[68] "He that is joined unto the Lord is one spirit [with him]." [69] Now, *to be in Christ, to be in the faith, to be in the Spirit* are all one for Paul, because it is the *pneumatic* who sounds the depths of the mystery in which are expressed the δύναμις and the ἐνέργεια which God put in Christ the Savior.

And actually, the interest of the Pauline mysticism lies largely in the fact that the communion of the *perfect* is established with the determinate person of Christ and not with a profound but obscure and badly defined Absolute, as is the case with Philo and the Neo-Platonists; and also in the fact that there is a true communion with the Savior and not, as in the Oriental Mysteries, a sort of divinization of the *mystos*. The *substance* of the Pauline Mystery is nonetheless the exact equivalent of the *substance* of one of these Mysteries, or *the establishment of a saving bond between the initiate and the Soter*.

Perhaps we can understand now why the Pauline Mystery has no stages of initiation. Actually, it would have no use for them. One enters into the Mystery by faith, and faith is a grace which God grants to those predestined for it and refuses to the others. To begin with, faith is practically the revelation of Christ, or the revelation of his existence, for who knows not Christ cannot have faith in him nor, consequently, participate in "the hope which is laid up . . . in heaven" for those who have heard "the word of truth, the Gospel" (RSV) and have believed it.[70] They are the ones who "are called according to his purpose." [71] Thus the trials of an initiation are superfluous, as is also the training imposed upon the believer in the Mysteries. The Lord himself gathers his own, those whom God has destined for him.

Under these conditions, it would be useless for Paul's Gospel to burden

65. 2 Tim. ii.10f.
66. In the fiction of the letter the Apostle is in captivity and chained as a criminal.
67. Cf. Rom. vi.5, 8–9.
68. Col. i.24.
69. 1 Cor. vi.17.
70. Col. i.5.
71. Rom. viii.28.

itself with an esoterism or with an organized Hermetism of structured symbolism, similar to the armor of the Mysteries. In his writings Paul often uses expressions which have apparently perfect equivalents in Hermetic literature; but in Paul they correspond to religious presentations and mystical ideas, and not to actual symbols.

It now becomes a question of knowing how the saving communion between the elect and the Lord is actually established. This is what I shall call *the form of the Mystery*. The subject is profuse and complex, but I shall dwell only upon the principal points.

V. The Form of the Mystery

A religion in spirit and in truth alone, apart from ritualism, would not have had much meaning in the time of Paul. In any case, it would have had no chance of success. In the Hellenistic world in which Paulism sought a place, men were accustomed to relating their hope for a blessed existence beyond death to mysterious rites of consecration reputed to be very powerful. *In order to be understood, Paul had at least to speak the language of his milieu.* To do so successfully certainly required no effort on his part, for his thought, formed in the same milieu, naturally assumed its usual expressions. The Epistles reveal four operative ways destined to *establish*, to *confirm*, and to *maintain* the precious κοινωνία: *baptism, the Lord's Supper*, which we call the Eucharist, *prayer*, of which I will say nothing, because there is in it nothing especially original, and *vision* and *ecstasy*, which go together.

a) *Baptism.* Baptism is not an acquisition of Paulinism: Paul *received* its use from the Christians who fashioned it, and they probably took it over from the disciples of John the Baptist. It was also currently practiced by the propaganda of the synagogues of the Diaspora and by the Jewish sects, either as a rite of initiation or as a means of purification. At this point I shall not attempt to clarify its obscure origins, but only to show what it was when Paul *received* it, and what he did with it.

Fundamentally, it was a rite of purification and of consecration. In the first Judeo-Christian community, whoever received it was *marked* for the Kingdom. But in the Mysteries, lustration, the sign and agent of sacramental purification and the means of liberating oneself from ritual impurity and inaptitude, united the *mystos* and the liberating divinity.[72] Recent archaeological discoveries, in revealing real pagan baptisteries,

72. *CXXXIV*, pp. 45, 81: *CLI*, pp. 35, 217; *CL*, p. 161; *CLXXIX*, pp. 219, 228.

emphasize with renewed force the importance of the baptismal rite in the Mysteries. Jewish baptism in all its forms, pre-Pauline Christian baptism, and pagan baptism are all, with a fair measure of accuracy, contained in the definition of *John's baptism* given by Mark i.4, "a baptism of repentance for the remission of sins," provided that the *metanoia* is understood as a transformation which, in the Mysteries, and doubtless already in the apostolic community, was the equivalent of *regeneration*. In *purifying* (if not *morally*, at least *ritually*) the one who receives it, baptism renders him capable of entering into communication with the divinity. The accent is put upon the *purifying virtue* of the operation.[73]

Let us see what became of this symbolic rite, in itself so widespread and so ordinary, in the Pauline Mystery.

We shall pass over the liturgy of the baptism, which remains rather obscure to us; but let us pause for a moment at the formula which connects the rite to the Christ. The Pauline baptism is administered *in the name of the Lord*.[74] This means that the baptized one enters into a direct dependence upon the Lord to whom he belongs; the *dynamis* contained in the sacred name, insofar as it expresses the being of the Lord, passes into the initiated one over whom it is pronounced. That is why in the Mysteries, in Hermetism, and in magic operations, the revealed (γνῶσις) knowledge of the true name, of the active name, appears from the very start to be essential.[75] We read in Acts iv.12: "Neither is there salvation in any other: for there is none other name under heaven given among men, whereby we must be saved."

This is clear: the salutary name is that of the Lord Jesus and the utterance of it effects an act of salvation.

The invocation of the all-powerful name is not everything in the Pauline consecration of the Christian; we see the Spirit intervene in it also: "Ye have been washed . . . in the name of the Lord Jesus Christ, and by the Spirit of our God" says 1 Corinthians vi.11; but since, for Paul, "the Lord is the Spirit," [76] the name remains most important—or, if one prefers, the factor of the *Spirit* enters into the factor of the *name*.

Such, then, is the first effect of baptism: it places the baptized in a

---

73. *Expiationem delictorum de lavacro repromittit,* says Tertullian, *De Praescriptione,* 40, in speaking of Mithra.

74. 1 Cor. i.13 and 15; vi.11. Cf. Gal. iii.27 and Rom. vi.3.

75. *CLXXIX,* p. 20, gives the text of a Hermetic prayer which reads: "I know your name [Hermes] which you received in heaven."

76. 2 Cor. iii.17. Cf. 1 Cor. xii.3 [Cf. Guignebert, "Contribution à l'étude de l'expérience chez Paul, Remarques sur 2 Cor." iii.15–17, in *I,* vol. 2, pp. 7–22, for the explanation of the Pauline formula. M. B.]

saving dependence upon the Lord. But what action does the rite itself exercise? Tradition replies: it purifies the faithful of his sins. Paul knows this, for he writes in 1 Corinthians vi.11: "But ye have been washed, but ye have been sanctified, but ye have been justified." [77] Yet, it is remarkable that *the Apostle does not insist upon this sacramental effect of baptism*, which is not enclosed within a symbol but constitutes a most efficacious operation by which man is cleansed of his sin. It may be said that he passes it as being self-evident on the basis of a notion already established in the faith, in order to linger over a more personal presentation, or in any case a presentation more profoundly related to the spirit of the Mysteries.

Paul sees in baptism, as it were, the mystical yet true and effectual union of the Christian *mystos* with the death of the Christ, who is the source of salvation. The descent into the water represents death, and the emersion represents the resurrection promised to the Christian. This twofold idea is contained in the following text of Colossians ii.12: "Buried with him in baptism, wherein also ye are risen with him through the faith of the operation of God, who hath raised him from the dead." A passage of Romans vi.3–5 permits us to grasp even more closely the Pauline presentation: "Know ye not, that so many of us as were baptized into Jesus Christ were baptized into his death? Therefore we are buried with him by baptism into death: that like as Christ was raised up from the dead by the glory of the Father, even so we also should walk in the newness of life. For if we have been planted together in the likeness of his death, we shall be also in the likeness of his resurrection." Thus did all the Mysteries associate, by a rite of assimilation, the fate of the *mystos* with that of a dying and resurrected Soter. Moreover, in associating the Christian *mystos* with the death of Christ, whereby sin was annihilated on the cross, baptism makes him die to sin. Thus, for the salvation of the faithful one, two specifically different notions are united: *that of his liberation from sin*, realized by the redeeming sacrifice to which the Lord consented and whose consequence is the *justification* of man and of the Cosmos and their reconciliation with God; and *that of his liberation from eternal death*, of the guarantee of his resurrection by that of the Lord. The two ideas are joined in Paul's thought, but he emphasizes the second. The image of Colossians ii.11 refers to it when baptism is qualified as *acheiropoietic circumcision*, that is, as the rite of introduction to Christianity, just as circumcision of the flesh is the rite of introduction to Judaism.

A short verse in Galatians (iii.27) expresses in a striking formula the

77. Cf. Rom. vi.4; Eph. v.25–27.

mystical operation of baptism considered from this point of view: "For as many of you as have been baptized into Christ have put on Christ." This means that the baptismal rite contains in itself a *virtue* which, like that of the taurobolia in the cult of Attis, establishes so close a bond between the *mystos* and the Lord that the *being* of the former is wholly permeated by that of the latter. To express this central idea of his Mystery, Paul uses even stronger words [78] and ends with the affirmation that we have already encountered in Galatians ii.20: "Yet not I, but Christ liveth in me." Similarly, the initiate of Hermetism said to the god: "For you are I and I am you; your name is mine and mine is yours; for I am your image." [79]

As a general rule, the entire Mystery is a game of similitudes of mystical symbols and assimilations which, viewed by down-to-earth, common sense, are nothing more than appearances or valueless approximations. But in the Mystery, the apparent parallelism of the gestures and acts between the *mystos* and the god, founded, it is true, upon justified mystical conventions, suffices to effect the necessary κοινωνία. The same is true in Pauline baptism.

If we were to pursue the study of the rite into its details and to analyze especially its sacramental content, the modes of its action and of its application, we would find in it an even stronger relation to the fundamental conceptions of the Mysteries. It is at this point that the contact between Paulinism and Orphism seems most apparent.[80]

In the Pauline Mystery, the baptismal operation does not concern solely the individual who undergoes it and derives from it his salvation *in the body of Christ*, together with the others who have been baptized; [81] it also constitutes the Church, "for by one Spirit are we all baptized into one body" (1 Cor. xii.13). This is a profound mystic reality, which can be understood only as the effect of a rite of admission.

b) *The Lord's Supper.* However, the communion with the Lord established by baptism is not definitive; Paul knows that it does not liberate the believer from the powerful instincts of the flesh. Hence a rite of confirmation is needed to assure such liberation. Moreover, it is necessary for the community to possess some means of demonstrating to itself its unity and the solidarity of its members in relation to the Lord. *The Lord's*

---

78. Rom. vi.5; 1 Cor. vi.16–17.

79. *CLXXIX*, p. 21.

80. I am thinking particularly of the baptism for the dead (1 Cor. xv.29). Cf. *CLXXX*, II, p. 128; *CXXXVI*, p. 119, n. 1.

81. 1 Cor. vi.15; xii.27: "Now ye are the body of Christ, and members in particular." The same concept in Rom. xii.5.

Supper is the answer to this double need, and is besides a correlative of baptism.[82] This rite has three aspects: (1) that of a memorial, a liturgical celebration of the death of the Lord: "For as often as ye eat this bread, and drink this cup, ye do show the Lord's death till he come" (1 Cor. xi.26); (2) that of a means of entering into communion with the Lord, and of realizing in this way the mystical symbiosis necessary for salvation: "The cup of blessing which we bless, is it not the communion of the blood of Christ? The bread which we break, is it not the communion of the body of Christ?" (1 Cor. x.16); (3) that of a means of establishing a communion among all those who partake of the *one loaf*, that is to say, the body of Christ: "For we being many are one bread, and one body: for we are all partakers of that one bread" (1 Cor. x.17).

Do not these strange formulas, considered in themselves and objectively, correspond to what is usually called a *mysterious* language, a language that is in violent contrast to that of the Synoptics? Reread, for example, the Sermon on the Mount. However, Paul is convinced that the Lord himself instituted this *mystic repast* "the same night in which he was betrayed," [83] by comparing his body to the Eucharistic bread and his blood to the wine of the cup of benediction. But there is no possibility that the Apostle spoke truly; he *received* the schema that he had speculated upon from the community of Antioch, which, according to all appearances, fashioned it, directly or indirectly. As Loisy so excellently declares: [84] "The alleged words of the Eucharistic institution have meaning only in the theology of Paul, which Jesus did not teach, and in the scheme of the Christian Mystery, which Jesus did not institute." But then what is the source of the rite and the words?

They are not from Israel. The Jews knew this communion at table and many of them awaited with great hope the *Messianic feast*; it is mentioned in the Synoptics.[85] Their sects, the Essenes and the Therapeutae, for example,[86] practiced *sacred repasts* [87] which strongly resemble the *sacrificial repasts*.[88] Above all, it simply indicates a *sign of fraternity*; nowhere can one perceive a trace of *theophagy* in it.

It did not come from the primitive Christian community. This community also knew a fraternal repast taken in common; it was called by its

82. 1 Cor. x.2–3.
83. 1 Cor. xi.23f.
84. *CXIII*, p. 208.
85. Matt. xxii.1–14; Luke xxii.30; Mark xiv.25.
86. [On these sects, cf. *LXXXVII*, pp. 223–46 and 318–26. M. B.]
87. Josephus, *Jewish War*, II, 8:5; *Antt.* XVIII, 1:5; Philo, *De vita cont.*
88. *LX*, II, pp. 568f.

initial ritual name, *the breaking of bread*.[89] No doubt it already symbolized, together with the union of the brethren among themselves, their union with the Master who had ascended to the Father; but nothing in it recalls the death of the Lord, which had at the time received no interpretation along the line of the dogma of redemption. The rite of communion was wholly derived from a habitual gesture of the living Jesus and was justified by the certitude of the invisible presence of the Resurrected One amidst the community of his own. Later, the necessary meditation of the disciples concerning the *scandal of the cross* added several interesting notions to this initial presentation of the Eucharistic repast—for example, the notion of a *memorial* of Jesus's last supper with his disciples. When the conviction arose that this supper was *paschal, the cup of benediction* was joined to the bread. It is of this stage of the Last Supper that the Synoptics speak,[90] as is apparent when one separates them from obvious Pauline additions. At the moment when the strictly Synoptic tradition of the *last supper* was beginning to take form, Jesus was supposed to have said no more than is found in Mark xiv.25: "Verily I say unto you, I will drink no more of the fruit of the vine, until that day that I drink it new in the kingdom of God." But this day tarried in coming, and the Christian community in pagan land instinctively related the breaking of bread to the ideas, common in their milieu, of the union of *mystos* with their god in a meal taken at *the table of the god.*

It is this type of presentation that Paul *received*, and unfortunately it is impossible for us to know with certainty what exactly he added himself. To believe that he merely conformed to Jesus's own instructions, given at the Last Supper and faithfully transmitted by the Synopsis, one would have to refuse to apply good sense in reading the texts.[91] There remains the possibility of a pagan influence.

The pagan world frequently practiced sacred and cultic repasts; these were closely related to the sacrifices. The sects constituted around the Soters especially made frequent use of these repasts,[92] at which sacred food was consumed which endowed the partakers with supernatural strength (δύναμις). Paul knew this, of course, and he very clearly noted his intention to substitute for the sacrificial repasts of the demons [93] the

---

89. Acts ii.42 and 46.
90. Mark xiv.22–25 and Synopsis.
91. [On the Eucharist in the Synoptics, see the study of the author in *LXXXVI*, pp. 530–34. M. B.]
92. *CLI*, index of words: Sacred repasts.
93. 1 Cor. x.20f.

repast of the Lord himself. Consequently, he conceived the notion that, as at the *table of the demons,* so too at *that of the Lord* more or less simple rites produced the same essential effect: *realization of the communion of the participants with the divine being to whom the repast belonged.* Among the pagans the supposedly efficacious rite was usually connected with the fact of *eating* and *drinking.* But eating and drinking what?

In antiquity, the idea of a communion established with the god by consuming him, in order to obtain part of the divine life, was very widespread.[94] For example, in the cult of the Thracian Dionysus, the participants tore apart, with their teeth and with their hands, the bull representing the god, and devoured its flesh in order to become *Bacchi* and assure divine immortality for themselves. Elsewhere "they devour the flesh of an animal conceived to be divine, and they believe that thus they identify themselves with the god himself and participate in his substance and in his qualities" (Cumont). It is possible that the ancient forms of the rite were no longer used in the time of Paul, that other *elements,* various *substitutes,* and even simple *symbols* had attenuated the barbarism of the old practice. The faith of the *mystoi* doubted neither the reality nor the effect of the salutary assimilation; the *how* probably did not embarrass them.

For a long time after Paul, Christian writers, less easily disturbed than our contemporaries who are captivated by the immutable originality of Christianity, noted the resemblance between the Lord's supper and the cultic banquets of the Mysteries.[95] This alone would suffice to make us believe that the influence which gave to the primitive *breaking of bread* the whole content of the Pauline Eucharist is to be sought in the realm of Hellenistic religion, and especially in that of the Mysteries.

The general idea dominating the Pauline Eucharist is that the Christians are united among themselves to the point of forming *a single body,* because they are all united with Christ, *in Christ,* by their common participation in the consumption of the Eucharistic elements, bread and wine, *which represent* his body and blood. *But how do they represent them?* This is the whole problem of transubstantiation, which I shall not discuss here. *Which are consumed where?* At *the table of the Lord,* in contradistinction to *the table of the demons.*[96] Numerous epigraphical and papyrological testimonies, not to mention the classical texts, assure us that the latter was

94. *CLVII,* II, pp. 318f.
95. Justin, *1 Apol.* 66, 4; Cyprian, *De lapsis,* 25; Firmicus Maternus, *De errore prof. rel.,* 18.
96. 1 Cor. x.21.

not an image, but a cultic reality.[97] A passage of Aelius Aristides (second century) tells us that the repasts given in the temple of Serapis were supposed to establish a close communion between the god and the participants.[98] Aristides presents this as a trait belonging exclusively to the cult of Serapis, but this restriction is certainly erroneous since, for example, Josephus [99] tells us that one could be invited into the temple of Isis to the repast of Anubis. While at the table of demons one did not eat *the body* nor drink *the blood* of the demons; the consecration of the meats—usually the flesh of a sacrificed animal—imbued this food with a very active δύναμις. The Christians were convinced of this for a long time.[100] For his part, Paul knew so well that the bread and the cup of the Lord were not simply symbolic that he claimed that whoever ate the one and drank the other unworthily would answer for his sacrilege: "He eateth and drinketh damnation to himself." (1 Cor. xi.27–29).

We already know that in the Pauline Mystery the concept of sacrifice is bound to that of expiation and of redemption, and I have pointed out that herein lies its originality, explained by the reality of the crucifixion. But does Paul see the *Lord's supper* as in some way a *sacrifice* in itself, a mystic renewal of Christ's death which makes us think of what the Catholics call *the holy sacrifice of the Mass?* This is nowhere said clearly, but I believe that it is probable: (1) because expressions like "Christ, our passover" (1 Cor. v.7), or "my body which is broken for you" (1 Cor. xi.24) might presuppose it; (2) because Paul compares his Lord's supper with the sacrificial repasts of the Old Covenant (1 Cor. x.18); (3) because shortly after him we find the concept established in the Christian presentation of the Eucharist; [101] (4) and especially because the practice of sacrifice is connected in the Mysteries with the notion of a saving operation.[102]

Altogether, and no matter what has been suggested to escape this conclusion, *the Lord's supper* introduces into primitive Christianity *an element of paganism.* Several ideas are found there: those of covenant, of ex-

---

97. Lietzmann, *XLIV*, IX, *An die Korinther* I,[2] p. 50, assembles the most striking texts. Cf. *CLV*, II, p. 734.

98. *In Serap., Or.* 8, p. 93 of Dindorf.

99. *Antt.* XVIII, 3:4. Cf. *CXCI*, p. 357.

100. Cf. in Cyprian, *De lapsis*, 23, the horrifying story of a little girl forced to take several drops of wine consecrated to idols. She was henceforth possessed, a fact observed when, a while later, in the presence of the Eucharist she drew back and, having received the sacred elements, vomited them.

101. *1 Clem.* 16, 11.

102. *CXXXIV*, p. 83; *CLI*, p. 63.

piatory sacrifice, and of a substitute in the expiation may be of Jewish origin; but it is the concept of sacramental communion in the body and blood of the Lord that is the focal idea of the presentation, and that is not Jewish. Neither is the related idea concerning the value and operative power of the consecration formula: "*This is my body . . . this is my blood,*" whereas analogous conceptions are commonly found in the Mysteries.

This very apparent relation becomes even more striking when one establishes in Paul's doctrine the connection between the *Lord's supper* and baptism. He who is baptized is, as we know, clothed with Christ; [103] henceforth Christ fills his being and lives in him; [104] thus he is joined to Christ's life, to his Passion, and to his resurrection. And we know that this is the fundamental idea of the Mysteries. We know also that in some of these Mysteries there are banquets of communion which renew or fortify the bond that unites each *mystos* to the god, and all the *mystoi* to each other *in the god.* Theophagy, or the consumption of the god in order to assimilate his *dynamis,* is no longer practiced with its former brutality, but it continues with alimentary substitutes or with representative symbols; it has lost neither its mystic reality nor its meaning. Moreover, the belief that by the means of blood, in the form of a bath or an aspersion, one assimilates the qualities of him from whom the blood came is very old. Blood is life, or, at least, its vehicle; [105] it is also the nourishment of gods and of demons. Ancient custom effected the realization of fraternal union by an exchange of blood, and it is also a widespread belief that he who drinks a man's blood acquires a magic power over his soul. But then, one remembers that *Jesus's death was not bloody.* Only John (xix.34), with symbolic intent and in order to represent simultaneously both baptism and the Eucharist, conceived the spear's thrust and the flow of water and blood that followed it. Hence it may be said that *Paul's Eucharistic structure is dominated not by historical memory, but by preoccupation with the symbolism of blood.* This gives Paul's presentation its principal richness; it is more interesting by far than the symbolism of bread.

We find in Egyptian papyri formulas whose kinship to Paul's seems most striking. A text, published not so long ago by Révillout,[106] declares: "May this wine become the blood of Osiris." Better still: another papyrus shows Osiris offering his blood in a winecup to Isis and to Horus for them

103. Gal. iii.27.
104. Gal. ii.20.
105. Lev. xvii.11: "For the living soul of flesh is its blood."
106. *Rev. égypt.,* 1880, p. 172.

to drink, in order not to forget him after his death, but seek him with ardent laments.[107] Does not this depiction correspond to the Christian's relation to Christ? The wine could, by an easily comprehended extension, represent all of the divine being's centers of action, as well as the being himself. Consider, furthermore, the following incantation: "Words to be said over the cup: say seven times: You are wine and you are not wine, but the head of Athena. You are wine and you are not wine, but the entrails of Osiris, the entrails of Jao." [108]

Rather than believing—as some people would like to persuade us to believe—that these texts are derived from Pauline formulas, which is highly unlikely, we must admit that the mysterious operation effected at *the table of the Lord* by these formulas and these symbols has its equivalents in other structures of salvation. In the true *Lord's supper*, the Paulinian, as he eats and drinks *substitute* elements, eats and drinks Christ himself and is imbued with the saving life of Christ. Since the Lord is the Spirit,[109] the Eucharistic elements are themselves *pneumatophoric*, and this is why Paul writes: "For by one Spirit are we all baptized." [110]

Is this a conscious imitation of the Mysteries? Assuredly not; but it is a development, in the same religious context, in the same mystic atmosphere, of a speculation tending towards the same object as the Mysteries. Seeking "means of grace," proficient ways of entering into efficacious intimacy with the Soter, Paulinism naturally adopted and adapted the means in which the mystic had acquired confidence in the milieu that had formed him. And historically the fact seems to be even easier to comprehend if we accept Paulinism as a complex doctrine that did not spring wholly from the initiative of Paul alone. The late date of the formulation of this Mystery, as well as the singularities of what I shall call the *Christian myth*, takes account of the differences which constitute its originality, especially the fact that the rites used in the *Lord's supper* do not function, as they did in the ancient Mysteries, *ex opere operato* and magically. Proof of this is to be found in the fact that, far from deriving a saving advantage from them, whoever uses them unworthily creates his own damnation. Thus the Pauline Mystery clearly establishes the same tendency as that already urged in all the Mysteries and to which they gradually yielded: *to demand of the initiate a certain prerequisite moral state.*

107. *CLXXVIII*, pp. 51 and 204.
108. Wessely, "Zauberpapyri," *Denkschrifft der Wiener Akademie*, 1893, p. 44; *CLXXVIII*, p. 205.
109. 2 Cor. iii.17.
110. 1 Cor. xii.13.

c) *Vision and Ecstasy*. The Pauline Mystery has still another means of entering into communion with the Lord: by *vision* and by *ecstasy*.[111] But these exceptional *charismata* belong only to the most perfect of the perfect, of whom the Apostle himself is the best example. Through these means, he lived in immediate and personal contact with the Lord.[112] In the practice of the Mysteries and of Hermetism, ecstasy [113] is the usual form of communion with the god. There are means of engendering it. It can be *passive* and take the *form* of a kind of trance in the presence of the god, as was Paul's state when he fell on the road to Damascus.[114] It can also be *active*, producing a sort of orgiastic frenzy which entails a *rapture*, the soul's trip to a divine place; it was such a state that evoked the Apostle's transport to the third heaven—"whether in the body or out of the body, I cannot tell: God knoweth." [115] The pseudo-Mithraic liturgy, published by Dieterich, opens with a prayer which reveals the *seer* ready to leave his body and his ψυχὴ (*anima animans*) in order to proceed in *spirit* (πνεῦμα) to contemplate the immortal Aeon. Is it not true that at the end of the perfection of his initiation the *mystos* is favored by an *epiphany?* [116] These visions are frequent occurrences in pagan mystic literature; as was the case on the Road to Damascus, they are usually filled with so intense a supernatural light that it cannot be borne by the bodily eyes.[117]

Conclusion

Thus we can no more doubt that Paulinism was organized and presented in the tradition of the Mysteries, in their atmosphere and according to their spirit, than the Apostle himself doubted it.[118] Obviously, there are *differences. Two of the principal ones* certainly favor the Pauline Mystery: (1) greater material facility in the access to the necessary *gnosis* and to the initiation; (2) greater realism in the sacramentalism of baptism and of the Eucharist. The sacred drama of the Mysteries (I deliberately use the most elastic term) probably remains more symbolic than the

111. Gal. ii.2. Cf. Acts ix.3–6; xvi. 9; xxiii.11; xxvii.23; etc., on the vision. 1 Cor. ix.1; xv.8; xiv.18; 2 Cor. xii. 1–4; etc., on the ecstasy.

112. 1 Cor. ii.10-16; 2 Cor. xii.1f.

113. This is ἔκστασις or ἐνθουσιασμός. Cf. *CXXXIV*, pp. 101f; *CLXXIX*, pp. 200f.; *CLXXVIII*, pp. 108f.

114. Acts ix.4–8.

115. 2 Cor. xii.3.

116. *CXXXIV*, p. 135.

117. Porphyry, *De Myst.* 2, 8; *CLIV*, p. 10, line 27.

118. 1 Cor. x.16f.

Pauline κοινωνία, in all of its parts and even in its liturgical banquet. As in the faith of the Apostle, the cross is not only a symbol, *to be crucified with Christ* is not only a formula or a way of speaking: it is a very real mystic *consummation.*

Let us remember, however, that the pagan *mystos* tended to identify himself with his god and when, by efficacious rites, he achieved his aim, he considered himself an Attis, an Osiris; whereas Paul no more dared to say that the *perfect one* was *a Christ* than he dared to say that the Lord, at the end of his exaltation, became God the Father. I think that at the root of this reservation lies a fundamental Jewish monotheism in relation to God, and a magnification of Christ which the Christian could not hope to attain in relation to the Lord. But, while in the *koinonia* of the Mysteries the divinity of the Soter is absorbed into the humanity of the *mystos*—for the latter becomes an Attis, an Osiris, etc.—in Paulinism the being of the believer is absorbed into that of the Lord; and if this represents a mystical advance, I relate it, too, to the same fundamental monotheism of the Apostle.

In Paul, on the other hand, the preoccupation with constituting the *body* of the community by the communion of individuals with the Lord seems much greater than it is in the *fraternities* of the mysteries. Paul endows the *Church* with a veritable existence. She is for him a person, who derives her being from this communion established by the faithful *in the Lord* (ἐν κυρίῳ). In the Mysteries, care for the personal salvation of the *individual* is predominant. For Paul, *personal salvation is, in part, a function of the life of the whole.*

Furthermore, what the *mystos* demands of his god is, essentially, saving assimilation, and not the principle of a new life, of a *palingenesis* coordinated with that of mankind and of the Cosmos. It is understood that the *mystos* who has achieved the *perfection* of the initiation finds himself freed of many constraints endured by the profane; in Paulinism, *life in the Lord* presupposes very precise moral demands, unknown or misunderstood by the profane; this is one of the points where the Jewish influence, and perhaps that of Jesus's teaching, is most evident.

Thus Paulinism represents and comprises a simplified, enlarged, and perfected Mystery; *it remains nonetheless a Mystery.* Its intrinsic attainments, which I could only sketch, are interesting; but it is of even greater interest when considered in relation to the origin of Christianity.

Jesus's initiative was limited to the announcement of the imminence of the Day of Yahweh, which Israel had awaited for so long: a day of happiness for the good, a day of terror for the wicked. The Nazarene related this Day to the great hope of the Messianic Kingdom, conceived as the Kingdom or the Reign of God, which would replace the reign of Satan on a regenerated earth. And he urged those who listened to the exhortations with which he strengthened his prophecy to effect within themselves the moral transformation (μετάνοια) that would please Yahweh and assure them a place on the right side in the fearful time of judgement. Few Jews had believed this message, and the event had proved that it was in fact only an illusion.

When the faith of the disciples, at first discouraged by the blow administered by Roman power, was reanimated, it became concentrated upon a certainty and a hope: the Nazarene was no longer dead; he lived close to God the Father, who had resurrected him to make him His Messiah, and he would soon manifest himself with all of the magnificence worthy of his rank. He would himself come to institute the Kingdom he had announced. What does this mean? Simply that those whom we call the Apostles had adapted Jesus's dream to the circumstances: they postponed its realization to the *parousia*, that is to say, to the glorious return, which they awaited every Sunday morning. But *they remained enclosed within the framework of the religion of Israel*, which they did not think of leaving, of transforming, or even of partially changing. Besides, they had no means of doing so, and were tolerated in Jerusalem only because they did not attempt it. However, their hope could have meaning only for the Jews. Now, it is obvious that very few Jews accepted this hope; moreover, why should it have appeared to be more certain when presented to them by the Apostles than when it was proffered by their Master? For logic demanded that after the illusion of Jesus had vanished that of the Apostles should also fade. It was saved from this misfortune and strengthened to the point where it became the beginning of a new religion by its transportation onto Hellenistic ground. But at the same time, its religious atmosphere changed.

In that Hellenistic world were the ruins of many religions; but there were also living religions, and above all an ardent religious feeling which aroused very precise aspirations towards a blessed survival of death, which was already called *salvation* (σωτηρία). The most widespread belief was that man, engulfed by nature in matter, could not by his own effort attain salvation, or even discover the sole way that would lead to it. The Mysteries, as well as Hermetism, made it their profession to discern this way, and claimed to command the decisive aid of an omnipotent Soter who would make easy the access and the way. Separated from the old national religions and alien in principle to the interests of the human City, they were concerned only with the *individual* and imposed upon him only the prerequisite of *faith*. By itself, the apostolic hope, born of the expectation of the joy and exaltation of Israel and thus fundamentally nationalistic, had nothing to offer to the Greeks, men who could claim nothing of Abraham's heritage. But, rejected by the Jews and rigorously attached to its own faith and confidence in Jesus the Nazarene who had become Jesus the Messiah, the apostolic hope had to be receptive to the Gentile drawn to this faith.

These came at first from among the proselytes who haunted the synagogues of the Diaspora. But, in order to win them, *it was necessary* to dispense with the legalistic constraints which as a rule separated them from complete Judaism. In reflecting upon this, that is, in instinctively comparing the intrinsic advantages to the inconveniences presented by legalism from the point of view of the extension of the faith in the Lord Christ, it was recognized that these constraints were outmoded, useless, and harmful; *this, specifically, is Paul's thesis.* To reject the Torah was to break with Judaism and thus to complete the separation that made Christianity an independent religion. It was even more necessary to speak to these people in a language they could understand, and to enclose within the words ideas acceptable to them. Our Hellenizing Christians succeeded in doing so without much trouble, by meditating, *within the categories of the religious spirit of their milieu*, on the very person of the Lord, on his role in the salvation transposed from the people to the individual, and on his mission. Paulinism represents the second stage of this meditation, whose first stage was at Antioch.

This then is the deep-seated reason why Paulinism assumed the appearance of a Mystery as I have tried to define it, and why it presented ἐν μορφῇ μυστηρίου (in the form of a Mystery) the conceptions, so foreign to the Synoptic tradition, which founded the basis of the Christian religion.

BIBLIOGRAPHY

Dictionaries and Reviews

ΑΓΓΕΛΟΣ *Archiv für neutestamentl. Zeitgeschichte und Kulturkunde* (Leipoldt, Leipzig, since 1925).

CE *The Catholic Encyclopedia* (16 vols., New York, 1917 *seq.*).

CW *Christliche Welt.*

DA *Dictionnaire des Antiquités grecques et romaines* (Daremberg and Saglio, 9 vols., Paris, 1877–1913).

DAC *Dictionary of the Apostolic Church* (J. Hastings, 2 vols., Edinburgh, 1913–17).

DACL *Dictionnaire d'archéologie chrétienne et de liturgie* (Dom F. Cabrol and Dom H. Leclercq, Paris, 1903 *seq.*).

DB *Dictionary of the Bible* (J. Hastings, 5 vols., Edinburgh, 1897–1904).

DCG *Dictionary of Christ and the Gospels* (J. Hastings, 2 vols., Edinburgh, 1906–1908).

EB *Encyclopedia Biblica* (Cheyne and Black, 4 vols., London, 1899–1903).

ERE *Encyclopedia for Religion and Ethics* (J. Hastings, Edinburgh, 1908–21).

EX *The Expositor*

JBL *Journal of Biblical Literature*

JTS *Journal of Theological Studies*

HRE *Real-Encyklopaedie für prot. Theologie und Kirche* [2] (A. Hauck, 22 vols., Leipzig, 1896–1909).

RB *Revue Biblique.*

RC *Revue Critique.*

REJ *Revue des Etudes juives.*

RGG *Die Religion in Geschichte und Gegenwart. Handwörterbuch für Theologie und Religionswissenschaft* [2] (H. Gunkel and L. Zscharnack, 5 vols., 1927–32).

RH *Revue Historique.*

RHLR *Revue d'Histoire et de Littérature religieuses.*

RHPR *Revue d'Histoire et de Philosophie religieuses* (The Protestant Theological Faculty of Strasbourg).

RHR *Revue de l'Histoire des Religions.*

TJ *Theologische Jahrbücher.*

TL *Theologische Literaturzeitung.*

TR *Theologische Rundschau.*

ZKG *Zeitschrift für Kirchengeschichte.*

ZNTW *Zeitschrift für die neutestamentliche Wissenschaft.*

ZWT *Zeitschrift für wissenschaftliche Theologie.*

I. General Books

I *Actes du Congrès d'Histoire du Christianisme,* Jubilé Alfred Loisy, Paris, 1927. Paris and Amsterdam, 1928, 3 vols.

II O. Bardenhewer, *Gesch. der altkirchlichen Literatur* [2]. Fribourg-in-Br., 4 vols, 1913–28.

III P. Batiffol, *Orpheus et l'Evangile.* Paris, 1910.

IV W. Bauer-Preuschen, *Griechisch-Deutsches Wörterbuch zu den Schriften des N.T.* Giessen, 1928.

V Baumgarten, Bousset, Gunkel, *et al. Die Schriften des N.T. neu übersetzt und für die Gegenwart erklärt* [3]. Göttingen, 4 vols., 1917–20.

VI H. Idris Bell, *Jews and Christians in Egypt.* London, 1924.

VII W. Bousset, *Die Relig. des Judentums in neutestamentlichen Zeitalter* [2]. Tübingen, 1906.

VIII W. Bousset, *Die Relig. des Judentums im späthellenistischen Zeitalter,* ed. Gressmann. Tübingen, 1926. A revision of the preceding book.

IX W. Bousset, *Kyrios Christos. Gesch. des Christusglaubens von den Anfängen des Christentums bis Irenaeus.* Göttingen, 1913; 2nd ed., 1921.

XI A. Brassac, *Manuel biblique.* Paris, 2 vols., 1908–09.

X D. E. von Dobschütz, *L'âge apostolique* (trans.). Paris, n.d.

XII L. Duchesne, *Histoire ancienne de l'Eglise,* 4 vols., 1906–29.

XIII R. Duval, *Anciennes Littératures chrétiennes: la littérature syriaque.* Paris, 1899.

XIV W. Erbt, *Von Jerusalem nach Rom. Untersuchungen zur Gesch. und Geschichtsdarstellung des Urchristentums.* Leipzig, 1912.

XV P. Feine, Theologie des N.T.[4] Leipzig, 1912.

XVI J. Felten, *Neutestl. Zeitgesch. oder Judentum und Heidentum zur Zeit Christi und der Apostel.* Ratisbonne, 2 vols., 1910.

XVII *Festgabe für Adolf Deissmann zum 60. Geburstag.* Tübingen, 1927.

XVIII M. Goguel, *Introduction au N.T.* Paris, 5 vols., 1922–26. Vol. III: *Le Livre des Actes,* 1922; IV: *Les Epîtres pauliniennes,* 2 vols., 1925–26.

XIX A. Gregory, *The Canon and Text of the N.T.* New York, 1907.

XX Ch. Guignebert, *L'Evolution des dogmes,* Paris, 1910; 2nd ed., 1929.

XXI H. Haas, *Bilder Atlas zur Religionsgesch.* Fasc. 9—11: *Die Religionen in der Umwelt der Urchistentums.* Leipzig, 1926.

XXII bis A. Harnack, *Gesch. der altchristl. Literatur.* 2 parts: *Ueberlieferung und Bestand,* Leipzig, 2 vols., 1893; *Die Chronologie,* 2 vols., 1897 and 1904.

XXIII A. Harnack, *Lehrb. der Dogmengeschichte* [4]. Leipzig, 3 vols., 1906–09. Since republished.

XXIV A. Harnack, *L'Essence du Christianisme* (trans. of *Das Wesen des Christentums*). Paris, 1907.

XXV W. H. P. Hatch, *The Organization of the Early Christian Churches* [2]. London, 1882.

XXVI E. Havet, *Le Christianisme et ses origines* [2]. Paris, 4 vols., 1873–84.

XXVII E. Hennecke, *Neutest. Apokryphen.* Tübingen and Leipzig, 1904; 2nd ed., 1923–24.

XXVIII E. Hennecke, *Handbuch zu den neutest. Apokryphen.* Tübingen and Leipzig, 1904.

XXIX H. Holtzmann, *Die Entstehung des N.T.* Halle, 1904 (*Relig. gesch. Volksbücher,* no. 11 of the 1st series).

XXX H. Holtzmann, *Lehrbuch des historisch-kritischen Einleitung in das N.T.*[3] Fribourg, 1892.

XXXI H. Holtzmann, *Lehrbuch der neutestamentl. Theologie* [2], ed. A. Jülicher and W. Bauer. Tübingen, 2 vols., 1911.

XXXII E. Jacquier, *Hist. de livres du N.T.* Paris, 4 vols., 1903. Since republished.

XXXIII E. Jacquier, *Le N.T. dans l'Eglise chrétienne.* Paris, 2 vols., 1911–13.

XXXIV M. R. James, *The Apocryphal N.T.* Oxford, 1924.

XXXV M. Jones, *The N.T. in the Twentieth Century.* London, 1924.

XXXVI H. Jordan, *Gesch. der altchristlichen Literatur.* Leipzig, 1911.

XXXVII A. Jülicher, *Einleitung in das N. T.*[7] Tübingen, 1931.

XXXVIII J. Juster, *Les Juifs dans l'Empire romain. Leur condition juridique, économique et sociale.* Paris, 2 vols., 1914.

XXXIX F. G. Kenyon, *Handbook to the Textual Criticism of the N. T.*[2] London, 1912.

XL   C. Kirch, *Enchiridion fontium historiae ecclesiasticae antiquae.* Fribourg-in-Br., 1910.

XLI   R. Knopf, *Einleitung in das N.T.*² Giessen, 1923.

XLII   P. de Labriolle, *Hist. de la littérature latine chrétienne.* Paris, 1920.

XLIII   H. Leclercq, *Manuel d'archéologie chrétienne depuis les origines jusqu'au VIII* siècle.* Paris, 2 vols., 1907.

XLIV   H. Lietzmann, *Handbuch zum N.T.*² Tübingen, 1925 seq.

XLV   H. Lietzmann, *Kleine Texte für theologische und philologische Vorlesungen und Uebungen.* Bonn, 1905 seq.

XLVI   A. Loisy, *Les Livres du N.T. traduits du grec en français avec introduction générale et notices.* Paris, 1922.

XLVII   G. Milligan, *The N.T. Documents: Their Origin and Early History.* London, 1913.

XLVIII   J. Moffatt, *Introduction to the Literature of the N.T.*² Edinburgh, 1912. Since republished.

XLIX   Moulton and Milligan, *The Vocabulary of the Greek N.T. Illustrated from the Papyri.* London, 1914 seq.

L   Eb. Nestle, *Einführung in das griechische N.T.*³ Göttingen, 1909. A revised edition by Von Dobschütz appeared in 1924.

LI   E. Preuschen, *Analecta. Kürzere Texte zur Gesch. der alten Kirche und des Kanons.* Fribourg-in-Br. and Leipzig, 1893.

LII   A. Puech, *Hist. de la littérature grecque chrétienne.* Paris, 3 vols., 1928–30.

LIII   Th. Reinach, "Judaei," in DA, cols. 619–32.

LIV   E. Renan, *Hist. du peuple d'Israël.* Paris, 5 vols., 1887 seq.

LV   E. Renan, *Les Apôtres.* Paris, 1866.

LVI   E. Renan, *L'Antéchrist*³. Paris, 1873.

LVI bis   E. Renan, *Saint Paul.* Paris, 1869.

LVII   E. Renan, *Les Evangiles.* Paris, 1877.

LVIII   E. Renan, *L'Eglise chrétienne.* Paris, 1879.

LIX   E. Renan, *Marc-Aurèle*⁵. Paris, 1885.

LX   E. Schürer, *Gesch. des jüdischen Volkes im Zeitalter J.C.* (Citations are from I⁴ [1901], II² [1898], III³ [1898].

LXI   G. B. Smith, *A Guide to the Study of the Christian Religion.* University of Chicago Press, 1917.

LXII   H. von Soden, *Urchristliche Literaturgeschichte (Die Schriften des N.T.).* Berlin, 1905.

LXIII   A. Souter, *The Text and Canon of the N.T.* New York, 1913.

LXIV   O. Staehlin, *Die altchristliche griechische Literatur.* Munich, 1924 (pp. 1005–1502 of vol. II⁶ of *Gesch. der griechischen Literatur*).

LXV   H. Weinel, *Biblische Theologie des N.T. Die Religion Jesu und des Urchristentums,* 2nd ed. Tübingen, 1928.

LXVI   P. Wernle, *Einführung in das theologische Studium*². Tübingen, 1911.

LXVII   R. Will, *Le Culte. Etude d'histoire et de philosophie religieuses.* I: *Le caractère religieux du culte.* Paris and Strasbourg, 1925.

LXVIII   Th. Zahn, *Einleitung in das N.T.* Leipzig, 2 vols., 1907.

LXIX Th. Zahn, *Grundriss der Gesch. des neutestamentlichen Kanons* [2]. Leipzig, 1904.

II. The Jewish Milieu and Primitive Christianity

LXX W. Bauer, *Das Leben Jesu im Zeitalter der neutestamentlichen Apokryphen.* Tübingen, 1909.

LXXI F. Boll, *Aus der Offenbarung Johannis. Hellenistiche Studien zum Weltbild der Apokalypse.* Leipzig and Berlin, 1914.

LXXII E. Bréhier, *Les Idées philosophiques et religieuses de Philon d'Alexandrie.* Paris, 1925.

LXXIII R. Bultmann, *Gesch. der synoptischen Tradition.* Göttingen, 1921.

LXXIV H. J. Cadbury, *The Making of Luke-Acts.* London, 1927.

LXXIV bis S. J. Case, *The Evolution of Early Christianity.* Chicago, 1914.

LXXV A. Causse, *Les Dispersés d'Israël. Les origines de la Diaspora et son rôle dans la formation du Judaïsme.* Paris, 1929.

LXXVI G. Dalman, *Worte Jesu,* I. Leipzig, 1898.

LXXVII E. de Faye, *Etudes sur les origines des Eglises de l'âge apostolique.* Paris, 1909 seq.

LXXVIII Fr. K. Feigel, *Der Einfluss der Weissagungsbeweises und anderer Motive auf die Leidensgeschichte.* Tübingen, 1910.

LXXIX M. Friedländer, *Die religiösen Bewegungen innerhalb des Judentums im Zeitalter Jesu.* Berlin, 1905.

LXXX M. Friedländer, *Synagoge und Kirche in ihren Anfängen.* Berlin, 1908.

LXXXI F. X. Funk, *Didascalia et Constitutiones apostolorum.* Paderborn, 2 vols., 1905.

LXXXII M. Goguel, *Jésus de Nazareth. Mythe ou histoire?* Paris, 1925.

LXXXIII M. Goguel, *La foi à la Résurrection dans le Christianisme primitif.* Paris, 1933.

LXXXIV M. Goguel, *L'Eucharistie des origines à Justin Martyr.* Paris, 1910.

LXXXV H. Gressmann, "Jewish Life in Ancient Rome," in *Jewish Studies in Memory of Israel Abrahams.* New York, 1927.

LXXXVI Ch. Guignebert, *Jésus.* Paris, 1933 (Coll. l'Evolution de l'Humanité, no. 29). English trans.: *Jesus.* New York: University Books, 1956.

LXXXVII Ch. Guignebert, *Le Monde juif vers le temps de Jésus.* Paris, 1935 (Coll. l'Evolution de l'Humanité, no. 28 [2]). English trans.: *The Jewish World in the Time of Jesus.* New York: University Books, 1959.

LXXXVIII F. Haase, *Altchristliche Kirchengesch. nach orientalischen Quellen.* Leipzig, 1925.

LXXXIX A. Harnack, *Lukas der Arzt, der Verfasser des dritten Evangelium und der Apostelgeschichte.* Leipzig, 1906.

XC A. Harnack, *Die Apostelgeschichte.* Leipzig, 1908.

XCI A. Harnack, *Neue Untersuchungen zur Apostelgeschichte und zur Abfassungszeit der synoptischen Evangelien.* Leipzig, 1911.

XCII A. Harnack, *Mission und Ausbreitung des Christentums in den ersten drei Jahrhunderten* 2. Leipzig, 2 vols., 1906. Since republished.

XCIII W. Heitmüller, *Taufe und Abendmahl im Urchristentum.* Tübingen, 1911.

XCIV G. Hoennicke, *Das Judenchristentum im ersten und zweiten Jahrhundert.* Berlin, 1908.

XCV G. Hollmann, *Die Bedeutung des Todes Jesu nach seinen eigenen Aussagen, auf Grund der synoptischen Evangelien.* Tübingen, 1901.

XCVI H. Holtzmann, "Die Apostelgeschichte," in *Hand Commentar zum N.T.,* I, 2. Tübingen, 1901.

XCVII F. J. Foakes Jackson and Kirsopp Lake, *The Beginnings of Christianity.* London, 5 vols., 1920–33.

XCVIII E. Jacquier, *Les Actes des Apôtres.* Paris, 1926.

XCIX A. Jülicher, "Zur Geschichte der Abendmahlsfeier in der ältesten Kirche," in *Theologische Abhandlungen Carl von Weizsäcker,* pp. 215ff. Fribourg, 1893.

C H. Koch, *Die Abfassungszeit des lukanischen Geschichtswerkes.* Leipzig, 1911.

CI M. Krenkel, *Josephus und Lukas.* Leipzig, 1894.

CII M. J. Lagrange, *Evangile selon saint Marc* 4. Paris, 1929.

CIII H. Lietzmann, *Gesch. der alten Kirche.* I: *Die Anfänge.* Berlin, 1932.

CIV J. Lightfoot, *Horae hebraïcae et talmudicae.* London, 1674

CV R. Lipsius, *Die Apokryphen Apostelgeschichten.* Leipzig, 1883 (Supplement, 1890), 4 vols.

CVI A. Loisy, *Jésus et la tradition évangélique.* Paris, 1910.

CVII A. Loisy, *La Naissance du Christianisme.* Paris, 1933.

CVIII A. Loisy, *Les Actes des Apôtres* 2. Paris, 1920.

CIX A. Loisy, *Les Actes des Apôtres. Traduction nouvelle avec Introduction et notes.* Paris, 1925.

CX A. Loisy, *Les Origines du N.T.* Paris, 1936.

CXI A. Loisy, *L'Evangile selon Luc.* Paris, 1924.

CXII A. Loisy, *L'Evangile selon Marc.* Paris, 1912.

CXIII A. Loisy, "L'Initiation chrétienne," *RHLR,* 1914.

CXIV A. C. McGiffert, *A History of Christianity in the Apostolic Age,* rev. ed. New York, 1920.

CXV Ed. Meyer, *Ursprung und Anfänge des Christentums.* Stuttgart, 3 vols., 1921–23.

CXVI G. F. Moore, *Judaism in the First Centuries of the Christian Era.* Cambridge (Mass.), 3 vols., 1927–30.

CXVII A. Omodeo, *Prolegomeni alla Storia del'età apostolica.* Messina, 1921.

CXVIII B. Pick, *The Apocryphal Acts of Paul, Peter, John, Andrew, and Thomas.* Chicago, 1909.

CXIX E. Preuschen, "Die Apostelgeschichte," in Lietzmann's *Handbuch.* Tübingen, 1912.

CXX Rendel Harris, *Testimonies.* Cambridge, 2 vols., 1916–20.

CXXI J. Réville, *Le Quatrième Evangile.* Paris, 1901.

CXXII H. Ropes, *The Apostolic Age in the Light of Modern Criticism.* New York and London, 1906.

CXXIII P. Sabatier, *La Didachè ou l'Enseignement des Douze Apôtres.* Paris, 1885.

CXXIV Fr. Smend, "Untersuchungen zu den Acta-Darstellungen von der Bekehrung des Paulus," AΓΓΕΛΟΣ I (1925).

CXXV H. L. Strack, *Jesus, die Haeretiker und die Christen nach den ältesten jüdischen Angaben.* Leipzig, 1910.

CXXVI B. H. Streeter, *The Four Gospels: A Study of Origins.* London, 1924.

CXXVII B. H. Streeter, *The Primitive Church Studied with Special Reference to the Origins of the Christian Ministry.* London, 1929.

CXXVIII L. Vénard, "Les Origines chrétiennes," in J. Brigout, *Où en est l'Histoire des religions?* Paris, 1911.

CXXIX J. Weiss, *Das Urchristentum*, completed by Knopf. Göttingen, 1917.

CXXX J. Wellhausen, *Einleitung in die drei ersten Evangelien* [2]. Berlin, 1911.

CXXXI J. Wellhausen, *Das Evangelium Marci* [2]. Berlin, 1909.

CXXXII H. Wendt, "Die Apostelgeschichte," in *Meyer's Kommentar* [9], Göttingen, 1913.

CXXXIII E. White, *The Sayings of Jesus from Oxyrhynchus.* Cambridge, 1920.

III. The Pagan Milieu

CXXXIV S. Angus, *The Mystery-Religions and Christianity.* London, 1925.

CXXXV S. Angus, *The Religious Quests of the Graeco-Roman World.* London, 1930.

CXXXVI G. Anrich, *Das antike Mysterienwesen in seinem Einfluss auf das Christentum.* Göttingen, 1894.

CXXXVII F. Baumgart, F. Poland, and R. Wagner, *Die hellenistich-römische Kultur.* Leipzig, 1913.

CXXXVIII J. Bernays, *Ueber das phokylideische Gedicht.* Berlin, 1856.

CXXXIX E. Beurlier, *Essai sur le culte rendu aux Empereurs romains.* Paris, 1890.

CXL E. Beurlier, *De divinus honoribus quos acceperunt Alexander et successores eius.* Paris, 1890.

CXLI G. Boissier, *La Fin du paganisme* [2]. Paris, 2 vols., 1894 (6th ed., 1910).

CXLII G. Boissier, *La Religion romaine d'Auguste aux Antonins* [3]. Paris, 1884.

CXLIII A. Bouché-Leclercq, *L'Astrologie grecque*. Paris, 1899.

CXLIV A. Boulanger, *Orphée, rapports de l'Orphisme et du Christianisme*. Paris, 1925.

CXLV M. Brückner, *Der sterbende und auferstehende Gottheiland in den orientalischen Religionen und ihr Verhältnis zum Christentum*. Tübingen, 1908; 2nd ed., 1920.

CXLVI J. Carcopino, "Attideia," in *Mélanges d'arch. et d'hist. de l'Ecole fr. de Rome*, vol. XL (1923).

CXLVII J. Carcopino, *La basilique pythagoricienne de la Porte Majeure*. Paris, 1926.

CXLVIII C. Clemen, *Der Einfluss der Mysterienreligionen auf das älteste Christentum*. Giessen, 1913.

CXLIX A. B. Cook, *Zeus: A Study in Ancient Religion*. Cambridge, 2 vols., 1914–16.

CL F. Cumont, *Les Mystères de Mithra* [3]. Brussels, 1913.

CLI F. Cumont, *Les Religions orientales dans le paganisme romain* [4]. Paris, 1929. Some citations refer to the 2nd ed., Paris, 1909.

CLII P. Decharme, *La Critique des traditions religieuses chez les Grecs, des origines au temps de Plutarque*. Paris, 1904.

CLIII A. Deissmann, *Licht vom Osten* [2]. Tübingen, 1909; 4th ed., 1923.

CLIV A. Dieterich, *Eine Mithrasliturgie*. Leipzig, 1903; 3rd ed., 1925.

CLV W. Dittenberger, *Sylloge inscriptionum graecarum*. Lipsiae, 2 vols., 1883; 3rd ed., 4 vols., 1915–24.

CLVI L. François, *Essai sur Dion Chrysostom, philosophe et moraliste cynique et stoïcien*. Paris, 1920.

CLVII J. G. Frazer, *The Golden Bough: A Study in Magic and Religion* [3]. London, 12 vols., 1911–22.

CLVIII J. G. Frazer, *Adonis, Attis, Osiris* [3]. London, 2 vols., 1914.

CLIX L. Gernet and A. Boulanger, *Le Génie grec dans la religion*. Paris, 1932.

CLX Th. Gomperz, *Les Penseurs de la Grèce* (trans. Reymond). Paris, 3 vols., 1903–10.

CLXI H. Graillot, *Le Culte de Cybèle, Mère des Dieux, à Rome et dans l'Empire romain*. Paris, 1912.

CLXII H. Gressmann, *Die orientalischen Religionen im hellenistich-römischen Zeitalter*. Berlin, 1930.

CLXIII F. G. Heinrici, *Die Hermes-Mystic und das N.T.* (edited by Von Dobschütz). Leipzig, 1918.

CLXIV H. E. de Jong, *Das antike Mysterienwesen in religionsgesch., ethnologischer und psychologischer Beleuchtung*. Leiden, 1909.

CLXV J. Kaerst, *Geschichte des Hellenismus* [2]. Berlin, 2 vols., 1917–26.

CLXVI P. de Labriolle, *La Réaction païenne. Etude sur la polémique anti-chrétienne du Ier au VIe siècle*. Paris, 1934.

CLXVII B. Latzarus, *Les Idées religieuses de Plutarque*. Paris, 1920.

CLXVIII F. Legge, *Forerunners and Rivals of Christianity*. Cambridge, 2 vols., 1915.

CLXIX J. Leitpoldt, *Sterbende und auferstehende Götter*. Leipzig, 1923.

CLXX A. Loisy, *Les Mystères païens et le Mystère chrétien* [2]. Paris, 1930.

CLXXI C. Martha, *Les Moralistes sous l'Empire romain, philosophes et poètes* [5]. Paris, 1886.

CLXXII L. Ménard, *Les Livres d'Hermès trismégiste et les derniers jours de la philosophie païenne*. Paris, 1866.

CLXXIII Th. Mommsen, *Histoire romaine* (trans. Cagnat-Toutain). Paris, 1887 *seq.*

CLXXIV A. Oltramare, *Les Origines de la diatribe romaine*. Geneva, 1925.

CLXXV R. Pettazzoni, *I Misteri*, Bologna, 1924.

CLXXVI R. Pettazzoni, *La religione nella Grecia antica fino ad Alessandro*. Bologna, 1921.

CLXXVII Ch. Picard, *Ephèse et Claros. Recherches sur les sanctuaires et les cultes de l'Ionie du Nord*. Paris, 1922.

CLXXVIII R. Reitzenstein, *Die hellenistischen Mysterien-Religionen*. Leipzig and Berlin, 1910; 2nd ed., 1920.

CLXXIX R. Reitzenstein, *Poimandres. Studien zur griechischägyptischen und frühchristlichen Literatur*. Leipzig, 1904.

CLXXX E. Rohde, *Psyche* [2]. Fribourg, 1898.

CLXXXI M. J. Rostovtzeff, *Mystic Italy*. New York, 1927.

CLXXXII L. Rougier, *L'Origine astronomique de la croyance pythagoricienne et l'immortalité céleste des âmes*. Le Caire, 1933.

CLXXXIII W. Scott, "Corpus Hermeticum," in *Hermetica*, 1. Oxford, 1934.

CLXXXIV J. Tambornino, *De antiquorum daemonismo*. Giessen, 1909.

CLXXXV J. Toutain, *Les Cultes païens dans l'Empire romain*. Paris, 1905 *seq.*

CLXXXVI N. Turchi, *Le religioni misteriosofiche nel Mondo antico*. Rome, 1923.

CLXXXVII N. Turchi, *Fontes Historiae Mysteriorum* [2]. Rome, 1923.

CLXXXVIII P. Vallette, *L'Apologie d'Apulée*. Paris, 1908.

CLXXXIX P. Wendland, *Die hellenistisch-römische Kultur in ihren Beziehungen zu Judentum und Christentum* [2]. Tübingen, 1912 (Lietzman's *Hdb.*).

CXC P. Wendland, *Die urchristlichen Literaturformen* [3]. Tübingen, 1912. Second part of the preceding. (Cf. Loisy, "Compte-rendu," *RHLR*, Nov.–Dec., 1912).

CXCI G. Wissowa, *Religion und Kultus der Römer* [2]. Munich, 1912 (*Hdb. der Klass. Alt. Wissenschaft*, V. 4).

IV. *Paul of Tarsus*

CXCIII B. W. Bacon, *Jesus and Paul*. New York and London, 1921.

CXCIV B. W. Bacon, *Story of St. Paul*. Boston, 1904.

CXCV E. Barnikol, *Forschungen zur Entstehung des Urchristentums, des N.T. und der Kirche: I. Die vorchristliche und frühchristliche Zeit des Paulus*. Kiel, 1929. II. *Die drei Jerusalemreisen des Paulus*, 1929; III. *Letzte Reiseziele des Paulus: Jerusalem, Rom und Anti-*

ocheia, 1931; IV. *Der nichpaulinische Ursprung des Parallelismus der Apostel Petrus und Paulus*, 1931.

CXCVI H. Böhlig, *Geisteskultur von Tarsos im augusteischen Zeitalter mit Berücksichtigung der paulinischen Schriften*. Göttingen, 1913.

CXCVII Ch. Bricka, *Le Fondement christologique de la morale paulinienne*. Strasbourg and Paris, 1923.

CXCVIII M. Brückner, *Die Entstehung der paulinischen Christologie*. Strasbourg, 1903.

CXCIX C. Clemen, *Paulus, sein Leben und Wirken*. Giessen, 1904.

CC A. Deissmann, *Paulus. Eine kultur- und religionsgeschichtliche Skizze*. Tübingen, 1911. Since republished.

CCI K. Deissner, *Paulus und die Mystik seiner Zeit* [2]. Leipzig, 1921.

CCII E. von Dobschütz, *Der Apostel Paulus: I. Seine Weltgeschichtliche Bedeutung*. Halle, 1926; II. *Seine Stellung in der Kunst*. Halle, 1928.

CCIII P. Feine, *Der Apostel Paulus*. Gütersloh, 1917–28. (*Beiträge zur Forderung christ. Theol.*, 2nd series, XXII).

CCIV P. Gardner, *The Religious Experience of St. Paul*. London, 1911.

CCV M. Goguel, "Essai sur la chronologie paulinienne," *RHR*, May–June, 1912.

CCVI M. Goguel, "La Mystique paulinienne," *RHPR*, May–June, 1931.

CCVII M. Goguel, *L'Apôtre Paul et Jésus-Christ*. Paris, 1904.

CCVIII A. von Harnack, *Die Briefsammlung des Apostels Paulus und die andern vorkonstantinischen christlichen Briefsammlungen. 6 Vorles. aus der altchristlichen Literaturgesch.* Leipzig, 1926.

CCIX W. H. P. Hatch, *The Pauline Idea of Faith in Its Relation to Jewish and Hellenistic Religion*. Cambridge (Mass.), 1917.

CCX E. Hatch and W. C. van Manen, "Paul," in *EB*; Hatch, cols. 3606–20; v. Manen, cols, 3603–06, 3620–38.

CCXI G. Heinrici, *Die Korintherbriefe*, cited in *Meyer's Kommentar*, V [8]. Göttingen, 1896.

CCXII H. Holl, *Der Kirchenbegriff des Paulus in seinem Verhältnis zu dem der Urgemeinde* (*Gesammelte Aufsätze zur Kirchengesch.*: II. *Der Osten*), 1st half-vol. pp., 44ff. Tübingen, 1929.

CCXIII A. Jülicher, "Der Brief an die Romer," in *Die Schriften des N.T.*, II.

CCXIV R. Knopf, *Paulus*. Leipzig, 1909.

CCXV R. Knopf, *Probleme des Paulusforschung*. Tübingen, 1913.

CCXVI W. L. Knox, *St. Paul and the Church of Jerusalem*. Cambridge, 1925.

CCXVII M. J. Lagrange, *Saint Paul. Epitre aux Romains*. Paris, 1916.

CCXVIII K. Lake, *The Earlier Epistles of St. Paul, Their Motive and Origin*. London, 1911.

CCXIX G. La Piana, "La primitiva communita cristiana di Roma e l'epistola ai Romani," in *Ricerche religiose*, May, 1925, pp. 210–26; July, 1925, pp. 305–26.

CCXX H. Lietzmann, *An die Römer*. Tübingen, 1928.

CCXXI H. Lietzmann, *Petrus und Paulus in Rom.* Bonn, 1915.

CCXXI bis A. Loisy, "La Carrière de l'apôtre Paul," *RHLR*, 1920.

CCXXII A. Loisy, *L'Epître aux Galates.* Paris, 1916.

CCXXII bis A. Loisy, "Les Epîtres de Paul," *RHLR*, 1921.

CCXXIII A. Loisy, "L'Evangile de Paul," *RHLR*, 1914.

CCXXIV A. Loisy, *Remarques sur la littérature épistolaire du Nouveau Testament.* Paris, 1935.

CCXXV E. Lombard, *De la Glossolalie chez les premiers chrétiens.* Lausanne, 1910.

CCXXVI V. Macchioro, *Orfismo e paolinismo. Studi e polemiche.* Montevarchi, 1922.

CCXXVII A. H. McNeile, *St. Paul, His Life, Letters and Christian Doctrine.* Cambridge, 1920.

CCXXVIII C. G. Montefiore, *Judaism and St. Paul.* London, 1914.

CCXXIX W. Mundle, *Das religiöse Leben des Apostels Paulus.* Leipzig, 1923.

CCXXX W. S. Muntz, *Rome, St. Paul and the Early Church.* London, 1913.

CCXXXI E. Norden, *Agnostos Theos. Untersuchungen zur Formengeschichte religiöser Rede.* Leipzig, 1913. (Review by Loisy in *RHLR*, 1913: "Les Ecrits de Luc," and in *RC*, Aug. 9, 1913.)

CCXXXII A. Omodeo, *Paolo di Tarso, Apostolo delle genti.* Messina, 1922.

CCXXXIII A. Pallis, *To the Romans: A Commentary.* Liverpool, 1920.

CCXXXIV J. Parry, "The Epistle of Paul the Apostle to the Romans," in *Cambridge Greek Testament for Schools and Colleges.* Cambridge, 1912.

CCXXXV P. Philippi, *Paulus und das Judentum.* Leipzig, 1916.

CCXXXVI W. Ramsay, *St. Paul the Traveller and the Roman Citizen* [10]. London, 1908.

CCXXXVII W. Ramsay, *Cities and Bishoprics of Phrygia.* Oxford, 2 vols., 1895.

CCXXXVIII W. Ramsay, *The Cities of St. Paul.* London, 1907.

CCXXXIX A. Sabatier, *L'Apôtre Paul. Esquisse d'une histoire de sa pensée* [3]. Strasbourg, 1912.

CCXL W. Sanday and A. C. Headlam, *A Critical and Exegetical Commentary of the Epistle to the Romans* [5]. Edinburgh, 1914.

CCXLI L. Schneller, *Paulus. Das Leben des Apostels.* Leipzig, 1923.

CCXLII E. Schwartz, *Characterköpfe aus der antiken Literatur* [2], II, V: *Paulus.* Leipzig, 1919.

CCXLIII E. Schwartz, *Zur Chronologie des Paulus. Nachrichten der koeniglichen Gessellschaft der Wissenschaften zu Göttingen*, Phil. Hist. Klasse, 1907.

CCXLIV A. Schweitzer, *Gesch. der paulinischen Forschung von der Reformation bis auf die Gegenwart.* Tübingen, 1911.

CCXLV Ch. A. Anderson Scott, *Christianity according to St. Paul.* Cambridge, 1927.

CCXLVI A. Steinmann, *Zur Werdegang des Paulus. Die Jugendzeit im Tarsus.* Fribourg-in-Br., 1928.

CCXLVII C. Toussaint, *L'Epître de S. Paul aux Colossiens.* Paris, 1921.

CCXLVIII C. Toussaint, *L'Hellénisme de l'Apôtre Paul*. Paris, 1921.

CCXLIX L. Vouaux, *Les Actes de Paul et ses lettres apocryphes* (Introduction, texts, commentaries). Paris, 1913.

CCL H. Weinel, *Paulus. Der Mensch und sein Werk; die Anfänge des Christentums, der Kirche un des Dogmas* [2]. Tübingen, 1915.

CCLI J. Weiss, *Paulus und Jesus*. Berlin, 1909.

CCLII J. Weiss, *Paulus und seine Gemeinde. Ein Bild von der Entwicklung des Urchristentums*. Berlin, 1914.

CCLIII P. Wernle, *Paulus als Heidenmissionär. Ein Vortrag*. Tübingen, 1909; 2nd ed., 1910.

CCLIV H. Windisch, *Der Zweite Korintherbrief* [2], *ap. Meyer's Kommentar*. Göttingen, 1924.

CCLV W. Wrede, *Paulus*. Leipzig, 1907.

V. Supplementary List

CCLVI W. Bousset, *Hauptprobleme der Gnosis*. Tübingen, 1907.

CCLVII F. Burkitt, *Church and Gnosis: A Study of Christian Thought and Speculation in the Second Century*. Cambridge, 1932.

CCLVIII F. C. Conybeare, *Myth, Magic and Morals*. London, 1910.

CCLIX E. de Faye, *Clément d'Alexandrie. Etudes sur les rapports du Christianisme et de la philosophie grecque au IIe s*. Paris, 1898; 2nd ed., 1906.

CCLX Ch. Guignebert, *La Primauté de Pierre et la venue de Pierre à Rome*. Paris, 1909.

CCLXI Ch. Guignebert, *Tertullien. Etude sur ses sentiments à l'égard de l'Empire et de la Société civile*. Paris, 1901.

CCLXII R. T. Herford, *Christianity in Talmud and Midrash*. London, 1903.

CCLXIII E. Herriot, *Philon le Juif; essai sur l'Ecole juif d'Alexandrie*. Paris, 1898.

CCLXIV Lebreton (S.J.), *Histoire du dogme de la Trinité, des origines au Concile de Nicée* [6]. Paris, 2 vols., 1927–28.

CCLXV Ernst Lohmayer, *Soziale Fragen im Urchristentum*. Leipzig, 1921 (Coll. *Wissenschaft und Bildung*).

CCLXVI A. Loisy, *Le Mandéisme et les origines chrétiennes*. Paris, 1934.

CCLXVII P. Monceaux, *Histoire littéraire de l'Afrique chrétienne depuis les origines jusqu'à l'invasion arabe*. Paris, 3 vols., 1901–05; IV, 1912; V, 1920.

CCLXVIII P. Monceaux, *Les Africains. Etude sur la littérature latine d'Afrique. Les païens*. Paris, 1894.

CCLXIX J. Réville, *Les Origines de l'épiscopat*. Paris, 1894.

INDEX

Achaia, 229, 246
Achan, 94
Acta Pauli (Acts of Paul), 28, 127–29, 171
Acta Petri et Pauli (Acts of Peter and Paul), 129
Acts of the Apostles, 28, 45–56, 90, and *passim;* its archaism, 54; authorship of, 46ff; its Christology, 84ff; its editor's intent, 52f; evidence of, *see* below; and Paul's Epistles, 52ff; place, date, and historical value of, 53–55; second edition of, 51ff; sources of, 49–53
—— evidence of: concerning Apollos, 228f; the Apostles, 61ff, 104ff; baptism, 79; first Christian propaganda, 102–10; foundation of Church of Antioch, 155f; Jesus as Messiah, 85f; Jewish Diaspora, 130; the Holy Spirit, 73f; Kingdom of God, 84–85; life of first brotherhood, 91ff; *parousia* in, *see parousia;* Paul, 49, 165ff, 174ff, 178f, 204f, 220–22, 234ff, 238ff, 249ff; the Seven, 69–70, 107f; the Twelve, 61ff
Adonis, 144, 145, 151, 184, 186
Aeacus, 147
Africa: debate in, on Canon, 28f; rejection of the Epistle to the Hebrews by its Church, 30

Agape (community meal): in primitive community, 70, 80f; as memorial of Jesus's death, 81. *See also* Lord's Supper
Agrippa I, *see* Herod Agrippa
Agrippa II, 254
Ahura-Mazda, 186
Alexandria, 145, 150, 181, 232, 238
Alexandrian revision of the New Testament, 35
Allat, 161
Amanus, 181
Ambrosiaster, 33
Ananias: and Sapphira, 92–93, 94; of Tarsus, 205, 251n
anawim, 2, 95, 97, 195
Andrew (apostle), return of, to Galilee, 58
Anthony the Healer, and Anthonists, 11–12
anthropology, Pauline, 262
Antioch, 145, 164, 167, 200, 206, 207, 218, 232, 233, 236, 240, 276, 297; appearance of, in first century, 157; Church of, *see* Church of Antioch; conflict of, 242, 244–45; Hellenists' preaching in, 103, 130ff, 157ff; Paul in, 186, 216, 237, 238, 244ff; Stephen in, 130
Antipater, 182
Anubis, repast of, 291